PRAISE FOR *MAN*

This stunning crisply-paced no
rylines in social-realist style. *M*
tious, exploring dilemmas around politics, genue. ....
moment in Indian history. Kavita A. Jindal brings her themes to life via a
gripping story featuring family dynasties, violent death, conflicts between
love and ambition, sex and betrayal, and an original take on the absurdities
of societal conventions in small towns and big cities.—Michele Roberts,
Author of the Man-Booker-Prize shortlisted *Daughters of the House*

Set against a tumultuous time in politics, Jindal unfolds the life and times
of Waheeda, a determined middle-class Muslim woman aiming to win a
seat in Parliament, whose personal life gets tragically entangled with Monish, the son of a business tycoon. Jindal uses her considerable story-telling
power to present a volatile mix of murder and mayhem, the clash of religion
and traditional practices with love, sex, greed, and power. The dialogue is
down-to-earth, the domestic space rendered in fine detail, and the cultural
landscape sharply observed. The rapid pace of the plot makes for edge-of-
seat excitement. Jindal's novel offers a telling commentary on the bigotry
of our times and the potential for women to play centre stage in public
affairs.—Saleem Peeradina, Author of *Heart's Beast: New and Selected Poems*

While exploring the tensions that exist between the personal and the political in an Indian Muslim single mother's life, Jindal has created a com-
pelling novel that is impossible to put down.—Manju Kapur, author of
Difficult Daughters

Manual For A Decent Life is a heart-searching novel with a wide sweep. Its
themes of Indian family, female identity and power struggles are of contemporary significance.—Russell Celyn Jones, author of *The Ninth Wave*

ALSO BY KAVITA A. JINDAL

Patina

Raincheck Renewed

MANUAL FOR A DECENT LIFE

A Novel

Kavita A. Jindal

BRIGHTHORSE
BOOKS

Brighthorse Books
13202 N River Drive
Omaha, NE 68112
brighthorsebooks.com

ISBN: 978-1-944467-23-4

For permission to reproduce selections from this book, contact the editors at info@
brighthorsebooks.com. For information about Brighthorse Books and the Brighthorse Prize, visit us on the web at brighthorsebooks.com.

Brighthorse books are distributed to the trade through Ingram Book Group and its
distribution partners. For more information, go to
https://ipage.ingramcontent.com/ipage/li001.jsp.

Cover Art © iStock.com/Elen11
Jacket design by Brent Spencer

MANUAL FOR A DECENT LIFE

ONE

A SINGLE MAGPIE, one for sorrow, on the drive. Waheeda's car slid up the paving; the bird scuttled to the shrubbery, pausing there, unafraid. It put its head to one side. Waheeda pushed open the back door to clamber out. The bird flew up into the Ber tree, shrilling.

She put her hand to her forehead in an automatic *adaab*, returning the gummy smile of the leathery gardener who'd set down his hosepipe to bend at the waist. Behind her Hira bounced out of the car, calling out 'hello, *mali*-ji,' and plucked a gerbera on her way to the front door, where she jumped up to reach the bell.

Waheeda looked up at her childhood home. When she was eight she'd been excited at moving into it, and being allowed to select her own space—innocently plumping for the largest bedroom. The house had taken two years to build, a rapid construction project overseen by her adoptive father, Aseem. 'For my family,' he would say with a flourish, the unuttered words being: *for the children I intend to have.*

It would feel so empty with his two sons gone. The house's façade betrayed none of the upheaval within, the paint remained fresh white with light-green accents on the mouldings over the front door and on the terrace balustrades.

Six months since she'd been here last, for the funeral of her brothers Rohail and Irfan. No new facts uncovered about the train fire that killed them. No one to blame or take revenge on. The family was holding it together. They were all good at that in their own ways: she, her mother, and Aseem.

When your younger brothers have died in suspicious circumstances you feel yourself an usurper in life. You are ambivalent about your good health, your veneer of defiant cheerfulness. You hug your daughter too tight each evening when you return home, so that if you're next to be taken away, she'll remember the intensity of your love. When you arrive at your parents' home you feel the mantle of their expectations settle on you. What will they ask of you? How will you measure up?

The front door opened and Ammi scooped up Hira to kiss her before releasing her. She hugged Waheeda, peering over her glasses into the car, as if expecting another passenger to appear. 'Isn't Nafis with you?'

Waheeda took a moment to compose herself. The driver was unloading their cases. The late-afternoon sun was mellowing. It was going to be a cool evening; she hoped winter fireflies would rise up in the back garden in the last warmth of dusk; she'd told Hira to look out for them. She swallowed. 'Ammi, I told you Nafis won't be travelling with us. He has work...an art gallery in Delhi has shown interest. They want large canvases and he hasn't produced any sizeable works recently.'

Everyone knew that her husband spent most of his time in his small lodge in Theog, ostensibly painting mountain scenery. They knew, but they asked after him. They marked his absence.

Her mother pushed her specs back up her nose and wiped under her eye. 'Doesn't he want to spend some time with Hira?' She spoke in a low tone, although Hira had skipped off inside.

'He was in Delhi just a few days ago—an especial visit to see Hira.'

Immediately she regretted her phrasing. She'd admitted aloud that Nafis came to Delhi to see his daughter, not his wife. When he visited Delhi now he didn't even stay with her, in his own home! He spent a couple of days with a friend who liked to visit Theog in return. Waheeda had to laugh. What else could you do? In those few years he'd lived in Delhi, Nafis had made no effort to acquire his own friends, complaining relentlessly about materialistic Delhiites. Now that he lived elsewhere he'd found congenial company in the city.

'When will he have an exhibition?' Her mother made no attempt to lead her inside for tea although their bags had been taken in. 'Is the gallery the same one that showed his work earlier?'

Nafis rarely offered his work to a gallery to sell, and when he was commissioned, he often didn't fulfil the commission. He marched to his own drummer. Waheeda didn't believe that he would produce what he'd been asked to deliver this time. 'I don't know. All I can tell you is…' she parroted his flat pretext for not joining them, '…he has some paintings to finish.'

Ammi opened her mouth, closed it, and Waheeda knew that she would not mention him again during her visit.

•

HER OLD BEDROOM was the same, the bed neatly covered by a faded bedspread, the one she loved. Its familiar print of blue and yellow sprigs reminded her of being a girl; of what she had left behind; of what she had made of herself. Hira was sprawled on the bed, banishing any aura of gloom with her infectious happiness. Waheeda had peeped into her brothers' rooms on the way and nothing had changed in them. That had made her chest squeeze up. But to find her room exactly as she liked it gave her a sense of peace.

She unzipped one holdall but before she could unpack Hira's clothes, her daughter said: 'Mama, I want to sleep in the sewing-machine room.'

Waheeda didn't ask why. She knew. Hira wanted to copy whatever her father did. When Nafis had rushed down from

Theog for the funeral he'd asked for a bed to be made up for him in the sewing-machine room. He'd explained to Ammi that he was an insomniac. It was better that Waheeda and Hira stayed together while he found 'another place for my head, where I can be lying churning, or up pacing, without disturbing anyone.'

Not that any of them had slept properly, for days, but late at night they had retreated into their own silent zones of grief.

She stroked Hira's fine straight hair. It had not been cut for a year and her bob had grown past her shoulders. When Waheeda was young, she'd wanted hair like this. Instead she had thick wavy hair which she now appreciated. She couldn't quite remember when she'd stopped wanting to have different hair or a different nose.

'Let me see if I can arrange it,' she said. Hira followed her downstairs, listening in as she had a quick word with Ammi. Waheeda dusted down the small cane bed in the room of bright yellow walls. She lifted the Singer sewing machine off the table—'this is very heavy,' she panted at Hira—and placed it on the floor. She arranged Hira's things on the wooden table: hairbrush, sketchbook, pencil tin, and the books she was reading to her. She cleared a shelf in the triangular corner cupboard for clothes. She made up the bed with crisp linens and on the tasselled violet eiderdown she placed Hira's beanie baby. 'All set.'

'Topar Khan waits on the pillow,' Hira adjusted the brown bear's position.

•

ASEEM'S DEEP TONES resonated through the house and Waheeda could hear him querying her mother as she came out of the shower. She sniffed at her wrists to inhale the scent of her rose soap before it dissipated. Later. She would greet him later. He would be impatient but it would have to wait until she was dressed and down for dinner.

His voice, drifting up, was firm and strong. Yet on the phone to her this past month, he'd sounded more faltering. Ever since the train fire she'd felt nothing but pity for him, and when he asked her for small favours, or for her opinions, she responded delicately, cooperatively. The last errand had strained her patience in the beginning. Aseem asked her to meet Chetna Mura, a lady of about forty-five, a fringe member of the Nulkazim Peace Forum party who had recently become more active. Aseem wanted to shake up and re-shuffle the Peace Forum's small Delhi operation. 'I think Chetna has greater potential as a fundraiser in Delhi circles than Faisal, what do you think?' he'd asked Waheeda on the phone.

'I don't want to get involved.' But she was thinking: *curious*. Faisal Ahmed was the political party's head in Delhi. Aseem thought of Faisal-ji as his brother. Faisal had been with him since 1970 when Aseem founded the party. Would he really replace him as the figurehead in the capital?

'Chetna would be a good front-person. Show how we are an inclusive party. Not limited to Muslims only. Or elderly men.' A pause. 'She has good contacts, Wija. I want you to meet her and give me your feedback.'

'I'm really busy with my work, Abba, and with Hira always waiting for me at home, alone with the maid, I really don't have time...'

'Wija, it's good for you to get to know some people.'

'I know plenty of people. I don't want to meet the kind of people you think it's good for me to know.'

'Who else am I going to send? I need someone I can trust; I need family...'

It was that word, *family*, that sense of his loss, which held her back from standing up to him. One last-ditch attempt to deflect his will that she become his antenna in Delhi. 'Can't it wait until your next visit? Aren't you coming soon?'

Aseem used his second card. 'I don't want to leave your mother alone here all the time. So, yes, I should be in Delhi more. But…I'm going to spend more time in Nulkazim…at least for another year.' He lowered his voice confidentially, 'I'd like a woman to meet Chetna. I'd like to know what *you* think of her. She may become our consistent 'face' in Delhi, after all.'

'OK, Abba. I'll meet her.'

He wasn't finished. 'After that, arrange a meeting with Faisal too.'

'What? Why?'

'All you have to do is find out diplomatically whether he wouldn't be slighted if asked to take a backseat. He would still be the driving force, of course. The main decision-maker. Always.'

'Of course,' she echoed back wryly. 'I'll make that clear.'

Although how was she going to elucidate 'taking a back seat' to a man whom she'd been taught to address respectfully at all times?

•

AT DINNER ASEEM presided over the table as normal but they were all subdued. Waheeda ached for her parents, sitting at this long table night after night, just the two of them, gazing at the six unused dining chairs, missing their two sons, missing the clatter of young people. Hira was too drowsy to chatter on brightly as she usually did.

Aseem's peculiar blue-grey eyes fixed on Waheeda. 'Did you have those meetings in Delhi last week?' His longish grey hair was slicked back. It struck her again how he'd lost that mantle of bravado he'd always had. Every time she saw him he'd aged a tiny bit more. His voice retained its dictatorial quality though; why had she imagined that it had become weaker?

'Yes, Abba,' she nodded.

Her mother looked at them both. 'What meetings?'

'NPF,' he said shortly.

Her mother appeared even more puzzled.

'Rehana,' Aseem explained more patiently to his wife, 'I requested Wija to help me with some party work in Delhi.'

Ammi shot her a you-didn't-tell-me squint.

'Let's talk in my study after dinner,' Aseem said to Waheeda. 'Yes, Abba.'

'How was the new driver?'

'Habib? Good. He drove carefully. He didn't speak much. Perhaps he's the strong silent type.' Waheeda had thought him a bit surly, but she knew from his size and muscularity that he'd been selected for security reasons, not his social skills. She didn't mind his reticence, she preferred to be quiet too, and anyway on this journey Hira had prattled on beside her.

When they'd finished eating, Waheeda carried Hira from the table and sang a lullaby to her. Usually she read to her at night, but in Nulkazim, Hira liked to regress somewhat and enact earlier babyish rituals. Waheeda was tired herself from the effects of the long drive and the pervasive sadness in the house, but she went into Aseem's study to give him her report.

'Should we install Chetna as chief?' he enquired straightaway.

What he was really asking was whether this was the right move to increase visibility of his provincial minor party. *I have no clue,* she wanted to reply. She had no interest in and had never been involved in party affairs. 'I don't know which of them is better with the media or knows more of the right people. Chetna was very forthcoming about her ambitions...'

She didn't say what she was thinking: It doesn't matter to *me* if the religion of one is a higher draw than the religion of the other in that city. She said, 'They aren't all that different in their operating style. Faisal-ji is male and Chetna is female... and younger...' Despite her initial reluctance, she'd enjoyed the meetings. There'd been a frisson in the discussions and she felt she was making things happen. Her reasoning skills were being deployed and she was being trusted to make decisions for Nulkazim Peace Forum.

'Hmm, I thought you'd say something like that. You're always fair.'

Surprised, she looked into his face. His wan eyes were encircled by a dark puffiness. Again she felt sorrow, for the loss of his sons, and for herself, for losing her little brothers. Her dear mother, destroyed and stoic. Ammi did have God, though, she had the verses she chanted, and a few times a day she unburdened herself to God, so that to everyone else she appeared unruffled. A picture of acceptance. Serene was the word most commonly applied to Rehana Zafar.

Aseem stood from his desk to go over to the console table at the side of the room. Waheeda's gaze got stuck on the blank wall behind his chair. Where were all the photographs? The portrait of Aseem's father that never left its place. Had it been taken down for cleaning? But *everything* was missing: the old pictures of Aseem with the extended Zafar family—all his cousins; and the newer portraits of her brothers; and the picture of Hira as a toddler on her first visit to Nulkazim's rose garden.

Before she could ask why the photos had been removed, he returned to set two pieces of origami on the desk. White chits perfectly folded into miniature triangles, upright on the green baize. At the lower corners of the triangles, the outermost layer of paper was tuned up in a sharp fold. She could only stare, a blackness beginning to spread in the pit of her stomach. What was this about?

He sat down. Said nothing. Her foreboding grew. They were playing a game. Why? What were the stakes? She didn't know, but she was damned if he would win. *I've been feeling sorry for you, but your machinations will never cease.*

'So, Wija, I also got some feedback from your meetings.'

'You did?' Her tone lifted in astonishment. 'Then why ask me to give you an account? And who reported to you? About *me*?'

'Faisal did.'

Then the meeting with him had been the opposite of what she'd thought she was doing. It was she who was being assessed in some way. It was her skill or tenacity on trial, not Faisal's willingness to step into the background for the good of the party. 'Did you lie to me? Did you go up to Delhi the next day and talk to him yourself?'

'No, I didn't.'

'You told me not to discuss it on the phone. So how did you get a report? You're full of deceit, a fraud—'

His blinking eyes betrayed how stung he was. 'A fraud? That's what living in Delhi teaches you? To call everyone a fraud? To speak like this to your elders?' He opened a drawer and brought out a mobile phone. 'Seen these?'

'You have one?' Waheeda hadn't known that.

'This is not tapped. This is how I got my report.' He opened the drawer again, bringing out another phone. 'I've bought a cell phone for you as well.'

'Oh.' She waited, still angry. He'd made a fool of her. Why? She pushed back her chair. 'If you've heard all the news, you don't need any more from me. I'll head upstairs—'

'But Wija,' he protested mildly, 'we haven't talked about your life yet.'

'Mine?'

'Yes, yours. I'm your father. Perhaps, I should say that I'm a concerned father. Would you agree that you've reached a crossroads in your life and you need some guidance as to what happens next?'

Waheeda felt her palms prickling. She was tempted to open her hands and look for answers in there. It would be written, wouldn't it? If this was a crossroads there would be a line, surely, a contour bisecting her life-line at the age of thirty-two, a line to show interference.

'Abba…' She couldn't help but reveal her surprise, and even

her vulnerability to his declaration of concern, 'my life is fine. I don't need guidance.' *Most definitely, I don't need your guidance.* She lowered her eyes, out of habit, so he wouldn't read her rebellious rejoinders. The white triangles loomed up at her; malevolent. Did both chits have the words *No* written on them? If form was being followed, then whatever the question, the answer was 'No.'

But she hadn't made an appeal. She had no need to escape. When she was sixteen, she'd made a request to leave Nulkazim, to go to boarding school, and he'd asked her to pick a chit from a bowl that had two pieces of paper in it. The luck of the draw. She hadn't realised until much later that both must have been marked 'Nulkazim.'

She *had* gone to boarding school in the end. After interventions from Ammi she'd escaped her stifling life. She'd relished her time at St. Ann's, up in the hills. She'd been lucky to stroll through its colonnade corridors and red brick buildings and to enjoy brisk walks in the forest around the school. She'd made friends for life there. St. Ann's had been her springboard to an independent existence as an academic in Delhi. Without her sojourn there she would not now be a history lecturer at Prajna College. If she hadn't determined her own path, in opposition to him…at sixteen, at eighteen, at twenty-one, at twenty-four—

His clipped voice brought her back. 'Wija, I cannot let you live as you are.'

She replied sarcastically, 'You want to kill me?'

Tears sprang into his eyes and she averted her own, warm blood rushing to her face. Her shoulders slumped. Stupid, stupid woman.

'You don't have a husband,' he said.

'I'm married—'

'He lives elsewhere. That doesn't count. You're a lone woman living in Delhi.'

'I'm not alone, I'm living with Hira.'

'I'm coming to that. You're at work most of the day and Hira is being brought up by maids. I want better for my granddaughter than that run-down rented house of yours.'

'You want to give me money?' Waheeda was confused.

'No. I want you to return to Nulkazim. I want you to bring Hira to live with her grandmother. She will care for her. You will both be comfortable.'

I don't want comfort. I want my freedom and I want my work. She tried to begin tactfully but Aseem ignored the words she found, addressing mild–mannered arguments to the air between them, as if the air was a sitting judge.

'What pittance do you receive for your work? Not much when you consider you're living in a city where your monthly salary wouldn't buy a meal for two at the Orient Express restaurant.'

'That doesn't matter to me.'

'Money will matter soon. And even if you claim it never will, although it will one day, I guarantee that; Hira matters to you, doesn't she? Look at your daughter's life. Tell me she is not better off here.'

Waheeda unclenched her jaw. 'What do you suggest I do with my life, Abba?'

Would he ask her to start a teaching career in Nulkazim? In a school maybe? Imagine. From a university lecturer to downgrade to a school. Did he know how suffocated she would be here, every step watched? There would be those who sucked up to her and those who maligned her. In this town, no one would be neutral. In Delhi, she could ignore the people who fell into camps; there was a whole population who had no idea at all of what went on in this part of the country. She could trust her close friends there. So many millions in Delhi; and so many thousands who couldn't care less what their local politicians did, much less who wielded backstage power in a small Uttar Pradesh town they'd never heard of.

'You should use your talents, Wija. I need your help in my work.'

Waheeda turned her palms up and scrutinised them. She shook her head slowly and a tear began in her left eye.

'Have I said anything at all that didn't make sense?' he asked.

She was silent; the tear left her eye and slid down her cheekbone. It was a small tear, just a tear of shock really, an insignificant tear; she could leave it alone. Let it show. Let her misery show.

'I need your support at NPF. You are my daughter. I cannot let you live a shabby life alone in Delhi.'

'I love Delhi.' Her voice cracked. 'I *love* Delhi.'

'You will be able to go there as often as you wish.' He gave a nonchalant shrug although the news he was imparting was yet another amazing dodge.

Visit Delhi whenever she liked?

'The flat in Sangeet Vihar can be yours, to use when you want. I travel there less often now. The main bedroom can be yours. The small room will be fine for me.'

•

REPLAYING THE SCENE, Waheeda would pinpoint this moment as her moment of weakness. He'd ambushed her, batting away anything she said and impatiently closing the discussion with: 'You will be making the decision, Wija, not me.'

She stood up at once. 'I'm glad to hear it.' She flicked her *dupatta* over her shoulder. 'I'll consider everything you've said,' she mimicked his mild-voice tactic. 'I'll let you know what I decide.'

Aseem pointed at the green baize. 'Pick a chit.'

'What? *No.*'

'You already know what is better for your daughter and even for you. But see what Fate has to say today. Today is as good a time as any.'

'What's written on the chits?'

'One says: Nulkazim.'

Translation: A life in Politics. Translation: Aseem wins. Nafis loses his wife and child. If he had any chance of bringing them to him, however slim, that chance would vanish. But other translations also jostled in her head: Love, security and care for Hira; family around Hira; comfort for Waheeda, and even if her adoptive father hadn't spelled it out, because he was cunning enough not to, she was sure the role of political heir was on the plate; hers for the taking, if she put the work in; if she stepped up to it; if she sank her faith in him. 'What about the other chit? What's written on that?'

'Nothing. It's blank. Because that's the state of your life now.'

How easily he slighted her. 'That first time,' she pointed at the chits, bitterness creeping in, 'both had the same word on them. "Nulkazim." There was no "St. Ann's." I didn't know it then. I realised your methods later. That was sixteen years ago, but don't think I've forgotten.'

'I know you haven't forgotten. Do you think I'd do the same again? You're grown up now. You should know it's not you choosing which chit will appear in your hands, it's your destiny.'

'You really believe that? After all that's happened...' She didn't think he did. But she also knew that even the most robust politicians were apt to believe what was suited to the moment, apt to be superstitious when needed and sceptical when required. When your career was based on the fickleness of people and on luck, as much as on anything you did, it helped to attribute let-downs, tragedies, and ill-will to another force, a greater force. At least Aseem was not invoking God; he knew calling on Allah wouldn't work with her.

Her life a blank? It wasn't true, but he was a master of psychological demoralisation. He knew how to turn someone's mind. It's what he did daily.

Where was Nafis in this equation? 'There is an option you

don't seem to have a chit for.' She liked the teasing quality she injected into her voice.

His eyes narrowed suspiciously. 'What's that?'

'Theog. My destiny could be in Theog.'

'What will you live on? And will you live in that garage that Nafis calls a house?'

'Nafis has enough money. He's managing on his income, isn't he?' She gripped the top of the chair and leaned forward. 'If you were keen to help me, you would buy us a bigger house there, and then—'

'—you would live happily ever after.' He completed the sentence with a snort.

The usual defensive streak took over on behalf of her husband. 'It could be. Somehow you missed that option.' *Because you want me here.* You're not packing me off to be with Nafis, not telling me to keep gossip at bay. If your sons were alive, you'd be saying something quite different. *If my brothers were alive...*

In truth, Theog was not an option. If she scratched out Nulkazim on a chit and wrote Theog the translation would be the same: the end of her independence. Worse, it could herald the start of a new and deeper depression for Nafis. It would end her university career, although she could do something low-key in the local villages or the closest town. Importantly, Hira would live in the same home as her father. But in other ways, her daughter wouldn't benefit. Theog didn't even have a choice of good schools as Nulkazim did. Hira could be sent to a boarding school. Waheeda's head buzzed with a sudden pain. *Then, without my daughter, my life really will be a blank. I will have made it so.*

She felt drained. 'Good night, Abba.'

'Wija, you can pick a chit. Then you can go.' He got to his feet and turned his back to her. 'I won't see what you're doing. Choose one.'

This was a strange psychology but it was working. She said, 'It doesn't mean anything if I pick a chit. It doesn't *mean* anything.'

She lifted one of the origami triangles. The paper dry in her tense hands. She looked up quickly. Aseem's back remained turned. She unfolded the paper. *Nulkazim.* Like all those years ago, the same neat black fountain-pen word. She picked up the other chit and without opening it crushed them both into her fist as she left the study.

TWO

She dropped the chits on her bed. She lay curled on her side next to them, with her cheek on the comfort of the thin cotton. She closed her eyes, wondering what Nafis was doing at this time of night. Pottering around in his messy living room/studio space?

If he returned to live with her in Delhi, no one would dare call her life a blank. When they'd married eight years ago, she believed in him. She was certain she understood him, that she knew him well, or as much as one human being could know another without dreaming their dreams. But she hadn't been able to follow him into that dimension he got lost in when he painted, or when he dragged on cigarette after cigarette, or when he cried fat secret tears.

It wasn't those things that kept them apart now. They couldn't speak without being cruel to one another. When Rohail and Irfan had died Nafis had done his duty, being the steadfast pillar that Ammi could lean on. He'd managed small kindnesses to Waheeda too, but two weeks after the funeral they were back to prodding a springy sensitive nerve when they spoke to each other, especially if they talked of the future. There seemed to be nothing left on his part but animosity. Waheeda tiptoed around him to avoid ructions. She could not, in her right mind, move to live with him in Theog.

She opened her eyes. Nafis would not be returning to Delhi. Everyone could see that. She was the last to know it. She sat up, switched on the lamp and smoothed open one of the crumpled chits. 'Who chooses: destiny or me?' she asked herself mockingly, scrutinising that one word. *Nulkazim.* Same immaculate handwriting as before. Same damn pen, probably. She unfolded the other triangle. Blank. She tossed the blank piece of paper towards the waste-basket. It missed and fell on the floor by it. She tore up the fragment that said 'Nulkazim' and put the shreds carefully in the basket. It was only a chit. It didn't mean anything.

•

THE NEXT DAY she took care to avoid Aseem, not wanting her mother to see her annoyance at his trickery. Fortunately, before she brought Hira down for breakfast, he'd already left for the party headquarters in the old part of Nulkazim. That afternoon, on the pretext of needing to mark some assignments, she left Hira on the back veranda with Ammi, both of them napping on the cushioned wicker chairs. She stood alone in each brother's room. The rooms were spick and span: cricket trophies lined up on Rohail's shelves; books stacked by Irfan's bed. She checked them—some were library books that required returning. Should she mention this to Ammi? Should she return them while she was here, without asking her mother? Wardrobes in both rooms heaved with the trendy clothes of men in their early twenties. Why had they needed six pairs of jeans each? And who had given them so many aftershave lotions—arranged in rows in their bathroom? Nothing had been given away or discarded yet, the rooms kept as if the occupants were away for a while, and would be back. Their starched kurta-pyjamas, their political uniform for campaigning days outside Nulkazim, hung ready for use. Next to them hung their office attire of short-sleeve shirts and light-coloured trousers. She ran her hands over their laundered shirts.

In her own room she weighed up the heap of students' essays, sifted through the notes for the research paper she was writing and reviewed the list she'd made in preparation for next semester's topics. She couldn't focus on any of these. Rohail. Irfan. Just boys. Sweet souls. Into nothingness. Foul play.

Rohail. Irfan. She'd nurtured them, been mini-mum for seven years, while she was still home. Rohail with his mischievous eyes and flashing temper. Irfan, who loved a cuddle, even when he was older. Both of them gone. In a horrible way. So horrible, she couldn't bear to imagine their dying moments.

She was alive. Pulsing to the tune of a chit.

Would Aseem actually anoint her his heir apparent? *She,* Waheeda, adopted daughter, who came in the package when he married the widowed Rehana, she would work in Nulkazim Peace Forum? *She* would campaign as her brothers had done?

What would Nafis, self-professed hater of politics, say? What could he say? He had an umbilical cord to state politics even if he pretended to ignore that fact. His father had been a stalwart of the party and his younger brother, Shakeel, was one of Aseem's most trusted deputies. Nafis and she had initially bonded over their dislike of the family business. They were above it; they were different. Watch the artist and the academic leap and bound into a distinct apolitical universe.

She wandered around the house to give time for the redness in her eyes to fade. A little stab to her heart as she straightened a painting in the hallway that led to two interconnecting receiving rooms at the side of the house. These windowless rooms had been designated the women's areas when formal or political functions were held at home. The painting was an abstract in soft grey and white by Nafis; it was the only one he'd gifted her mother. It hung in this hallway because Aseem didn't think much of it. He didn't want it displayed in the sitting or dining room, where he was likely to see it often.

•

ASEEM RETURNED HOME in the early evening, just as a cool mist settled outside. Waheeda heard the car and stepped into the kitchen, joining Hira who was 'helping' her grand-mother prepare dinner. 'Nani is making *aloo gobi* for me,' Hira informed her seriously. 'Because I don't like *bhindi*. And I don't want *dal*.'

Ammi was chopping a cauliflower into tiny pieces. 'I'll cook it for Hira just with *jeera* and *haldi*; how she likes it. But why does she seem only to eat *aloo gobi* and mild chicken curry? She's too fussy!'

Those are the dishes Nafis cooks. 'She's not the only six-year-old who's fussy; surely you remember, Ammi.' Rohail had been a picky eater even at twenty-four, but she didn't name him. Nasreen, the maid, would be first to wail if the boys were mentioned, even if her employer, Rehana, never cried. At least not in public.

At the stove Nasreen was frying the onions for the *bhindi*, and watching the potato cubes set to boil. 'Don't add too much chilli,' Waheeda reminded her. The maid's young daughter was also in the kitchen, hovering by the stove. 'How are your studies going, Munni?' Waheeda asked her. 'Do you still like Geography best?'

Nasreen answered for her daughter. 'She doesn't go to school anymore. *Behenji*, if you need another maid in Delhi, please take Munni with you. She will look after Hira very well.'

'She doesn't go to school? Why?' Nobody in the kitchen met her eye. Waheeda knew that her mother paid the fees for Nasreen's children. Surely she was still doing so.

Munni lived in the village with her aunt while her father and mother both worked in Nulkazim. Nasreen had been with her mother many years. As a maid in a busy household she had no time to tend to her own children and they'd been left in the village, where the whole family was now relatively better off compared to their neighbours. Waheeda assumed Munni was staying in Nulkazim with her mother just for the holidays.

Hira skipped up to Munni, 'School finished?' she asked.

'Now will you go to work? Do you want to be a doctor like me?'

Another embarrassed silence filled the smoky kitchen. Munni shook her head at Hira. The back door was ajar and she went to open it fully.

'Remind me, how old is Munni?' Waheeda asked Nasreen. The girl was short and filled out; it was hard to tell if she was a teenager or younger.

Nasreen threw the *bhindi* into the *karhai* and shrugged. 'About thirteen. Maybe twelve. Maybe fourteen. She is a smart girl, *behenji*; take her with you to look after Hira.'

'I already have a maid,' Waheeda murmured, 'but I'll keep her in mind and also ask my friends.'

She was lying. She did not want to be responsible for thirteen-year-old Munni moving to Delhi to be exploited. Later at the dining table she asked her mother, 'Aren't you paying school fees for Munni?'

Ammi nodded. 'But she's decided not to continue.'

'She's decided? Or her father? Abba, surely you can speak to him and insist she goes to school.'

Aseem had been concentrating on eating but he stopped chewing his chapatti and looked up. Before he could speak, Ammi interjected, 'It's not entirely her father's decision. Munni doesn't want to go to school. Her father is pleased, but he's not forcing her either way, since he's not paying the fees anyway.'

'Munni doesn't want to go to school? Why not? If there's a problem, we can look at another school for her.'

Her mother darted a glance at Hira. 'It's not so simple, Wija.'

'Why doesn't she want to go to school?'

Ammi gave her an impatient look and fluttered her eyes towards Hira and Aseem.

'Hira, if you've finished,' and Waheeda could see that she had, 'can you switch on the television for me?' Hira slid off her chair with alacrity. Waheeda called after her: 'Wash your hands first.'

Aseem bent his head down to his plate and seemed engrossed in eating again.

'Why?' Waheeda repeated. She didn't care if her mother wanted to shield him from whatever the reason was. She was already prickly from the previous evening and now he was sitting at the head of the table, imposing his presence on the conversation she wanted to have.

Her mother lowered her voice. 'She finds it difficult. There are no separate girls' toilets in the school. What with getting her period…and the boys' behaviour…'

'You can have a toilet built,' Waheeda said loudly.

Aseem raised his head, realising she was addressing him.

'You want me personally to have a toilet built for Munni?'

'Yes, you can do that surely?'

He stared at her like she was an idiot. 'Nasreen's village is far away. Am I going to start building toilets in schools there before I do so in the villages of Nulkazim?'

'Fine. Start nearby and extend out and then make a special dispensation to build one there. You can do that.'

He pushed his plate away in disgust. 'You want me to be a builder of *toilets*. You do realise, Wija, that people are clamouring for roads and electricity…when they come to me to sort out issues, to put pressure on the minister, it's about *infrastructure*—'

'You don't think this is important?' Waheeda was so angry she pushed aside her own plate. 'I think it's *really* important. Why can't you use your influence for something like this for once?'

A light went on behind his dull grey eyes. '*You* build the toilets. If you join the party, as we discussed last night, you can be the toilet-builder.' He seemed to smirk.

'It's not a joke.'

'I'm not joking.'

She breathed out noisily through her nostrils. Like a sick mare. She picked up her plate, intending to take it to the kitchen, although she knew that as soon as she did so, Ammi would call for Nasreen to clear up the table and bring out the oranges and grapes.

'There's something you should know.' Aseem's tone was purposeful. 'Even if you have a separate girls' toilet constructed at Munni's school, the probability is she won't attend. Not everyone wants to study. Not everyone has just one reason for giving up. And now that she's already stopped, the likelihood is that she won't go back.'

Why does he treat me like an idiot? She went into the kitchen and deposited the plate by the sink. Maybe she *was* being silly. She'd become impassioned on Munni's behalf and now he was telling her that she wouldn't be any good to this young girl. Munni was sitting on a stool with a steel thali on her lap. She licked her fingers, having hastily swallowed a mouthful of her dinner at Waheeda's abrupt entrance. Waheeda retreated to the dining table to leave her in peace. There were other girls like Munni. Many of them wanted to study further. They *should* go to school. Education would offer some protection from the worst tribulations awaiting them.

'Just one other thing.' Aseem spoke as though they were continuing a calm discussion. 'The building of toilets is between us.' As though her decision had been made. 'You won't mention your agenda to anybody just yet. You don't want to be a complete laughing stock.'

THREE

April 1997
Delhi

WAHEEDA SET DOWN her canvas case in the bedroom in Sangeet Vihar. It felt odd to occupy the main bedroom of the flat while Aseem settled himself into the smaller room. He would have to use the tiny guest bathroom by the front door. She offered him the choice as they arrived, but he'd pointed to the larger room, with the attached bathroom, 'That's yours now.'

She shouldn't be discomfited; they'd made a deal. This was a part of it. The next few times she came to Delhi she would be on her own. He'd already indicated that once she was supervising operations in the capital he would prefer to stay back in Nulkazim.

She looked at herself in the mirror above the sink. Her hair needed combing and fastening back again after the long drive. She should wash her face too; it would refresh her, set her up for the appointments ahead. She knew what she would encounter, especially from Chetna Mura. In political circles what they were saying behind her back was: 'Waheeda is naïve.' It wasn't a compliment. Perhaps they were right; yet she felt a certain pride at that description. They may as well have said, 'She is idealistic.'

She splashed warm water on her face and scrubbed it dry. *I have a lot to learn, but I don't think it's necessary to do everything as others do.* She dabbed on powder from her compact and a slick of eyeliner. Lip gloss. Yes, presentable. The individual who looked back at her was the person who nodded placidly at Aseem's exhortations on etiquette, the person who followed Umair-ji's scripts to the letter for speeches. The person who harboured the ambition of being her own woman. The chrysalis would split—the real Waheeda would harden her wings. *What here, in this bathroom that smelt of Dettol? She would become a force?*

In the park across the road an *Amaltas* tree was in full bloom. She admired it from the window of the sitting room. Not for nothing was this laburnum called 'golden rain shower.' Bright yellow petals carpeted the ground under it, while the drooping branches remained laden with soft yellow flowers. With a pang she remembered the rented home she'd given up, where an *Amaltas* dominated her neighbour's front yard. April was always golden there. At least visually. Hadn't someone, a poet, said April is the cruellest month? Another jolting memory. Two years ago in April her brothers had stopped by unannounced.

Shake off that recollection. Don't be critical of them. Not now.

She was fully aware of the absurd nepotism in her current position. Even so, she'd not swanned into politics with a sense of entitlement. Not like Rohail and Irfan, who, to her surprise, had fallen easily into the role of young-blood politicians: obvious heirs and leaders. To her then-disapproving eye, they had been boys displaying the inherent flaws of youth.

Remember only happy moments with them. Togetherness. Love. Protection. How when they were little they convulsed into giggles when she danced with the yellow lampshade on her head. She liked that: dancing with a lampshade hat. How she read to them; made up secret passwords for their games; and adjudicated in their disputes. But that April. Rohail's long legs planted on her blue *dhurrie*, his contorted lips informing her that Nafis had abandoned her. *Tell me something I don't know*. It must have finally become crystal-clear in Nulkazim that Nafis was spending all his time in Theog. 'We're here for you,' Irfan offered shyly, not quite into his defender role.

Rohail and he would set Nafis right. Rohail was tough-guy matter-of-fact. 'We're travelling on to Theog and I'll break Nafis's legs when I get there.' Irfan sheepish, his thoughts not in concert with his older brother, but unable to contradict him. Waheeda losing her cool. 'What kind of louts are you? Is this what being in politics teaches you? *I* asked Nafis to live in Theog for a while. For his *health*. Do you understand?' The two of them looking perplexed at each other. She'd punched Aseem's number into her telephone. 'If *anybody* harms Nafis I'm *never* coming home to Nulkazim. *You* can explain why to my Ammi,' she told Aseem, handing over the phone to a glowering Rohail. Aseem had calmed him down and commanded him back to Nulkazim.

•

IT WAS IRONIC that she'd been reduced to defending Nafis in his absence. She had not sent him to Theog, or if she had, she'd meant it as a temporary measure. When she'd told him he was free, she hadn't known that she was sealing a permanent contract. Four years had passed since *that* conversation. Nafis's deep depression seemed to have lifted in Theog, and so had any affection he had for her; lifted out of him and evaporated! But what she'd done was not wrong, and it couldn't be undone.

That was in late April, too, with the neighbour's *Amaltas* glowing like paradise while Nafis dulled into his own abyss. He'd spent the month muttering '*I can't stand it.*' His grumbling would start as she got dressed for work in the mornings. One night, after Hira had fallen asleep after bellowing and squalls, and Waheeda knew that in his studio-room Nafis had been holding his head in his hands or his hands over his ears or smoking furiously out of the window, she'd thought of a solution.

When he entered their bedroom it was late, past midnight. He switched on the bedside lamp at his end and padded to the bathroom. She heard him dip the mug in the bucket and splash his feet. He came to the bed and drew his top sheet on himself. She sat up. 'Why wait?' she asked him. 'Why wait to live the life you really want? If you truly believe that a house in Theog will make you happy, that living there will make you content, that the beauty there will feed your art, then don't imprison yourself here.'

Nafis seemed stunned. He sat up too, turning his back, adjusting his pillow behind him.

'Do you think I want to be the person who restricts you? Don't I know enough about that?' Waheeda gripped her knees to stop her voice trembling. 'Do you think I want to be the person you can blame for your unhappy life? Do I want that? If we're keeping you here, Hira and I, from a sense of responsibility, and that's all that's keeping you here, and you won't smile or laugh or finish anything—not a song, not a painting, then you must ask yourself: are you going to stay depressed forever? And is that what your wife wants? Is that any help at all to your wife?'

'What are you saying? Do you want me to leave you?'

'No, you misunderstand me. That's not what-'

'Wija, I really don't know what—'

'I don't want you to do anything for me. If you want to make me happy—do something for yourself. Whatever you want, do it. Just promise never to point to me ever in your life and say this person is the reason I didn't live my dreams. That,' she said, tears filling her eyes, 'is not why you married me.'

She felt him shift, heavy on his side of the bed. He turned his face away again, staring at the simple striped curtains drawn across their window. It was a while before he spoke. 'You want to be the person who sets me free?' He leaned across to his bedside lamp, his hand resting on the switch. 'Because you love me or because you hate me?' His voice was soft. He switched off the lamp and lay down.

'I don't hate you.' She spoke into the darkness.

•

WHERE HAD FOUR years gone? They'd passed in a flicker. There was an art to loneliness and she was now an expert. She blinked at the laburnum, flourishing in the park, making people happy. No, she wasn't going to be lonely; not on this second-last day of April. She was going to have a very pleasant evening dining with her friend Lara. It had been a while since they'd met and there was so much to fill her in on.

The sun streamed in through the glass pane, causing a light perspiration on Waheeda's neck. She turned the fan speed up to five. The fan began to judder on the ceiling and she twisted the dial down a notch. She could hear Aseem in his room, murmuring into his cell phone. She walked towards the kitchen just as Bhavna, their part-time help, brought out a pot of boiled water. She'd anticipated Waheeda's request.

They'd departed Nulkazim at dawn, in a three-car convoy, for security. Habib and two cars remained with them here at Sangeet Vihar while the party workers who'd accompanied them took the other vehicle for their own errands. Waheeda poured hot water into a large mug and added two heaped teaspoons of instant coffee. She took a chair at the square dining table, stirring in a spoonful of sugar, trying to list the day's commitments in her head, but fast-forwarding to the evening and Lara's company. She must ensure that she had some clear hours with her closest friend, who was visiting from Singapore, where she now lived. They'd met as freshers at St. Ann's when they were sixteen and they'd remained close ever since, supporting each other's endeavours along the years. Waheeda had lived in a *barsati* at the top of Lara's family home when she was studying at university in Delhi. Aseem had allowed her that degree of independence only because he'd met Lara's parents, and been assured by Santosh Auntie, Lara's mother, that she would keep a *very* close eye on her guest-tenant.

Waheeda smiled to herself, anticipating that Lara's wicked wit would lift her spirits. Even though she'd been slightly annoyed by their last phone conversation, and at Lara's patent shock at her decision to join NPF, it would be wonderful to be with an old friend. She would feel human, a cheerful talkative human, and be herself.

Aseem stepped out of his room, grey eyes gleaming. 'I've just been invited to a party by Arun Selvani. Of all people. I can't stand the chap. But Chetna says that this is an important social gathering, a big 'do' and we must go. We must see and be seen.'

'When is this important gathering? Tomorrow?'

'Tonight, and you must—'

'This evening?' Waheeda laughed. 'It's a last-minute invite,' she said dryly.

She imagined that Selvani, whoever he was, wasn't fond of Aseem either, but that Chetna had engineered this.

'We are attending. I've said so. And you must come with me.'

'Abba, I can't. I'm seeing Lara this evening. She's flying back to Singapore tomorrow. It's the only opportunity I have.'

'This may be an *important* event. I keep telling you it's good for you to meet people.'

She chewed at the inside of her cheek. 'I would come with you…but I've already made plans with Lara. That's important to me, too.'

'Can't you do both?'

The bell rang and Chetna whooshed into the flat. 'Namaskar, Adaab, good morning, Aseem-ji.' She'd stuck on a black bindi that was almost as large as her forehead. Her kajal-smudged eyes rested fleetingly on Waheeda. 'Ready for your meetings?'

Waheeda dunked down her coffee. She suspected that Chetna had a crush on Aseem. He did not encourage her, it was true, but he couldn't be unaware of it. 'I'll be a couple of minutes.' She retreated into her room to gather her things.

When she emerged, Chetna said, 'Take your friend to the party. Then you can work and play: two-in-one, strawberry and cream.'

'What?'

Aseem grunted at her as he started down the stairs. 'Bring Lara to the party.'

She followed him to Chetna's big car, where her driver busily opened doors as they appeared. 'I can try to persuade her. But—'

Aseem took the front passenger seat. Chetna and Waheeda sat at the back on plush beige upholstery. Waheeda sighed openly. Even if Lara agreed it would hardly give her any proper time with her friend.

Aseem wound down his window and called over Habib, who had appeared from nowhere, as he did, to stand to attention by Aseem's Honda and Waheeda's Fiat. 'Take a break now. We'll be out late tonight.'

They disembarked from Chetna's car at the porch of a brand-new, five-star hotel. Chetna strode forward, up the black marble steps, surprisingly quick in her sari. Aseem and Waheeda followed in her wake. The air conditioning in the hotel coffee shop made the atmosphere cold and damp, and Aseem wrinkled his nose. Waheeda knew he was thinking about the waste of energy—one of his bugbears. A tang of smoke hung in the chill. Brass railings gleamed around the booth where Romy Fernando was waiting for them. He was a Mr Fixit for a prominent business mogul. Chetna made the introductions. Romy had a round face, an easy grin, and a short body that tended to plumpness. He fired off some questions about Nulkazim Peace Forum, focusing on Aseem's plans to break out of being a provincial party. 'We never put up a candidate for a national election before this last one,' Aseem said. Waheeda knew this to be a lie, but Aseem always glossed over his own long-ago failure at the polls. 'This time, our candidate was very close to winning in Patharghat. Literally, two hundred votes behind. Imagine.' He stopped suddenly and his face slackened. She knew he was trying to steady his features, he'd let himself think about what had happened just after the results.

Luckily they were all distracted by a plate of *kathi* rolls being served by an over-obsequious waiter. Romy had pre-ordered these. He tucked into them with relish and genially began to include the women in the conversation. He mentioned that he was just back from a road trip in the United States. 'Route 66,' he informed them, between mouthfuls. Chetna responded with news of her shopping trips to Saks Fifth Avenue. Waheeda had never been out of India. With nothing to contribute she thought it reasonable to excuse herself for a few minutes. She stepped out into the lobby to dial Lara's home number.

'Please,' she pleaded as soon as Lara was on the line, 'please say yes to a favour.'

'You know I never do that until I know what it is.'

'I have to attend a party this evening. It's a last-minute thing but Abba insists I don't miss it. I don't want to miss seeing *you*. *Please* come with me to the party. I'll pick you up; I'll drop you home whenever you say, and we'll get some time to talk.'

'You mean you're cancelling on me?'

'I'm not cancelling. If you say No, I won't go to the party. Although I have to be there.'

'Well, put like that...' she detected a smile in Lara's voice. 'I'll come with you, but if I can't stand it—'

'I'll drop you home whenever you say, I promise.'

'Deal.'

Waheeda breathed out with relief. 'Wonderful. I'll come by at eight. Bye.'

'Wait! What do you want me to wear?'

Precise quick-thinking Lara. Waheeda sometimes forgot

how differently she'd begun to dress from her peers. 'Indian dress,' she said, and could picture Lara nodding to herself, glad she'd asked. It wasn't a party after all, or not for Waheeda, it was just another work occasion.

She returned to the coffee shop, finding Chetna ready to go, onwards to the next person she wanted to introduce to them. Aseem and Mr Fixit both looked pleased, perhaps they'd come to some understanding. Romy raised his hand and almost instantly the waiter was at his elbow presenting the bill. Romy signed it with a flourish while Chetna raised her brows. 'You have a tab here?'

'My office is next door.' Romy gave a slight shrug, pointing in the direction of an adjacent building. 'I'm here pretty much every day. Those *kathi* rolls are my brunch. They send the bills to the office.'

'He's got it made,' Chetna remarked as they slid into her car. 'Nice life, eh?'

·

WAHEEDA PARKED OUTSIDE Lara's home in Defence Colony at eight that evening. She tooted and looked up at the second floor, at the terrace where she'd rented the room. For six years she'd lived with the Sabbarwals and they'd looked after her like she was their own daughter. She'd moved out when she married Nafis to set up her own little home. It had been a condition of her accepting his proposal. They would live in Delhi. She would not leave this city to go to live in Lucknow where Nafis's family home was. He'd been fine with that. Then.

She tooted again. If she got dragged inside they'd be late for the party. Lara appeared, trailed by Santosh Auntie, who flung out her arms. Waheeda got out of the car to offer and receive hugs. Everyone told everyone how good they looked. Santosh Auntie asked how Hira was, and Waheeda reached into the back seat to produce the small album she'd brought along, filled with recent photographs. They went into the house to look at the photos, Lara cooing over Hira and Waheeda in turn exclaiming how cute Lara's two daughters were growing up to be. Lara had their picture in her wallet. The Sabbarwal sitting room was just as it used to be, and Waheeda noted that although there was a discreetly positioned photo of Lara's children, half hidden behind the fronds of a plant, there were no photos of Lara or her husband, Vijay.

It was half an hour before they returned to the car. 'So where are you taking me?' Lara dawdled as she settled into the passenger seat, almost closing the door, then opening it again to check her *dupatta* was not caught in the frame before she slammed it shut.

'We're going to Arun Selvani's home. You've heard of him?' Waheeda frowned in concentration, trying to remember the best route to New Friends Colony.

'The industrialist? Paper, sugar, paints, electronics, that Arun Selvani?'

'Yes, finger in every pie, that one. My dad and he can't abide each other, but now Arun's invited him to this dinner he's hosting of the great and good, so Abba feels he ought to show up. Otherwise it'll be a snub. And he wants me to attend, too. All of this was decided just this morning! And I don't want to see any Selvani, Melvani; I want to see *you*.'

'I don't think I should be going along—' murmured Lara, but Waheeda cut her off.

'Of course you can. Abba knows I've come to get you.'

Waheeda sensed Lara's right leg tense up like she wanted to press down on the brake. 'Maybe you'll find the networking useful too,' she said quickly. Lara worked in communications for a pharmaceutical firm in Singapore. It was a long shot that there would be anyone there she wanted to meet professionally, but it was something positive to say.

'The Selvanis are nouveau,' pronounced Lara with false hauteur.

A giggle escaped Waheeda. She was so pleased to have her friend along. She felt young, free, happy. 'Yes, darling, I know. Unlike the Sabbarwals. Even so, influential people will be there, or so my father says.'

'Hmm…are you taking me to a mansion of gold taps?'

'I have never been to their home. I don't even know them!'

'Wija, are you sure we'll get to talk to each other? So many questions I have for you!'

'Let's see how it goes, Lara. We'll leave whenever you want. I've so many questions for you, too.'

'I'll start first. So: you've given in. After you always said you never would. I just can't think of you in this sleazy line of work…'

Waheeda felt her face tighten. 'Sorry,' Lara said. 'I mean it's all right for some people, and I don't mean to be rude about Aseem-ji, of course, it's just you were the last person, although I understand now that—' she bit her lip suddenly. 'How *are* all of you? After what happened. Every time I asked you on the phone you were so vague. Like you think your phone is tapped. What actually happened in the train fire? Did you find out?'

Waheeda couldn't hide the tremor in her cheek.

'Sorry, sorry,' Lara flapped her hands in dismay. 'Just concentrate on driving, darling. Too many questions already.' She went completely quiet.

When they were stationary at a red light and Waheeda wasn't monitoring the traffic on all four sides, she felt able to compose herself. 'I already feel useful in my new role.' She spoke defensively, to the windshield, out of context, but Lara nodded encouragingly at her side. 'The charity I've set up, the Golden Oriole Trust, to build essential structures in schools…it's part of what I'm doing. It's not related to NPF, but…I wouldn't have one without taking on the other. If you see what I mean.'

There were some things Waheeda couldn't articulate. The

palpable satisfaction when she could contribute to further the education of women, and young Muslim girls in particular. 'Essential structures' was a euphemism for toilets. Her charity concentrated on building either those or girls' changing rooms, but there were occasions when it was appropriate to talk about the exact nature of the work it undertook and other occasions when it was not. Why was it so difficult to articulate her belief that she was achieving *more* than she had before? Lara knew that she'd loved her job and had got along with the people she worked with. Naaz, a colleague in the history department, had become a great friend.

'Where I'm placed now is inspiring in an utterly different way!' She'd spoken out of context again, but Lara gave an understanding nod. Waheeda chewed at the inside of her cheek. If she examined herself fairly, she would have to admit that in the last few months she'd been grabbed by a heady sense of what was attainable. She could become a member of parliament. It wouldn't be easy to let go of such ambitions, however secret they were for the time-being. Lara knew her well, she knew Waheeda was quiet but steely with her aims.

She assumed Lara didn't approve, but she also assumed she would stand by her, no matter what. That was another thing that didn't need articulation. Waheeda wasn't expecting the little dig that came from Lara, who asked oh-so-gently, 'What does Nafis make of this?'

Lara had got on really well with Nafis. They played *Antarakshari* and sang together. Lara always won because Nafis didn't have a good stock of film songs in his memory that began with the *b* sound or the *l* sound. He'd wing it by singing his own compositions. Lara would disqualify him. When Lara told Nafis that an unpublished, unrecorded, unfinished song couldn't be counted he didn't sulk and walk away. If his wife had said such a thing it would have launched a major quarrel.

What does Nafis make of this? Lara didn't need Waheeda to spell out what he might be thinking. But then Lara didn't know the whole story. She didn't know the messy details of Nafis's low period; she had only heard the glossed-over version that Waheeda had provided.

When it became apparent to him that the move from Delhi to Nulkazim had been orchestrated with more in mind than just Hira's well-being and solace for Ammi, he said coldly, 'Why does everyone become a politician when there's nothing else left for them to do?'

That stung. Waheeda replied, 'Why don't you ask your brother?'

Shakeel was not just the mainstay of NPF in Lucknow, like his father had been before him; he was invaluable to Aseem, his trustworthiness never in doubt. In the last three months, she herself had begun to depend on Shakeel when they were out on the road. Being a relative, he could accompany her in her jeep and provide a shield against gossip and potential unfitting behaviour from the male village leaders and committee members she had to meet.

Shakeel would not be drawn on what Nafis said to him about her. If indeed she was mentioned when the brothers spoke to each other. When Nafis came to Nulkazim to visit Hira, he stayed only a day each time, and he barely spoke to Waheeda. One time, late at night, he found her alone, pacing in the sitting room, her mind was too agitated to rest when he was in the house. He stepped up close. 'NPF,' he bit out through tightly-set teeth. 'Remember the one thing we both agreed on: We would never join the family firm. And now here you are.'

'You brought me to this point.' Somewhat honest, but also spiteful, so that he would never mention past promises again. He hadn't continued the conversation.

•

'WHAT DIFFERENCE DOES it make what Nafis thinks?' she

asked Lara. 'He's gone from my life.' It killed her to utter those words lightly, she hadn't spoken them aloud to anyone before. This is what friends were for. They knew when your heart was breaking and you were covering up. She parked among the throng of cars outside the tall gates of the Selvani residence. As they entered the imposing gates, Lara and she paused for a moment, looking at the two-storey mansion within, at its calm tasteful exterior, and at each other. 'We are so prim, aren't we?' Lara mischievously pushed Waheeda towards the front door.

Waheeda wore a black silk *salwar-kameez* suit; the *salwar* had silver embroidery on the *ponchha* and silver threads danced along the length of her black chiffon *dupatta*. Her hair was left untied, for a change, and hung down below her shoulders in natural waves. Her *kameez* was demurely cut, with a V neck and loose raglan sleeves flowing to just above her wrists.

Lara was wearing a cotton sleeveless *kameez* in a bright lozenge-pattern of pink and purple. She'd matched it with a purple *churidar* and a short *chunni* draped on one shoulder. With her curly hair, wild as ever, her twinkling eyes, her thin bare arms, and vivid clothes, she looked anything but prim. *That word must be reserved for me.*

Halfway up the drive a man directed them, above a cacophony of voices spilling out, to enter the house from the glass doors that opened onto the front lawn. Waheeda glanced quickly around the large room they were in: mostly women, shrill conversation because it was too noisy to speak normally, and waiters threading themselves in between guests, holding silver trays laden with *shammi* kebabs, *hariyali* kebabs and *paneer tikkas*.

She couldn't spot Aseem. She couldn't see anyone she knew, not even Chetna Mura. It struck her that Chetna hadn't overtly said that she would be attending. Lara helped herself to food and drink; she held a square black napkin in one hand and a glass of cola in the other. She proclaimed the snack she had just eaten 'delicious.'

'Let's just find Abba so he knows I'm here.' Waheeda led the way further into the room and out at the other end, Lara and she squeezing themselves behind a waiter carrying a tray of used glasses. They were in the main hallway of the house and could hear a hubbub from another room to the right. Waheeda peered in. Unlike the larger drawing room they'd been in, this was a smaller room filled with dark paintings, all in a bottle-green hue and executed in the same shadowy style. Perhaps they were figurative, but it was hard to tell without standing close up to them and getting used to the play of light and shade in each image. The air conditioner blasted away and around a semi-circular bar at the centre wall stood a cluster of men. There was Aseem, deep in conversation.

She walked up to the small group and realised in that instant that she was in the wrong room; this was one of those parties where the separation of the sexes prevailed. She would have to mingle among the women. This room of dark paintings was where the men would remain in their congregation, drinking whisky, smoking cigarettes and talking business. Not that women couldn't be accommodated, they would be if they were pushy enough and had an interest in whisky, cigarettes or business, but she could see that Aseem would not want her here. He introduced his little group politely and after Lara and she had greeted them she locked eyes for one moment with him, sending him a silent message of understanding.

She left the room, Lara trailing behind her, and she winced as she turned to her friend. 'Sorry.' This was the kind of party Lara loathed. They returned to the larger drawing room. Waheeda noticed how different it was to the room they'd left; here the décor was contemporary and more formal, with the furnishings mostly in navy and cream. Lara was magnanimous. For a moment. She said, 'Oh, I can see why he wanted you to be here. This is quite a scoop of Delhi folks. I've spot-ted a few people I know. But Wija, this is not my scene. Let's leave right now. Your dad won't even notice. You can come back later after you've dropped me home.'

'Where do you want to go?' They stood in their own huddle, their backs to the rest of the room, so that they could hear each other.

'Let's go to India Gate. Let's buy jasmine *gajras* like we used to. Remember when we used to walk and talk, walk and talk, with *gajra* tied on our wrists?'

'We can't walk around in the dark.'

'No, but we can buy some *gajras* anyway. And we can talk in the car.'

'OK, let's go.' Waheeda was secretly glad that Lara shame-lessly gave in to nostalgia when she visited India. Some of the best evenings of her life had been those 'walk and talk, walk and talk' evenings spent with Lara, the two of them sniffing at the jasmine strands wound around their wrists, because Lara wanted to imitate dissolute men visiting dancing girls, as a joke, and not be feminine and wear the *gajra* in her hair. Just the thought of spending the evening emulating the past made Waheeda's heart lift, but she didn't say any of this to Lara.

In unspoken agreement they wandered out of the room and towards where they assumed the kitchen to be. It would not do to be seen leaving minutes after they'd arrived. They passed a dining room where long tables were being set up for a buffet. It would probably be served at midnight. Lara pushed ahead into the kitchen. She smiled cheerily round at all the staff and asked where the back door was as if it was a perfectly natural question. A young saucer-eyed girl wordlessly pointed.

They took the indicated exit, with Lara holding the door open for Waheeda, who stepped out hurriedly into the dark and straight into something. She stopped. She'd bumped into someone. But Lara had stepped out behind her now and pushed her forward again. She was forced to bump into someone's chest again. 'I'm sorry, so sorry,' she spluttered as she, Lara and one other person moved away from the door and further onto the dark patio. There was another series of 'sorry, so sorry,' while they got used to the light and she made out the form of a tall man. 'I didn't see you there,' she said. 'I didn't realise you were just coming in. I'm sorry.'

'It's all right. Were you leaving the party?' There was a hint of amusement in his voice. 'Is it so boring?'

'No, not at all. We're coming back,' she said hastily. 'I mean, I'm returning. We just decided we needed to get some…uh… *gajras*.'

There was a pause in which she could sense Lara suppressing laughter.

'*Gajras?*' repeated the man. He reached out his palm to the wall of the house. A white light came on. Waheeda saw that he was young and casually dressed. The light bounced off his rectangular glasses and picked out the green tinge of stubble on his jaw.

'*Gajras* will suit my reading,' he said. 'Will you bring back some for me? If you *are* returning…'

'Yes, sure,' she forced out an obliging smile. She pointed behind him. 'I guess going round the patio will bring us to the front drive, yes?'

'What reading?' Lara asked, hanging back to chat.

He put his hand out to Lara. He must've guessed she was an NRI. Waheeda hadn't noticed a change in her but Lara's mother always said that she behaved like a foreigner and it was obvious to everyone. As Lara shook his hand the white light caught shiny flecks of his hair and the glint in Lara's black eyes and the glimmer of the silver bangle she wore.

'I'm Monish,' he introduced himself. 'I'll be reading from my novel later. That's why I was invited. And you are…?'

'Friends,' said Lara. 'Friends of the family. I'm Lara and this is Waheeda.'

Waheeda came forward and returned the clasp of his hand with slight pressure of her own. She believed in strong hand-shakes, when she did shake hands, which was not that often anymore. 'Hello, Monish.'

He looked puzzled. His eyes moved from her to Lara. He looked her up and down swiftly and then Waheeda received the same quick assessing sweep.

'I didn't think the Selvanis would do *literature*.' Lara swung her face up to Monish. 'I thought it was politics and business tonight. Are you sure you're not a writer-politician? So many are. Maybe you're someone we should know but don't recognise?'

'I'm not a politician,' he said gravely, looking down into Lara's face. 'Are you?'

'No. But Waheeda has just—'

Waheeda didn't let her finish. 'We must go now,' she cut in, 'if I'm to make it back to your reading.' She absolutely didn't want Lara to go on a conversational detour and tell this man about her life, that she was a 'hovering' politician, a wanna-be who would declare her hand when she was trained and ready.

'Yes, you *must* return in time for the reading. What a *good* idea.' Lara sounded genuinely enthusiastic. 'Bye, Monish. Nice to meet you.'

They started off but then Lara turned back. 'What's your novel called?'

'*Dalchini ka tukda.*'

'Oh.' Lara's mouth made an exaggerated 'O' of surprise while Waheeda stood there with no immediate remark to make. '*A bite of cinnamon,*' she thought. How odd.

Monish smiled at them like he was used to this reaction. 'I write in Hindi,' he explained.

'Yes, I see.' Lara giggled. 'Well, good luck with the reading. Waheeda will see you later.'

'With the *gajra*?' He raised his thick straight brows at Waheeda to remind her.

'That's right,' she assured him, wondering whether she should switch to speaking in Hindi. 'Will you be in the smaller drawing room? The one with the bar?'

'Oh no, I won't be downstairs.' He pointed to a room on the first floor. 'My reading will be held up there. See those windows. That room.' Lara and she gazed up towards a set of three window panels, nodding in unison.

'I'll start at ten-thirty,' he said. 'Ten-thirty, sharp.'

FOUR

HABIB APPEARED AT the driver's door as they got to her car. Waheeda waved him away. He stepped back, frowning heavily.

'Who *is* that burly surly guy?' Lara chuckled at her own rhyme.

'My bodyguard.' Waheeda was apologetic as she turned the key in the ignition. 'Actually, he's my driver, but he's also supposed to guard me. And I'm guessing my father uses him to spy on my activities. He ultimately reports to my dad after all.'

'Hmm. Aseem-ji has his reasons, I'm sure. Does he think you're in danger?'

'Ever since Rohail and Irfan…he's been a bit paranoid… he mistrusts the whole world…'

'Can you talk about it, Wija? What happened exactly? It *was* on the day after the election. Was it politically motivated? And who?'

Waheeda shook her head. 'We don't know the truth yet.' She shook her head again. Her voice came out tremulous. 'I can't talk about it right now.'

•

ON THAT DAY of the election in May 1996, NPF had come very close to winning its first seat in parliament. It was Aseem's dream to have representatives in the Lok Sabha. Bir Sultan from Patharghat constituency came second by just 230 votes. It was a big deal for NPF. They had expected it to be close but not so close. This amazing result was a surprise as much to them as to the other candidates. Her brothers had stayed overnight at Patharghat, where they'd gone to oversee the voting. They'd decided to travel by train as they were in a large throng of young men. All the vehicles were with Bir already. Everything at the disposal of the party had been made available for him.

Waheeda had heard that the group was jubilant on the return journey. Then suddenly they were engulfed in fire. The carriage they were in and those on either side were in flames. The news reports said: fifty charred bodies were pulled from the three bogeys that caught fire. The news reports said: The cause of the blaze is not known. It was believed to have started in one bogey and spread to the other two. The news reports said: The train was stopped and passengers were evacuated. Only seven people survived from one of the three burnt carriages, probably the last one to catch fire. The survivors could shed no light on the circumstances of the outbreak. The Railways Minister has announced that the fire was *not* caused by a short circuit. The cause of the blaze is being investigated. Most bodies have been identified from belongings. Some bodies are unaccounted for.

Rohail and Irfan were somewhat identifiable. Some semblance of their remains and their things were claimed by Aseem. Had he taken what he was given? She hadn't dared ask.

After the funeral, she had heard Aseem raging at Umair in his study at home. Umair, who was older than Aseem, and of even grander parentage, had been his deputy from the beginning, right from 1970. At that time Umair had wanted a grand name like National Muslim Union, but Aseem had stubbornly stuck with his local place "Nulkazim" and had insisted on "Peace" in the party's name.

Umair usually worked in a hidden office, behind a sliding wall of books in Aseem's office. In her head Waheeda had always referred to Umair's office as 'the inner sanctum,' where Umair sat a desk with six telephones on it. From there he pulled the strings that needed pulling and received the news of the world: all the rumours and gossip that he needed to know.

But on the days after the funeral, he circled Aseem in his study, or rather the two men circled each other, and Aseem's grief could not be contained by Umair's soothing interjections, because Umair had for once failed to find out the truth. Aseem had many enemies but it couldn't be established if one of them was behind the fire or whether it was a genuine accident. It was difficult to believe the latter. Her brothers were prime targets for anyone who felt threatened, who wished to douse the flicker of Nulkazim Peace Forum forever. Anyone who wished to finish Aseem. They had succeeded, almost.

She'd overheard Umair advise Aseem, 'Don't roar at the local police chief, in the way you just did, my friend. Whatever you think of his investigation and inconclusive result. If he's protecting someone there's nothing we can do. I can dig deeper and deeper. I really am trying. But don't antagonise him, because *you* need him, too.' Aseem had growled something in response. Waheeda had been startled at just how patient Umair was being, letting Aseem curse him.

She had always thought him supercilious and brash, with his long shrewd face, shock of white hair, and sneering expression. Perhaps he'd been like that just towards her. Or perhaps that was her impression from when she was very young. He was thought to be among the best speechwriters in the business. Now that she uttered words he wrote, even sentiments that she didn't personally agree with—that she amended or skipped as she spoke—she had come to respect his eloquence in Hindi and Urdu and even local dialect.

•

A BUS SWERVED too close to them on a roundabout and she felt Lara shiver. 'I won't be able to drive in Delhi again. I won't be able to stand it.'

Waheeda pulled herself back to where she was. An evening out with Lara. 'Don't tell Falguni,' she said with a smile in her voice. Lara and their mutual school-friend Falguni always ended any evening out with an argument. Was life better in Singapore or India? Was it ok to shudder at Delhi's madness if you lived in a sterile dictatorship?

'Have you seen Hyper lately?' Lara asked.

Waheeda laughed and grimaced simultaneously. Falguni was a law unto herself. She'd been part of their close-knit clique in St. Ann's. How Waheeda had ended up in a group that included the profligate Falguni Lava, she couldn't say. They were polar opposites but life is full of strange occurrences and friendships. Although her current relationship with Fal was strained. 'I haven't seen much of her. She's very jealous of my friend Naaz and—'

'Ah, your new best friend,' interjected Lara. 'Your colleague from the history department.'

'Yes. Like I was saying—'

'Do you see Naaz much?'

'Yes, I do. Whenever I can.'

'And why not Madam Hyper?' Lara smiled at first. Because she half knew the answer. Then she narrowed her eyes. She'd been having her own troubles with Fal.

'I can't trust her.' The simple truth. 'Not like I can trust you and Naaz.'

Fal was as unpredictable as she was striking: tall, with green eyes, long brown hair and an insolently sexy manner. You never knew how she would react and what trouble she would stir up. In the last year, on the two occasions that Waheeda had met her for lunch or a coffee, Falguni had discussed Lara's marriage, making Waheeda uncomfortable. What was Fal saying about Waheeda and Nafis to other people? When Waheeda moved to Nulkazim, Fal had expected to become her Delhi confidante. She liked to pump Waheeda about her political aspirations and early tactics and wanted to know all the details of what was going on at the NPF HQ. Waheeda was wary. She didn't even need excuses not to see her erstwhile friend now, because she was infrequently in Delhi, and when she was, she was rarely free.

India Gate was illuminated, the sandstone arch glowing orange, the flame to the martyrs burning brightly. The lovely old lamps lining the avenue were lit, lending a magical quality to the calm centre of the city. Waheeda stopped the car and rolled down her window. She would have to catch the attention of a *gajra*-seller if there was still one about. She wasn't keen to let Lara out of the car to go wandering off, or to accompany her, dressed up as they were. There were some ice cream vendors dotted around on the lawns and also a balloon man, but she couldn't make out any other street traders. It was probably too late. She looked at her watch. Nine-thirty.

'I'll drive around a bit,' she said to Lara, not wanting to give up on the idea. 'Keep your eyes peeled for a *gajra*-seller.'

Lara looked attentively out of the window as Waheeda circled the roads around India Gate. 'How is Vijay?' Waheeda asked. 'Is he really managing to carry out his research on the Central Indian tribes while minding two kids in urban Singapore?'

Lara's face glowed, as it always did at any mention of her husband. Waheeda envied that look. 'He doesn't really look after the girls all day, even if he gives everyone that impression. We have a helper, you know. And it's me who struggles to cope; I'm always frantic between work and family. The logistics are down to me!'

'But you're happy…' Waheeda murmured.

'Yes, of course. Did I ever think life would bestow two precious gifts on me—my two wonderful girls? Did you ever imagine me a mother?

'No.' Waheeda giggled. Lara had been completely

unmaternal until the day she'd given birth, at which point she had metamorphosed into a devoted parent.

'I found one child and work manageable,' Lara mused, 'but two is just chaos. But still, far better to have two than just the one—' She checked herself. 'Vijay's research is going well. He travels back and forth from the tribal regions when he needs to.' She scowled suddenly. 'He just doesn't broadcast the news that he's in India.'

'Or that he's passing through Delhi?' questioned Waheeda. She wondered if the family scandal that Lara had created with her marriage five years ago was any closer to being forgiven or forgotten. Was the acrimony between Lara's mother and her mother's sister settling down to a bearable level?

'He barely transits through here and tries not to be spotted,' Lara conceded. Her eyes grew angry and became an even fiercer black. 'My cousin is a bitch. She won't let it rest. What can you do?'

Waheeda took that to mean that Vijay was not accepted yet, and it would be a while before he could attend Sabbarwal family gatherings, if ever. Surely, one day, everything would be just so much water under the bridge, but only if Harleen, Lara's cousin, would 'let it rest,' as Lara put it. Waheeda had heard from Falguni, who mysteriously cultivated a friendship with Harleen, that Harleen could still spout endless bile about the absent Lara and about the husband Lara had supposedly pilfered from her. Lara insisted he was Harleen's *ex*-husband when she proposed to him, an important point to note, according to Lara. 'When I met him for the first time,' she would say, 'when I visited them in Bhubaneshwar, they were already in the divorce courts. Harleen had filed the case. How can she accuse me of stealing a husband that she'd already discarded?'

It was complicated and feelings all around continued

to run high, so Waheeda didn't bring up Fal's barbed little updates, not wanting to upset Lara any further. She wanted to maintain the sense of fun and freedom of the evening. It was so infrequent.

'Isn't it time to return to the party?' Lara tapped her shoulder. 'You should drop me home now.'

'Soon.' Waheeda guided the car into another wide circuit around India Gate. She spotted a man with a basket that looked like it would have flowers in it. She beckoned him over. '*Gajra? Chameli*?' She was delighted when he said 'yes,' proffering his round shallow basket. Lara and she examined the left-overs in there. The jasmine was turning brown at the edges.

'We'll take them all,' said Lara grandly to the man. She turned to Waheeda. 'And now you can take me home.'

The perfume of jasmine filled Waheeda's nostrils as Lara sorted out the strung flowers on her lap. 'Six for me, six for you, and that leaves two for that novelist chap.'

'I'm sure he thinks it's a joke. He's not really expecting me to turn up with a *gajra* for him.'

'No, but it'll be funny if you do.' Lara was obviously taken with the idea. 'It'll be a good excuse to go to his reading.'

'I'm not sure—'

'Oh, you really *must*. I think it will be very interesting.'

'All right, I'll go. I'll give him the flowers from you.'

'Good. You'll have to tell me what his reading's like when I next call you.' Lara was winding three strands around her left wrist. 'What if he writes in complex and *bilkul shesht* Hindi? Are you going to understand it all?'

'Of course. My vocabulary and fluency improves every day. My speeches are all in Hindi...'

'Oh Lord. Wija. Speechifying all day in Hindi. I wasn't *thinking*...so much to discuss, so much to ask.' She flapped her garlanded hands in front of her face. 'Next time...all my questions, next time. Except...' She glanced sideways at

Waheeda. 'Your take on the Babri Masjid quandary.'

Waheeda concentrated on the dark road, and responded slowly. 'Nafis has a view. For once, I agree with his thoughts. But…it's not something I can speak about very firmly, you understand. So many factions…and no one seems to want to learn the lessons of history. Destruction in the past doesn't have to mean destruction in the present day or in the future. No one even properly understands the precepts of their own religion. Anyway, the issue is at stalemate—'

'Nafis thinks what?'

'Nafis thinks the Indian judicial system will grant the right to all faiths to pray at the sacred site. Not that anyone really knows when and where Ram was born. But let's leave that aside. Nafis thinks the court might split the site. No one will be happy with this. He thinks a protected place of meditation to bring people of all beliefs and all spiritualities together would be best, but—'

'Nafis is overly idealistic, as usual,' Lara cut in. 'Do you really think we Indians could ever be so sensible?' A snorting giggle from her. 'What would our politicians have to do to divide us if we could drop the religious animosity? Our politicians would be *bereft*.' She brought her hand up to her cheek in exaggerated remorse. 'Oh Wija. I forgot for a moment whom I was speaking to.'

Waheeda braked outside Lara's house. 'Go.' She pushed her playfully out of the car. 'I have no time to defend myself. Give my love to everyone.'

•

SHE DROVE TOO fast to the Selvani residence. Habib would probably note the time she returned. When Aseem discovered she'd been gone so long, and been alone in the car at this hour, he'd be furious.

She decided to re-enter the house the way they'd left, through the kitchen. There was now a uniformed security guard at the entrance to the rear patio. '*Hanh-ji?*' Questioning but deferential.

She pointed in the vague direction of the upstairs room with a finger. 'I'm just going to Mr Monish's reading.'

He stood aside. She felt the tiniest bit silly holding two *gajras* in her hand. In the hallway she paused at the foot of the stairs. Which room was the reading in? Probably one on the left, she thought, as she climbed the stairs, because Monish had pointed to the windows from the back patio. The doors to the rooms were closed. From one of them on the left, she heard muted clapping and wah-wah appreciation. She turned the handle and peeped in.

Directly in her line of sight sat Monish on a pile of floor cushions under the windows, a glass held in his hand, his head leaning back into the wall. The clapping died down and a warm whisky-soaked voice began a ghazal. It was Ghulam Ali singing his most sentimental song...*chupke chupke raat din....* The applause had been coming from the speakers. There was no one else in the room.

Monish looked straight at her when she opened the door, as if his eyes had been closed and he'd been disturbed. He unfolded his lanky legs and came to the door. 'Come in,' he said and when Waheeda, not quite knowing what to do, had taken a step in, he pulled the door half-closed.

She felt even more foolish than she had before, her hand tightening on the jasmine strands she held. 'You're not reading...' she began, and stopped and looked around the room and turned back to the half-open door. Something was not right.

'Come in, Waheeda,' Monish said again. 'Do sit down.' He gestured to a second pile of floor cushions. He sounded gentle, unthreatening.

A strange feeling took hold of Waheeda. She felt instinctively that although something was not quite right, it wasn't the man who was wrong. The man was someone she could trust. She took another step into the room, but remained standing. She should not remain here long. She cast her gaze around again. A stereo system, shelves coming half-way up the walls from the floor, all lined with CDs, a double bed at the other end of the room, on which was flung a squash racket and a blue towel. Monish looked very much at ease in the room and suddenly it dawned on Waheeda as to who he might be.

'You live here,' she said accusingly.

He responded with a mock-chastened expression. 'I don't live here…well, not all the time. But this is my old bedroom, yes.'

'Let me guess—you're a Selvani son.'

'That's a funny way to put it. I'm Monish. Just Monish. But yes, my surname is Selvani.'

'And you write? Hindi novels?'

He shook his head regretfully and grinned, showing small even white teeth. He held out his hand to the flower bracelets she clutched in hers. 'For me?' he asked.

She handed them to him in a sharp, annoyed movement, her hot graceless hand touching his for a moment. He received the flowers with an expression of pure pleasure, bringing the two jasmine strands to his face, inhaling, and then laying them down carefully on the flat top of the disc player, running his slim fingers along the petals. He didn't remark on how wilted they were.

'Do sit down.' He seated himself where he'd been before.

She was embarrassed now, embarrassed about the flush on her face, and of standing awkwardly looking down at him, at his knees, where his jeans were stretched because of his bent legs.

'Don't run away, *gajra* girl,' he said. 'You like Hindi novels? Or is it novelists that you like? That's why you came up? To hear me read?'

'Lara thought you really wanted a *gajra*. She asked me to bring these to you.'

'I did. I appreciate you bringing these back for me.' He gestured at the braids he'd set down so carefully, and Waheeda took the opportunity to sit on a floor cushion too, tucking her legs to the side. It was too awkward standing up when he was sitting down. A few moments passed in silence. If only she could rattle out questions the way Lara did, but she couldn't quite collect her thoughts. He was a Selvani, he was not a writer, this was his idea of a joke, Lara and she had fallen for it, but then who exactly was he and what did he do and why didn't he live here all the time? Was he abroad? Was he working or studying? Could she ask? Before she could articulate any query, he spoke: 'So who is your favourite Hindi novelist?' Behind his glasses, his eyes were very unusual in shape, sloping downwards at the outer edges.

'I haven't really read any.' She felt slightly ashamed admitting that. 'We read Premchand's short stories in school and I was always moved by those.'

'I read Premchand, too. Same curriculum, I guess.' He stretched his legs out. His feet were bare, they were long and slim to match his hands. 'I haven't read any Hindi novels either.' He laughed. She made a rueful face at being taken in.

His eyes were on her face and when she realised he hadn't stirred; when she knew with a bizarre excitement that his eyes were very keenly on her; she moved her own gaze firmly to one of the CD racks. Most of the discs were of ghazal or qawwali artistes. He pushed away the glass she'd seen him holding earlier—it looked like a tumbler of whisky on ice—he pushed it to the wall, behind him. 'Do you like this kind of music?' he asked her, waving his hand towards the rack she'd been studying.

'Yes, among other things.'

'I wonder if I have your favourite ghazal in my collection here. Assuming that you have a favourite.'

Waheeda didn't have *one* particular song that she cared for above others; there were several that she could call equal favourites. For the sake of conversation she'd have to pick one. What came to mind was '*Tum apna ranjho ghum.*'

She mentioned it, adding tentatively, 'I'm not sure if you would class it as a proper ghazal. It is from a film, after all.'

'You like it; that's all I wanted to know. But your choice shows sadness. Are you particularly unhappy today?'

Waheeda smiled, inexplicably overcoming her natural reserve. 'Actually, I was particularly happy today. After a long while.'

'You *were*. You're not now?'

'I am,' she insisted. Then she felt the need to extricate herself from this place of unexpected confession to which he had somehow led her. It felt too intimate. He would understand if she stood up to leave. It wouldn't be rude to do that.

Monish addressed her again. 'What are you doing here? At this dinner? No, that's not what I meant. I meant…I meant…'

'My father was invited. He wanted me to accompany him.'

He frowned. 'But you weren't with him when I met you. You were escaping with—'

'Lara. You see, she lives in Singapore and tonight was the only time I could see her before she flies back tomorrow. I brought her along…I'm sorry.' Again she was discomfited. 'We took liberties with your invitation.' He would surely think of her as a complete freeloader.

'Not my invitation,' he waved away her apology. 'No matter. And your father is?'

'Aseem Zafar.'

He looked bemused. 'Your father is…is…'

She helped him out. 'He is the founder of the Nulkazim Peace Forum. It's a political party although it doesn't sound like it.'

'Here in Delhi? There's a place called Nulkazim?'

'No, it's in Uttar Pradesh. It's where we're from. The party is fairly local.' She decided to keep it brief. 'A minor player in the scheme of things.'

'I see.' He looked at her in that searching way she was finding very flattering. The irises in those downward sloping eyes were a dark brown. His lashes were thick and short. His spectacles were unsmudged, the black wire sitting neatly on the curve of his cheek. 'I get the feeling he must be an important man there.' She felt his stare; she could tell when he was looking at her hair, and then her clothes, and her wrists and fingers. She kept her own eyes mostly on the floor; let him look if that was what he wanted to do. She felt elated and silly in equal measure at her own irrational response to his interest. She was certain that when he stirred it would be to put a *gajra* in her hair.

She felt him draw up his legs and stand up. He knelt by where she was sitting. 'Waheeda...'

I was right, she thought, looking up startled. *He's going to tie a gajra in my hair. How odd to be able to predict that.*

But there were no flowers in his hand. He just had a mundane question to ask. 'Do you like Jagjit Singh?'

'I...yes...he has such an amazingly rich voice. Why?'

'I have tickets to a concert next week. I'm going with a group of friends, mostly girls. Would you like—'

The door of the room swung open. A woman in a pink *mocaish* sari, scattered with fine sequins, stood framed in the doorway, a harried look on her pretty face. 'Oh,' she exclaimed, startled. 'Monish, I didn't realise you had a friend over.'

Monish and Waheeda stood up together. She knew they both looked guilty although there wasn't a reason to be, except that from being strangers they had crossed a boundary.

'Not a friend, Ma,' Monish said. 'This is Waheeda. One of your guests.'

Waheeda folded her hands. 'Hello,' she said, stepping to the door. 'I'm Waheeda Rela.'

Mrs Selvani reproduced the exact puzzled frown she'd got earlier from Monish. It was clear she was running through her guest list in her head. 'I'm Aseem Zafar's daughter,' Waheeda said.

She watched Mrs Selvani's expression change to relief followed by faint disapproval, before she directed her gaze at her son.

'Monish, dinner is served now. It would be good if you could look after *all* our guests.'

'I'm coming down in a moment,' she heard him mumble behind her.

Waheeda made her way back to the blue and cream drawing room via the buffet table, where she let her plate be filled with small portions of eight different dishes. The crowd had thinned and many ladies were sitting on sofas and chairs with their dinner plates. Obviously, a good proportion of the guests had either gone home or moved on to other commitments. She found a seat next to someone she knew, Tina Matni, the fashion designer. Tina owned sixteen emporia around the country, always wore chocolate brown and dark pink, had a small head with bald patches showing through her thinning hair and a voice like a ship-horn.

'Waheeda,' Tina bellowed as soon as she'd sat down, 'Is it true that your father has persuaded you to join his party and help him campaign in Nulkazim?'

Waheeda nodded.

'Your brothers…any more news on that investigation?'

Waheeda shook her head. She looked at her plate for a moment, her throat closing. She had a fork in her hand. She arranged a navy-blue paper napkin on her lap and balanced her plate on it but set down her fork, hoping no one would notice.

A movement drew her eye to the doors of the room. Monish had appeared and he was handing out plates and napkins to those who hadn't yet made their way to the buffet. Once he'd finished that task, he began a circuit of the room, greeting people and cracking jokes with them. When he turned his head slightly towards her and Tina, she looked down hurriedly, acutely aware that his eyes were on her. He must have known that she was staring at him. He must have felt it.

'There comes my favourite person,' declared Tina, as he made his way towards them. 'Hi, honey,' she said, as Monish bent to embrace her shoulders. 'I didn't know you were back living at home.'

'My flat's being painted. I'm here for a few days.'

'Only a few days. Your mother will be sad if you don't stay longer.' At his slight shrug, she continued in a high voice, as to a miscreant child, 'Were you hiding upstairs all this time, naughty boy?'

'Yup. But now I've been asked to "look after" our guests. Pratish gets the gentlemen, I get the ladies.'

'Of course, honey. Because the ladies *love* you.'

Monish held out a folded paper napkin to Waheeda. 'You look like you need this,' he said.

Waheeda instinctively accepted it, then murmured, 'I already have one, thank you.'

But Monish seemed not to have heard her and he continued his tour of the room. He turned back just once when Tina called out to him, 'Monish, will you find some white wine for a lady?'

He gave her a thumbs up sign and disappeared. Tina turned to Waheeda. 'Arun's not serving wine tonight. But Monish will open a bottle for me. Would you like a glass, too?'

'No. I don't drink.'

'Of course.'

There was a strange undertone to that "of course." It carried a range of messages. Disbelief? Or 'silly of me to ask, when you obviously don't.' Or even 'you poor unsophisticated thing, you.' It didn't matter, thought Waheeda. She had become used to this. She was no longer exasperated by innuendos that she couldn't decipher.

She placed the extra napkin which Monish had given her on a round glass table by the sofa. The fold opened up to reveal something white—a note—placed inside. She snatched up the napkin, gently dabbed it at her lips and slipped it into her black clutch bag at just the moment a waiter arrived with a glass of white wine for Tina.

•

AFTER THE DESSERTS had been served and then the masala tea, finally, finally, Aseem appeared in the drawing room to signal that it was time to leave. Waheeda made a special effort to find Mrs Selvani and thank her before she left. She didn't recognise Mr Selvani, and Aseem didn't bother pointing him out to her. There was no sign of Monish. She followed Aseem obediently to his car and handed her car keys to Habib, who would drive it back. Habib made to speak to his boss, but Aseem, who had obviously had a very good time, said 'Tomorrow' as if he didn't want to be bothered with a report just then.

Once he was driving, he launched into an exhaustive round-up of the evening and whom he'd spoken to about support and whom he'd spoken to about making new contacts and also how some idiot had sketched out a strategy to him whereby he would be able to deal with the BJP without getting swallowed up by them, yet receiving their endorsement. Or perhaps the man wasn't an idiot, just very cunning.

Waheeda knew she was meant to respond. 'Really? What strategy was that? BJP to endorse a Muslim party? How, when and why? Just for the Nulkazim constituency, to join forces against Congress?' And also, 'That sort of deal will make us losers in the long run, for sure. What compromises will we have to make to keep that support?' She thought all this, but didn't want to initiate a serious discussion at this time of night.

Aseem turned his head for a second. 'Where did you disappear to?'

'I dropped Lara home. I'd promised her I would whenever she wanted to leave.'

'Did you take Habib?'

'No.'

'You should *always* take him with you. How many times do I have to tell you that?'

'Lara and I barely got an hour together to talk. *After two years*. I do need to spend some time with my friends, Abba. I couldn't have Habib with us.'

'You can't drive alone at night; it's a grave risk and I'm not having it.'

'Sometimes I need time alone. I can take care of myself.'

He must've been in a good mood overall, because instead of raising his voice, or grunting in bad temper, he shook his head impatiently, his face clouding with an expression of long-suffering resignation, but he said no more. From his hooded eyes she decoded that Habib would get stricter instructions for the future.

•

IN HER ROOM she retrieved the folded napkin, took it into the bathroom and latched the door. She unfolded it standing at the sink. What had Monish written?

It wasn't a note to her. It was a ticket to a Jagjit Singh concert the following week. She handled it carefully, reading the sparse details on the front (Kalyani Auditorium, 8.30 pm, Seat 7, Row 3) and the small print of no import on the back. She held it up to the light. Nothing written on it. It was not a note.

In the plain rectangle of mirror a flushed face looked back at her. She raised her hands to her cheeks. Her fingers were feverish, blood pounding at the tips. This was silly. He was just a young man. Even if his demeanour, his considerate manner and his easy confidence had made her think that he might be in his early thirties, he looked so youthful, so boyish that he might only be in his early twenties.

He was a Selvani. He was almost certainly a playboy type, the kind of crowd Fal ran with. Although Falguni's pack would be slightly older than his, wouldn't it? And Fal preferred rock concerts to ghazal recitals. But why had Monish given her this ticket? What did he want with her? If she showed up, then what?

She zipped the ticket into the inside pocket of her holdall and got into bed, her mind and body still fizzing. Much more to the point, she thought, was the question: what did she want with him?

FIVE

ON THE RETURN journey to Nulkazim the next day they travelled in a three-car convoy as before. Aseem's personal driver, Jivan, had come by train to Delhi and he drove Aseem's car with Waheeda and Aseem in the back, screened by tinted windows. Habib drove her Fiat ahead of them. Their car was followed by another that held party workers, who ran to fetch them tea and snacks whenever they stopped.

Aseem carped about the building-works on both sides of the highway. He pointed with disgust to a new 'Chicken Shoppe' that had replaced an old-fashioned roadside stall. 'There's going to be a "Chicken Shoppe" in Nulkazim,' he said heavily, 'did you know?' She did. She didn't like the idea either, but you couldn't halt development or cultural changes. There was a market for fast food outlets, that's why they were expanding.

'Next we'll have a McDonald's opening there.'

At his grumpy tone Waheeda gave a complicit smile agreeing with his sentiment of thinking it a fiasco if that should happen. She looked intently out of the window to avoid conversation but she couldn't quite block him out; he moved on to criticising the huge advertising hoardings selling "things people don't need." She vaguely heard "gullible customers." She wasn't really noticing the hoardings or the film stars on them touting Parker pens and fridge-freezers. Here was a new national heartthrob, peddling a mobile phone text package. "200 texts a month included in the plan." How much had he been paid by that telecoms company? She gazed into his euphoric face as it flashed by and she remained staring blindly at the scenery, re-playing the scene in Monish's room. How imprudent she'd been. But what to make of his apparent interest in her? The sweet intensity of the moment she handed him the *gajras*. Stop. She was reading too much into the attentiveness of a man who was a practical joker. It was irrational to think he was attracted to her, even if it was true that she was attracted to him. They moved in different worlds; there would not be an opportunity to meet again. But he'd given her a ticket. If this wasn't another prank he would be there. They would meet again.

They halted at a crossing and hawkers dodged between the stationary cars, hoping for sales. Aseem rolled down his window to buy fresh coconut slices. He bit into one and chewed. She refused his offer of a slice as did the driver. A girl selling single stems of roses wrapped in cellophane knocked on her window. Waheeda could see her although the vendor couldn't see in. She was young, probably just twelve or thirteen. Waheeda opened her window and stuck out a ten-rupee note. She told the girl to keep the flowers as the traffic began to press forward. *Go to school*, she wanted to utter, but of course, it would sound plain stupid if she did. Who knew what the circumstances were? She caught Jivan's disapproval in the rear-view mirror. She knew what he was thinking, because sometimes he tended to say it: '*Choti*-madam, her bosses will take the money. You are just encouraging these people. This is not charity as you think it is.'

She turned her face to the window. The roses had reminded her of Monish. Well, everything did, at the moment. She shook her head at herself. Jasmine, roses, all the same, any flower equals a man I met last evening. Whom I may never have a conversation with again. A peculiar sadness enveloped her. She had felt able to speak freely to him. It was a puzzle why, but if she went to the concert, they would talk, and she would solve the puzzle. There was no harm in that, surely.

'Abba, I didn't have a chance to mention to you before,' she rubbed her left cheekbone as she spoke, 'but Naaz invited me for dinner next Thursday. She's holding a gathering of women, well-connected women, she said, and she wanted me to speak to them about The Golden Oriole campaign for separate toilets for girls in rural schools.'

Aseem gave a light shrug. 'If you really think it's worthwhile… If you think any of these people will be truly influential…or future donors…' Another small shrug, followed by a decisive nod. 'It will be good for your profile, Wija; you should accept. Maybe there will be a journalist in the gathering.'

'If I go,' she smoothed her *kameez* on her knee, 'I'd like to stay on for the Friday. I have a ticket for a concert by Jagjit Singh and I'd love to go.'

'I didn't know you had a ticket. You bought it? When?'

'No, Lara gave it to me. She said she thought of me as soon as she was offered it. She herself was not going to be staying in Delhi that long, but she took the ticket for me.'

'I didn't know you were that fond of Jagjit Singh's music.' He appeared surprised.

'Maybe Lara was mixing up Nafis's tastes with mine. But I would really like to attend this concert. I don't often get the chance for this sort of thing.'

'Will you stay with Naaz or at the flat?'

'I think I'll stay at the flat.'

He gave her a stern look. 'Don't go driving off anywhere without Habib.'

'Abba, I won't take him to Naaz's place. And I won't have him tag along if Naaz and I go out somewhere together. It gets very stilted. We did agree that it was OK to visit close friends on my own.'

'Not if it's late at night,' he said grimly. 'Habib will drive you to the concert. And he will drive you to Naaz's if you're going to be late.'

•

IT WAS WONDERFUL to have the evening at home with Hira, who didn't leave her side and stayed curled on her lap after dinner. Hira and her grandmother filled in Waheeda on all the activities of the two days that she'd been away. Eventually Waheeda hoisted Hira off her lap. 'School tomorrow.'

Hira was settled permanently in the old sewing machine room. Waheeda didn't mind Hira's choice, the room was small but it was bright and cosy for a young child. Her brother's old rooms were still places of mourning and memories; their possessions very slowly being given away or stored elsewhere. Nafis was given Irfan's room when he stopped over, but he only stayed a night each time, and barely seemed to sleep. Ammi had moved the sewing machine to Rohail's room. It stayed covered up and unused.

'Brush your teeth for a whole minute,' Waheeda instructed Hira. 'Don't be lazy.' She tucked her in and sat on the bed stroking her arm until she fell asleep. Warm drowsiness and innocence filled the room. Waheeda breathed in, slightly dizzy with love for her daughter. She leafed through the two red notebooks on Hira's bedside table. 'Zahira Rela,' Hira had written in her neatest handwriting on the covers. One was her English Grammar exercise book, the other was beginner's French. Waheeda didn't know why Hira had picked French for her language option, but seven-year-old kids seemed to want to do what their peers did. Waheeda didn't remember being like that, but who knew? Hira's best friend had chosen French. 'Fine, you too,' Waheeda had said, thinking that as long as Hira could read and write Hindi and English, it didn't matter whether she studied the basics of Sanskrit or Urdu or French or Russian.

Hira kept two framed pictures on her bedside table. One was of herself, laughing with eyes scrunched up, a forest of deodar trees out of focus in the background. Nafis had taken the photograph in Theog. He had made two copies of the enlarged print: one for himself, placed in his bedroom in Theog; and the other for Hira. Waheeda knew why he loved this image of his daughter. It was the opposite of the crying toddler that he hadn't had the patience for. The other picture was of Nafis, so Hira could kiss her Abba's photo 'good morning' or 'good night' or both, depending on her whim. The glass on this snapshot was smudged.

How handsome Nafis was. How charming she'd thought him when they first met. How unconventional in his lifestyle, because he was an artist, rebelling in a political family. 'Head in the clouds, but a good heart,' his father had said about his older son on being questioned by Aseem. Well, now Nafis lived on a level with the clouds. Good for him. She picked up the frame looking into Nafis's face. The photo didn't do him justice—you couldn't see his stunning light brown eyes and perfectly slim nose. He had an incredible smile. When he used it.

She looked at Hira, asleep on her back, arms loosely bent. Hira had large eyes in a small heart shaped face. She had not inherited Nafis's eyes or Waheeda's dimples. The most noticeable features of her mother's and father's faces were missing in Hira, although she had the shape of Waheeda's eyes, her nose was like her father's and she had his lighter skin tone too. Strangely, overall, she bore a close resemblance to Waheeda's mother, Rehana; and since Hira and she had come to live in Nulkazim in early 1997, everyone had remarked on it.

Waheeda examined Hira's laughing photograph. She remembered that visit to Theog, in 1994, about a year after Nafis had taken up residence there. Hira and she had gone for a few days in June, in her term break. Waheeda had seen pictures of the cottage but even so she was unprepared for the breathtaking beauty of the location. Nafis had a good eye, she conceded that. The cottage was surrounded by pine and cedar trees and further outwards lay acres of neat apple groves. Waheeda had flippantly referred to the cottage as a *hava mahal*, a wind-palace, the room in the gardens of grand mansions or palaces which the ladies retreated to in high summer. A room of maximum windows to enjoy cooling breezes. But Nafis had taken it as veiled criticism of the house. That set the tone for their time there. Everything she said was misconstrued. Although the house *was* small. It wasn't a family space. The living room was essentially his studio. She had begun to feel that Nafis was building a solo life, with no thought of what would suit his wife and daughter.

It was only on the last night of her visit that they had both mellowed. They had lain down in the main bedroom together after Hira had fallen asleep. That was to be the last time. She hadn't known that. She remembered drifting into a blissful sleep, her legs stretched diagonally across his. She'd awoken at some point in the night and moved her legs. Nafis had mumbled in his sleep and turned on his side, his back to her. She put her arm around him, she fitted her fingers under the soft flesh of his belly, she fitted her naked body to his solid back. He had put on weight since she'd seen him last. She smiled as she squished his waist and fell asleep again.

She waited for him to visit Delhi but it was three months before he turned up. One September evening she returned home from work to be told by Florrie that Nafis-saab had called and she was to call him back. Hira jumped about, seconding Florrie, 'Yes, I spoke to Abba. He said to call him.'

She felt a flutter of nerves. On the phone Nafis said 'I'm coming to Delhi tomorrow. I need to buy art supplies and I want to see Hira.'

In that order? Is that how his brain worked?

'Tomorrow.' Nafis repeated. 'Is that all right?'

'Yes.' What did he mean? 'It's your home.'

But it wasn't his home, she thought, when she sat propped

71

up in Hira's bed later. She was reading the tale of the monkey and the crocodile, but she wasn't doing the best acting job, her brain in some turmoil. When she'd returned from Theog in June she'd realised that the accoutrements of his life had all been taken away from their rented home in Delhi. This was now a female household: One history lecturer, one domestic helper and one little girl. The only hints of a male presence were the clothes left in the wardrobe: Nafis's formal jacket and shoes, and his wedding day sherwani.

She left the college early the next afternoon, whispering to Naaz on her way out that Nafis was arriving that evening. She stuffed assorted papers into her bag: minutes of some committee meeting that she was meant to read, new instructions for academics, updated college rules for students, blah blah. She threw some unmarked history essays on the passenger seat. She'd have to snatch time somehow for those. Nafis had taken her usual parking spot by the front of their house. He was here already? Early? She parked across the road. She let herself in quietly, heading to the bathroom first to wash her face to dispel the heat from her forehead. She wanted to appear fresh when she walked into the sitting room to greet Nafis. She heard a sound in the spare room. Florrie was spreading two thick quilts on the floor of the room that used to be Nafs's studio before he had emptied it.

'What…' Waheeda frowned in at her.

'Nafis-saab said.' Florrie stopped smoothing down the upper quilt.

'He said make up a bed in here?'

Florrie nodded. Waheeda bit at the inside of her cheek. She picked up the single flat sheet—floral-print—that Florrie had brought out, went to the shelf where she stored the linens and found a soft cotton double-sized sheet that would look neater on the spread quilts. She ran her fingers down the stacked linens looking for a matching pale yellow sheet for the top, single or double, as long as it matched. Things that weren't complementary hurt Nafis's eye.

When the bed was made to her satisfaction she walked slowly to the sitting room. She'd been tuning into Hira's excited babble and Nafis's deeper tones, but what they were saying had been drowned out by the mortification thrumming in her head and the re-opened wound in her heart. She squeezed Hira to her for a whole minute until her daughter began to wriggle away. To Nafis, who only said 'hello,' she merely replied, 'How long are you staying for?'

'Two days. Maybe three. All right?'

What was this ' all right' that he kept asking her? 'It's your home,' she muttered.

But Nafis was behaving like a visitor. He was replicating her behaviour in Theog. She'd let him dictate the style and pace of life there; it was his space and she had not interfered. Now he was doing the same in Delhi. They spent a stilted first evening, Hira's beaming countenance in direct contrast to their sombre moods.

Waheeda was grateful to see that he was in a better mood the next evening. She'd hoped for that in the morning when she'd dressed for work, donning a grey cotton sari with a purple border and a pair of earrings that Nafis had bought for her. Just before she left home she'd rummaged in a box to find the amethyst and silver bracelet that was part of a set with the earrings. She'd gone to Florrie to help her close the clasp; she found it impossible to put the bracelet on one-handed. Nafis was at the dining table with his morning tea and she noted his eyes sweeping appreciatively over her. She knew how he liked to see her in a sari. In the evening she shook her hair out of the clasp as soon as she got home and pulled a wide comb through her waves.

She let Nafis put Hira to bed, let him sing her to sleep. She waited in the sitting room, a magazine on her lap, staring at the wall. She heard Florrie make up her own bed in the ante room off the kitchen, close the kitchen door and switch off the lights. She heard Nafis come out of Hira's room. She bowed her head to the magazine. Nafis came to the door. 'Reading?' he asked.

Stupid question, but this is what they were reduced to. She nodded and wondered what to say. *Come in, sit down, hold my hand.*

'You don't have enough light,' he came up to the sofa and switched on the lamp by her elbow. 'The way you squint at things, I wouldn't be surprised if you had glasses the next time I see you!'

On that topic, she wanted to say, *about when the next time will be, we need to have a conversation.*

But he stood above her, looking awkward now, and she decided to stand up too. He began to walk out of the room but she called him back. 'Nafis.'

'Yes?'

'Are you going to bed now?'

'Sort of.' A note of caution in his voice.

She held out her arm. 'I need help removing this.'

'Removing what?' he asked, his smile breaking out, his eyes not on her arm but on her waist where the sari folds were tucked in.

'My bracelet. I can't do it one-handed.' She dangled her wrist in front of him.

He moved closer, bending his head to fiddle with the bracelet.

Let me put my head on your chest. Hold me tight.

The bracelet was unclasped and he opened her palm, placed it there and closed her palm over it. She remained standing by him, not moving, her breath halting. He'd stopped smiling, he appeared to be thinking. She leant into his chest. Nafis raised his arms, wrapping them lightly about her. She put her arms about his waist.

Her ear was pressed into his chest, her eyes closed, when she realised he'd said something. What had he just said? Something that sounded like 'when you come to Theog.'

He disengaged himself, standing back slightly. His breath was short but his full lips were clamped in a stubborn line.

'What did you say?' she asked.

'When you come to Theog. Not here.'

She stared at him. Abruptly she left the room.

As soon as she was alone anger rose in her, such fury that she could barely contain it. Did he think that by withholding his affection she would capitulate and come running to Theog? What was she—some sex-starved creature? Was she meant to give up everything to be granted a night with her husband?

Why did he think this imbecilic policy would work? Or did he not care? He hoped that she would leave him alone, never approach him! She had visions of him spending his evenings in the old colonial club in Theog—the one she had not been taken to, because children were not allowed and Hira couldn't accompany them—visions of a cheerful Nafis playing bridge with a coterie of women, young and middle-aged, all willing to flirt with him. Willing to go home with him? Did they smuggle him into their bedrooms under cover of darkness…

She threw the bracelet at the wall and flung herself into the spare room. 'If you have someone else you should just say.'

Nafis had changed into his white kurta-pyjama. He stood by the large open window, moonlight behind him. The jamun tree in the side passage outside whispered in the soft breeze. An acrid smell hung in the air; he must've just smoked a cigarette. He turned into the room to frown at her. 'No. You're reading it wrong. If you come to live in Theog you will see.'

Her eyes on his broad chest visible under the light muslin. 'And if I don't come?'

'You will. In time. It's the right place for us.'

Such belief. Such idiocy. It made her want to thump him and cry. There wasn't a life there for her or Hira. Not the life she wanted for them both. He'd already spent his inheritance on buying the cottage. Who would earn for the family? He hadn't had a show of his paintings in years.

'If you leave this window open too long the mosquitoes will come in and get at Hira.' Her voice trembled as she pointed. 'You know that, Nafis.'

She returned to what was now solely her room.

SIX

May 1997
Nulkazim

WHEN SHE ENTERED party headquarters in Nulkazim old town she could hear the buzz following her right from the ground floor reception to Aseem's office on the first floor, past his two reception rooms. Bir Sultan from Patharghat had announced that he was leaving NPF. He had been their best hope of getting a seat in parliament in the next elections. Was he running scared? Had someone threatened him, blackmailed him? He wouldn't say. Other than to personally apologise to Aseem and tender his resignation from the party, he'd said nothing.

Despite all the whirring fans the heat penetrated the thick walls and the air in the office smelled stale, like old samosas. Waheeda joined the five men in their conference circle. She let them talk.

Umair was emphatic. 'He's a coward.'

'He has a family,' Aseem reasoned. 'We can't blame him.'

'No one's touched a hair of *his* head. Has he suffered like—'

'He saw what happened to us as a warning.'

'All our work in Patharghat...'

'Down the drain—'

'Are we going to nominate another candidate?' Rahim, a deputy leader, steered the conversation on. 'If we're going to field someone at the next election, we should decide it soon, between ourselves. We won't declare until the time but at least we know what we're working towards.' He placed both palms on the arms of his chair. 'We mustn't let everything we've done get sidelined. We *have* to keep it in people's minds.'

Waheeda wondered if Rahim wanted to be nominated. In the past Aseem's plans had not been so big, but somehow he'd been persuaded by his deputies that NPF should fight a national election. Umair had encouraged it. Perpetual Bachelor Umair. 'We'll have much more bargaining power with an MP, or two, in Delhi; much more regional power…and most important, more Muslims in Parliament.'

'We don't have anyone in Patharghat as popular as Bir Sultan,' Aseem said.

'Jehangir Wazan's party came third in the last election. Behind us. But *third*. Out of many.' The short man, the statistician. 'We could have a strategy.' He glanced meaningfully around the group. 'If we joined forces with him, we will have a fantastic chance…'

Jehangir was a rival political force to Aseem. Waheeda had met him a few times. He could be as intimidating as her adoptive father. He did have the same old-world courtesy though, especially towards females. But he could be gruff with Aseem with whom he had a chequered history.

'Jehan is never going to *join* forces with me,' Aseem spoke slowly, eyes hooding. 'But there are other ways of supporting each other. Let me consider what it is possible to ask without insulting him.'

'But who are we going to put forward in Patharghat?' Rahim, insistent, impatient.

'Who is interested?' countered Umair. 'Do you want to stand?'

Rahim blanched. 'No.'

'But earlier, before we selected Bir, you wanted to be nominated—'

'—yes, but not this time. Not just yet.'

'I see.'

Another man spoke up. He was the youngest in the group and evolving into a fiery speechwriter in the Umair mould. 'Perhaps Waheeda *didi*?'

A heavy silence followed his suggestion. Waheeda hoped she'd concealed the tremor that went through her. They wanted *her* to stand against the thugs in Patharghat? She couldn't show them how afraid that made her. She would have to exist within the innards of a security platoon every time she visited the constituency. She should speak up now. Say something. But what to say? I'm petrified. You want to throw *me* to the wolves? She should say: oh, good idea. Just what I was thinking. This is the challenge I seek.

Umair coughed to draw attention to himself. 'Waheeda has a fan club in Dhoonpur. She's made a real impression with the ladies. That's half the votes, almost. I had picked Dhoonpur as a possible seat for her.'

This was the first Waheeda had heard of this. She pulled up her jaw that she'd let sag in astonishment. She herself was fond of the villages in the Dhoonpur constituency; it was a less violent region and through the Golden Oriole charity she'd organised three new toilets to be built in the schools there.

Everyone was silent again. Waheeda looked around the group of five men. Five! Not six. Where was Shakeel? Why wasn't he here? Was he ill or had they stopped including him in these important conferences? She had a sinking feeling that he'd been left out because nominations would be discussed. As a senior deputy Shakeel had as much of a right to ask to be selected as anyone here. But he'd been excluded. No, he was unwell. That was the reason for his absence. Not the fact that the complicated lives of his brother and sister-in-law were having an adverse effect on his career. She would ring him to see how he was, but she would say nothing about the meeting.

The youthful speechwriter said: 'Jehangir Wazan will field someone in Dhoonpur, too. He did last time. Didn't get anywhere but he'll break up our bloc votes. No chance for Waheeda *didi*. Patharghat is a better bet.'

'Leave it with me.' Aseem closed the discussion. 'I will speak to Jehan first and then consider what to do.'

•

ON THE WEDNESDAY that Waheeda was departing for Delhi, with just one car as she'd insisted, Habib and her, no other escort, Aseem hurried out to the drive as they were setting off. She rolled down the window.

'I managed to get hold of Jehangir finally. Caught him before he went for his morning walk. He said he'll see you in Delhi on Saturday morning.'

Waheeda got out of the car. Aseem and she moved a few feet away to talk privately. 'He wants to meet *me*?' She shaded her eyes with her hand. This early, and the sun so fierce already. 'You are sending *me* to talk to him?'

Aseem let out a sigh. Behind him, at the far end of the lawn, the gardener was on a stepladder, pruning the lower branches of a tree. Her adoptive father looked directly into her eyes, his grey eyes holding hers with a magnetic force. 'Yes, *you*. He wants to speak to the proposed candidate for Patharghat...although...don't mention that it may not be you in the end...'

She raised her brows and hoped the slight buckling of her knees had gone unnoticed. He wasn't set on her being the nominee? *Thank heaven.* 'What do you want me to say?'

'Would he be willing to make his candidate step aside if you stand? Whatever it takes. That's the ideal scenario. See if he gives you a hint of whether he will make trouble for you. I think Jehan will agree that his party won't stoop to rabble-rousing and crudeness against you. He would have to rein in some of his people a bit...but don't put it like that, of course. If you can convince him to act neutrally towards you…that's one hurdle down at least.'

'But he's small fry.' *Like us. Who was going to tackle the big parties?*

'It's still one hurdle down, Wija. And our Bir Sultan came second in the election, don't forget. Only 200 votes behind. Some people in Patharghat don't think we're small fry or they wouldn't have—' He stopped.

—murdered your sons.

'Take Jehan seriously, Wija; this is an important meeting. Do your very best. He is not a soft touch.'

'That I know.'

•

ONCE SHE'D ARRIVED in Delhi Waheeda felt guilt for the first time about using Naaz. Instead of the 'important dinner' she'd claimed had been arranged for Thursday, it was she who had invited herself over to Naaz's home and burbled something to her friend about seeking more publicity for her charity. She found that Naaz had rounded up her elder sisters-in-law as the type of folk she thought would be useful. The two sisters were seasoned socialites and although they didn't have much in common with Waheeda she could see that they were glad to meet her; it gave them something new to talk about at their soirées; the fact that they knew a woman who was cutting a swathe in the murky politics of Uttar Pradesh. That's what Naaz had told them and Waheeda didn't disabuse them of the idea. She was willing to be the entertainment; it made her feel better about her ruse. She knew they would spread the news about the toilet-building too.

Naaz's husband, Deepak, was away on a work trip. Waheeda promised Naaz that she would come to lunch on Saturday, to give her company. The two of them would have a relaxed meal together. 'A proper catch-up,' as Naaz put it.

•

On Friday evening Waheeda stood in the foyer of Kalyani auditorium feeling utterly lonely and exposed in the midst of a heaving crowd. *You're used to doing everything alone, then you stand in a place packed with other humans, and because you have no one to chatter to excitedly, you feel close to tears.* If she hadn't sent Habib off for his dinner, telling him to be back for the end of the concert, she would have slipped away, back to her flat. She glanced down at her ticket and then around the foyer again. *You are being silly, Waheeda Rela. Chin up.* She didn't expect to see many people she knew. Most of the people around her were a generation or two older. She recognised one or two faces but she flickered her eyes away. If they came up to her she would greet them, but she hoped they hadn't noticed her.

Was Monish here? She was too shy to circle the foyer on her own looking for him. When it was time to enter the auditorium she took her seat in the third row observing that there were indeed three or four scattered groups of younger people. Her own seat was at the edge of one such babbling, thrusting group of friends. Turning left to run her eye over the row she found Monish, comfortably ensconced four seats away from her. There were four young women in between them, all of whom he seemed to know well. *Does he always promenade with a harem in tow?*

Monish smiled a greeting at her and she nodded at him, decorously. He responded with a deep incline of his head. He was sensible, she decided. He had understood what would be acceptable to her in a public situation. He leaned forward to introduce his friends to her. He didn't mention that he'd personally given her the ticket. The young women surprised her with their laid-back friendliness. They seemed to have no edge. Or be annoyed that a stranger was part of their ensemble. The girl in the seat next to Waheeda was called Sasha. Huge round glasses. Trendy green frames. Raucous laugh.

Sasha was under the impression that Waheeda was a distant friend or family member, because she said, 'Oh yes, Monish said he had to give away a ticket because someone connected to his mom's charity was a huge fan of Jagjit Singh. That must be you, Waheeda.'

His mother ran a charity? 'I'm only indirectly connected,' she said hastily.

'He cancelled Sunita. Not that she really minded.'

'Oh. I'm sorry, I didn't know that.'

'Sunita didn't mind; I just *said*. Monish will make it up to her. Take her to a concert that's more up her street. He's a generous man, as you know.'

'Er, yes…yes. So Sunita prefers different music. But *you* like Jagjit Singh?'

Sasha let out a short guttural laugh before whispering, 'I like all kinds of music; I'm not fussed. I'm certainly not obsessive like Monish. He was super-keen about being here tonight. He offered me a ticket a week back, as a little thank-you for doing up his flat and I said yes, I'd come along.'

'You're an interior designer?'

A bitter chuckle. 'I did the course. I have the diploma. But I don't like running a business and I don't like working for anyone. So I just design for friends. It's much more fun. I did Kriti's flat last year. She was very particular about her style. So *bossy*. But Monish basically let me do what I liked.' She turned towards Monish then back to Waheeda. 'Do you know Kriti?' she asked.

Waheeda leaned forward. 'We were just introduced.' She nodded at the girl who sat by Monish, then sat back in her chair, feeling faint. The girl was utterly gorgeous.

Well, the only good thing about her being so beautiful was that it was very unlikely that anyone here would link Waheeda to Monish. She was not in that league, nor was she wearing the uniform of the pack. She slid her eyes left, her attention diverted from the stage, where the musicians were warming up. The four girls were all wearing tight denim jeans and chiffon blouses. Their hair was carefully askew; waved and curled, but then clipped at the back or in a loose up-do. Waheeda used to play with her hair, long ago, but not anymore. If she wore jeans now, it was in the privacy of her own bedroom in Nulkazim. And a politician's hair should be neat, not tousled. It should be neat all the time.

She'd agonised over what to wear this evening. First she'd picked out a dark red suit with a colourful *lehiri dupatta*. She held it up against her and looked in the mirror. It looked so good that she worried it would draw attention to her. That wouldn't do. She must not look like she'd dressed up. She should be simple, as if this was a normal evening out, and there was no ridiculous anticipation befuddling her mind. She went to the other extreme, bringing out a white *chikankari churidar-kurta* set. 'I'm not changing my mind again,' she'd muttered, 'but what can I do to jazz this up a bit?' She added a *chunni* printed with soft blue and white spirals. The only jewellery she wore was a silver button-fastening-chain on her kurta, the silver smooth with age and use. It had belonged to her mother and Waheeda had appropriated it from her wardrobe when old-style fastenings had briefly come back in fashion. Little beads of silver hung down from each of the four closed buttonholes.

Waheeda fiddled with these beads as she waited for the star to appear on stage, her thoughts flitting away from the concert completely, although she gazed straight ahead. She worried that if she looked at Monish, he would know her confusion. He couldn't really be interested in her; there was no way; just look at the women he hung out with.

The audience began whooping and cheering. Jagjit Singh had appeared on stage, radiating solidity and charisma. True to a Delhi audience several men began shouting out their requests and messages before Jagjit had even sat down to take his place at the microphone set up for him. He appealed for silence and calm, cleared his throat and sang one note. The crowd hushed. Waheeda checked her watch: nine-thirty, the concert starting only an hour later than advertised.

She tried to concentrate on the stage as Jagjit's deep melodious tones flowed towards her. The singer and his musicians were seated on a Persian rug on a raised dais. Jagjit was playing the harmonium himself, while behind him sat an old gentleman with long white hair, wearing a black kurta, who played a keyboard. The tabla player, on the other hand, was a young chap with wavy hair, wearing black trousers with his matt gold kurta. The violinist, in rust kurta-pyjama, with a side-parting and glasses, sported a suitably solemn expression to match the sound emanating from his strings.

In the row behind Waheeda an over-excited man kept going 'Wah Wah. Wah Wah. Wah Wah.' It's only the second song, she thought, even if it is Ghalib's *Dil–e-nadaan*. Sasha nudged her, turned round to stare pointedly at the man behind, and then exchanged an amused glance with her. Waheeda leant forward slightly and let her gaze slip again to the left, till it halted on Monish. He turned his face to her, sensing her stare, and their eyes locked for an instant. With an effort, she turned back to the stage, staring at it blindly as the ghazals slipped by, Jagjit's famous and much-loved timbre not registering in her brain.

SEVEN

MONISH KEPT HIS eyes fixedly on the stage. His thoughts rushed helter-skelter, dipping into old memories and then back to the present. He was only vaguely listening to the singer that he so admired. What was wrong with him? All the pressures of the day bearing down on his shoulders at this moment. He'd thought it as he left the office earlier this evening and the thought rapped at his head now: he had become jaded in his gilded cage. Been there, done that, so what? He was too young to feel as he did. That part of his father's nagging was true. Monish felt set to turn his back on life, even as he was prepared to keep up pretences for the sake of his father's money. Clash of his two selves, that's what he'd dub the movie of his life. The recluse and the money-man; he was both.

Kriti rustled in her handbag for something and he was diverted for a moment. She pulled out a tissue, and then applied lip gloss in the dark. Her attention returned to the stage and he went back to his thoughts, keeping his gaze away from Waheeda, who was further along at the end of the row. If they tried to communicate with their eyes as had inadvertently happened a few minutes ago, someone would soon notice.

Strange that in that first instant of seeing her he'd been vividly reminded of Shabnam, from his school days. Waheeda's dimples, in that first insincere smile, caught in the white light of the patio-bulb, had brought back to him his last school term; even the very last day.

Then, when she'd arrived accidentally in his room with the *gajras*, he'd looked more closely at this woman, and the more he saw, the more curious he became. There was a disconnect between her internal and external personas, he was sure of that. Like him, she was someone inhabiting another self, although he could see no reason why. In the few seconds he'd spoken to them out on the patio Lara had come across as the extrovert, of course, but she also seemed more normal. Waheeda had said Lara was her close friend. Lara was sharp and smart, and Waheeda was…what? Aloof. Like Shabnam, she was graceful, but reserved and cautious. Like Shabnam, maybe he couldn't have her.

Shabnam had been in his class from X B through to XII B, the economics stream. She came from an overly conservative family and had not been allowed to join social activities after the school day, ever. Nor did she bunk off. But in the last term, Monish, who had harboured a secret crush on her for two years, despite his series of girlfriends, had tried to entice her out. He invited her to parties, to the farmhouse, for a picnic, to a movie after the last exam. Her dimples had flashed, she'd smiled at him warmly, very warmly, but shaken her head, and sweetly said, with no hint of regret 'I'm not allowed.'

I know that, he'd thought, but what I'm asking is, do you *want* to come out with me? She'd not answered that unspoken question, obviously.

•

HE REMOVED HIS glasses and put them on again, adjusting the tilt. He liked them to be evenly balanced. Waheeda was not Shabnam. For a start, she was older than him, although he felt that he would have to lie to her about how many years older she might be than him. She was married, separated, had a child. She'd returned to live with her father and mother. She was helping Aseem Zafar at his party HQ after the death of her brothers. He'd found out a bit about her, but there again, there was not much to go on. There was more he needed to know. The crucial point was that she was here. She was here because she wanted to see *him*. It was a mini-triumph and he smiled broadly in the direction of the stage.

This whole episode was amusing. That evening at his parents' home, when she'd been in his room, he'd forgotten himself and ogled, remembering Shabnam. It took a moment or two for him to realise the effect he was having. The fresh sheen on Waheeda's face. When he realised he'd caused this reaction, he felt a sudden euphoria. He'd struck upon the idea of giving her a ticket to the concert and wondered at himself. What insanity was this to try to date a guest of his parents?

But she was here. Her presence made him feel boyish. Excited. After the concert, he'd like to take her to his flat. He wanted to squeeze those delicate wrists in his hands. Preferably as he lay on top. Unexpectedly, all he wanted was simple. He laughed softly. He hoped his boisterous companions for the evening wouldn't scare Waheeda off. What was Sasha whispering about him?

Jagjit was singing a Noor Jehan classic, written by Faiz Ahmed Faiz, *'Mujhse pehli si mohabbat mere mehboob na maang.'* 'Don't ask me for the same love as before, my beloved.' Someone in the audience had shouted out this request beforehand. Kriti began weeping at his side. Love is never the same as in the first flush, he wanted to tell her, but Kriti knew that, which is why she was weeping. He patted her arm and she put her head on his shoulder for a moment and sniffled.

Kriti was a loyal friend, at least to him, but she had been unable to sustain a romance with any man beyond three months. Something about her high and low moods, her narcissism, apparently. That's what he'd heard from her exes. Although he'd gone out with her for a whole year when they were just out of their teens and he'd not found it problematic. Not in the least. Perhaps he'd been besotted the whole time.

Her disorder had not been diagnosed then anyway; it must've become worse when she entered the stage of 'real life.'

Kriti's early stab at marriage when she was twenty-two hadn't worked out; that three-month timeout again; although why each partner couldn't give it more time to settle he didn't understand...anyway, she decided to buy a flat in the same building as him. He'd cut loose from the parental home front. More ammunition for Dad's complaints against him.

But Kriti had felt some comfort in being near him at her time of need. For her he would always provide a shoulder to cry on, no questions asked. When you'd been friends with someone since you were fifteen, then gone steady at nineteen, then reverted to being friends again...

...although occasionally they were lovers, when it suited. But he'd never been interested in co-opting her into a girl-friend role again and she would know better than to want that. If there was one person privy to his own melancholia, his own struggles with who he was, it was Kriti. He watched her wipe away copious tears. Odd that she should sob so much at this particular song, but as he well knew himself, the power of ghazals made them all over-emotional.

•

WAHEEDA STOLE A glance at her watch. It was just after eleven o' clock. Jagjit Singh's effusiveness and banter had kept the audience wildly animated thus far. The man in the row behind hadn't been able to suppress his exclamations of 'wah wah' for too long and as the concert wore on he was joined by many more. She slid a glance to the left again, leaning forward, and exchanged a half-smile with another of the girls. The ghazals were having a profound effect on her now that she'd started listening to them. She was filled with sorrow, restlessness, the urge to follow her heart, to dream, to love. At the same time, a part of her brain continued its practi-cal prattle: '*Focus*, Waheeda Rela. Tomorrow's meeting with

Jehangir Wazan. What are you going to say if he refuses any form of collaboration? How are you going to convince him?' And yet another part of her brain remarked: 'Why is Monish here with all female friends? Is one of them his girlfriend, the proprietorial one beside him?'

On the stage Jagjit was pleading with the audience to let him go. Twice he said he was on the last song and twice the audience had roared last requests and stormed the aisles, although they had returned to their seats in response to his entreaties, and inevitably he'd had to sing some more. He launched into a crowd-pleasing Punjabi song 'in honour of Delhi': *kainde ne raina, tere kol raina*. And then he gave in to yet another 'last last request,' and sang *'yeh daulat bhi le lo.'*

Waheeda was acutely aware of the words as the song progressed, 'Take my wealth, take my fortune, steal my youth if you must, but return me to the monsoon of my childhood, the paper boats, the rain.' It was overly nostalgic, as songs went, but it made her eyes mist up thinking about Hira, who *was* a child. Hira must have a happy childhood, that was the one thing her mother could provide for her. Blinking as she looked around she spotted Monish's eyes on her and she turned her face to the ground, noting the black stains and worn strips on the flooring, its indentations and scuff marks. To the reverberation of emphatic claps and shouts and group adulation streaming towards him, Jagjit Singh left the stage and the audience began its slow drizzle out into the entrance hall, an amenable, humming mass, in which Waheeda moved steadily if distractedly. Monish was walking beside her. She slowed her pace. He dipped his head. 'Do we get to talk?'

'If there's a private spot,' she answered, in as low a voice as possible. She hadn't hesitated before replying with an honest answer.

His forehead creased. He waited for conversations to start up around them before he asked, 'Will you come to my flat?'

'Yes.' Waheeda surprised herself. 'But just let me think a moment...I've got a driver whose job is to keep an eye on me and ensure I'm driven home safely...'

In her head the thread continued. If she told Habib she would come back later herself, he would get an earful from Aseem and so would she. Possibly Habib wouldn't budge, but follow her. It would be better to say she was having a late supper at a hotel coffee shop with friends and he should wait there.

'The Siroi Lily hotel,' she said quickly to Monish. That was the closest one to the auditorium. 'The lobby. In twenty minutes?'

His friends converged around them. 'I'll try to get there as soon as I can—' he murmured, as Sasha said to Waheeda, 'Wonderful to meet you. Bye, Waheeda.'

She said goodbye to each of them, nodding at Monish as graciously as she could manage. Kriti linked her arm in his and led him away.

•

'Does the son of a business tycoon become a business tycoon?'

'Is that your way of asking me what I do when I'm not writing Hindi novels?'

Waheeda was perched, improbably, she thought, on a sofa in Monish's flat. *At least I'm not in his bedroom this time.* The sofa was long and grey, a contemporary-looking structure, with deep, flat arms. Waheeda sat straight-backed at one end, while Monish lounged at the other end. Two squarish armchairs were placed opposite the sofa, one upholstered in deep grey; the other silver-grey with a wide black velvet stripe down the middle. There were black cushions strewn about, some velvet, some linen. Everything looked new. This must be Sasha's work; she'd ask him later.

At the Siroi Lily hotel she'd instructed Habib to wait in the car park, telling him she would call for him after supper.

Monish had met her in the hotel lobby, where she'd waited fifteen minutes for him, and brought her here. She'd never known herself capable of such subterfuge. But now was not the time to question herself. It was Monish she wanted to question, about himself.

His flat, on the top floor of an unobtrusive four-storey building, was not what she'd expected at all. For a start it was small. True, the location was great: a quiet lane, yet very central. She knew about the working women's hostel that was in the adjacent block, and the Doll Museum in the vicinity that she'd visited with Hira and Naaz, but she'd never been in this apartment block before. The entrance area was smart and well-maintained, but in an old-fashioned way. A surprising twist on entering his flat: everything in it new-fangled. The front door opened into the main living area. On the right the sitting area, and to the left a round glass-topped dining table, supported on a column of black granite. When Monish ushered her in she'd looked ahead at the narrow hall with a door on the left and at the end of the hall, another door on the right.

She could smell paint. She tried not to wrinkle her nose. She met his eyes. 'Are you in business?' It would be much too bald to ask, 'What do you do exactly?'

'I work in the family office.' He answered her question reluctantly, it seemed, with a small shrug. 'I manage one of the companies.'

'The paper mills?'

'No. Paint products.'

No more detail than that. She would have listened to him talk at length about wall paints. But he stood. 'What will you have to drink?'

'Limca.'

'I don't think I have any Limca! But now I know that's what you like, I'll keep it in stock for next time.'

He *was* flirting with her. Next time, was there to be a next time?

He opened a door leading off the dining room. Into a kitchen, she guessed. She heard a fridge open. 'Will Sprite do?' he called.

'Yes, that's fine, thanks.'

He set a glass of Sprite on the metallic black table by the side of the sofa.

'Do you mind if I have a drink?' he asked.

'No, go ahead.'

'I mean, a *drink* drink…whisky.'

'That's fine.' She wanted to laugh, but it felt mean to do so.

He disappeared back into the kitchen and she looked around the living space. The floor of the dining area was laid in a pretty black-and-white mosaic, demarcating it from the sitting space, which had a parquet floor. A clever idea. Sasha's? The walls were painted cream. So he was not utilising all the hues of 'Vani Paints.' She'd seen the advertisements of bright blue walls in boys' bedrooms and dark pink walls in a woman's bedroom. Was he fed up of colour? There were no pictures on the walls, just chrome lights, with cream shades in a fluted fan shape. There was a silk rug at her feet and on impulse she removed her sandals. She *loved* the texture of silk under her soles.

When he returned with his tumbler of whisky he seated himself a few inches closer than before. She shifted slightly away from him, into the arm of the sofa.

'Thank you for the ticket to the concert,' she spoke formally, 'I really enjoyed it.'

'I'm glad you came. I wasn't sure that you would, daughter of a politician.'

Waheeda's eyes rested on his face. She allowed herself a half-smile. She sensed that it would spoil the mood of their getting-to-know-you chat if she revealed that she was a rookie politician, too. There was something of a slur in the way he'd said "daughter of a politician." Unless he spoke mockingly of everyone and everything; that might be a trait he had.

She looked up at the stacks of CDs filed in tidy chrome shelving all along the wall behind the armchairs. Underneath was a complicated sound system, all matte black and steel with a row of knobs she couldn't tell the uses for. The speakers, too big really, were placed at two corners of the room. He must be serious about his music listening experience.

'Actually,' she met his eyes again, and surprised herself with her honesty, 'I'm the daughter of a pen-repairer.' She could count on one hand the friends who knew that about her.

Monish took a sip of his drink, his eyes afar, evaluating something. He turned to her to speak. 'Aseem Zafar was a pen repairer? I thought the Zafar family prided themselves on their noble lineage. Viziers in the court and all that.'

'I'm his step-daughter. My father, the pen-repairer, died when I was four. He lived in Calcutta. That's where I was born.'

'There's a story there…' he looked for sadness in her but she kept her face down.

'Yes—a long one. Too long to go into right now. My adoptive father met my mother at exactly the same time that he decided to found the Nulkazim Peace Forum. 1970. It's part of the whole Aseem Zafar myth. He found love and politics all at once! So my story; his unexpected marriage to a widow—my mother; my adoption; it's all tied up with the founding of the party.'

'Next time…will you tell me the whole story?'

She laughed, happy at the suggestion of a next time. 'Yes, perhaps.'

'Do you have any memories of your father?'

'Just one or two. I recall scenes in which he was present. I remember I bumped my head under the sink once; he was shaving and I was getting in the way, I suppose. I remember crawling by his legs, I remember his legs vividly, but I don't remember his *face*, and I remember hitting my head on the sink when I tried to stand up and say something to him.' She tailed off. 'Aseem has been my father since I was six. To his face I'm supposed to address him as "Abba."'

'Has he been a good father?'

Best to duck this one. 'Everyone tries to do their best as a parent.'

'I don't believe that.' She was taken aback at his vehemence. 'Not *my* father. He's a tyrant. And he relishes being one.'

'Maybe he thinks he's doing what's right for you. You just don't agree with his method.'

Monish stretched his arm along the sofa, so it reached her shoulders. Her neck tingled. 'I don't agree with much of what he does, that's right.' He grinned, his eyes half-closed and she noticed how his thick lashes pushed just past his downward sloping lids. 'To say we don't get on would be putting it mildly.'

When she said nothing, he added, 'I'm not his idea of a proper son. I'm not "go-getting" enough. That's what he said just this evening. Before I came to the concert. I'm not committed to expanding the Selvani empire. I *am*; but whatever I do is not good enough for him.' He paused.

She was still taking this in.

'And then there's the marriage issue…' He darted a glance at her as he continued. 'I won't get married despite his badgering, and soon all the best families will be offering me their rejects rather than the pick of eighteen-year-olds. It bothers *him*. He should butt out of my life, don't you think?'

She took the plunge with the question that had been bothering her. 'How old are you, son of a tycoon?'

Monish sat a little straighter, looking towards his CD racks. 'Thirty. *Actually*,' he mimicked her way of speaking, 'I'm the son of a flower seller.'

She was breathless, not at that revelation, but with relief

that he was older than he looked. What with that thin face, that black beauty mark below his lip, which made him look feminine, but was as seductive as it would be on a woman, the thick wavy hair, the black-rimmed spectacles, and the long very lean body, he had the appearance of someone much younger. But a response was required to his statement, although what she wanted was to touch his lip and the soft black dot under it.

'Arun Selvani is not your real father?' She knew she sounded suspicious. This could be another one of his jokes.

'Oh he is; he is. But when I was born, Waheeda, he was a florist. He had a stall on a road near GKII. That is our origin. Well…by the time I was born he had three kiosks and had started looking at other investments.'

'He built up the business to this…conglomerate…all in the space of what? Thirty years?' She was impressed.

'You won't find a man more ambitious than him. He did have a good head for business, I suppose. Still does. He bought real estate first and then diversified with the profits. He was lucky, of course. And he had a good wife. You know, he was so far-seeing he chose an educated wife from the city instead of a girl from his village. He always said, "When we're rich, she'll know what to do."'

'And she did,' Waheeda finished for him. 'It does remind me of someone I know, though. A similar story. I mean about the aspiring man marrying someone more educated and better-looking…' She tailed off; she hadn't wanted to imply Arun Selvani was unattractive; it was just that Aseem always referred to him in terms that made her think he was ugly.

Monish didn't look too concerned. 'Who does it remind you of?'

'A friend from St. Ann's. Her father has the same sort of trajectory. He was a migrant from a village and he married a model from Bombay. She was much in demand because she had light eyes and light hair. Although I guess he proposed to her when he was already wealthy.'

He nodded. 'After he'd made his first *crore*, probably. Who are we talking about here?'

She got the feeling he knew who. 'I may have said too much. Their daughter, Falguni, is my friend. I don't want to—'

'Falguni Lava? I know her well. The Lavas are family friends.'

'Oh, I didn't think that you would know each other.'

'*Everyone* knows Fal. Or rather, Fal knows everyone in Delhi worth knowing.'

'Yes,' she conceded, 'everyone knows everyone,' which was why just being in his flat was immeasurably stupid.

'You're a friend of Falguni's? From that boarding school in the hills that she was sent off to as punishment?' A mischievous spark in his eyes. He slapped a hand on the sofa. 'Now I can get all the dope on you!'

'*No!*' She knew she sounded panicked. She took a breath. 'No. Please…please don't mention to her that I was here…in your flat; at this hour…*Please* don't ask her about me.'

'Okay,' he said. 'Okay…I promise.' He lifted her chin. 'No, look at me, you can trust me. I will never mention you to Fal. Ever. You have my word.'

She bent to retrieve her sandals. Her progress buckling them was arrested by Monish placing his hands on her wrists. He sat on the rug bringing his face level with her bent head. When she glanced up he took her hands and brought them onto his chest. Her fingers fanned out across the pale green stripes of his shirt. He kept his fingers pressed on top of hers, his eyes fixed on her face.

She let her fingers lie splayed on his chest for a long moment. *I could close my eyes. I could fall forward into his embrace. We might tip onto the rug. That wouldn't be very dignified. But nothing I do here will be dignified.*

She pulled back her hands. 'I must go. Right now.'

He rocked back on his feet. 'I didn't mean to frighten you.'

'You didn't.' She didn't trust herself to say anymore. Her husky tone must have conveyed that it was herself she was afraid of.

He lifted his arms in the surrender gesture. 'I won't touch you,' he said. 'If that's what you want. I swear. You don't have to go.' He pointed to the furthest armchair. 'I'll go sit there.'

She finished buckling her sandals.

He stood. 'Waheeda, I'll go sit on the balcony.' He pointed comically towards the glass doors. 'We can talk. You don't need to leave. I won't touch you. If that's what you want.'

She offered him a tight little smile. 'I must leave now.'

'I'm sorry.' He picked up car keys from the narrow sideboard in the dining room.

'Nothing to be sorry about.'

'Damn Fal. She's ruined my evening. Listen, you do understand that I can be very discreet. I will never mention you to *anyone*.'

'Good. Thank you.'

'So you will come back?' he asked, opening the door.

She didn't reply, walking out into the corridor as if she hadn't heard. The flat opposite him had a green door and a stencilled pattern around the spyhole. They took the lift down in silence and got into his car without either of them saying anything. As they neared the hotel, Monish eased his foot off the accelerator, letting the car dawdle, while other traffic overtook them. 'I hope you'll visit me again. Will you, Waheeda? I thought we were getting on well.'

'I…yes…of course…I'm sure I'll see you again.'

'Cool. When?'

'When I'm next in Delhi. I live in Nulkazim, I'm not sure if you know.'

He took his eyes off the road to look at her for a moment,

but seemed to be waiting for more, so she said, 'It'll be a few weeks before I'm in Delhi again.' She hesitated. 'I'll let you know. And I'm sorry about this secrecy, but…I have my reasons. It might be too much of a hassle to arrange to meet.'

'Too much of a hassle for you?'

'No, I meant for you.' It would be a huge hassle for her, but she didn't want to give him any more information.

'How long are you here for this time?'

'I'm leaving the day after tomorrow.'

'What are you doing tomorrow?'

'I've got a meeting in the morning. After that I'm seeing a friend…'

'In the evening?'

'No, I'm seeing her for lunch. In the evening I've nothing planned but—'

'Come over tomorrow. This "one day I'll be back" sounds like a false vow.'

'I do mean it. I'll let you know…'

His lips pulled into an artificial smile. The car surged forward as he pressed the accelerator. 'Another phrase that sounds false,' he said. 'I don't like "I'll let you know." If it's going to be, it'll be tomorrow. You know where I live. Seven p.m., eight p.m., nine, ten, whatever time. I'll be home.' He looked across at her. 'Did you hear that?'

They came to a stop within a dark shadow in the forecourt of the hotel, away from the marble stairs of the entrance and the quadruple gilt doors.

'I'll be home,' he repeated. And then, 'I'll wait here now to ensure your driver is around to pick you up.'

'It's all right. He's extremely reliable. You can go.'

'I'll wait. Goodnight, Waheeda.'

'Goodnight.'

She walked as confidently as she could into the hotel lobby and found an overstuffed armchair of gold and brown stripes to sit on for a few minutes. Somehow it was already two in the morning. The lobby was deserted, except for three staffers in dark suits, two behind the high reception desk and one behind the bell desk. She felt their eyes on her. She rose to make her way to the washroom. This arrangement didn't really work. It called attention to her: a lone woman waiting in a hotel lobby. She'd have to think of something else. 'For what?' she asked herself impatiently splashing water on her face. She'd have to think of some other arrangement for what. For a tryst with Monish? Hadn't she just decided she couldn't risk seeing him again?

She returned outside to the bright illumination of the marble entrance and asked the doorman to call for her car. 'Driver Habib,' he said into his microphone, and she knew the announcement would be rumbling in the ground below, in the sour recycled air where the drivers waited for their pampered employers to put a full stop to the day. She tried not to peer into the shadows to the right of the steps, where Monish had parked his BMW, and she tried not to appear self-conscious. She was holding her head up too high, looking into the distance, or looking down at the broad step, at the black diamond shapes inset in the white marble, anything to avoid meeting the doorman's puzzled, appraising gaze. A dressed-down upmarket prostitute? A woman with no friends, at this hour of the night-morning?

Habib drove up in her white Premier Padmini. Incongruous though he looked in it, by the time he'd jumped out and settled her in the back, the doorman had snapped to attention. He must've clocked Habib's heft, his alertness to what was around him, and his deference to his passenger. The doorman was at her window, bowing and calling her 'Madam.' '*Namaste*, Madam, see you again, Madam, thank you, Madam,' for the note she put in his hand.

'It really has become *very* late tonight,' she said to Habib.

The roads were empty, except for trucks lumbering into the city. 'You can have tomorrow evening off…you told me once you had some nephews in Delhi, yes? If you want to go see them, you can.'

'*Chutti?* Sir didn't say to take time off…'

'Yes, well, it's up to you. Or you can stay home. I'm not planning to go anywhere tomorrow evening. But if I change my mind, Naaz will come to get me. You should have tomorrow evening off, anyway.'

'Yes, *Didi.*'

'Now, about tomorrow morning,' she said briskly, 'we'll need to set off at nine-thirty sharp. It might take us an hour to get across to Rafi Marg in the morning traffic.'

She let her head rest back against the seat. Re-tune, Waheeda Rela. Re-tune to Jehangir Wazan. Her heart may be racing and her ears buzzing with Monish's last words 'Did you hear me? Tomorrow evening. I'll wait for you,' but she could ill afford to lapse into ridiculous dreaming. She *had* to plan for the meeting in the morning.

EIGHT

Jehangir Wazan's spartan office was in a low whitewashed building on the backlot of a bungalow. The building was forty years old and it showed. A weedy male receptionist ushered Waheeda into an empty meeting room on the first floor and left her standing by a rickety metal table in the centre. 'Salaam aleikum,' Jehangir greeted her, entering with a young man who was not introduced to her. She pinned him as an assistant when he asked Waheeda if she wanted tea or coffee, departing with their requests.

Jehangir said: 'How is Aseem-ji? How is the elegant Rehana-ji?'

'Everyone is well. As well as can be in the circumstances…'

He grimaced in understanding. 'You have a daughter, I hear. What is her name and how old is she?'

On Waheeda's reply, he exclaimed, '*My* daughter is also called Zahira. But she is much older than your little girl, of course. *My* Zahira is twenty-eight.'

She wondered how long they would exchange these family queries and niceties. But she had to respect the pace of the meeting as he set it. He invited her to sit down, gesturing at one of the scruffy woven-plastic chairs, but he remained standing by the window, looking at the patchy lawn and the trees. His stance, face turned away from her, unnerved her. The assistant returned with two teas and when he was gone, Jehangir said, 'Tell me your plans for Patharghat.'

Right, here we go. He was wrong-footing her already. Sitting down, she had to look up at him, and explain herself. Ask for favours.

At sixty-three, Jehangir was a few years older than Aseem. He had a hooked nose, a salt and pepper moustache, short grey hair, heavy brows and a prominent dimple in his chin. In the past he'd been unable to join forces with Aseem because they both wanted to be in control. But they had a healthy respect for each other and could be amiable acquaintances outside of politics. Jehangir had always been more conservative than Aseem, and he was also a Muslim who fully practised his religion, but Aseem had informed her that lately Jehangir had been aghast at the noises emanating from the majority of the national Muslim leaders. They seemed to lack a belief in pluralism, tolerance, and Hindu-Muslim cultural fusion. They seemed to be opportunistic and want to play the victim card. They didn't talk up the illustrious Muslims who played major roles in India's independence movement and the setting up of the country's institutions. Where were the role models, other than in Bollywood? Why wasn't the Hindu rightwing rhetoric being countered in a better fashion? In their own way, they were becoming less secular and more extreme.

Aseem and Jehangir both strongly believed in *Ganga Jamuni tehzeeb*, in the idea of nationhood that Lala Lajpat Rai gave voice to in 1920: 'The Indian nation, such as it is, or such as we intend to build, neither is nor will be exclusively Hindu, Muslim, Sikh or Christian. It will be each and all.'

But Aseem and Jehangir were disillusioned men themselves, anxious about the lack of representation and respect for their communities and the lack of money that flowed into these communities. Waheeda thought of them as chips off the same block. She knew Jehangir preferred his lifestyle in Delhi to life in a small town or in a rural district. For that reason, Aseem was far more influential than him in the Nulkazim region and its outlying areas. But Jehangir's small party had not stopped contesting elections, targeting the same voters as Aseem, and he had thus remained a niggling thorn in Aseem's side.

Observing him, Waheeda thought that he lacked Aseem's personal charisma. It was a shame that he divided votes that might otherwise go to NPF.

'I'd like the contest to be clearly defined,' she said. *What did that even mean? Nothing.* She faltered on. 'You may have heard that Bir Sultan has resigned.' *Of course, he must know that.* 'I'm thinking of standing from Patharghat for the Lok Sabha, as my father told you.' She licked her lips. 'Whenever the next election is called.'

Oh dear, she wasn't saying anything of actual use! Be bold, Waheeda Rela.

'I'd like you to withdraw your candidate if I stand in Patharghat. I mean, I *will* stand and I'd like you to support me. If not overtly, if not publicly, at least behind the scenes. I *need* your backing. If I'm to have a chance. Perhaps the time has come for cooperation, Jehan-ji? Our parties should work more closely together. We have the same aims, after all.'

He was listening carefully to her, so carefully that it seemed even his hawkish nose was paying attention. 'You're a daring girl,' he said. 'Not scared after what happened to your brothers?'

She suppressed the urge to say, 'Don't call me a girl.'

'Thank you for your kind words,' she murmured. 'I'm not brave. I'm committed.' She spoke a bit louder. 'There are things I can do. I should be allowed to do them, to implement my ideas. If I win, I can be a force for change. That's what I'm looking at as my goal. That's what drives me.'

'Yes, indeed. Aseem Zafar's daughter, in one sense, after all. He did say I would be impressed by you.'

'Do you agree that even if you can't endorse me, as I understand you may not be able to, you will ensure no one stands against me from your party?'

'But are you not scared?'

'Jehan-ji, to tell you the truth, I am scared of many things. Death is just one more to add to that list. What I would find disheartening is putting in a great deal of effort, and losing just because there were some things I could have dealt with but were not dealt with…such as the agreement I'm now asking from you…'

'It was clever of your father to send you to ask. I can't be rude to a lady.'

She responded with the briefest of her fake smiles. NPF had poured most of its resources into Patharghat for Bir Sultan. They had massive support in the community now; the election result had made that clear. But if Jehangir insisted on fielding a candidate against her, and that candidate was a man, she would expect an erosion in support. Despite the fact that the current Chief Minister of Utter Pradesh, Mayawati, was a woman, and there were women politicians from U.P. constituencies in the Congress and BJP, she didn't feel confident about the chances for a Muslim woman in Patharghat. She clenched her hands.

Jehangir seemed to be distracted by something outside the window. He wasn't looking at her anymore. His gaze was on the crown of the peepal tree.

'It's a big decision, I know,' she said. 'I'm asking a lot from you. But it will be worth it.'

How could it be worth it to subvert the chances of your own party? Let him mull on that. She shouldn't defeat her own objective.

'Let's look at the greater good of getting ourselves representation,' she said.

He didn't reply.

This is useless. Why did Abba send me to meet him?

Jehangir spoke into the room, although he was considering the air, and not looking at her. 'We will have a candidate in Patharghat. We have to keep a root in the constituency. The root may be weak but it is there and we must nurture it. However…with your father's current authority in the area I doubt that our nominee will make too big an impression.'

'Who? Do you have someone in mind? Someone from the area? The same contender as last time?' She didn't ask '*male or female*,' being quite sure of the response.

'Whoever it is, he won't make a big impression.' He looked out of the window and Waheeda had to strain to hear what he was saying. 'He will run his own small campaign, but he won't impede you. I will tell him to treat your campaign with respect. Your main opposition is mighty. Congress. BJP. Mayawati's BSP.'

At last he looked directly at her. 'You will need a miracle.'

She stood. 'Thank you for meeting me. And...for your... encouragement.' She had nothing to thank him for other than a begrudging promise of civilised behaviour. Which was more than she would get from the other parties.

'I wish I could do more for you.' He said it quietly.

She had a feeling he meant it.

'If you think of some other way that I can be of help, do be in touch.'

A thought struck her. 'Jehan-ji, do you *have* to field a candidate in every constituency as us?'

His eyes fixed on her attentively but he didn't respond.

'What about Dhoonpur?' A sudden excitement rose in her; she might get a concession out of him after all.

His eyes swivelled around the room as if the tiny new cobwebs in the corners were spying on them. 'What about it?'

'Could you leave Dhoonpur to me?'

He pretended he hadn't heard.

She pressed on. 'It's one of my options. I could stand from there at the next election.' She gazed too eagerly into his face.

He remained grave and silent but she detected an almost imperceptible nod. She put a hand on her heart and bowed with respect and gratitude. He touched a hand to his forehead in a long goodbye.

It was only in the back seat of the boiling car that she felt able to exhale. Slowly. Habib started the engine and they joined the thick syrup of Delhi traffic. Dhoonpur. The two syllables beat on her heart. They tasted of grit and victory on her tongue. Jehan-ji had not insisted on having a candidate there, although he hadn't shown a visible or recorded sign of a pact with her. That would leave him free to change his mind if he was so inclined when the time came. But she would hold him to it. She would remind him of his nod. She clasped her hands tightly together, one hand sealing an accord with the other. Dhoonpur. Her selected constituency.

•

She rubbed at her red eyes as she sank into a wicker chair in Naaz's air-cooled veranda. They were shielded from the afternoon sun and the heavy humidity by the unrolled chicks, the bamboo blinds lined with pale blue fabric creating an enclosed private space.

'I'm tired.' Waheeda yawned. 'After that concert last night. I don't feel like doing much more today, other than eating and sleeping. And I want to have a long chat with Hira once I'm back in the flat.'

'How is my chweet-chweet Hira?' Naaz fanned away the flies that had managed to dodge the screens and fly in. 'Call her from here, call her now, then I can speak to her, too.'

'She won't be home yet; we can call later this afternoon, before I head back to Sangeet Vihar.'

Naaz loved to spend time with Hira, playing games with her and making up nonsense stories. Even now, Hira chatted to Naaz on the phone as if they were buddies. Often they were cooking up some scheme or other whereby Hira was "required" in Delhi by Naaz for a visit to the zoo, or a fun fair, or for Eid shopping and even Diwali shopping. Naaz had recently given up work and Waheeda looked carefully at her, at her face and her body. Naaz returned her stare and

Waheeda smiled indulgently. She hadn't wanted to question Naaz last Thursday evening in front of her sisters-in-law. 'So you're not missing the history department?' she asked lightly. 'What are they going to do without you?'

Naaz tossed her head. She'd piled her hair into a bun at the top, but she still looked hot, with tendrils of hair damply caught in perspiration. 'They'll cope.' She touched her tummy, with a meaningful glance.

'Are you—' Waheeda asked and at the joy that broke out on Naaz's face she knew the answer was "yes." She hugged her. 'Congratulations, I am thrilled.'

'Not as thrilled as I am! And we've made it past three months.'

Waheeda was happy to talk about Naaz's pregnancy all through lunch. She would let Naaz take the lead if she wanted to move on to other topics. She wouldn't rush her friend; she knew how much this meant; the agony and confusion of the last few years, Deepak and Naaz praying to their respective gods for healthy offspring. Waheeda was content to talk about babies all afternoon, if that was what Naaz wanted.

'How was the amazing Jagjit Singh? And how did you wangle a ticket at short notice?'

Waheeda described the entire scene at the concert and ran through the playlist, as Naaz hummed snatches of each song she listed. She didn't answer the question of how she'd got the ticket but Naaz seemed to have forgotten about that. As their plates were cleared away, and they were left alone on the veranda, Naaz leant forward. 'How was your meeting this morning?'

'Reasonably successful.' Waheeda knew she sounded cagey. She examined the Bourbon biscuit she'd picked out of the open packet on the table.

Naaz stirred sugar into her milky coffee. 'Can't you talk about it?'

She shook her head apologetically. 'I prefer not to. There

are some decisions we have to make back at HQ. Once things are confirmed, or there's something concrete to announce, I can tell you.'

'All right. What have you been doing that you *can* talk about?'

She'd been waiting for this opening. 'I met some new people at this party I attended with my father,' she began. 'A couple of weeks ago. Actually, I wanted to ask you some questions about—'

'Ooh, delicious gossip.' Naaz leant close again.

Waheeda laughed. 'I've none to offer. I was going to ask you about someone called Monish Selvani. He mentioned he knew Falguni. It struck me that you might know him too?'

'You mean the paper mills, home appliances, *those* Selvanis?'

At Waheeda's nod, 'He's Arun Selvani's older son, isn't he? I don't know him personally. But I've heard of him. Isn't he the offbeat one? Not Daddy's favourite. The younger one, Pratish, sticks with the father.' Naaz sipped from her cup. 'Who are the other new people you met? Anyone interesting?'

'No, not really.' She let a gap ensue before trying again. 'Naaz, about Monish Selvani, I wanted to ask—'

'Yes?' Naaz sat back, screwing up her eyes.

'What do you know about him?' She hoped she sounded fairly neutral.

'Why this interest in him particularly?'

'Just curious.'

'Me, too.' Naaz grinned at her, her square jaw softened by her pregnancy. 'I'm just curious, too. Very-very curious.'

Then she relented. 'Let me think. What does the rumour mill say? Hmm…he's got tons of girlfriends. That translates as the group he moves in has a lot of girls. More girls than boys, now, in fact. You know why? The boys are getting married, the girls are not. Or if they are, they're backing out of their marriages fast and going single again. Obviously, this applies to just that slice of super-rich kids.'

Waheeda nodded sagely. Naaz would start analysing social structures next, but she couldn't prod her anymore. Eventually she'd give her the information she wanted.

A teasing gleam in Naaz's eyes. 'Like I said, the boys are getting married, but not Monish. He refuses. Some relic of philosophy or principle. I forget which. Drives his papa crazy-crazy. But he's young, he'll change his mind.' She tore the wrapper off a packet of Krackjack biscuits. She'd eaten six Bourbons already. Waheeda was wondering whether to chide her, when Naaz asked, 'What did you make of him, Wija?'

'Who, Monish?' She shook her head in a vague manner. 'I just met him for a short while.'

'Even so. I don't know him, Wija, and it seems like you *do*. You must know more than me.'

'Not really. I'm out of that kind of gossip loop. What I wanted to know was—"

'—whether he had a serious girlfriend.' Naaz was triumphant at Waheeda's inadvertent blush. 'I knew it! I knew it as soon as you uttered his name.' She patted Waheeda's hand. 'Don't look so dismayed. It was written on your face.'

Waheeda looked around quickly. 'Volume.'

'Oops. Sorry.' Naaz giggled. 'Don't look so worried.' She kept her tone low. 'Only I can tell. Because I know you so well.'

Waheeda hoped she'd reset her face to neutral.

'If you're not an insider in their snooty band,' Naaz commented, 'it's hard to know which ones are ex-girlfriends and which ones he's currently dating. They all seem to stay chummy these days.'

'They're not snooty,' Waheeda interrupted and Naaz raised her shapely brows. 'You know his friends, too?'

'I met some of them…they seemed friendly enough.'

'Huh. Well, I can't tell you anything more about him. It'll

be easy enough to find out, a couple of calls. Although this is a dangerous question to ask. The rumour mill works overtime here and *you* know how much truth there is in what it churns out. But if you really want me to find out about his love life—'

'No! Thanks but no thanks. It's not that important.'

'If you say so.' Naaz settled her hands on her stomach. 'What's he like?'

'Nice. He's…nice.'

'I see. And?'

'And nothing. I'm going back to Nulkazim tomorrow. To real life.' She looked at her watch. 'Shall we call Hira now?'

It was only when Waheeda was leaving later that afternoon that Naaz referred to their lunchtime conversation. 'If you want me to find out anything about you-know-who, just ask. It's not difficult.'

'I don't think there's a need for that. Thanks all the same.'

'Well, I'm always here. If you need me.' Naaz squeezed Waheeda's hand.

Waheeda hugged her. 'I'll remember that.'

NINE

REAL LIFE COULD be put off by a few hours. Even though real life was good, she had nothing to complain about. She lay on her bed, trying to nap, trying to ignore the strange routes her brain was taking. She should count her blessings. All she had to do was look around to see many who were a hundred times worse off than her. Start near to hand, with Bhavna, who lived in the servant quarter at the back of these flats, who cleaned the flat when it was empty and came in to cook and wash when it was occupied. Then there was Habib, often making do with the car as a place of sleep, other times with temporary quarters, as he drove her about on her quests. Being a bodyguard was a tense job and that's probably why he rarely smiled.

Waheeda had a roof, plenty to eat, and a proper career. She'd embarked on something that brought light to her eyes and energy to her soul. It had made her strong, determined, ambitious. Her fledgling career even seemed to make successful friends jealous, Falguni being the first one who came to mind.

Most of all, in her real life, she had Hira. The blessing, the heart, the goodness of the world, the unselfish, the kernel of what the universe meant and what she'd been put on earth for—Hira to clasp and to love and to bring up.

She had everything. Almost. An element of fun was missing from her life, and occasionally she worried that by the time she was brave enough to follow her instincts she'd be on the highway to dementia. But why would she raise herself from the bed, shake her head at her tired eyes, step out under the looming clouds for a brisk walk to the local chemist, lie back down again, perspiring, but with cooled cotton pads soaked in rosewater over her eyes? *What was she doing?*

She was bathed, dressed and driving to Monish's flat. She was wearing her red *churidar kurta*. Habib had taken up her offer of time off but Bhavna was hanging around the car. Was she keeping tabs on her in Habib's absence? 'Just going to have an early dinner with a friend,' Waheeda said. 'I'll be back very soon.' If Bhavna was waiting for her return, she couldn't be too late. She didn't have much time.

Monish opened the door before she rang the bell. ' I heard the lift come up; thought it might be you in the hallway.'

He looked happy; she wondered if a similar happiness emanated from her.

·

SHE WONDERED ALL the way home if it was possible to hide such joy; would it be as noticeable to everyone as it had been to Naaz? Maybe you pursed your lips and scowled to hide the singing of your gleeful heart. That's what she would have to do, she thought, as she parked the car back in Sangeet Vihar. Scowl at Bhavna.

At Monish's flat there'd been food laid out on the table for her, but she'd said right away about not having much time and he'd seemed to understand that eating was not her priority. She'd accepted a Limca with ice and sat on the grey sofa, in her previous spot, attempting to make conversation about the décor of the flat. Had Sasha chosen the ceiling lamp? she asked. She hadn't seen anything like it and she couldn't decide if she liked it or not. Six fluted cream shades protruded from a chrome globe. Maybe her taste was not contemporary enough. She hadn't travelled. What did she know of interior design trends?

She shut her eyes when Monish kissed her and kept them firmly shut after that. A part of her rose to the ceiling and settled on the chrome globe and somehow this part of her had open eyes to watch in fascination as the Waheeda on the sofa with the clamped-closed eyelids had not resisted when Monish had lain her down, as gentle as the laying down of flowers. She remained in that detached observant mode even as clothes had been loosened, then removed. Her limbs wove around his but now she wasn't speaking either. She was a shut-eyed tongue-tied idiot who hoped he wouldn't break the spell. Twice or possibly thrice, Monish hesitated, paused, began to speak, but her eyes and mouth had tightened. He'd sensed that it was best to say nothing and best not to stop half-way.

She finally opened her eyes when she was sure he wasn't watching her because his head was buried in her neck as his breath came back slowly. But he must have been very aware, because the moment she opened her eyes, he lifted his head. 'Sleeping Beauty wakes up at last. Oh thank God.' He started laughing. He wasn't wearing his glasses, they'd come off early on, before he kissed her, and she saw how his eyes ruched downwards at the corners as he laughed helplessly.

She started laughing, too. Maybe she was meant to feel bad about her uselessness but she found the way he said it funny, and she could feel the laughter bubbling out of his belly, still stuck on hers. This was more intimate than what had gone before, this holding on to her shoulders and her on to his and the shaking of their stomachs in unison.

•

MONISH STOOD IN the balcony gulping his scotch. After his third swallow he felt the burning of the liquid reach his stomach. Food, he needed food; he went inside to the dining table. He lifted the lids off the dishes he'd asked Malti to prepare for the evening. He spooned some cooked cabbage into a chapatti, rolled it and bit into it as he returned to the balcony.

What a disaster the evening had been. A strange first encounter, but he was still laughing. Disaster or not, it had ended well.

Even so, during the course of the hour that Waheeda had been in the flat, he had been assailed by moments of huge uncertainty, wondering what in hell he was meant to do. They'd started out all right. He understood she couldn't stay long and she didn't want to eat. She wanted him, he'd caught the right vibe about that at least. He gave silent thanks to Sasha for equipping his living room with a broad comfortable sofa, one that could see action. Because once Waheeda had closed her eyes and seemed to float off elsewhere, he hadn't known how to move them both, either to the rug or to the bedroom. If he spoke a whole long sentence he worried that she would open her eyes, fasten her clothes and leave. He did try half-sentences—*Are you OK?* being one such that received no response. Every time he stopped to think he realised that her fingertips were pressed into his back. Later it was the pressure of her legs around him that had given him the confidence to keep going despite the crazy silence and those tightly shut eyes. Was he so damn ugly? Was she pretending he was someone else?

It had been a weird evening but he'd done fine. He must've passed some test. He hoped. And he had to admit that one of the times that he'd paused to wonder what was going on exactly, one of the images that had come to him was a cliché from Hindi films. Here was the shy bride in her red apparel, and here was the groom pushing her down. Although in the movies it was always a flower-bedecked four-poster-bed where this took place.

Nulkazim

'REPUTATION IS EVERYTHING.' Umair's long face elongated further as he intoned these words. A sepulchral sage. Waheeda would've been amused at his seriousness if she wasn't feeling pity for Bir Sultan and his daughter. Umair had informed her that Bir had resigned because he was being blackmailed.

'His daughter had an abortion while her boyfriend was abroad doing his masters, and the lovelorn, sad letters she wrote to him have been copied to the local press. Bir has to step out of the public gaze. They won't publish if he goes away.'

'He told you himself?' Waheeda pressed her hands on her knees.

'No.' Umair pulled his chair a little closer. 'I found out… like I always do. Bir must protect his daughter's reputation and get her married. Save his family from being shamed. We all understand that.'

'Of course. I suppose the shame is not the boy's. It must be owned by the girl, right? I suppose the boyfriend's family won't stand up for her—'

Umair compressed his lips. 'Whatever you may think, Wija, you can't swim against society's norms without consequences. Society is what it is.'

'We make society what it is, Umair-ji.'

'The newspaper will not publish snippets of the letters if Bir is not a candidate.' He ignored her intervention. 'One editor told me that all the editors and proprietors have seen the letters, so the girl's reputation is in shreds anyway; but at least not publicly. The editor said his arm is being twisted—'

'By the goons?' Waheeda sat back, unnerved. Patharghat would be a tough nut to crack, if play was at this dirty level. She was a woman, she would always be in danger of assault and abuse and fabricated smears. 'And the committee thinks *I* should be the next candidate there.'

Umair wheezed out a breath. 'What do you think?'

'Should I discuss this with Abba as well?'

A sudden twinkle in his eyes. 'I'll pass on the message. I have a feeling you know what you want.'

Waheeda chewed her inner lip. 'Not really. But I felt with

Jehan-ji that…I felt that he would leave Dhoonpur open for me.'

Umair's eyes squeezed shut for three seconds. When he opened them, he said, 'Dhoonpur it is.'

Her eyes widened. 'Just like that. You agree?'

Umair was conspiratorial again, his voice low. 'I have news. There's likely to be a by-election there at some point. WW Singh has cancer. He's spending a fair amount of time at the hospital in Bombay.'

How did he ferret out his information from all quarters? She thought about the elderly gent, WW, the incumbent Congress MP. Did Umair think he was so ill that he would die soon? Or give up his seat? She didn't like to ask. She was feeling sorry for WW, having to battle cancer.

'When he's gone,' Umair said, with no hint of emotion, 'internecine rivalry will destroy both his lieutenants. There is no love lost between them. Those brutes will fight each other and divide the party's votes.' He placed his palm flat on the low table between them. 'We'll draw up a campaign schedule for you that will touch on all the areas surrounding Dhoonpur, but we'll make sure you concentrate on the villages and communities that make up WW's constituency.'

TEN

June 1997
Delhi

WAHEEDA HOVERED AROUND Naaz as she settled herself into
a corner table at Nathu's sweet shop in Bengali market. Naaz
hailed the waiter, ordering tea and an uthapam. She brought
out a book from her handbag and gave Waheeda a little push.
'I'll be fine. Go now, or you'll have even less than the two
hours you've given yourself. It's already past six p.m.'

'You remember where to meet me later?'

Naaz waved her away. 'Yes-yes. I'll text you when I'm
parked there. Go now, Wija.'

Waheeda looked back once from the door. Naaz was scru-
pulously wiping the formica table with a tissue. Waheeda
walked on to Monish's building, her steps slow because of the
pulsating heat, and also, after all the dithering and arranging,
at this nth moment she was reluctant to go up to his flat. It
had been three weeks since she was last here. In the interim
they'd spoken a few times on the phone; she'd called him
from her mobile when she'd had the opportunity. Each time
he'd asked when she'd next see him and twice she'd tried to
tell him that this wasn't the start of anything, that, in fact, she
couldn't see him again. Once he'd discovered her goal was to
be an MP, he wouldn't want to see her anyway. It was difficult
to express on the phone, when she only had two minutes to
speak to him, wary as she was about long calls. She would tell
him in person today.

She thought back to her previous visit. Rushed and mad.

It made her smile, she couldn't help it. She gave the littered pavement the benefit of her full beam. As she'd left his flat that last time he'd asked for her phone number.

'I can't give it to you…I'll explain why another time…'

He'd brought an A4 sheet from his study and written down his numbers, all five of them: two work numbers—one a direct line; his cell phone; his home phone and the farmhouse number, where he said he often spent the weekend. Waheeda brought out the sheet daily in her room, studying those numbers, but she'd exercised restraint and only called him a few times.

More restraint was needed today. She lost it pretty much immediately on entering his apartment, flashing an exhilarated smile at his happy hello. Then she remembered, and stood awkwardly in the centre of the silk rug. He came close for a hug but she stepped back, gesturing at the glass doors that led to the balcony. 'Could you close the curtains?' she asked.

Monish stared at her, searching her face for clues. 'You look different,' he remarked. He looked out towards the balcony and she followed his gaze. Dusk was falling and the sky was yellow with the sun's rays shooting through the smog. Intermittent irritable horns sounded from the surrounding roads, even though his apartment had a quiet aspect and was four floors high. His rooms had been air-conditioned before her arrival, that was considerate, she was already feeling cooler and fresher.

He said, 'No one can see in.'

'Still…'

He closed the cream drapes. They were double muslin, not completely opaque. The room darkened but there was enough light to see each other. They were now in a grey dusk, altered versions of themselves, dark silhouettes with softened features.

'Please sit down, Waheeda.'

She knew he meant on the sofa, but she chose the armchair opposite it. He didn't seat himself on the sofa as she expected; balancing himself on the arm of her chair instead. 'I know why you look different. Your hair's tied up.'

Don't sit by me, because I can't concentrate on what I've come here to say. Don't sit by me because I will want to pull you on to me and really, that won't do.

Monish removed the clasp from her hair and set it on the narrow table between the two armchairs. He ran his fingers through her loosened hair, bringing the strands to the front. 'I like your hair loose.'

She sat still, electrified. He was much cleverer than her in some ways. At ease on the arm of the chair, touching her. He was so much more assured than she could be in a situation like this. She'd come with many things to say, especially that what had happened last time, couldn't happen again. He seemed to have sensed that and begun breaking her resolve already. He ran his fingers through her hair again and as he did so the back of his hands lightly stroked her nipples through her *kameez* and her chiffon *dupatta*.

Waheeda closed her eyes just for a second, to think. Instantly Monish was pulling at her hands, pulling her up to standing. 'Let me show you the rest of my flat,' he said. Somewhere inside her she was amused and understanding. He didn't want her to close her eyes through it all again. She wasn't going to. She allowed herself to be led into the hall, glad he had hold of her hands, that their bodies were touching, that he'd ignored her standoffish signals. *One more time, she could have him one more time.*

'My study.' He pointed into the room on the left. It was crammed with stuff.

Two desks along the left wall. The far one in black metal, with a monitor and a keyboard on it. A large computer was wedged on the floor between the desks. The second desk looked exactly like a walnut bureau that Falguni had in her home, that she'd commissioned from the furniture designer

Brijesh. It had the same smooth finish, the rounded shape, the bronze fittings. She guessed it contained a panoply of drawers behind the plain outer panels. Falguni's desk had three hidden drawers that were not easy to access unless you knew where they were. Or if you had ample time to scope out the desk, pressing on hidden hinges, or pushing back mini-panels after removing an outer drawer.

'It's a beautiful piece, isn't it?' Monish asked, mistaking her interest for admiration. His fingers holding hers, his fingers cool, hers warm.

'Yes.'

'It's from the designer—'

'Brijesh.'

'Oh, you know him?'

'I've seen some examples of his work. It's quite distinctive.'

Falguni's round bed had also been made by Brijesh. There was a hidden ledge under her bed, where Fal kept her tape recorder running. But the ledge would have been Fal's request, knowing her, not part of the regular design.

Waheeda cast a quick backward glance into the study as Monish pulled her on. A single high-backed chair; a bank of fitted cupboards; towers of CDs by the far wall; shelves for books and videos. A sports bag on the floor and a squash racket propped against the cupboards.

They were at the closed door on the right. He opened it and ushered her in. 'My bedroom.'

It surprised her. Large and airy, walls painted in dove-grey; a wide window with the split air conditioner set high in the wall above it and a curtain rail just below the air conditioner. Heavy drapes in cream cotton embroidered with a subtle grey paisley pattern. Sculptured metal half-loops held back the drapes. Had Sasha made all of these selections? Whoever had, the result was lovely. The room was appealing and peaceful. A light-grey eiderdown covered the big bed. It was completely smoothed, and the material precisely folded under the pillows at the top. How come everything was so neat? An armchair by the bed faced a black cabinet on the opposite wall. It must be a television cabinet, the kind she'd seen in hotel rooms; a lacquered or stained-wood creation where the doors would slot into the sides when opened.

Monish placed his hands lightly on her shoulders as she stood by the bed. Behind him she could see a wardrobe and another door which she supposed led to the bathroom.

'Do you like my room?'

'Yes, but—'

'But what?'

'Could you close the curtains?'

She received a searching look before he went to the window to pull the thick drapes together. The room became completely dark. He switched on a floor lamp by the cabinet. It spilled a halo of yellow light around itself and they were bathed in a faint glow. He held the top of her arms, indenting them with his thumbs. Waheeda could barely draw her eyes off the big bed, but she looked up at him and said, 'We haven't talked.'

'I know.' He steered her to the chair and asked her to sit. He propped up pillows on the bed and sat back on them, stretching out his long legs, then crossing one over the other. He was barefoot. She noticed how slim his feet were and the sparse black hairs on his big toes. She wanted to abandon her chair, sit by him, put her feet on his and lay herself on him.

He turned towards her. 'Let's talk.'

She swallowed. There were a hundred important things to say but she didn't know where to start. All that came to mind was: 'Are you always this tidy?'

A rueful grimace. 'Yes, I have a bit of an obsession with orderliness. Do you mind?'

'No. It's hard work being this neat.'

He grinned and she loved everything about his face at that

moment, the small white teeth, the sharp lines of his thin jaw, the beauty spot under his lip.

'I have Malti,' he said. 'A gem. She's my housekeeper. She used to be a nursery teacher. Her husband died in an accident. After all the expenses and without his salary, her income wasn't enough for her and her daughter. I told her I'd give her the same salary as my personal assistant at work, if she became my personal assistant at home. She comes in daily, usually when I'm at work. She knows how I like things. She cooks for me when I need her to. She runs some errands. She never gossips with the other maids in the building or with my office driver. She's a real find. The kind of employee I want to keep forever.'

Wow, he was evangelical about his Malti. But she understood. Everyone in Delhi complained about how difficult it was to get staff, how no one was loyal to families as in the old days. Schools and servants, it was what everyone talked about. If Monish had found someone he trusted, and who coped well with his regulation tidiness, she could see he would be delighted.

He seemed to be waiting for her to lead their conversation. 'Are you obsessive about music, too?' she asked, remembering what Sasha had said at the concert.

'Not obsessive, no. I have a great interest. I'm building a collection of every Hindi film song released from 1931 to 1981. Fifty years of *filmi gana*. I'm also collecting most of the semi-classical music recorded since 1902, as they become available in new formats. Although most of that is stored at my parents' home. They have a lot more space than I do here.'

His palpable enthusiasm made her smile.

'So, tell me,' he said, 'do you like old songs? Any particular one? Any specific singer?'

Waheeda considered. Her brain was in turmoil, he wasn't to know that, it was chattering to her, chiding her. Statements burning a hole in her head, things she needed to articulate.

'I like listening to Talat Mahmood,' she was slow to reply. 'His voice calms me, I think.'

Nothing was calming her here, though. How and when to blurt out: "I haven't told you but I'm a rookie politician. I may be just starting out but I'm aiming for the Lok Sabha. Just being here with you is a risk. I mean, risking my career, naturally, but also possibly my *life*. Perhaps putting you in danger, too. No, I'm not being melodramatic. What with all the fanatics out there, who knows who can take an axe to whom? Do they need a reason? Never. They just need a rumour or an excuse to take offence. You know that as well as I do. You know a woman can't get away with much, even if a man can. As for the mixing of religions—let's not even go into what some people think."

What had he said? What? Oh, which particular Talat Mahmood song would she choose to listen to? She found herself confessing that she disliked love songs. That sparked something off and he asked her another question. Another song question! She was only vaguely aware of what she was telling him because she was carrying on two conversations. To herself: What am I *doing* here? What is my family going to think? Nafis, will he understand? My mother, what will she say? Aseem—he will go ballistic. I can't even begin to imagine his reaction. My Hira—what will she think of me?

If anyone should find out, anyone at all, other than the only two people I trust, Naaz and Lara, then...I could lose *everything*. Losing the party nomination would be the least of it. Once her reputation was tarnished, how would she recover it? Impossible.

Did I not steel myself to tell him straight out, rightaway?

Monish bent his legs, the soles of his feet flat on the bed-spread and his weight leaning back onto the bedhead. Padded grey linen. He looked very comfortable. After a few silent moments he asked her which restaurants she liked to go to in

Delhi. Evidently he assumed they needed to make more conversation. She told him she preferred quiet old-fashioned cafés
like Bankura and she mentioned a couple of dosa restaurants.
She didn't say that Nafis had liked the *dhabas* in Paharganj,
although she was not fond of them. Nafis and she hadn't had
much money and they didn't dine out on the scale that she
presumed Monish did.

She got the impression from the tone of his questions that
he knew she was married. But also that she lived apart from
her husband. He seemed to think she was looking for a new
academic post in Nulkazim, because he asked about academia
as though he was truly interested in what life was like as a
lecturer. Had she given him the idea that she was looking for
a job? She couldn't remember what she'd said about herself.
Not much. She was being thoroughly absentminded; even
about what she was telling him at this moment.

'You haven't asked *me* anything for twenty minutes.' He
removed his glasses, setting them carefully on the bedside
table. 'Is there anything you want to ask me?' Puzzled eyes.

'Not today.' *There are things I want to tell you.*

He adjusted the pillows behind his back and re-crossed his
legs. 'Have we talked enough?'

So that was the end of conversation as foreplay. He was
laughing at her, patting the space beside him. 'Come and sit
by me, *gajra* girl.'

•

MONISH DREW OPEN the drapes, threw open the glass doors
and went onto the balcony. A strong wind had blown away
some of the smog and a silver half-moon was hanging in the
velvety warm sky. A rare sighting now compared to when he
was a child. These days the Delhi smog obstructed everything
and poisoned his throat and lungs. It's why he liked to go on
holiday to places where the air was grit-free. He gazed down
at the residential cul-de-sac that his balcony overlooked. It

was quiet below, people ambling genially, some scurrying women aiming to get home before it became late and unsafe for them on the roads.

Naaz had parked at the kerb down there earlier. He'd told Waheeda about this quiet lane that went nowhere. He'd explained it was a discreet spot to be dropped off or picked up. Only the people on his side of the building overlooked it. The girls who lived in the adjacent working women's hostel often hung out here, too, until eight p.m., which was their curfew time. But it was not usually used by outsiders to the vicinity.

So. He ran his hand through his hair. Another evening that had not gone how he'd expected. He wandered inside to find a Talat Mahmood disc, laying a few on the floor before selecting one. Waheeda claimed he was her favourite old-time singer. Soothing voice, according to her. Let's hear the songs, let's see if it made him feel close to her, if it made him feel he knew her any better. He pressed play. Out in the balcony he convulsed with laughter as soon as he heard the first words of the opening song, '*Phir Wohi Sham, Wohi Gham.*' 'Again the same evening, the same sorrow, the same loneliness…'

Waheeda had said that although she thought all the music he loved was beautiful, she found the lyrics of most of the songs defeatist.

'Defeatist?' He'd been incredulous. 'This wonderful tender poetry, defeatist?'

She was firm. 'Yes, overly sentimental, completely defeatist. "If my love doesn't come to me, I will die." "I will go to my love's door, and I will do something to make her mine; or I will die." "I cannot live without my beloved." It doesn't work like that does it?' she said. 'People carry on. 'They don't lie down and play dead when their beloved disappears.'

He wondered immediately about her husband, and whether she loved him, and what had happened between them, but it wasn't the right time to ask. He didn't want reminders of the husband looming over them just before he took her to bed. But he'd imagined that afterwards there would be time. They would be relaxed and they would snuggle for a bit, and he could ask her the more intrusive questions that he was holding back on. She was obviously wanting to ask him something too, he just didn't know what. He'd tried gently to give her opportunities to come out with whatever it was, but she'd seemed faraway. Oh well, he'd thought, there would be time to chat later.

So wrong. There'd been no 'later.' Hardly a few minutes to relax. He'd turned her on her side and filled his hands with her breasts and let his neck slide down to rest on his pillow. He'd begun to breathe slow and deep, rhythmic. Waheeda stirred, removed his hands, sat up. 'I must get dressed.' Her tone urgent. He'd wondered, but pointed wordlessly to the bathroom and drawn his sheet over himself, right up to his forehead to give her the privacy he sensed she needed. This time there was no laughing; she seemed solemn. Regretful?

He must've drifted off because he woke to a touch on his shoulder. She folded down the sheet from his face and smiled into his sleepy eyes. She reached out her thumb to the corner of his eye. A light caress. 'I'll wait in the lounge.'

When he came out in his jeans and a T-shirt, she was seated at the dining table rubbing contemplatively at the glass top. She'd switched on the air conditioning and all the lights in the dining area. She stood as he appeared. 'I have to go soon. My friend Naaz will be arriving at the lane where you said to be picked up.'

'Already?' He was astonished. 'Now? It's…It's…' He looked for the time.

She didn't meet his eyes; her gaze on the floor. He lifted her wrist to read her watch.

'Really?' he asked. 'You told her to come at *seven-thirty*?'

What had she expected—wham, bam, thank you ma'am?

Is that what she wanted and he hadn't understood? He ran his hands through his hair in disbelief.

'I…' She looked into his face. 'I did ask her to come before eight.' She rubbed at her cheek. 'I wasn't going to… because…I was going to—' She shook her head. 'I have to be somewhere else for dinner.'

He touched her arm. 'Plan it better next time. Stay the night. Or half the night…whatever suits you. I can drop you wherever you want, whenever you want. You don't have to bother your friend.'

She shook her head again, made a face, and said in rush: 'I can't come here again. I can't see you.'

He felt hurt. Stupid for being hurt. What had he done wrong? He'd tried so hard to be sensitive to what she wanted.

'It's not anything you did.' Her left palm pressed flat on the dining table. 'It's just not a good idea.' She didn't seem able to say more.

'That bad, huh?' He gave a small false laugh. 'I didn't please you.' He didn't believe that, but something was wrong. Obviously.

She put her hand on his chest. 'No…it's not about that at all…not at all.'

'So what's the problem? Suddenly you don't like me anymore?' He didn't believe that either. Not when she'd been clutching him like he was a life raft.

'It's difficult for me. My life isn't like yours. I'm not sure you understand.'

'Try me.'

'There are some things about me you don't know—' She hesitated.

'Like the fact you're married. I know that.' He wanted to help her out.

'What else do you know?'

'You have a daughter.'

She nodded and ran her fingers along the glass. He could

see he hadn't hit upon the problem yet. 'Your husband lives apart,' he said. 'But I understand what the world is like. Are you afraid of your husband?'

'Not quite.'

'Is he likely to lose his rag if he finds out? Does he get violent? Beat you?'

'No. No! Nafis is...not like that. What he will do if he learns about this, I don't know, but in any case he should never find out—'

'I understand. I can keep quiet. I'm not a boastful boy! You've told me enough about Aseem-ji for me to know what *he's* like. It can be our secret, Waheeda. It's not an issue. Don't you trust me?'

Her eyes pierced his. 'I trust you. I probably shouldn't, but I do.'

He waited. She said, 'There's something I haven't told you.'

He felt himself clam up. He knew a coldness appeared on his face because she looked at him anxiously. 'My work...'

'It's about that?' He was surprised.

'Yes, you see I...I'm...'

'Looking for work in Nulkazim,' he filled in for her. 'I know.'

'It isn't quite like that. I've joined my father's political party. I've set up the Golden Oriole charity that I've told you about. But, in addition, I'm beginning to campaign. Just starting...'

It took him a moment to understand. 'You're not looking for a new post as a lecturer?'

She shook her head. She laid her warm hand on his arm.

He moved his arm away. 'Are you telling me what I think you're telling me? You're campaigning for yourself?'

He knew from the defensive look in her eyes that he'd got the point.

'*Why didn't you tell me earlier?*' He couldn't stop the anger, and his raised voice revealed it.

She compressed her lips, which made her dimples appear

in her cheeks. She said nothing, but a slow flush rose in her face. Even though she was dark-skinned, he could see it mounting over her cheeks and up to her forehead.

He pulled out a chair and sat down, breathing, counting, his elbows on the table, head down, his fingers interlaced. It made him furious to be made a fool of. One, two, three... Control. He heard her sit and stole a look up as he counted. Twelve, thirteen, fourteen. Control. She was calm, watching him. At the count of seventy-two he felt his anger dissipate. She hadn't told him for the same reason he hadn't told her his real age. And he wasn't going to tell her just yet that he was twenty-eight, not thirty. Not at this juncture. If she had lied to him, he had lied to her. He looked up. 'I understand.' He spoke in his normal tone.

She scraped back her chair, rummaging in her handbag for the phone that had started ringing. 'You see now why this is such a bad idea.'

'Really? *Such* a bad idea?' He feigned hurt, but more playfully than before.

'You know what I mean.' She gave him a wobbly smile and whispered into the phone, 'I'll be right down.'

They stood in unison. He held her arm. 'Wait.'

It was madness but there was hope lurking in her eyes, he could see it, and there was hope hiding in his heart. 'That explains so much,' he said. 'We can deal with it. Let's talk. I mean really talk. About this.'

•

HE'D PULLED HER to the sofa. He'd asked all the questions he wanted answers to. He'd convinced her they could find a way around all the hurdles she was throwing up *if* she truly wanted to see him. Her phone buzzed again. She answered it, covered the mouthpiece, and looked at him apologetically. 'Naaz is pregnant. She's been waiting downstairs a while now and she's desperate to go to the bathroom.'

Monish took the phone from her. 'Come up, Naaz.'

Waheeda snatched her phone away. 'Never do that. Never.'

Idiot, he'd thought, Monish you're an idiot. Of course you shouldn't speak on her phone. You'll have to learn to behave completely differently. You've just been rashly promising all kinds of stuff and then you make a basic mistake. What an idiot!

Naaz came up to the flat. A big jovial woman, with large eyes and a wide laughing mouth. Monish could see that she had a great affection for Waheeda. He could also see that she would do anything for those she loved. He liked her. If a woman like Naaz had come to him at his office looking for work, someone whom he instantly deemed capable, energetic, and kind, he would have taken her on; he would've created a position for her if he had to. He hoped Naaz had a good feeling about him, too; she would be crucial if he was to meet Waheeda regularly.

As they were leaving, he said to Waheeda. 'Wait a moment.'

'Why?'

He picked up the hair clasp on the side table. She'd forgotten about it. 'Do your hair,' he said, 'the way it was when you arrived.'

It was a little thing but he was just showing off. He wanted to prove he understood. All of it. The danger. The clandestine nature of anything they did together. The risk she was taking to be with him.

•

TALAT MAHMOOD WAS on song four. '*Sham-e-gham ki qasam*.'

Monish put his head in his hands. "On this evening of sorrows I swear, I'm sad today, come to me, come to me now, my love." He adored this melody by Khayyam, but Waheeda was right. If you paid attention to the words, they were pretty mournful. He poured himself a scotch on ice. A double would do after the revelations of this evening. Hell, a double Patiala peg was needed. He twisted the ice tray, scattering cubes onto the counter instead of the bowl he'd placed beneath the tray. He scooped the cubes into his tumbler and added another shot of whisky. On the balcony he raised the full glass to the burnished half-moon. 'Evening.'

The moon mocked Monish. It often did. In that sense it was in cahoots with his father.

Yes, moon, he said, Insanity. I know. I'm being loony to enter this relationship. Not just because of the risks and the faff of secrecy. But because I'm low on the pecking order. This is a woman whose priorities are other.

Lunacy, folly, fault of the half-moon, call it what you will. It was his choice. No one had compelled him as they did in other aspects of his life. He, Monish, was ready for a change from the normal. He, Monish, had made promises.

He'd offered to work out a fail-safe plan each time of how they could meet. It was something he'd have to do if he was going to see her regularly. The next meeting was set. He'd come up with the ploy of accidentally meeting at the flower show at the end of the month; he'd heard a passing remark from his mother about the dahlias and carnations she was looking forward to seeing. The suggestion had gone down well. Naaz could stay and enjoy the show while he whisked Waheeda away and back. Waheeda had expressed concern about Naaz being overtired, what with being pregnant, but Naaz had waved her doubts away. For the moment, it was all good; there was a plan. But he was going to need more ruses than one pathetic flower show.

He stepped inside to change the plaintive song wafting out to him. Talat *bhai*, don't weep so much. Look at me, I'm choosing celibacy. Yep, one fuck every three weeks or so was in effect celibacy. Worse, he'd offered his fidelity, although Waheeda hadn't thought to ask for it. She'd looked almost shocked. He couldn't help speculating what that look had meant: she expected fidelity; she didn't expect it? He couldn't make out. Other than that inadvertent stare she'd ignored his avowal. But he knew her now, a bit, and he knew what was required of him.

He must've been crazy in that moment. 'Perversity,' he said aloud to his sound system. But it wasn't perversity, it was what he wanted. An excuse to put a stop to going out too much. An excuse to stay home. He needed an excuse just for himself, to do what he really wanted to do. And he needed more from Waheeda. He didn't properly know her, despite their two couplings, and that was the attraction, wasn't it? If someone had told him yesterday that he would be putting in this effort to date a *politician*, his mirth would've surely choked him to death.

He pushed at the skip button, cutting Talat off in mid-croon. Let's find a happy song, Talat *bhai*, shall we? Nothing defeatist. He pressed play on '*Milte hi ankhen dil hua diwana.*' Somewhat appropriate. "As soon as our eyes met, my heart became crazy for someone; the story of my life became the story of her life." Monish hummed it as he moseyed to the kitchen to heat up dinner. In his elated gut a foreboding of jeopardy insinuated itself. He ignored it. 'Let's just see how it goes.'

ELEVEN

September 1997

THE MINIBUS FILLED with the smell of sweet oranges. Waheeda's stomach rumbled. Someone at the back was eating the fruit. She was seated, as always, in the first row behind the driver. The citrus scent intensified and her nostrils twitched. Someone was distributing oranges to everyone in the bus. Soon, one would reach her. She would stick her thumb into the middle and peel the loose skin in one go. She was so hungry, she'd eat half of it in one bite.

When Prem got to the front, he offered her the nubby green fruit from a plastic bag and also a *peda* from another plastic bag. '*Prashad* from the temple we halted at earlier,' he said. 'You must have it.' Waheeda regretfully accepted both. She didn't want to eat the *peda*. She mumbled something about eating later, drew out a tissue from her handbag, wrapped it around the sweet confection and placed it in a side pocket. She let the orange drop into the bag and looked out of the window in disappointment. Tradition dictated that one should always eat *prashad* but she'd had her fill of temple sweets for the day. Prem was one of her steadfast aides, and the only Hindu male in the campaign minibus today, other than the driver. They'd halted at the temple because the driver wanted to pay obeisance; others in the coach had disembarked and milled around. She couldn't grumble to Prem about too many sweetmeats. Prem and at least two of the ladies in the group had gone in for a swift veneration. There were only a handful of women on her team and these two ladies who travelled often with her made offerings at every place of worship when given the opportunity: every *dargah*, *gurudwara*, or temple: it didn't matter which paltry god or goddess it was dedicated to, or if it was Hindu, Jain, Sikh, Buddhist. Being in her entourage was giving them a free ride to each place of worship in the Nulkazim region and just beyond its boundaries. She herself had started out with enthusiasm, getting in and out of the bus at every medium-sized shrine that someone pointed at, but now she saved herself the effort. She saved herself for the important mosques where she was a special visitor, and the *dargahs* and temples that were famed, and she'd given instructions that worshipful halts were to be limited to three a day, *maximum*, one of which was to be the driver's choice. God was supposed to be everywhere, not residing in these man-made structures, and she was sure God could see her, hear her, and know what she was thinking or doing without her telling him when she entered His Holy Premises. Even if it felt automatic for every Indian to enter a temple and clang the bell *Hear me, God*, or kneel to place your forehead on the floor, *Look at me bow to you, God*, or for Muslims to face Mecca; to her it felt like everyone asked for favours from the Almighty and if she did that, too, she was just the same. One of a billion, asking, asking...

Yet. When she entered a hallowed monument, she felt unable to leave without closing her eyes and uttering a prayer for her family and herself.

The only person she knew who never gave in to the temptation to pray was Nafis.

Her stomach growled. When no one was looking she might unpeel that irresistible orange. Was Shakeel eating one? She looked across the aisle. He was chewing the last of his fruit and also watching her. He always sat in the first seat by the door. From that vantage point he could both guard her and check if she needed anything. He understood her nods and grimaces. He knew when to come to her rescue if she was suffering unwanted attention or if someone had sat by her too long or spoken to her too forcefully. At the moment a smile played about his mouth. He must know she was peckish but couldn't stand the thought of a *peda*. She disliked all milky sweets. Only her family and closest friends knew this about her. Shakeel was family. Before he'd become her lieutenant he'd been her gentle brother-in-law. What strange cards fate had dealt them.

Shakeel leant forward to speak to the driver, instructing him to stop if they passed an appropriate snack store on the way back to Nulkazim HQ. He asked for the air conditioning to be turned up. 'On top speed already,' the driver replied.

It was late afternoon, the sun burning into the windows on the left side of the bus and they still had a couple more hours to drive. Shakeel could pull across the flapping icky curtain of his window, she thought, but no, of course, he couldn't, because it would be a security breach to not know what was going on outside.

It had been a good rally in Dhoonpur town. She had never had such a large turnout before nor such an enthusiastic response to her coded calls for a change of political direction. After the rally they'd taken a return route that enabled her to go on a short walkabout at a village that fell on the border of the constituency. She felt that they'd been welcomed with more than basic politeness and with genuine inquisitiveness. News of her toilet-building schemes had reached the women and her educational promises had fired up the youths in the local office. She'd asked the NPF overseer in the little town nearby to set up a basic women's committee. It was only a first step, but it meant that next time she would have a forum in which to hear the views and issues of the female inhabitants of the village. Today, they had half-hid beneath their head-coverings and veils and not looked her in the eye. Still, it had been a satisfying day's work.

The only low moment was not being able to refuse the kindness of a fresh glass of goat's milk. The headman's wife wouldn't take no for an answer. Waheeda had tried all the excuses she kept up her sleeve, except the truth: 'I heartily dislike milk.' Her stomach turned a bit at the memory of that stainless steel tumbler, the sips she took while attempting not to grimace, the coughing fit she'd resorted to, the praise she'd sung.

Everyone on the bus was wilting from the heat and the ebbing of adrenalin. Somehow when they'd been walking under the sweltering sun earlier no one had seemed affected by the temperature. Shakeel's foot tapped on the metal floor of the bus, revealing his impatience at something going on in his head. Waheeda noticed his shoes. New. She'd been too caught up to spot them earlier in the day. Dark blue trainers. They should've looked incongruous with his white *churidar*, but he had on a long navy kurta, and the overall effect was quite stylish. That blue suited him. He was so much like Nafis; even his eyes were exactly the same light-brown. She should've bought Nafis a navy shirt—he would've looked good. She closed her eyes. Maybe she could still buy one as a present from Hira to her father.

She looked out of the window at the rice fields ready for harvest. The dirty pane reflected Shakeel; he'd turned towards her. She often chanced upon him observing her. Partly, it was his job. *But what was he actually thinking?* What did he make of his sister-in-law becoming, in effect, his boss? She sometimes felt bad about that fact. Overriding her spasms of guilt, though, she felt gratitude, for his unruffled manner, his protective instincts and the respect with which he treated her.

He really should be next in line as the party's candidate for Parliament. Her own brothers had been so very young and Shakeel would've had his turn before them, if all had gone according to plan and if life was fair. But Aseem's energies were focused on tutoring her and making her the party's priority candidate at the next general election. Shakeel had been harnessed into giving his all for her sake. Their local MLAs did have strong set-ups in three or four constituencies, among them Patharghat. One day the party would be able to field more candidates. There would be openings in the future. *When I have achieved something myself and am more influential, when I am deputy leader or leader, I promise you, Shakeel, I will give you all the opportunities you deserve.*

For now there was a lot of spade work to do in Dhoonpur. The constituency comprised one town and 683 villages. Because it lay within the broader District of Nulkazim, over the years it had partially been brought under the umbrella of Aseem's informal largesse. It was up to her, Waheeda Rela, to woo the population in the villages currently controlled by other parties. She carried Aseem's ambitions on her shoulders: at the next election, his puny party *would* register on a national level. Small though the party was, smaller than a speck of pollen in the large bloom of Indian political parties, she knew how dedicated its workers were and how motivated by the belief they had a chance. They'd been so close to a win.

Shakeel worked tirelessly and uncomplainingly, but it wasn't the same story with his wife, Parveen. She'd grown colder and colder towards Waheeda, while Shakeel had never been cross with her, or even with Nafis, as far as she knew. He'd accepted without comment, without embarrassing her with incredulous brows, or icy pinched looks, the version of her marriage that explained how Nafis *needed* to paint in the mountains far away while Waheeda was required to lend her support to her father's cause.

Shakeel was instrumental in perpetuating this myth because people asked him the questions they didn't directly ask her.

She'd once overheard him explain that Nafis inhabited a terrain too rarefied for politics but that he fully supported his wife's ambitions and had especially asked Shakeel to look after her. At that moment she'd felt terrible, tears pricking her eyes. Later she'd tried to express how grateful she was, but Shakeel brushed her away with, 'Never thank me. Please, none of this English idea of thank-you's. You're my sister-in-law, you're *family*. I will always do what I can for you.'

On the road he remained inscrutable. She didn't know what he was really thinking, but she did sometimes wish that she didn't have to be so dishonest with him. She couldn't confide in him about the true circumstances of her relationship with Nafis without betraying her husband: first, his despondency and lack of adjustment in Delhi and then, after Hira's birth, his fickleness and lack of responsibility. Perhaps Shakeel knew his older brother's nature better than she did; he sometimes hinted that he wasn't surprised at the outcome of their marriage. She couldn't confide in him about Monish either. That would be the most foolish betrayal of herself and all of them in the family, near and distant.

She turned her neck for a stretch in the other direction. Shakeel looked away, out of his window, into the blazing sun. It was too strong and he turned inwards, riffling through the papers in the concertina folder on the seat by him. All the administrative work for the day's agenda. Waheeda quickly peeled the orange within her bag, and popped the segments into her mouth.

•

THEIR COACH PULLED up at a busy level crossing. The barriers were down. Beside them stood a horse-drawn cart, overloaded with bales of cloth. The horse had pitch-black blinkers on. Waheeda felt the horse snorting, although she couldn't hear it inside the minibus. She stared at its flaring nostrils, its flicking tail, its aura of fatigue, and the whip in the hand of the *tonga-wala*. Blinkered horses always seemed terrified, flinching at the clamour around them. For a moment she felt empathy with this horse and had to resist the urge to bring up her hands to the sides of her eyes in imitation of the poor creature. If the barriers stayed shut awhile, the horse would get some respite.

Did the horse really need its blinkers? Would it be alarmed at the belching vehicles around it, would it be distracted and not listen to its master? Wasn't it cruel to be blinkered?

It was the sort of idle question she could discuss with Monish. They often had silly conversations, but somehow she believed that they had honest conversations. She actually voiced her opinions to him, on a multitude of topics, which was so rare for her now. He, in turn, seemed to speak the truth about what was in his mind. She'd begun to understand him, his needs and moods. If she mentioned this horse to Monish he'd offer to procure a pair of horse blinkers so that the two of them could properly experience limited vision. Or he would mock her: 'You've read *Black Beauty* too many times, that's your problem.'

She smiled at that, and then remembered to turn into the streaky window to hide her expression. Their relationship, just four months old, was not ridiculously smooth. But they had fallen into a pattern, whether she admitted it or not. It was not a one-off each time as she pretended. She rubbed her cheekbone. Stop that core lie to yourself, Waheeda Rela. The first time, the second, and the third, it had been easy to behave as though she was snatching at a moment that wouldn't happen again. Therefore, the joy that overwhelmed her after, would not be repeated. She could let herself be a bit rash, a bit dazed. She could look at a bird gliding in a stream of wind at dusk and feel her heart soar with it. Monish had brought that sort of happiness into her reach.

She dug out her appointments diary and casually flicked

through it. When next? When could she see him again? *Neutralise your face, not too much soaring could be allowed*. It didn't fit in with the scheme of things. Because it would have to be wouldn't it that just as she emerged from her introverted state to create a public face, that's when she would meet a man she could be with. Contradictory directions. That's what life was like. Offering her a public vocation and a bond that could only be hidden. Hello life, when will you become less complicated?

She turned the pages to the last week of September. She had an appointment in Delhi with Chetna Mura who needed mollifying after her cold war with Faisal had erupted into a concrete spat. They might as well have built a wall between the two factions. But the Delhi office needed to be unified. Aseem and she were working out a separation of duties that she would put to Chetna when she took her out to dinner to schmooze her. On that afternoon, though, before dinner, there was a window of precious time. If Naaz could be persuaded to have a pretend outing with her. If Monish could take a half-day off work. She'd check.

I was known to be eminently sensible. I can't work out why I'm going against the grain now, but I don't care. Her practical voice spoke up: Once before you followed your heart to the displeasure of your adoptive father; and look how your marriage turned out. Waheeda shut the diary and put it away.

She did not regret marrying Nafis. He had given her Hira, who was the sparkling centrepoint of her existence. Waheeda didn't hate Nafis, as he claimed, despite their ructions, even if he appeared to positively dislike her now. She still felt that she couldn't have married anyone else. Not only had there been no one else in the picture, there hadn't been anyone who had stirred her so.

Until four months ago. The current truth was that Monish only had to insist that it was time to meet, and she would find a way to see him, deceit and all. Those hasty phone calls, when she was alone and certain no one could overhear, working out logistics. Oh, the convoluted logistics. He did come up with schemes, she had to hand it to him. One time he picked her up from South-Ex market, where she'd ostensibly gone shopping with Naaz. Another time, because it was early evening on a week day, she'd made her own way to his flat, arriving at the allotted hour. He had a plan in place if he was running late. He left his spare door-key under the floral mat at Kriti's front door. His friend, the gorgeous one, lived on the floor below. Even though Waheeda felt a pang every time he mentioned Kriti, she'd decided it was better that she always pretended to be visiting her flat. When she entered Monish's building, she would declare to the security man in the lobby: 'Kriti Khanna, third floor,' sweeping by imperiously, as Monish had instructed. The guard never attempted to stop or question her. What use was he if he was cowed by any superior-sounding woman? But he would never risk his job by offending someone whom he deemed a genuine visitor to the apartments. That's just how it was. In any case, the security was more for show, as Monish said. There was the back entrance to the building that the servants used, and although there was another guard stationed there, Monish sometimes used it when he took the stairs from the carpark and he'd never been quizzed. 'The guard probably knows who I am,' he'd said, 'But it's still laughable that we *pay* for this lax security.' He assured her that Kriti had no clue that he was occasionally leaving a single key under her mat. Waheeda had made him promise not to mention her visits, even in passing, to any of his friends, however much he trusted them.

•

THE BARRIERS AT the level crossing creaked up, and their minibus overtook the tonga and the tired horse, swerving too close to it. She closed her eyes. She felt someone slip into the

space next to her on the seat. She opened her eyes, pulling
her bag onto her lap so that there was more space for Nita,
one of the three ladies in her travelling group today. Nita was
forty-ish, she was married to a Muslim man, they'd been college sweethearts, and eventually they'd married, some years
later, after she'd refused every other proposal brought to her
by her family. She was a brisk outspoken woman who wore
block-printed cotton saris, because block-printing was Nita's
father's business. Whenever she received a compliment on
her perfectly starched and flawlessly tied sari, she would tell
you exactly where you could go to buy the same design if
you wished. Waheeda had heard that Nita's husband was not
entirely pleased that his wife was part of Waheeda's entourage, but he'd been a recipient of Aseem's influence in the
past, and his wife had agreed with alacrity when Umair had
asked if she would join Waheeda's team.

'Do you mind if we have some music on the bus?' Nita asked.

'Go ahead,' Waheeda replied, watching as Nita spoke to the
driver and returned to her seat at the back. Barely a minute
after the driver had turned on the radio, a new song blared
out, a risqué song full of double-entendres, causing Waheeda
to cringe. Shakeel was up out of his seat and he chose a cassette tape in consultation with the driver. It was a '*bhoole bisre
geet*' compilation. "A catalogue of forgotten songs." In actual
fact, songs from old movies that they all knew. Much more
appropriate. She nodded her approbation as '*chanda o chanda*'
played through the speakers. Possibly a bit boring for the
others but far less chance of embarrassing lyrics being aired.

The three women at the back began to sing along and then
some of the younger men did, too, and she was happy for
them. They needed to enjoy these long drives if they were
to volunteer more regularly. She wouldn't disconcert them
by turning around to look. Scrutinise the fields beyond the
road instead, rice crops in some, resting earth in others, and

reflected in the pane, Shakeel observing her. Aseem's dream of the next generation *could* have been transferred on to him, but Aseem had recruited her, his daughter, bloodline or not. But *if* one day she was an MP, and *if* one day Shakeel was, too, then there would be two Relas in Parliament. Waheeda grinned at the flying grit outside. This is how dynasties start, how they become entrenched, how they cease to think of other possibilities.

Hira was the only Rela of her generation for the moment. As far as Waheeda was concerned, Shakeel's children, when he had them, could try their hand at creating a political dynasty. She did not want her daughter to grow up to be a politician, or an artist or even an academic. There were other careers in the world, other than those of her parents or grandparents. There were other jobs that were fulfilling and well-paid, and she hoped Hira would find one of those. She hoped Hira would not be buffeted about by circumstances the way she had been. When she thought about Hira, her hand lifted to her heart, and the only desire she felt was to shield her from hurt: physical and mental, to protect her from sadness and untoward happenings.

This was an unreasonable desire but no parent could help it. Her own Ammi, when she was widowed, must have wanted to buffer Waheeda from harshness and sudden losses, especially that of a husband. But she'd had to endure the breakup of Waheeda's marriage. Maybe this was why, when Nafis visited Nulkazim, Ammi continued to spoil him rotten. Maybe she coiled herself around the hope that they would all come together as one happy family under her roof. Maybe she spoiled Nafis, and also Shakeel, because they were the only son-substitutes she had left. Waheeda's eyes misted. She wiped the backs of her fingers delicately over her eyes. No one must notice she was crying. She mustn't show weakness. She peeked across at Shakeel and he glanced away.

145

TWELVE

Delhi

IN THE CUL-DE-SAC a group of girls, all holding lit cigarettes, a couple of motorbikes parked by them, with four young men forming a protective half-ring around the girls. Their voices floated up to Monish on his balcony. He'd stepped out to talk to the moon but she was obscured. He looked down indulgently at the women, understanding their reluctance to enter their hostel and be locked up until dawn. It was a few minutes to their curfew time of eight p.m. Another three minutes and the girls would head to the main road to check in at the gates of the working women's hostel. The motorbike boys would wend their way back to their mummies.

He himself felt too restless to relax in his own home. The muggy-sky evening didn't help, the air heavy with diesel fumes even up on the fourth-floor. His head was still whirling in anger from the confrontation with his father just as he left the office. Usual stuff, but Monish wasn't dealing with it very well. He should take his mind off his own dilemmas. Go visit other people's problems. Better yet, be entertained by a friend who didn't expect much of him; who'd be ecstatic that Monish had showed up. On this whim, and because he was missing Waheeda, but he couldn't talk to her this evening, or about her to anyone, he set off to see Gaurav. He would be able to talk about Falguni, the person Waheeda and he knew in common. She worked at the same advertising agency where Gaurav was a media buyer. Gaurav had got married a few months before and Monish had not seen him since.

146

On arriving at his friend's house, or rather the house that belonged to Gaurav's parents, he was ushered to the first floor by a youth he was unfamiliar with, a new member of their domestic staff. Monish remembered that in the months leading up to the wedding there'd been huge renovations. Gaurav's old room had been expanded into a suite. The newly-wed couple would have their own space: a small sitting area, a bedroom, and a mirrored bathroom as requested by the bride-to-be.

'I know my way,' he said to the youth, who tailed him nonetheless. Good training. He knocked, then pushed at the partly-closed door. Oh, Oh. He'd disturbed them. Gaurav and his wife were on a couch that faced the outsized new television, sitting close, watching a film.

Gaurav jumped up like an over-excitable puppy when he caught sight of Monish. He clicked a button on the remote control. 'Monny!' Rushing to the door and shaking his hand with fervour. 'I haven't seen you since the wedding, man! Where've you been hiding? Have you been abroad?'

'No, I've been here. But you two have probably been coochy-cooing at home and that's why I haven't seen you around.'

'We go out a lot and it's *you* who's always missing from the get-togethers. Take a seat. It's great you've dropped in. I haven't seen you for yonks.'

Monish nodded at Gaurav's wife. 'Hello Diljit.'

He looked at the screen where a scene from a recent Hindi film was held on pause. 'I'm sorry, I'm interrupting your movie night. I won't stay long.'

'Don't be ridiculous,' Gaurav pushed on his shoulders, forcing him to sit down. 'Every second night is frickin' movie night here.'

Diljit vacated the couch, a black look on her face. To Monish she was polite. 'Hello, Monny. It's true we haven't seen you at all since our wedding reception.'

He winced. He didn't know how to tell her that she couldn't call him Monny. Only very old friends did that. To be fair, she was just picking up on how her husband addressed him. He wouldn't say anything now because already there was tension in the room; he sensed an unresolvable husband-wife argument hanging in the air.

Gaurav turned to his drinks cabinet and pulled down a ledge. He set out two glasses and held out a bottle with a flourish. 'I'm going to open this Blue Label in your honour.' Monish began a protest about how he wouldn't stay long but Gaurav overrode him. 'We need some ice, Dilly,' he said. 'Bring us some ice.' He handed her a silver ice bucket. 'Recognise it?' he asked. Monish nodded. It had been his wedding gift.

'It's very nice, Monny.' Again Diljit managed to sound civil to him while glowering at her husband.

'Ice, Dilly,' Gaurav said. 'And some chilli cashews. *Dost aaya hai.*'

My friend is here. Monish felt that Diljit was about to throw her embroidered slipper at Gaurav's head but she grasped the ice bucket and left them. Monish looked at the screen. 'You two should get back to your movie.'

He'd met Diljit a few times when she was engaged to Gaurav. Their marriage had been arranged by their families but once they'd chosen each other and the engagement formalities were over they'd been permitted to go out as a couple. They'd seemed very much in love. Monish remembered that at one of his parties they'd spent the entire evening huddled by the sideboard, their hands roving over each other in the dim light. No one had nudged at each other to 'look-see.' In a couple of months they'd be married, everyone knew, and it wasn't especially noteworthy to witness their passion. It wasn't illicit. Diljit hadn't called him 'Monny' then. She was a bit shy, slightly in awe of him, or not him exactly, but his last name.

Gaurav settled beside him on the sofa. 'I can't stand these movies.' His droopy moustache drooped further and his long sideburns flared wider than before.

'Oh, you watch them for her? How sweet.'

'What to do? I don't get sex unless I watch one of these films with her. We have to see the whole damn thing to the end. We *know* what the end will be. Still, I must sit here like a moron. And some nights, even after that sacrifice there's no sex. I mean, women! Too tired; headache; movie finished too late.'

Monish looked around him. There was a new sculpture of a standing Buddha placed in the corner. 'Why are you telling me this?' he asked Gaurav mischievously. 'You want me to have a word with your wife? Tell her to give you more pity-fucks?'

'Oh shut up, you bastard,' Gaurav growled. He fiddled with the remote. 'Let's watch the cricket highlights.'

Diljit returned with ice and a bowl of nuts. She dragged a round pouf-stool towards the coffee table and perched on it. She turned down the volume of the soaring cricket commentary to almost-mute. 'Why haven't we seen you?' she asked Monish. 'Have you been hiding out with some secret girlfriend?'

Right on the money. How?

'No. But you might have hit on the problem. I haven't felt like going out. I find I like solitude. But maybe all I need is a new girlfriend. Could you introduce me to some of your attractive friends?'

She sized him up with a cool look. 'My friends want to get married. They don't want the kind of relationship you're looking for. Even if they fall for you at first, they won't thank me later for introducing them to you. I won't do it.'

Gaurav snorted. 'Dilly, how about that friend of yours who was here yesterday? The one who has made up her mind that she *must* go to Tahiti for a long holiday. She dreamt she lived there in her previous life. Wasn't she saying she wanted to find a rich guy to take her to Tahiti? Well. Looky who's here-'

'There's no need,' Monish interjected hastily. 'Not now that I know all she wants from me is a ticket to Polynesia. It won't work.'

'She's hot, man,' Gaurav said.

Diljit pursed her lips.

Monish wondered if Gaurav was being deliberately obnoxious. He shook his head. 'Thanks, but no thanks.' He turned to Diljit. 'I totally get what you're saying. I agree. I wouldn't want to put you in an embarrassing situation. Forget I asked.' He'd been joking anyway, but he didn't want to make a point of it. 'In fact, Diljit, I doubt any of your friends are as pretty as you.'

Her expression softened. He smiled, thinking it was quite true that she was good-looking; she had the features that were commonly sought after in north-Indian brides, but that he himself didn't find particularly appealing. She had golden skin, a high forehead, a long fine jaw, a longish straight nose, and almond eyes. She had the face of a noblewoman in a Mughal-era painting, but not the curvaceous body. She was slim to the point of boniness. The sleeveless knee-length dress she was wearing revealed her thin golden legs and tanned spaghetti arms.

Gaurav busied himself pouring their drinks, adding water in his own glass from a jug on the cabinet, and tinkling in extra ice for Monish. 'What about you, Dilly? Shall I fix you a drink?'

She pouted. 'Mom and Daddy-ji are expecting us to join them for dinner downstairs. Pour me a drink later.'

Monish rose and began to make his excuses. Gaurav's heavy hands on his shoulders pushed him down. He spoke over Monish's protestations. 'My old friend has come to see me for the first time in months. We're going to have a

Tandoori chicken takeaway. With our drinks.' He gestured expansively. 'Dilly, can you place the order. For delivery now. *Kalmi* kebabs also.'

Diljit fetched the phone, thumping it into her husband's hand. 'You do it.'

'Number?' Gaurav looked around for help.

Diljit flung down a brown leather address book. He began to dial and as he did he issued more instructions to his wife. 'Send us the dal from downstairs,' he said. 'And raita also. Oh, and chappatis. Tell Mom and Daddy-ji that Monny is here with me. They'll understand.'

'Ah, but will *she*?' Monish murmured, as she huffed off.

When Gaurav had placed the takeaway order, he sank onto the couch slurping greedily at his drink. 'You know, Dilly gets in a mood when my really old best buds visit. Man, I don't know why.'

'Do you always treat her like this when 'old best buds' come round?'

'Yup.'

'Well, that's why.'

'Cool it, Monny. Don't *maro* a lecture. You know nothing.' He sank his lips into his glass and gulped. 'It's all very well being agreeable all the time to girlfriends. That's a different story. Anyone can do that, be nice to someone they're not going to marry. Put up with their fits and fancies. When you get married, you feel the responsibility. You're in charge of looking after this person *for life*. It's not about being *nice* any-more. You're on parade, every day and night. Being a man, a provider, a fixer, a son-in-law, a distributor of favours, a son taking his mom's side, a good lover, a good husband....And wives nag. I mean, from Day One. Suddenly, it's like don't drink so much, don't swear, change your aftershave, why are you still speaking to your ex-girlfriend....I tell you, Monny, *you* won't last six months.'

I know, Monish thought, that's why I'm not getting married. Despite the friction with Dad. I'll ruin some poor girl's life. And she'll ruin mine. The streak of sadness that ran through him like a mineral deposit would intensify. He stayed silent. He couldn't leave now; he'd have to let the evening play out. Gaurav was feeling pressured, that was clear, but Monish couldn't tell if it was just from adjusting to marriage or something more. Gaurav was a man with a strong conscience although he hid it under his bluff exterior.

Monish sipped from his glass, rolling the whisky in his mouth to savour it. 'How are things at work?' he asked casually.

'All good. All's the same in my department.'

'Does Falguni Lava still work at Vault?'

'Fal? Yes, of course. Soma will be mad to let Miss Lava go.'

Gaurav had told him in the past that Falguni was a disruptive force. That when she did show up in the office she irked her colleagues. More often than not she didn't bother going in. Every once in a while she brought in new business through her contacts and Soma was pleased. Vault also had the advertising contract for Jessie's Corn Puffs, the product, that in all its flavours, had made Falguni's father very wealthy. He had diversified into many different food products and Vault handled most things for the Jessie's brand. Soma couldn't sack Falguni without risking the loss of that lucrative account.

'In fact, she's been given yet another title,' Gaurav said. 'Did you hear?'

'Fal? No.'

'Yes, madam is now associate director. I thought you would've heard from that guy who lives in the flat opposite you.'

'Choppy Sodhi?'

'Ya. Because she's still following her old modus operandi. This time Choppy got the chop. Ha. Ha. Poor guy, it's a big loss for him. Didn't he mention it?'

'No. I play squash with him. The bastard always thrashes me even though he's five years older. But we don't talk business. It's not Choppy's style. What happened with Fal and where does he figure in this?'

'Oh, she went into DB's office. Sat there and chatted for a while. After tea and all sorts, he finally said, "Fal, what do you want?" She said, "your advertising account for Vault." He said "Choppy has always had our biz and we're very happy with him. We've no need to change." But it turned out she wasn't going to budge till she got something. And he couldn't fend her off. So end result was he hived off a sliver of work to Vault. Just the pedestal fans, I think. But Choppy's agency is small. It really hurt him. Meanwhile Madam Fal is floating around being a director.'

There was a knock on the door and Gaurav went to hold it open. The youth who'd brought Monish upstairs entered with a large tray. The aroma of tandoori chicken and raw onions filled the room. Monish felt bad that Diljit would have the smell in her bedroom all night. The door to the bedroom was behind the couch and he decided to close it, peeping in as he did so. Just a large bed. Wardrobes on one wall. No space for anything else. A print of Guru Gobind Singh above the bed. Gaurav's parents insisted on a picture of a Sikh guru adorning each room of the house. *Over the bed?* Monish would not be able to tolerate a guru checking him out like that. But maybe Gaurav was avoiding a clash with the Buddha statue that now dominated the couple's private lounge space.

White takeaway boxes were neatly arranged on the tray that the youth set down.

'What about the dal and chappatis?' Gaurav asked.

'I'm just bringing it,' replied the young man. He nipped downstairs to reappear shortly with another tray loaded with dishes and plates.

'Paper napkins,' Gaurav barked.

'Coming, sir.'

Gaurav helped himself. Monish wondered about Falguni and Waheeda. Close friends when they were sixteen. That's what Waheeda had said. He couldn't imagine it. What had they been like? Had Waheeda been as fond of revelries as her friend? He didn't think so. He'd seen Fal high on all kinds of substances and he couldn't visualise Waheeda like that. She had never even been tempted to try alcohol, she told him. He peered into space through his glasses, trying to imagine a teenage Waheeda at a dance party. He knew she'd been to those, they'd laughed fondly about the music that inevitably came on at each one. *Saturday Night Fever*.

Gaurav waved a hand in front of his face. 'My, my,' he said. 'Lost in dreams. Please don't tell me you were fantasising about Miss Lava.'

He handed him a plate, giggling. The whisky had certainly relaxed him. 'Don't go there, Monny.' He wagged a finger. 'Oh no. You're no match for that volcano. She will swallow you and spit you out. She'll turn you to toast.' He thumped his fist on his knee and laughed uproariously. 'Your famous charm will be charred. Ha-ha.'

Monish picked up a chicken leg and tore a piece off with his mouth.

THIRTEEN

November 1997

I'M GOING TO faint. Waheeda struggled to stay upright on the stage and continue with her speech. She'd experienced the same sensation at last week's rally. The virus that she'd caught wasn't finished with her yet. She hadn't cancelled today's assembly because a junior journalist from a respected news magazine was following her on her public outings for a week. She began to regret her decision to keep going with her schedule. There wasn't even a mike-stand or a lectern to clutch on to. There was supposed to have been a microphone set up, as usual, but it wasn't working and there wasn't time to wait while attempts were made to fix the sound system. She'd been handed a loudhailer.

She began her greeting: 'Sisters and brothers, you've been waiting here for an hour; I thank you for your patience and for being here…' But then she was interrupted by the head-man of the village, who was among the dignitaries seated on the stage. He said the poor quality of the loudhailer was distorting her voice too much and advised her: 'Speak as loudly as you can, they'll hear it at the front and later they'll repeat it to the people who can't hear.' He motioned for her to move to the centre of the stage and position herself at the very edge.

She steadied herself, her gaze on the large crowd. The local organisers had done themselves proud (other than the glitch with the mike); they must have bussed in people from several surrounding villages. After apologising that she could only project her voice so far she began again. Her own hands distracted her, she was unused to having them empty. She tried clasping them in front of her. It felt odd, probably looked odd, but she pressed her palms together to give her some forcefulness to keep going. She'd shorten her speech. She wouldn't be able to keep this up for long, not with how weak she was feeling.

Although it was a beautiful temperate day she was obliged to squint into the slanting sunlight of late afternoon. The stage was canopied so that the VIPs behind her, sitting in a row, were shaded. No shade for her, now that she'd been pushed to the front. She adjusted the *dupatta* on her head, a pause to draw breath before resuming her speech. She felt sick. Nauseous. She paused again to swallow that feeling, to control it, ignore it. Keep talking. Emote.

A mass of faces, all male; a mix of bare heads, white rural-style turbans, and white *topis* surged forward. The few women in the audience hung back in small groups at the periphery, keeping their distance from the throng. Today they would hear nothing of what she said, but they would watch her intently, her figure small from far away, and later they would decipher her from her attire and her gestures and what was repeated to them of her words. She noticed a boy held above the horde on his father's shoulders. He looked younger than Hira, he must be only six or seven; she could see the alarm on his face as the crowd closed in tighter. She wanted to stop speaking and to point to the father: Move away. There's no need to hear me. Take your son out of the throng. But the father was listening in rapt attention. She moved her focus back to what she was saying.

'When the time comes, vote local. Vote for those you know. Not for those who flit here when they need you. I understand *your* needs. I will work for the entire community and a vote for me is a true reflection of our strong community. A reflection of the intelligence and maturity of the people of Dhoonpur. We have worked and lived in peace for gen-erations, nay centuries. Let us not forget that. Let us not be persuaded by petty agendas. Together, we will better the lot of each person here. *Each person here*, every one of you listening to me today....I wouldn't be here speaking to you, I wouldn't have left my job as a university lecturer in a big city, unless I truly believed that this sacrifice would lead to something bigger than me; that it would lead to deserved progress for our region and for our communities...I'd like to stress by that I mean every single person—woman, man, and child in the Dhoonpur community...' and the boy had begun to sway on his father's shoulders. His eyes closed as he toppled forward. Waheeda had the sensation that she was toppling backwards. She leant forward to counter that, halting her speech. She pointed at the child who had mercifully been caught and was being cradled on his father's chest. A multitude was pressed around them and Waheeda shook her head in impatience, gesturing for people to move aside. But no one in the crush behind the father understood what she wanted and they were craning forward instead.

'What is it?' Shakeel was right at the front under the stage, speaking to her in English.

'That boy needs air. He must get some air.' She pointed again. Shakeel cut a swathe to where she indicated and cre-ated a space around the father and his boy.

Waheeda returned to her speech, switching back into Hindi: 'Today you will not hear false promises from me. I won't repeat what you hear regularly from your current MP. But my hope is, on another day in the future, I will stand here having already brought to fruition my plans: for an extension to the school, for social cohesion, for a medical clinic in each village, a good supply of drinking water to every part of every village in the constituency and proper roads in the main areas instead of mud tracks.'

•

WAHEEDA RELA *ZINDABAD. Zindabad. Zindabad.* The party workers began the chant, the crowd picked it up for about six repetitions, and the youth team kept it going until she'd walked to the clearing where the campaign bus was parked. She leant her hand on the dusty bus for support. 'I'm feeling faint,' she muttered to Shakeel. 'I need to get home as soon as possible. I'm afraid I'm going to—'

A tape-recorder was shoved in front of her face. It was the young journalist. Waheeda shook her head tiredly. She hadn't even heard the question. She couldn't do an interview at that moment. Interviews were excruciating even when she was well. Her unguarded opinions were pounced on. She'd learnt that this was another arena where she couldn't speak the truth. It took energy to circle around the same bland answers endlessly.

'Waheeda has flu,' Shakeel had stepped in front of her. 'Should I fix an appointment for you another day?'

The woman addressed her. 'I was hoping to record an interview today.'

Waheeda put her hand to her throat and looked into the journalist's face hoping she would understand she meant: a) she'd lost her voice and b) she would puke if she had to speak.

'Could we meet in Delhi then?' the journalist asked. 'When you're next there?'

Waheeda nodded. Shakeel drew out the little notepad he kept in his kurta's side pocket, reconfirmed the woman's contact details and promised to set up something soon.

Waheeda leant her head on the bus, uncaring that her hair would be streaked with dust.

'Oh no!' Shakeel looked up from his notepad. 'You look bad.' He spoke louder to the group around them. 'We need to requisition a car. We should get Waheeda-ji to her home as quickly as possible.'

The NPF local organiser stepped up and whispered to Shakeel.

'Wonderful,' Shakeel said, 'Thank you.' He took Waheeda's arm. 'We're taking his car.' He led her towards the other end of the clearing, where a few cars were parked. The man whispered something else. 'Unless you want to rest at his home. The ladies will look after you. He thinks you might prefer that. Stay the night in the *zenana* and return to Nulkazim tomorrow. His wife and daughter are very keen to meet you anyway.'

Oh no, she thought. 'No,' she said aloud, making an effort to speak normally. 'I'm very grateful, but I want to get home if possible. My daughter…'

Shakeel settled her in the back seat of the car. 'I'll return later tonight with your car,' he said to the man. 'I cannot thank you enough.'

'It is our pleasure. My son is in Nulkazim; he can collect it from you tomorrow. There's no need for you to drive back tonight. I'll call my son and let him know. It's no problem at all. I hope Waheeda-ji feels better soon.'

As Shakeel got into the driver's seat, she saw him glance towards the campaign bus. She caught his fleeting expression of anxiety. She tapped his shoulder.

'Shakeel, could Nita come with us? Would you ask her?'

Relief crossed his face. She turned to look as he walked back to the bus. No one in her travelling group had got in yet. They were all standing around observing the two of them in the car—Shakeel and her. Shakeel returned to the car with his concertina folder and a small holdall which he placed on the front passenger seat. Nita followed and sat beside her. Waheeda let her head fall back on the seat. She closed her eyes as they drove off. She'd guessed correctly. Shakeel's concern had been for himself; for tittle-tattle about him and her. Parveen would be mad if she heard anything. Maybe she was already mad at him for no reason. The amazing rumour mill, it ground out whatever. If you were in a party that was opposed to hers, why then Waheeda Rela was a slut, a runaway, a woman who couldn't keep her husband happy, a pretender to the throne, a useless novice, bad blood. If you were in NPF, you dismissed these ideas as rubbish, but secretly you wondered who she was romantically involved with. There had to be someone to link her with. Otherwise gossip wasn't much fun, was it? The husband was far away. She'd put that flirtatious young speechwriter dude in his place. He was out of the picture. But the brother-in-law was always by her side. And if they drove off together into the soft dusk, just the two of them, without a chaperone, well then…

•

SHE FELL INTO a fevered sleep.

She awoke sobbing. A truck had crashed into them. She'd breen thrown onto the road. Hira was in this car, too, a bottle-green car (she'd never seen a car that colour in real life). Hira was thrown from the car and, miraculously, she'd landed on Waheeda and was saved injury. Thank heaven. But Waheeda was bleeding and sobbing.

Nita pressed her hands to Waheeda's cheeks.

'I'm OK; I'm fine.' Waheeda was embarrassed. 'A dream. It was just—a nightmare—'

Shakeel pulled over to the side of the road. 'Do you need anything?'

'I must call Hira. I want to talk to her. To know she's fine.' She pulled out her phone with shaking hands but there was no signal.

Shakeel gave his phone to Nita. 'Keep trying,' he said. 'We'll get reasonable signal strength at some point. Waheeda, you rest. Please.' Grim-faced, he drove on.

Nita dampened a hanky with water from a plastic bottle and pressed it onto Waheeda's perspiring forehead.

'Don't fuss,' Waheeda said weakly. 'Just try my home. I want to speak to my daughter.'

Later, she slept better. They'd got hold of Hira, who was safe at home, and was keen to tell her mother that she was diligently doing her maths homework. She'd taken out two new books from the school library: one to read herself and one for her Mama to read to her.

FOURTEEN

Delhi

NAAZ'S BOY BROUGHT joy and pain to Waheeda in equal measure. When she held his tiny newbornness and gazed into his little wizened face, she wanted to wrap her spirit protectively around him the way she'd done with Hira. The baby had a mass of dark curls. Waheeda stroked his hair gently, with just two fingers, giving his head a light relaxing massage. It would be incredible to have another child. That was a loose thought; it wasn't on the cards for her.

She envied Naaz and Deepak their joint elation. She was glad to be of some help to Naaz, offering tips from her own experience. This baby was not a wailer like Hira had been. He was altogether more easy-going. Although his arrival did change a few things in Naaz's household.

'I can't drive you around anymore,' Naaz said as Waheeda nodded understandingly. 'I have a plan.' Naaz's eyes glimmered.

What was she cooking up?

Naaz held out a key.

'What's this?'

'The guest suite on the ground floor has its own door to the garden. You must've seen. This is the key to that door. If you get Habib to drop you here for dinner and say you're staying overnight to help me with the baby, then you'll be free. Habib can pick you up the next morning for wherever you need to go.'

'I see. Does that mean—'

'Yes. Monish can be your secret chauffeur instead of me.

You can come and go from the guest suite. No one should notice in the dark.'

•

'KABIR, THEY'VE NAMED the baby Kabir,' she said to Aseem on the phone. The flat in Sangeet Vihar was quiet, just her occupying it, and the tinges of dusk entering the rooms. No Bhavna fussing round the place. 'Yes, it's a beautiful name. Yes, I know what to say to Chetna tomorrow. I will smooth it out…' Another rumpus with Faisal. But Waheeda would butter her up tomorrow. 'I'll be staying overnight at Naaz's place,' she informed Aseem. 'She likes to have me there. Deepak? He's back to his normal travel schedule. Yes, of course, Habib will drive me everywhere. But there's nowhere for him to stay at Naaz's home. The car gets so smelly if he sleeps in it overnight! He can drop me off in the evenings and return to Naaz's in the morning. Chetna has changed the time? She called to tell you but not *me*? Right! Fine, I'll go early.'

She checked her watch after the call. six-thirty p.m. She'd told Habib they'd leave for Naaz's at eight. Monish was meant to pick her up at nine. But if the next morning she was to leave Naaz's home earlier than she'd envisaged, then she wanted to spend more time this evening with her. She decided to go up to the quarters at the back of the flats to tell Habib they'd go over to Naaz's soon, as soon as he was ready.

'Ha-bib,' she called up from the bottom of the spiral concrete stairs. There was no answer. She climbed up to knock on the door. A long silence ensued. Then Habib's voice, in an angry grunt: '*Kaun*?'

'It's me.'

Some scuffling, and the door opened, Habib looking uncharacteristically crestfallen, blocking her view into the room. 'Ji?' he mumbled. 'You need me?'

'I just came to tell you that I want to leave earlier.' She peered past him to take in what she could. 'In fifteen minutes.'

'Ji, *didi*.' He shut the door. She'd glimpsed playing cards laid face-up on the floor. Like a game of *teen patti*. A visitor with Habib, a man, thick-necked, bearded. Sly eyes. She faltered outside the door wondering whether to say something. To ask who that unfamiliar man was? Were they gambling? She turned away. Habib was entitled to a private social life.

•

'You look tired,' she said to Monish as he drove and she sat in the backseat, head ducked down. 'Are you working on an important deal? Is that why you stayed so late at work?'

'I haven't come straight from work but…I'll tell you when we get to my place. I can't talk to you at this angle.' She remained silent at his short temper.

In his flat she ran her fingers from the corner of his eye down his cheek and neck. His cheek was bristly. 'What happened?'

'Oh, the bane of my life, what else? I meant to come home and shower before I picked you up. But he called just as I got home. We ended up having an argument. Then I came to get you.'

Usually when she saw Monish, he was freshly showered, his hair damp and his body smelling of the neem soap he used. This evening he was in his work clothes—dark trousers and a light-blue shirt. A slim black belt on his slim waist. Socks and shoes. She had gotten used to seeing him in jeans and a tee. Barefoot.

But if he was going to become her chauffeur she would see him in all sorts of guises.

'Your father called?' she asked. 'About something important? Or just to chat?'

'He was calling from Geneva airport. He's about to board a flight home. The Prat was supposed to pick him up at the airport but the poor little sod is in bed with a cold. So Dad thinks *I* should pick him up tomorrow morning at six-thirty. Notwithstanding the man's got two drivers.'

'Will you be picking him up?'

'Yes.' Monish sounded like he was being invisibly strangled. 'He likes me to jump to it. He doesn't care if I have other plans. Not that I'm doing anything at six tomorrow morning, other than hoping to sleep before work, but I mean generally. *He* comes first. He likes to make sure of that.'

'You could always say No. If you don't want to be treated like this. You could say no to everything.'

'Of course,' Monish said mockingly. 'Especially today. I could tell him to piss off. He's returning with details of numbered accounts in Switzerland and I should infuriate him. I'm glad I don't take your advice all the time.' He took off his glasses and rubbed his eyes. 'Sometimes, Wija, you make sense. But not today. No. I must go and be a compliant son to ensure I'm not cut out. He often threatens to part-disown me, you know, says he'll give the numbers of a new Swiss account just to Pratish. He knows that gives me the wobbles.'

'You don't have to live under his yoke,' she persisted. 'You could go out and get a job.'

'What's got into you?' He sipped his drink. Then he said, gently, as though talking to a child, 'No job is going to fund my lifestyle.'

'But if you didn't want to be beholden—'

'It comes with the territory. We're talking about money. Maybe you didn't understand—'

'I did, and I don't want to hear about it. It is *wrong*. You don't *have* to be involved—'

'I didn't realise you felt so strongly,' he said. 'But surely you know that rich people remain rich because they look after their wealth. They pay a lot of attention to keeping their earnings.'

'Don't be patronising, Monish. Undeclared bank accounts in Switzerland, or anywhere else for that matter, are illegal.'

How baffled he looked at her stupid preaching, as if he couldn't quite believe what he was hearing. Then his eyes narrowed. 'Nafis wasn't loaded, was he? Or you'd not be so condemnatory.'

She compressed her lips. She wouldn't rise to his jibe.

'Where does Aseem Zafar keep his money?' he asked. 'Sewn into a mattress? In safe deposits? In a sack of potatoes?'

'I don't ask for the details.' She strove for a measured response. 'It doesn't go out of the country. That's the main thing. Otherwise, it's money stolen from the country. We're a small party anyway; it's not as if coffers are overflowing. And Abba has a lot of property, it's true, but that's not liquid money. He doesn't seem minded to liquidate it.'

'I see. What you're really saying is, everyone draws their own lines. Admit it. You would put your money abroad if you had enough to do so.'

'I don't know if I could do that. Perhaps I would be one of those few people who blindly and faithfully followed the rules.'

'You'd pay taxes.'

'Yes.'

'Don't be an idiot. Nobody pays tax.'

'Salaried people do. You know that and I know that. I paid my, admittedly low, tax when I was working. You, Monish, have a choice. You could pay more into the country. You could change the ratio of your black and white…'

He gave a short cheerless laugh. 'Put even more into the politicians' pockets you mean. It's hardly going to go into infrastructure is it? It's a bloody waste. You wait, Wija. If you get to Parliament, you'll be singing a different tune. You'll be out to Switzerland to open your account as soon as you can. I *guarantee* it.'

She bit at her cheek. 'You guarantee nothing on my behalf.'

He held up his hands. 'You're very appealing when you're angry. I was just teasing you.' He linked his slim fingers in hers and squeezed her hand. Her hand remained passive and he squeezed it again. 'Let's listen to some music,' he said. 'Let's not talk about money.'

But he couldn't help himself. Standing by the CD rack he said, 'Life is miserable without money. No one can disagree with that. I know money can't buy happiness, but it eases life.'

'I don't disagree,' she said quietly. 'But you don't have to become a criminal.'

Monish shut his eyes. She'd irritated him. She could hear his loud controlled breathing as he turned to put on some music. 'Something from the 1970s,' he said. 'Is that all right?'

She nodded and he returned to sit beside her.

'Shall I tell you what I find funny when I go to Geneva?' he asked.

'If you must.'

'There's a bunch of flunkies who like to take me out to lunch. They urge me to increase and diversify our deposits. They invite *me* and not fat Prat because I'm the older son. They think I'm the future. They don't know I'm the pariah. For one, that gives me hope, that Dad doesn't blare his opinion of his sons to his foreign bankers. Anyway, at lunch, they like to talk about the *endemic* corruption in India. How nothing works. How rotten all the systems are. "Too much corruption in your country, it's tough for businessmen," they tell me very sympathetically.'

'That's funny?'

'Considering *they're* living off the proceeds of the world's black money, yes. I laugh a lot at lunches in Geneva. Sometimes helplessly. They just think I'm wonderfully high on white wine.'

Waheeda smiled, imagining him laughing at the bankers and them laughing at him. She snuggled into him. He put his hand on her hip and pulled her close. She let her head dip towards his shoulder. He moved his hand to her hair and removed her hair clip. She shook her hair loose. He looked at his watch. 'It's a quarter to twelve,' he said, 'Shall I drop you back by three?'

She nodded. 'Or earlier. You need to get some sleep too.'

'Let's aim for three. Don't worry about me. I can catch up on my sleep tomorrow evening. And the night after that. And the night after that! And the whole week after that!'

'I understand what you're saying. I'll try to find dates for us more regularly.'

He removed his watch and set it on the side table. He pulled her up and they went into the bedroom.

'I must have a quick shower,' he said. 'Give me a few minutes.'

She sat on the bed listening to the water running. When he opened the bathroom door, there was fog behind him and the somewhat bitter smell of neem soap clouding him. He had wrapped a towel around his waist. She had not seen him like this before. He caught her gaze and he placed a hand behind his ear and stuck out his hip. 'Do I make a good model?' He raised the towel to show his upper leg and his bottom.

She laughed. 'Not really. But your bum's cute.'

He undid the towel to give her a full-frontal flash and then tucked it in again at his waist. She reached out her hand.

The doorbell rang. *Ping ping. Ping ping. Ping ping.*

She stood up. Monish frowned. 'Who could it be?' she whispered.

He picked up the alarm clock on the bedside table to look at the time again. 'It could be for me,' he said doubtfully. 'But it's late. They must have the wrong flat. Could be someone for next door.'

The bell was pressed again and sounded its high call three more times. Monish opened his wardrobe and pulled on a T-shirt. Then he pulled on jeans, zipping them carefully.

'Don't answer,' breathed Waheeda.

'I won't,' he whispered. 'They'll go away soon.'

He was wrong. Twice more the bell sounded its three notes, with hardly a pause between each impatient press on it. There was the sound of some scuffling at the front door and then a girlish voice called 'Monish, Monish. It's urgent. I have something important to ask you.'

The voice was raised a decibel. 'Are you there? Monish? I *know* you're home.'

They heard a male voice, a hushing tone. Something about, 'He's not there.' But the girl was calling again, 'Monish. I have something important to ask you.'

Waheeda realised that the girl was drunk. Or high on something. She wasn't slurring. It was the insistence, the serious enunciation, and the insensitivity to the racket she was making.

'What's so important?' muttered Monish to himself. And to Waheeda, 'If she keeps this up, the Sodhis will come out to shut her up. She won't care if she wakes the entire block! Let me deal with this.'

He put on his glasses and left the room to the sound of the bell. It was still on its *ping ping* when he opened the front door.

Waheeda stood against the closed door of the bedroom, listening. She wrapped her *dupatta* around her. She realised she was barefoot; she'd kicked off her sandals in the front room. And her hair clip was lying on the coffee table.

He couldn't let in anyone, he *knew* that. Not with her there.

The piercing voice floated in clearly. 'Monish! I knew you were home. I told Vivek that you would be, that you like to hide out. I heard the music playing.'

'Kriti, shh. It's late. What do you want?'

'Are you going to keep us standing here?'

There was a footfall and the sounds of movement. Waheeda imagined that Monish had blocked the entrance. Or had the girl slipped through? She held her breath and stood unmoving.

'Kriti…' Monish was speaking softly. 'I was working…'

'Working? At this time? I thought you might've fallen asleep and left the player on.'

'So you decided to wake me up?'

'Yes, *yaar*. I have something important to ask you. Vivek and I need to know, what are the words to that song. You know that Rafi one.'

'Er, which one exactly, out of the thousands he sang?'

'The Rafi one.' She was insistent. "*Sheeshe mein tumko bhi utaare chale gaye.*" That's the last line. But I can't remember how it starts. We must have the words. Because, I told Vivek —Oh, this is Vivek.'

'Hi.' Vivek greeted Monish loudly, making Waheeda wince inside the bedroom, even though he wasn't as strident as Kriti.

Monish was the only one speaking in a lowered tone. 'Hi.' She could just make out his reply. 'I was working…I need to finish something…'

'You have the song, Monish. We just need the words. I told Vivek those lyrics were simply the best. Let's listen to the song and I'll write down the words…'

'Not now, Kriti. Not now…'

'Why, *yaar*?' Over loud.

Waheeda was tempted to go out and have a good look at Kriti. The gorgeous one. Who'd sat next to Monish at the concert. Why did she assume that she could walk into his flat whenever she liked?

Monish began his excuses again. 'I said I was working—'

'I told Vivek, you'll know the words for sure. And you'll have the song. He hasn't even heard of it. We can listen to it—'

'I can't invite you in…' Monish was actually *pleading*.

'What? You're joking!'

'I was working on something important—'

'Why are you behaving like this? You're being fucking mean.'

'…Kriti, I…'

'Why are you being fucking mean? Just because I've got Vivek with me?'

'It's not that...'

'It must be. Because I've come with Vivek.'

Waheeda wondered if Vivek was squirming. He should be.

Kriti went on. 'If I'd come alone, you'd be all "come in Kriti. Stick your face in a cushion Kriti, doggy style, baby; three times, baby."'

Waheeda's palm flattened against the door while her blood chilled.

She imagined Monish freezing up, too, but after a moment she heard him, his voice not as quiet as before. He addressed himself to the man. 'Vivek, why don't both of you call me when you're not sozzled, and I'll give you the words to the song. I've got some paperwork I have to finish for a meeting tomorrow morning; *you* know how it is. Call me in the afternoon; in fact, *any* time after noon; hell, I'll sing the song for you from my office.'

'Sing it now!' Kriti demanded. 'We're not high, are we Vivek? We'll remember the words.'

'Tomorrow.' Monish spoke with finality. 'You're not listening, Kriti. I have work to do. Good night.' The door shut.

Monish didn't return to the bedroom. Perhaps he was standing at the door, waiting to ensure his visitors would leave. She strained her ears to listen. Outside the door she could make out the angry murmur of the girl, 'what a bastard, I can't believe it,' then the half-soothing, half-embarrassed tone of her friend Vivek; the girl, again, 'what a fucking b.'

'Have they gone?' she asked when Monish eventually pushed at the bedroom door.

'Yes. They went back down to her flat.' He sighed. 'There's much I can control, but I can't control who'll ring my doorbell.'

'Even at midnight?'

'Midnight, shmidnight, she can come here at any time. That's what she's used to…' He sat down on the edge of the bed.

'Is it true?' Waheeda asked.

'Is what true?'

She didn't deign to respond. Monish knew what she'd meant. He stood up again. 'You want an account of my life, Waheeda? An account of my life and friends?'

Waheeda found herself having an almost helpless reaction. 'Fucking is not friendship,' raced to her tongue, but she bit her lip in time. He gave her a hard stare. He'd read her mind anyway.

'I'm getting a drink.' He went to the kitchen. She could hear him open the freezer and get the ice tray out. Then he was back and sitting on the edge of the bed again.

'Sit down.' He spoke gently, setting his drink on the bed-side table. 'You're standing there like a stricken rabbit.'

She took the armchair instead of the space next to him that he'd indicated.

'So what do you want an account of?' he asked, his eyes seeming to slope further downwards than normal. 'My life and friends before I met you? All my lovers? Or just my history with Kriti?'

'I don't want an account of anything.'

Monish took a quick sip of his whisky. 'That's what I thought.' He took another sip, a long one, before he spoke again. 'You know when people get drunk, sometimes old sores well up; old resentments get spilled…'

'You manage never to spill anything.'

'You can see I have more practice at holding my drink than most.' He allowed himself a slight smile.

'I'll have a drink, too.'

'You will? What?'

'My usual, a Limca.'

He put the drink in her hand, wrapping his hands around hers as she took it. She stiffened and he stepped away to sit on the bed again.

'For what it's worth…' he began, and she saw he was not looking at her, his eyes on the closed curtains at the window. 'For what it's worth, there's no account to give for the last few months.'

Then almost immediately he asked, looking into her eyes this time, 'Would you lie to me about anything?'

'Me?' Waheeda almost sputtered. 'Lie to you? No. Why would I need to?'

'Exactly.' Monish raised his glass to her in a toast. 'That's what makes us.'

He drained his glass and set it back on the bedside table. He lay back on the bed and closed his eyes. 'I won't bite. You can sit next to me.'

Waheeda felt rather than heard his mild sigh when he realised that she hadn't budged. She looked across at his face, his eyes closed, waiting. She was angry and jealous, but these were emotions she should deal with later. She shouldn't even let him see how the thought of him with Kriti was killing her. Of course, she had questions, dozens of questions, all about Kriti, but she wouldn't ask them.

'We need to change that sombre expression,' Monish said, opening his eyes when he felt her weight settle beside him. He tickled her under her ribs. She fidgeted and tried not to squeal like a child. He sat up and continued tickling her, relentlessly, until she was rolling on the bed laughing, but then he whipped up her *kameez* to place his hands on the skin of her abdomen. Her amusement faded immediately. Monish pulled at the knot of her *salwar*. It came undone. Waheeda pushed away his hands, and held on to the string, turning on her side to re-tie the knot. 'I can't.'

He lay down beside her, bringing his arm across her chest, and pulled her back towards him. 'All right,' he said in her ear. 'All right.'

He would be disappointed but she wasn't over her Kriti

shock. She lay within his arms, her back to him, and they listened to each other's breathing for a few minutes. 'What is it with you women?' he asked. 'Your favourite position involves doing nothing.'

He was teasing her. He swung himself out of the bed. 'I'm going to get a drink.' And before she could say anything, 'Yes, I know, I just had one.'

When he returned, he propped up the pillows and leaning back on them, he extended his left arm to her. 'Come here daughter of a pen repairer. Let's just hug to our heart's content.'

With her snuggled up comfortably on his left, her head on his chest, he picked up his drink in his right hand, looking for all the world as if he was in his most natural state. Despite his youthful face, he seemed patriarchal in this pose.

Waheeda smiled.

'What's so funny?' he asked.

'You're so theatrical.'

'Me? You must be more theatrical than me, Wija. You're the one who's speechifying all over the place. All those crowds. All that beating on a tin can, repeating yourself. Remembering your lines.' He grimaced. 'I would never be able to stand going on the campaign trail. I like the quiet life.'

'Quiet life? Your type of quiet life requires a huge supply of cash.'

'I know. We've just talked about that. But I do go to the office and run a business, doing what I'm meant to do. Responding to the whip.'

'Just to secure your income?'

'What else?'

'I don't believe you. You pretend you're not competitive, but you are. Last time, when you were talking about the new advertising campaign—'

'I do the minimum. I just sit there behind my nice desk. The agencies bring the concepts to me. They do the work.'

'Are you saying you don't want your paint products to out-sell all the others? You do, don't you? I know what you're really like, Monish. If you weren't leading the market you'd be tearing out your hair!'

'Still, I've a quiet life,' he said. 'Compared with you.'

He looked into the distance and grimaced again. 'How can you bear it? Addressing hordes of people, and then having to climb into the bus where even more people want a piece of you.'

'I can deal with it. The adrenalin keeps me so high…I can't explain it. It's a daily shot of adrenalin! And the bus—those are my people! They're working on *my* campaign.'

'That's what I mean. How can you bear it? All those men in your party, wanting something from you, wanting a promotion, or a promise. And some of them dreaming of getting close to you, being the favoured ones, getting intimate, touching your hand, ripping off your clothes—'

'Monish!' She was startled. 'They're not like that.'

'Can you really say that, Wija? Some of them, those young party workers, running around for you, doing their utmost, can you swear that none of them fantasises about tearing off your clothes? Do you know what men are like?'

She narrowed her eyes at him. 'I'm finding out.'

He was unfazed. 'You know which ones are the most ambitious? The ones that look at you with puppy dog eyes.'

'How do you know?' She was surprised. He'd never been in a campaign bus with her; how did he know of the more fervent aides? Like the speechwriter who'd tried to get too close to her.

'I have the same thing in my office. Position and the possibility of wielding power. All my assistant managers have puppy dog eyes.'

'Are you talking about your male employees?'

'I've picked women to be the assistant managers.' There

was a mischievous grin on his face. 'They're efficient and they work hard. They rarely slip up. They just want to please me.'

She turned to look at him. She had no doubt they were vying to please him. 'You are truly mean,' she said.

A glaze of sadness came over his dark irises. 'You're the second person to tell me so tonight.'

Waheeda was instantly sorry. She pressed her cheek against his in silent apology.

FIFTEEN

MONISH WAITED UNTIL late morning to call Kriti from his office to apologise and to give her the lyrics of the song. He'd deposited Dad at home, promised Ma he'd come by for a long lunch with her soon, just her and him; and he'd instructed his secretary, Chanda, not to put through any calls, unless it was Kriti. In the end he'd not slept even an hour the previous night and he had a solid headache.

No one answered the phone at Kriti's flat. He tried her cell phone. 'I'm in a meeting,' she huffed and hung up on him. Of course she was outraged at his behaviour. He had never turned her away before and he expected to grovel for forgiveness. He wondered if she really was working. Was she in her boutique, overseeing a new window display or checking the ledgers? Should he go around there to make it up to her? He decided against it. Most likely she was lolling at home in her flat, with that Vivek chap she'd been with.

He tried again after a couple of hours. She answered her home number this time. When he spoke, she cut him off. 'Don't call me ever again,' she said. 'I don't want to speak to you.'

'Kriti, I'm sorry...'

'Monish. Just don't. Don't. You *were* my friend.' She hung up on him again.

He called her once a day for the next few days to make a stab at offering explanations. She insisted that she wanted nothing to do with him. He gave up; best to wait until she cooled down a bit. One woman's demands were enough, he reckoned, thinking about the subterfuge involved each time he met Waheeda. For the time being, at least, he wasn't in the mood to entertain another woman's *nakhras*.

One evening he spotted Kriti in the lobby of their building. It was cool and she was wearing a light cardigan over a long skirt. He caught her arm to make her face him, to begin an apology, but she wouldn't look at him. She brushed his hand off and turned to her mailbox, inserting the key to unlock it. She stuffed her post into her tote bag and walked away.

The next day Monish instructed Chanda to order one dozen black Baccara roses to be delivered to Kriti's boutique. But she didn't call to acknowledge them. He asked Chanda to send a box of pastries, again to the boutique, so she could share them with the girls there. He used to do that fairly regularly at one time. He used to be more thoughtful. Again, she didn't call.

He let it be after that, although from the few phone conversations he'd had with friends, usually making his excuses about not being able to attend this or that bash, he realised that they were aware of a rift between him and Kriti. It would mend in time, he thought, but he hoped it wouldn't be long. Inadvertently he'd hurt his closest friend; the person who always stood up for him. Kriti used to speak up for him even to his Dad, not that it helped Monish's case—the opposite, in fact—but he found it sweet that she tried. She had been on his side.

•

AT LEAST WAHEEDA made an effort to put things right with him by finding another date in November. She'd fixed press meetings during the day and would stay the night with Naaz. But Deepak, Naaz's husband was at home that week, and Waheeda was wary of coming out late at night. 'Naaz will drop me off for an early dinner with you,' she said. 'She's going to see our old colleagues from the history department. She'll tell Deepak I'm joining them for dinner, too.'

Kismet was not in his favour that day. He received a call that afternoon from his friend Gerry. Caught on the hop, Monish couldn't find a reason to tell Gerry that he couldn't stay over as usual. He rang Waheeda. 'Just to warn you I have a friend staying with me.' He hurried on before she could say anything. 'You can't not come. Don't even think of cancelling, Wija. Gerry's turned up suddenly. He does that sometimes. But don't worry. He's not from here, he's from Australia. He won't know who you are; and he won't care.'

'I don't—'

'You can use a false name if you like. I'll tell him you're just a friend I'd already invited for dinner.' He had meant to surprise her with an early birthday present. There probably wouldn't be a chance to give her the watch he'd bought for her. There probably wouldn't be a chance to touch, even; they would just have to look at each other and have their fill that way. Damn.

'I don't—'

'It will just be the three of us for dinner at home. He's safe, I promise. *Don't* cancel on me.'

•

SHE COULD HAVE said no. But that warning note in his voice had compelled her. Naaz suggested that Waheeda take some flowers for Monish, as a dinner invitee might do, and introduce herself with a false name.

'Hello, I'm Sulekha,' Waheeda said on entering the flat, and the Australian man said, 'Hello, I'm Gerry. Gerry with a G.' He shook her hand enthusiastically.

She gave him her polite smile, clutched at the bouquet she was holding and ignored the amused look Monish cast at her. 'Call me Sue,' she said.

'I don't think I've met you before, have I?' asked Gerry.

'I wouldn't think so. I see Monish very occasionally. I live in Calcutta. I'm just in Delhi for a few days.'

Gerry beamed at her. 'I'm just here for a few days myself. But I pass through Delhi twice a year at least. If Monish is in town I stay a couple of days with him.'

Waheeda flashed her bland smile again. Monish had never mentioned Gerry to her before, but then she hardly knew what went on in his life, other than what he chose to tell her in the brief moments they had together.

She handed Monish the flowers without a word.

'For me?' His voice had an upward lilt. 'Thank you so much.' He held the yellow lilies in one hand and opened random cabinets with the other looking for a vase to put them in. Not finding one tall enough he settled on a white plastic pail that he found in the kitchen. He filled it with water, placed the flowers in it and stood the pail in the corner so the lilies could lean against the wall. He took care to ensure the plastic wrapping protected the wall. Then he bustled in and out of the kitchen while Gerry and she chatted in the sitting area. She longed to follow him into the kitchen and kiss the back of his neck and wrap her arms around his leanness. She sat sedately making the effort to ask Gerry the usual questions.

Gerry was as tall as Monish, but heavier and sturdier. He had unremarkable brown hair, dark brown eyes and a very square jaw. He was freshly shaved and he wore shorts and a polo shirt. The shorts made her smile. It was the mark of a foreigner. To dinner in shorts in autumnal Delhi. Of course, he was just lounging at Monish's pad and there was no need for him to be formal. She could see that he was very much at ease in the flat. It turned out Gerry lived to hike in the lower Himalayas. He returned to odd jobs in Melbourne, saved up and returned for long trips to India. This time Dharamsala had been his base. She would never have thought that a Gerry-type and a Monish-type would be friends but they seemed to get on very well. They'd known each other for four years. They'd met on an overbooked flight to Melbourne when Gerry had been upgraded to business class. He'd ended up sitting next to Monish. She gleaned all this from Gerry although a few times she had to ask him to repeat what he'd said. She'd never heard an accent like his. For his part he seemed completely used to Indian accents and Indian English. He understood everything she said. Even the Hindi words she slipped into. She found that he constantly used an expression: '*Chalta Hai.*' He obviously liked it. *It will do. Life goes on.* He didn't use it pejoratively, but as a mantra.

Gerry practiced yoga daily and didn't drink alcohol or smoke. He looked on indulgently when Monish brought over his tumbler of whisky. It turned out he didn't drink Coca-Cola either. Or Limca. 'I'll make *nimbu-pani* for him,' Monish mock-groaned to Waheeda. 'I'm used to his pickiness.' He disappeared again into his little kitchen.

Gerry followed him and Waheeda felt free to move about, too.

'Where is Malti?' she heard Gerry ask Monish as she stood in the dining area. 'Isn't she cooking for me?'

From the kitchen Monish flicked a quick glance at Waheeda. 'She's cooked us a very nice dinner,' he told Gerry. 'But she had some family matter to attend to, she couldn't stay. She'll come in early tomorrow to do the washing up, don't worry.'

'I'll do the washing up,' Gerry said.

Monish shrugged. 'Suit yourself.'

He came out of the kitchen holding three dinner plates which he handed to Waheeda. She set them out on the table. He'd told her that Malti usually worked for him in the afternoons: cleaning, washing clothes, ironing, cooking. But, of course, thought Waheeda, if he was entertaining guests, she must help him out regularly in the evenings too. Monish made sure that, when Waheeda was due to visit, Malti was given time off. Waheeda had never seen his domestic assistant and she fervently hoped that Malti had no inkling of her.

Gerry brought the dishes to the table. He was vegetarian. Monish said, 'I know Wa...*Sue* doesn't mind veg or non-veg; so I'm leaving the mutton biryani that was prepared for her in the fridge. Let's keep it simple, we'll all have just dal and vegetables, cool?'

She nodded her affirmation at him. Gerry was garrulous in an entertaining fashion. She liked that, because she didn't have to contribute much to the conversation. She was enjoying listening to the two of them. As they ate and talked, Gerry admitted to Waheeda that his world was very different from Monish's sphere.

'So is mine.' She smiled but didn't elaborate.

'I thoroughly relish it when Monish splashes his money on me,' Gerry said, 'but I also feel guilty. But thanks to him the few days I spend in Delhi are amazing—I go to all the best restaurants and clubs. It's a whole different life!'

He helped himself to his tenth chapati. Waheeda had counted without really meaning to. He didn't seem to mind that they were not fresh off the *tava*; they were lukewarm from being in the insulated tin. 'But for myself,' Gerry continued, 'I don't really want material things. I'm not interested in wealth. I *couldn't* work in an office all day. I'd go raving mad.'

Monish wrinkled his nose. 'I don't much care to work in an office all day either.'

'You don't even have to work. You're sorted, mate.'

'I *have* to go into work.' Monish responded. 'Every week day. At least for now; and some years yet. No one quite understands that.'

Gerry raised his bushy brown brows teasingly. Waheeda

got the feeling they'd had this conversation before.

'"He works hard for the money…"' Gerry sang. He gave her a wink and laughed.

'He does,' she agreed. 'For the money. But not as hard as Onetta.'

'Why do you make it sound like I'm doing something wrong?' Monish asked. 'Or something lesser than Onetta the restroom attendant? What else would you work for if not money? And why wouldn't you do the loftier, better-paid job if you could?' He stopped to chew and swallow, frowning at her and Gerry. 'Money smooths life. Ask somebody who doesn't have it.'

'I don't,' Gerry retorted promptly.

Monish looked at him appraisingly. 'True,' he conceded. 'What do you have? You don't even own a home.'

'I don't need one.'

Monish grinned wickedly. 'No…because you have the comfort of strangers. The hospitality of poor Indians who live in the mountains. The air of the Himalayas. The currency exchange in your favour…'

Gerry reddened, all the way to his high hairline, including his ears. His face was as pink as his sunburnt neck and his nose shone a brighter pink. Monish laughed. 'All that may do for you, man,' he said, 'but it doesn't do for me. I want the house, the holiday home, the pool, the tennis court, the life-style I'm used to, acres of land to call my own, bank accounts to call my own. Everything my absolute own.'

'I know, I know.' Gerry turned to Waheeda. 'I'm sure we're boring you.' He'd recovered his composure. 'We always have the same old discussion. It's something to do with the air in Delhi. You can't help but talk about property, buying and selling, and therefore, money. Everyone bandies about these big numbers. And even I get swept up in it.'

Waheeda inclined her head in agreement. She looked at

her watch and scraped back her chair. 'I'm so sorry,' she murmured, 'I have to leave now.'

Gerry seemed astonished. 'It's not even dinner time for most *Dilli-wallas*,' he said.

'You're right. It's just that…I…have another appointment.'

She looked across at Monish who checked the clock on the sideboard. Nine-thirty.

Naaz would be waiting in her car downstairs in the cul-de-sac. She was generally on time.

He pushed back his chair too. 'Wa—Sul…' he stumbled again over her name, 'Sue is a very busy lady.' He waved his hands at Gerry. 'Keep eating. Please. I'll just see her out to the lift. I think she has to get back to her aunt's home. Her aunt is strict!'

Gerry stood up to say goodbye to Waheeda. 'I can tell you're not from Delhi,' he joked. 'You're obedient to your aunt!'

Monish pulled the front door almost-closed. Waheeda was about to start down the stairs to call the lift from the floor below but he held her hand.

'Come back soon,' he said. 'I have a present for you that I couldn't give you tonight.'

'I don't want any presents.'

'Too bad. You're getting one from me. Fix a date soon. Next week?'

'I'll try,' she said.

'We're not having much luck, are we?' He squeezed her hand and bent forward as if to kiss her, but she ducked. 'Not here. I'll call soon.'

•

HE STOOD OUTSIDE the door of his flat hearing the noisy lift click-clack up to Waheeda on the floor below. He'd wanted to grasp her dense hair and grind his mouth into hers before she left. Instead he called out pretend-cheerily, to no one, 'Speak soon.'

Earlier when he was in the kitchen looking for serving spoons Waheeda had come in for a moment to leave her used glass by the sink. He'd let his hand rest on her hip for *one* second. She'd looked so panicked that he'd moved away from her immediately. He'd said, 'Gerry doesn't matter.'

'Every single person who knows matters,' she'd whispered back fiercely.

He entered his flat, kicking the front door shut with his right heel.

Gerry was spooning out the last of the yogurt with relish.

Monish felt too grim to talk and went past him into his bedroom. He needed a moment to clear the anger on his face. It wasn't Gerry's fault. He scrubbed at his nails in the bathroom before returning. He paused by the study door which was weighed open by Gerry's humongous rucksack. He stepped in and opened a cupboard to bring out two quilts and two sheets. Gerry would be comfortable using one quilt as a mattress on Monish's rug in the living room. What else did he need? A pillow. Monish pulled down two from the top storage shelf. He stacked the linens and pillows on a chair. He'd told Malti to go early so she hadn't set all this up, as she usually did. He needed pillowcases. He opened a cupboard and found them.

Gerry had cleared the dining table and was at the kitchen sink running water over their plates and dishes. Monish found himself laughing, although nothing was funny. He brought over his glass from the table and poured more whisky into it, his grip clenched and angry on the neck of the bottle.

'Leave it,' he said to Gerry.

Gerry dried his hands on a small towel and followed him to the sitting room, addressing his back. 'She's not your usual type.'

Monish stiffened but turned round with what he hoped was a relaxed smile.

'She…Sue…is just a friend. I thought I'd said.'

Gerry had the grace to look chastened. 'Yes, you did say that.'

Monish set his drink down and slumped into an armchair.

His phone rang twice and then stopped. That was Waheeda's signal. She was safely on the way home with Naaz. On Naaz's phone and also on Waheeda's he was in the Contacts list as Manisha Doctorwala. He'd keyed it in himself. On his phone she was Moonraker.

Gerry knelt before the rows of CDs and pulled one out of the rack. He motioned to the player. 'Will you put it on or should I?'

'Go ahead.'

Gerry slid the CD into the player. It was an instrumental sitar composition—Gerry's usual choice.

SIXTEEN

December 1997

'THIRD TIME LUCKY,' Monish thought as he wrapped up the watch in silver paper for Waheeda. A whole five hours of together-time lay ahead, and he could stop feeling like a monk and more like a lover.

Waheeda's birthday was in a couple of weeks in mid-December. He'd bought the watch in September when he'd visited Singapore. He'd enlisted Lara's help there to ensure he bought something that Waheeda would actually accept and wear. Lara had chosen an inexpensive but classic piece: plain white face with black roman numerals, slim case, matte gold. Lara said that Waheeda would like the double strap in honey-brown leather. 'She notices details and this will suit her. It will look different from any other watch she has.'

In the store he'd pointed to a Gucci stainless steel ladies watch which was all the rage in Delhi. He himself wore a similar style—the men's version. Lara had laughed at him. 'Wija will not wear a brand like that. Don't be silly,' she'd said. 'She wouldn't accept it for a start. But even if she did, to not hurt your feelings, she wouldn't be able to use it. How would she explain it? Just stick with something low-priced and smart, and she can tell anyone who asks I sent it to her.'

Monish set the gift-wrapped narrow box on the bedside table. It had been the only thing he could think of to buy for Waheeda. Strange, though, how customs were so different everywhere. Lara had told him that for the Chinese giving clocks or watches as a gift was taboo. It brought bad luck. 'But not in the emperor's day,' she'd added. 'It's a fairly recent thing; only in the last hundred years, maybe?' He'd thought Indians were the most superstitious people in the world but every time he heard of another Chinese custom he'd been unaware of he decided that the Chinese were far more superstitious.

He'd asked Lara if she had other suggestions. Perfume? Make up? He knew Waheeda barely used the latter, it was one of the reasons he found her so attractive, but if there was something that she did like, then he could purchase it for her. Lara had grinned at him as if he was being nosy about Waheeda's beauty secrets and she wasn't going to be the one to tell him anything. 'A subtle lipstick,' she'd suggested.

He didn't tell her that he detested lipstick. It wasn't a gift he liked to give unless a friend specifically requested that he return from his travels with lipsticks in such-and-such brands in such-and-such colours. Yes, sometimes he'd seen Waheeda put on a neutral shade of lipstick before she left his flat. He'd also noticed that she used an eye-pencil when she was leaving in the day time. He guessed it was so that she didn't appear dishevelled. Certainly, when she arrived, her face seemed fresh scrubbed and her dark complexion naturally smooth and radiant. It was the look he liked best. Not that there was any point informing anyone of his preferences; he'd learnt that a while back. He remembered watching Kriti make up her face once. They were both about to turn twenty—that was the year they'd gone steady for some months. After sitting around for half an hour in her bedroom, at first quite taken with the spectacle of her applying something from this tube and then that tube, and then an eyeshadow compact and a blusher compact, he became impatient about heading out for their dinner. She was brushing mascara on her lashes. 'You don't need all that gunk on your face,' he said. 'Without make-up you truly are the most beautiful girl I've ever seen.' She stared into the mirror, her mouth held open in a funny face as she finished brushing up her lashes. She set down her brush and turned to him. 'I'm not doing this for you. I'm doing it for me.'

•

MONISH PLACED A card next to Waheeda's gift. He'd not written in it or signed it. But at least, on Waheeda's birthday, it was something for her to open in Nulkazim. She could leave it out in her room and not worry. He'd tell her she could write any friend's name in it. But she would look at it and remember him. And if she wore the watch daily, she'd remember him every time her wrist with the double strap came into her vision.

It was time to go and collect her from Naaz's home. He'd been rushing again today, first late for his squash game and then stuck on the way home in traffic chaos. He'd given Choppy a lift back, too, from the club as his wife was using the car that evening. The two of them sweated up his car and Monish had the airconditioner on high. They'd talked mainly about Choppy's little boy. The boy was asthmatic and Monish was adamant that he should continue with his swimming lessons because in the long run it would be good for him. Monish knew nothing about children, but Choppy humoured him by listening to him, and then putting forward his own view. Choppy was good like that. All those typical things people said about Sirds, their boasting, their aggression; it was funny that all his Sikh friends, whether they kept long hair or not, were completely unSird. Choppy was the gentlest man. Except on the squash court, where he annihilated Monish.

He'd been ravenous when he finally got home and he'd eaten more than he usually did for dinner. Then he'd showered and tidied the bed and the bedroom. He went into the bathroom to check himself in the mirror once and use the eyewash on his bleary eyes. The traffic fumes had really got to him. He reached into the top shelf of his wardrobe to pull out the jute bag that contained his disguise. Ten-thirty. He needn't change now; he could put on the disguise when he swopped cars. It was dark enough that nobody would see. This evening he hadn't parked his car in the cul-de-sac behind the building as he sometimes did. He took the lift down to the car park and drove out.

He parked by the shed-like structure that was called 'the manager's office' at 'Bittu Transport Company,' the private taxi firm owned by his friend. The shed was made up of a large room with a desk, a smaller room for storage and an attached bathroom. At this time there was no one around, just the guard for the parking lot. The guard knew he was a friend of the boss with permission to come and go. Monish headed over to the one taxi that was stationed behind the manager's office. The key had been left in the ignition for him. He'd told his friend that he was engaged in industrial cloak and dagger stuff. Whether his friend believed him or not didn't matter; he followed the code: he didn't pry further, but arranged matters as Monish wished. Monish drove out of the lot, stopping again a few streets away to don his disguise. He pulled on a dark blue safari suit over his jeans and shirt. He got into the passenger seat and flipped down the mirror. He put on the fake beard and moustache; it was an easy-wear item, the elastic went behind his ears, and he adjusted it over his chin and mouth, which it completely covered. Close up it wouldn't pass for real, but driving in the dark and scut-tling into his building, it did the job. He tied a narrow white band of cloth around his forehead. Lastly, he bunged on the blue turban he had 'borrowed' a couple of months ago from Choppy. He checked in the mirror. Yup, he was transformed, he was a Sird driver, complete with epaulettes on his safari shirt. In the top pocket he carried a letter addressed to 'Mr Selvani,' so that if a sentry at the building stopped him he would show whose flat he had been sent to, to deliver the note from his imaginary employer.

He waited across the road from Naaz's house. A few minutes later Waheeda appeared. She bent to the front window to check it was him, said hello, heard his voice, then slid into the back. He could tell instantly that something had happened. Her face was animated by a strange light from within, but he couldn't guess whether it was good news or bad news. He didn't ask. It was always awkward when they tried to chat in the car, what with him concentrating on driving an unfamiliar vehicle and her hiding low in the back.

He dropped her outside his building and she went on ahead to his flat while he parked the taxi in the street behind. When he came up he asked, 'What's wrong?' even before he'd taken off the turban and the beard.

She sat on the sofa looking pensive, her bare feet stroking the silk rug. Her white *kohlapuri* slippers had been slipped off at the edge of the rug. They were at an angle he didn't like, the tops touching and the heels apart. Footwear left like that bothered him. He laid the disguise, piece by piece, neatly on the chair ready for the return drive.

'I wasn't expecting it to happen so soon,' she said. 'It's sudden. I don't feel ready for elections. Although it's what I was building up to. It feels strange…but at the same time it's electrifying…'

'What're you talking about? What elections?'

'Haven't you heard?'

'Heard what? Has your doddery Congress chap in Dhoonpur popped it?'

'Monish! He isn't doddery; he's very ill. And no, he's also very much alive. Umair-ji's information is rarely wrong, but in this instance…well, it seems he really has the will to keep going despite his advancing cancer....Haven't you paid attention to the news today? The President disbanded Parliament this afternoon.'

His mouth fell open. He hadn't bothered with the news after a cursory glance at the paper in the morning. No one had told him at work and Choppy hadn't mentioned it in the evening. 'Disbanded Parliament?' he repeated, struggling to understand. 'That has never happened! For Chrissakes, *why*?'

She shrugged. 'They couldn't keep it together—all the warring sides and each with their own agendas. No coalition or one party could form a majority or win the confidence of the House.'

He nudged her slippers so that they lay precisely side by side before he sat down beside her. 'What now?'

'There will be fresh elections all over the country. They announced it will have to be before mid-March.'

'No, please.' He put his head in his hands. 'Bunch of bloody jokers. They played musical chairs in parliament and didn't do an iota of governance. Not an iota! We had to bribe all comers, all corners, all parties. Now they can't hold it together. What a waste of resources for your wonderful country, Wija. They'll send it to hell in a handcart.'

Waheeda's forefinger tapped her thigh. She grimaced but made no response.

He covered her hand with his. 'Sorry! I hadn't heard. As you can tell from my ranting. Parliament dissolved, oh boy.' He lifted her legs and put her feet on his lap. 'What are you going to do, my lovely?' She adjusted her position so she could lean back into the wide arm, propping two cushions behind her. Her turquoise blue sari flared on his lap. He slid his hand underneath her petticoat to stroke her ankles.

'I've been on the phone for hours. Talking to Abba and Umair-ji. Officially, I'll decide when I'm back in Nulkazim.

We'll have a proper meeting. But I'm leaning towards…' She paused.

'Yes, what?'

She smiled but it was a quivery smile. 'I'll lose, you know…'

'Why? What have you decided? Are you going to stand? Where?' He pushed up her sari to place his hands on her legs.

She was faraway. 'I can already see what defeat will look like…what it will *feel* like…it's not what I want.'

He ran his hand up and down her legs. He liked her soft skin. Her legs were so smooth, he thought they might have been waxed recently and then lotioned up daily. For him? He looked at her delicate, anxious face. It was crunch time in her life, and he was wondering whether she'd waxed her legs just for him. Wake up and smell the coffee Monish. He leant towards her. '*What* have you decided, Wija? You're not being very clear.'

'I will stand. In Dhoonpur. I don't have a choice. I can't back down, not if I'm serious, not after what I've been saying in my speeches. I thought I had a bit more time to prepare. But now it's less than three months…there's no chance really…'

'Winners don't talk like that.' He bent forward to kiss her forehead. 'You've got to believe.' He sat back. 'On the other hand, if you don't have hope, why stand?'

'To show I meant everything I said. To repeat that I'll carry on my work and my betterment schemes regardless of the outcome. I won't say that last bit, of course, but whatever happens, I will go back. And re-start the longer-term campaign.'

'For the next election in five years?'

'It may not be that long…'

'Aha.' He laughed. 'Still hoping for a by-election. Have you put a curse on your cancer-ridden non-doddery congresswala?'

'No, Monish. I don't wish him ill. I know I sound horrible, and it's easy to think these things, but to wish him ill or wish him dead is more horrible than I want to be. But the truth is the truth and neither he nor I can hide from that. If his doctors say he hasn't got long, then maybe he hasn't. He's outlived all predictions though, so who knows how many years he can go on. Who knows how many more times the Dhoonpur electorate will be so obligingly loyal to him?' She swung her legs off his lap. She moved to sit closer to him and curled her legs up on the sofa.

'Maybe not this time?'

She grimaced. 'This time…I think I know what the result will be. I guess the point is I've been proclaiming myself a candidate, no, *the* best candidate and I can eat my words or I can go into the field and battle.'

He put his arm around her waist and hugged her to his side. 'Are you going to stand somewhere else as well?'

She exhaled very slowly. Then she put her arm around him. 'Perhaps we shouldn't talk any more about this. About what I can and can't do.'

'You don't want to tell me?'

She shook her head. 'It's not that. We'll be here hours talking. And I've just been through this whole debate on the phone. And more to come tomorrow. Patharghat frightens me, Monish. The people who run the other parties' offices there have no compunction about using extreme violence. They seem to think they're untouchable. More so, if it's aimed at Muslims. They'll go scot free and NPF will be blamed for any trouble. I won't stand there. We don't have the capacity to run two campaigns anyway, one of them somewhere entirely new.' She laid her head on his shoulder. 'Losing in one con-stituency is enough, isn't it?'

'First off, stop saying that. You don't know. Anything can happen. Look what happened at the last election. Frankly I'm surprised WW survived in Dhoonpur. Congress were routed everywhere else.' Under her *pallu*, he held the folds of her sari in his fingers. 'Anything can happen.' He tugged. 'Like your sari can magically come off.'

•

HE DROPPED HER back at Naaz's at four in the morning. Initially the plan had been for five a.m. but Waheeda decided that dawn was too risky. Some people were up and about at five, she said, elderly walkers and devout temple-goers. Naaz's husband Deepak was on a trip to Karnataka, which was where he sourced some of the crafts and textiles that he exported. At least they'd had the time at night, because he was away. Waheeda was never willing to risk creeping out of his house when Deepak was around. She didn't want to get Naaz into trouble with her husband. He would definitely disapprove, she'd said. And not just that, he might feel obliged to ring Nafis and tell him. It's not as if Deepak and Nafis got on well, but Deepak would be furious, she was sure of that.

Monish suspected that it would be a while before she fixed a date with him again. The elections would take up all her time and energy. He'd wondered if she was going to break up with him before she left. Or if he was meant to do the breaking up. The moment had certainly come this evening. Come and gone! He couldn't believe how his heart had sunk. In free fall. He realised he wasn't ready to give her up yet. She would have to be the one to call it quits. She almost did. But couldn't bring herself to say the words. He'd felt again, that delicious power. He, Monish, was her weak spot. She might be strong in many ways, but she was completely weak for him. Completely. Well, almost.

When she was re-tying her sari in the bedroom, he'd said, 'I was going to suggest spending New Year's Eve in Ranikhet. You'll take time off from campaigning, won't you? You won't be out that evening or the next day?'

She'd looked at him cautiously, her fingers busy with her *pallu* pleats. 'I'll be home,' she said hesitantly.

'So, I was thinking I'd come to Nulkazim. Take you off somewhere overnight. You make some excuse to—'

'*No.* Never come to Nulkazim, Monish. Never.'

When had she become so ruthless? He sat on the bed. 'Fine.' He spoke coldly. 'You don't mind if I go with other friends, do you?'

She bit her lip. 'Of course not. I hope you have a great time.'

Her tone told him she hoped he had a dire time. She was twisting her fingers, tying the waist pleats of her sari. He waited until she'd tucked them in.

Just as he spoke, she did, too. 'You first,' he said, gesturing.

She bent to her open handbag on the floor and brought out the watch box. She placed it on the bedside table. 'I will understand if you don't want to…' She paused.

That was when he felt himself plummet. He would hit the ground on his feet, of course he would, and he would be unhurt after his fall. But just at that moment, he was shocked at himself and his lack of breath.

As if from far away, he heard himself ask, 'If I don't want to what?'

She wrapped her blue woollen shawl over her shoulders. 'If you don't want to…I'll understand…completely understand.'

Then his feet were safely on earth. She couldn't even bring herself to say 'If you don't want to see me again.' His pulse was quick and he was happy again. Could he make her say it? Or was it such anathema to her?

'If I don't want to what?'

She lifted her bag off the floor and combed her hair with the fingers of one hand.

'You know…'

'I want,' he said. He picked up the watch box and slid it inside her bag. 'Call me when you can. Text me when you can. Tell me when you're free to meet. Deal?'

In the sitting room, before he put on his beard et al, he kissed her forehead, and whispered, 'Good luck. Show them.'

Then he'd put on the safari suit and saluted before leaving. 'Madam, your taxi will be at the front of the building in five minutes.'

SEVENTEEN

January 1998

CHANDA KNOCKED SOFTLY on Monish's open office door and stood on the other side of his desk.

'Yes?' He raised his head irritably. The schedule for the national elections had been announced that morning. On New Year's Day! He was way too hung over to digest the information correctly, but he was trying. He'd only got home after a four a.m. breakfast at a hotel coffee-shop. He'd not gone to Ranikhet after all, but stayed in Delhi and done the usual drink/dance communal thing at a rooftop nightclub. In the rest of the world, they had a holiday. Or some countries did. Not here, not when they had too many public holidays anyway; more than any other country in the world. India was top. For this one thing, at least.

He frowned into the newspaper he'd been reading. Polling would take place in four phases across the country. In Uttar Pradesh it would take place on two dates in February. The vote-count would not happen until early March when the last polls had closed in another part of the country.

He'd told Chanda to hold all calls. She was busy at her desk when he'd come in late and unshaven. But the other two secretaries who shared the large office with her were missing. He didn't mind. Those two must have partied, either with friends or family. Why didn't Chanda have some fun sometimes? She'd probably had a low-key evening with her parents.

He wanted some quiet time to think; to make some decisions—how was he going to handle himself; his social life;

his life, full stop. Everyone was supposed to make resolutions, right? Mom had started pressuring him to see (*what's the harm in meeting them?*) the lovely marriageable girls she kept discovering. She had never nagged him to this extent before. He used to enjoy the time he spent with her, their long lunches; and now she just upset him every time.

'Mr Gaurav called twice, Mr Monish.' Chanda ignored his peevishness.

'Oh.' Monish checked his phone, which was on silent. There were two missed calls from Gaurav.

'Did he say what he wants?'

'It's his wife's birthday party tomorrow, sir. Mr Gaurav said you didn't confirm your attendance.'

What had he said last week when Gaurav had invited him? 'I'd love to…I'm not sure if I'm free on the second.… Yes, I'll let you know…I wouldn't want to miss Diljit's party.'

He nodded at Chanda. 'I'll call him now.'

She turned to go, her maroon bangles clinking. As ever, she was neatly turned out, on this new year's day in navy tailored slacks and a cream tunic patterned with dark red blooms. Whether in Indian or Western outfits, she always wore matching glass bangles. 'Nice,' he said, nodding towards her arm, to make up for his tetchiness. 'Nice colour on you.' She had an ongoing infatuation with him. He complimented her infrequently so as not to encourage any pointless hopes. He did notice her matching bangles every single day—he just didn't remark on them. At the same time he was careful to maintain her steadfastness towards him, by being as good as he could to her. Making sure that her loyalty to him would come above any boyfriend, or a husband when she got one.

He checked the election schedule in the paper again and texted Waheeda. 'What's your polling date?' She would take her time to text back, when she had a chance to be by herself.

Whatever the actual date was, it would be a while before *he* saw her. Not till after the count, he guessed. In theory she could meet him when she was next in Delhi. But it was likely she would only visit for urgent and important meetings, and spend the rest of the time on the campaign trail. He felt a bit sorry for himself. But, hey, he was a free man. It was his choice to be a temporary *brahmachari*. Not so, Waheeda. Immediately he was sad on her behalf. What she really wanted was a man she could come home to, someone who would hear the day's woes, someone she could nestle into, someone with whom sex was regular, and not such a big deal.

He couldn't even explain to himself that protective emotion that overcame him when he took her clothes off. It was such a shame that her soft shapely body was never flaunted; it was just him, Monish, who embarrassed her when he tried to praise her. But that admiration was probably the reason she hadn't given him up. He knew and she knew that after him there would be no one else. She couldn't find romance within her party, even if that was the natural inclination. It would be even more asinine than going out with him. And outside of her political circle? Well, which man would be fool enough to take on the mantle of disguises and complex webs of deceit required? Which man would not crow about his conquest? No, her only hope of a loving relationship would be if she got back with her husband. That wasn't going to happen. It was why Monish liked to give and give, of himself, when he was with her. Mind, not all for the sake of altruism. Some part was for his own sake.

•

HE DIALLED GAURAV's number. 'Celebrate and commiserate,' Geaurav said cheerily. 'Isn't that what friends are for?'

'I'll be there, buddy. Remind me what we're celebrating and commiserating.'

'Celebrating Dilly's birthday: sweet twenty-six; Commiserating:

another year down the drain for Gaurav the Great. Ambition unachieved.'

'What was Gaurav the Great hoping for?'

'Moving into my own home.'

'Ah, well…you'll get there, buddy. By the way, is Kriti invited tomorrow?' Monish hadn't seen her at the club the previous night.

'Ya, she's coming.'

'Shall I give her a lift there and back?'

'Monny…' he knew from Gaurav's hesitation that he wanted to be diplomatic. 'Not sure what happened between you two…anyway, Kriti has already organised her lift here. And I've promised to take her back if she's stranded here late.'

'Sure. But it's a bit much for you to drive her back. I'll do it.'

'I don't know…' Gaurav sounded doubtful. 'Will she accept a lift home from you?'

What the hell had Kriti said? 'I think so.' He would make it happen. 'She's sulked like a child long enough.' Someone should repeat that to her. 'See you tomorrow.'

•

LATER THAT AFTERNOON he called in Chanda. He'd received a short text from Waheeda informing him of the poll date in Dhoonpur. 'The process starts,' she'd written. 'Nominations, candidate lists, checks. Will explain another time.' That was one of her oft-used phrases. 'Will explain later.' Meaning when she saw him, face to face. But when was that going to be?

'Chanda, there are a couple of things I want you to organise.'

She raised her pad and pencil. A soft jingling of the bangles. 'I was looking into a new venture of my own in U.P.' he said. 'But it's stalled. Because of the damn elections. Bunch of clowns in Parliament. What do you think?'

'Hmm, yes, Mr Monish.' Noncommittal as ever.

'I want to order the local newspapers from these ten towns.'

He lifted his own notepad to read the names. She wrote down the nine random constituencies in U.P. he'd picked in addition to Dhoonpur. 'How do you think Mayawati will do?' he asked.

She shrugged. 'I don't know, sir. I don't follow the politics there so closely. The papers you want…in what language?'

'Ah. Any Hindi or English local paper.'

'*You* will read all of these, Mr Monish? Do you want to assign someone to—?'

'No, Chanda. This is confidential. I'll flick through them when I have time. Could you put them in a plastic bag daily — opaque bag—and stack them there,' he pointed under his desk.

'There's one more thing,' he said. 'Even more confidential. Please sit down.'

A worried look crossed her face. 'I'm fine standing, sir.'

He jotted some arbitrary numbers on his notepad. He cleared his throat. 'The reason I'm asking you to sit down is because I have a favour to ask of you. I find it strange to ask you when you're standing.'

She pulled out the chair and seated herself. 'Please ask, Mr Monish.'

'I am going to entrust a task to you, Chanda. For next Sunday. No one must know. I must have your word.'

•

ON ENTERING GAURAV'S drawing room he saw that Kriti was already there, resplendent in a green silk dress, ensconced in a group. Her eyes slid away from him, but she'd noticed his arrival. She turned her back. So, she was determined to cold-shoulder him. He spouted his initial greetings and began a slow orbit of the room, knowing their mutual friends were watching him with amusement. Still, he felt confident enough to go up to her.

'How are you?' he asked. She turned her enormous eyes on him, but didn't answer.

A woman standing beside her said, 'Monish, your *best* friend is not speaking to you. What happened? What *did* you do?' He couldn't miss the schadenfreude in her tone.

His lips pressed into a thin line and he gave Kriti a curt nod. 'We'll talk later.'

We've got to talk, is what he meant; he hoped she understood. She'd had her public revenge now. She could not have missed the gloating their rift was causing. Really, she should be malleable by the end of this party; he would bet on it.

He looked around for comfort. Diljit was making a bee-line for him, but he'd already pecked her cheek, wished her a happy birthday, handed over a bouquet of flowers, and heard her complaint that Gaurav should have taken her for a holiday to Bali instead of throwing a bash for his mates. A hand-wave from the left corner of the room caught his eye. The Ranjan sisters. The younger one was waving like she was marooned. He went over. When he'd loved them, he'd loved the older one more. Definitely. She was smiling serenely.

'Hello, hello,' he said, 'Thought you two had disappeared.'

'More like you've disappeared; that's what we hear.' Neha, the younger.

Seema, the older, keeping her own counsel, as usual.

'What else do you hear?' he asked. Big mistake. There was an uncomfortable silence.

He turned to look into Seema's eyes. 'How's your love life?' She smiled again. It was a coded, happy smile.

'None of your business,' chipped in Neha, her tone happy, too.

So, they were going out with someone. Who? He looked around the room. Someone there, someone he knew? He would hear soon enough if he began socialising again.

They were both in artfully torn jeans and white shirts. Neha wore a long strand of blue beads and Seema a jade pendant. Both wore their long hair in a single plait down the back. Monish had gone out with them two years ago. He reckoned they'd had a blissful six months. But how were they ever going to get married if they came as a package? Didn't every woman want to get married?

'Marriage on the cards?' A mean question, but they deserved it for hiding some rumour from him.

Neha looked at the floor. A loud cackle from Seema. 'Who'll marry theatre actresses?' she asked rhetorically. 'Only theatre directors. And who wants *them*.'

'What's up with you?' Neha raised her head, smiling at her sister's retort. 'How's *your* love life?'

He made a sad face. 'Not so good. Empty...pretty much...'

'Oh!' The two of them looked at him in bewilderment and dismay.

'And on top of that, you've lost Kriti!' Neha couldn't stop her exclamation. 'What happened?'

He touched them on the shoulders to draw them into a little circle. 'She's been sulking over a silly little incident. You two can help me tonight...unless you're leaving later with someone here.'

That cackle from Seema again. 'No one *here*,' she said.

•

THE HOUR GREW late, the drink stopped flowing, the dinner plates were cleared away, the guests dwindled, but Monish hung on, dispatching the Ranjan sisters to keep Kriti chatting. Diljit was dancing, although Gaurav had pointedly switched the music off before he stationed himself at the front door to see off his guests. Eventually Diljit realised and she stopped dancing mid-twist. She stumbled. Monish got to her and looped his arm in hers to keep her from falling over. Don't fall on your face at your own party, Diljit.

'Monny.' She slid her hand on his shirt front. 'Look at these.' She touched her ear where floral diamond earrings gleamed.

'New?' he asked. And then quickly remembered the right thing to say. 'Very pretty.'

'My birthday present from my hubby.'

'Very, very…uh…pretty.' He needed a better vocab for diamond earrings. Good Lord.

What had she been complaining about before?

But here she went again. 'We should have gone to Bali. Like we did for our honeymoon.'

Naïve thing. It's Bali or diamonds, he wanted to tell her. Not both, darling. Especially from Gaurav, who wants neither Bali, nor diamonds, but a Home Loan from the bank.

Diljit reached up to remove his spectacles and try them on. 'Your eyesight is really bad, Monny,' she cooed, peering wildly at the empty room through his glasses.

Gaurav appeared. He grasped the specs off her face and handed them to Monish, who unhooked his arm from Diljit's.

'It was so good that you came. Glad you stayed till the end.' Gaurav put an arm around his wife's waist and pulled her to him. 'Could you do me a great favour and drop off the sisters? I know it's in the opposite direction to you—'

'It's not a problem. I meant to, anyway.'

'I'll take Kriti back—'

'No.' Monish spoke sharply. 'It makes no sense when she's in the same building as me. I'll give her a lift—'

Gaurav looked past Monish at the wall. 'Will Kriti go with—'

'Of course. I'll tell her now.'

He went up to the three girls. 'Gaurav has to take Diljit up, as you can see. I've been asked to drop you off.' He looked at the sisters, then at Kriti.

She said nothing. The sisters moved to the door, bringing her with them. Kriti sat in the front and the sisters squeezed in at the back of his sports car. At this hour, motoring was a pleasure. The roads were empty, the air smelt cool and calm, and a half-moon graciously beamed down on them. It seemed to Monish that even the thieves and the roadside dwellers were quiescent, lulled by a tranquil pre-dawn.

Neha and Seema giggled when they disembarked, jumping out of the back, all flailing legs and arms. They leaned in to smooch him, teasingly, now that they were home. Neha spoke across him: 'Goodnight, Kriti dear. Are you going to be silent all the way home?'

And to Monish, 'Enjoy your ride with Miss Frosty.'

He waited until the lights came on at their first floor flat and Seema opened the window to give him the thumbs up. They were safe. He drove home.

•

BACK AT THEIR building, he put his foot in Kriti's door. 'Let me in. We must talk.'

He stepped into her front room. An orange-shaded lamp was aglow in a corner, casting a soft light on her sofa of square purple cushions.

'I really don't have much to say to you.' She scowled.

He stood by the cane rocking chair, his favourite seat in her home. 'It's a new year, Kriti. Let me explain and maybe you can forgive and forget. That evening I was in a really foul mood, I just couldn't deal with anybody and when you turned up with what's-his-name…'

'You don't even know Vivek,' she spat. 'Why do you have a problem with him?'

'I don't. You know that. Bring him up for dinner one evening. If he's still on the scene.'

Unexpectedly, she was tearful. Oh dear. Wrong thing to say. Idiot.

'I don't understand how you could be so cold, like you were that night…' She shook her head. 'How *could* you treat me like that after all the times you've told me to come up to you whenever I want, whatever I need…We were *friends*. Real friends.' Her tears dropped down to her zigzag rug, but he didn't touch her. He was afraid she'd push him away before he'd restored their relationship.

He spread his hands out in a helpless gesture. 'I know it was unforgivable. I'm so sorry, Kriti. I'm sorry…'

'But *why*?' Angry again. 'There was a woman hiding in your bedroom—you should have just said. I mean, I'm hardly going to run in there to claw at her, am I? What do you take me for?'

'No, no woman,' Monish said hurriedly, and received a strange look from her.

'I know it's no excuse at all,' he said slowly, 'but you have to believe me. I was in a really low mood; I'd had an exceedingly shitty day…' *If only I could tell you the truth.*

Kriti blinked a few times. 'Your dad hassling you?' she asked.

Monish nodded glumly. 'Mom, too, now. All I need is Fat Prat to start on me.'

She sighed. 'Okay. Good night.' She looked outwards towards her balcony, dismissing him.

He gazed at the wide, low neck of her dress, the smooth stretch of her creamy skin from her ear down across her shoulder to the tops of her small breasts.

He held out his hand. 'Friends?'

She clasped his hand lightly, but didn't look too convinced, her palm cool against his.

'Good night,' she repeated.

'Kriti, you know you can come up to me any time. I will never turn you away again, whatever is going on with me. I promise.'

He thought: I hope you don't need me when Waheeda is with me, because then I'll be in an impossible situation. But what are the chances?

EIGHTEEN

January 1998

OUT ON THE veranda Waheeda chopped peeled apples into small pieces. She separated a portion for herself onto a smaller plate, liberally sprinkling it with *chaat masala*. She stacked fresh custard-apples in a bowl, handling the fragile fruit with delicacy, and brought out spoons and plates from the kitchen. Relaxing in her wicker chair, she thought how comforting the sun was in its winter-afternoon weakness. It shone like a benediction onto her arms and onto the silky heads of Hira and her friend, who were kicking a football on the lawn. Ammi was watching the children from the kitchen window. How things had changed. Waheeda had never kicked a ball in her life! She used to play French Cricket with her friends.

Hira's friend was showing off with the ball, spinning it on the toe of her trainers.

She smote it with the side of her foot so that Hira had to run diagonally to reach it before it went into the flower beds. Hira kicked back hard and the ball flew towards the veranda. Waheeda raised an arm in involuntary self-defence. The ball hit a chair and bounced down. Hira's friend ran to retrieve it.

'Do you want to stop now and have some fruit?' Waheeda offered, but the girl shook her head. Hira's expression changed to one of discomfiture, an expression Waheeda remembered well from her own childhood. She turned to see Ammi behind her, about to rebuke Hira. 'She knows,' Waheeda said quickly. 'She knows she kicked too hard for playing about on this lawn. She won't do it again.'

She offered Ammi a bite from her plate. 'I like apples without *chaat masala*,' Ammi said and before Waheeda could proffer the other plate she returned to the kitchen. Waheeda ate the small plateful of fruit, reminiscing in episodic scenes about her own childhood. Hira was being brought up the way Waheeda had been: diplomatic, knowing what to say to whom, knowing the appropriate behaviour and dress code for each occasion, knowing that *tehzeeb*, good manners, were important. Waheeda wondered if Hira would feel the need to break out of here; out of Nulkazim; out of Uttar Pradesh. Out of India? If Hira was anything like her parents she would rebel. But nicely. Courteously.

She laughed at that. She would tell Monish about the football. It made her sad that she couldn't tell Nafis. Hira would chat to him and fill him in on her life, but Waheeda had lost the knack of having a normal conversation with him. He only ever spoke to her to voice his displeasure over something or the other. He'd called this morning knowing she had a day off from campaigning. He'd said: 'Why do you need to be in this election? Why do you want to join the low life?'

She'd replied: 'Should we leave it to the 'low life' to rule us? Should a thinking person just carp about politicians but not step up to do something themselves? I've told you before and I'll tell you one more time: I want to provide education for girls, in all the districts in the state and at every level.'

Nafis snorted. 'You've got your charitable foundation. Use that platform for everything you need to do. Don't give me a rigmarole about politics.'

'A charity has less power. A charity has to negotiate with the local government. A charity can't provide the other things that are required to make education feasible for the older girls. I keep telling you, Nafis, and anyone who'll listen. Toilets are needed. Regulations are needed. Laws have to be enacted. You can't do that from the outside.'

Nafis replied in a different voice. 'Be careful. I've spoken to Shakeel. He should double your security.'

'Oh.' She didn't know what to think. He was frightened for her. He wanted to frighten her. Didn't he know she was secretly panicky? 'What did Shakeel say?' she asked. 'Have you spoken to Abba?'

'No, I haven't spoken to your Abba,' he said wearily. 'And I'm not going to. Shakeel tells me everyone knows what they are doing.'

'Will you take Hira away from here before the voting day?' she requested before he hung up on her. 'I don't want her to see the…well, when the results come in…it'll be mayhem… it's better that she's away with you in an apolitical space.'

•

CONSTANT HONKING ERUPTED on the main road. Monish stood from his desk to go to the window. An accident? A traffic jam, more snarled-up than usual? He opened the light-blue vertical louvres, looking down through the gaps. An open vehicle with loudspeakers attached left, right, and centre-front, followed by a fleet of cars and mini-vans. Garlanded men in the open-top, waving, giving the victory sign, folding their hands in a demure *Namaste* whenever they spotted a lady looking at them. A Delhi politician on the campaign trail. Blaring his message; disrupting the traffic. Monish could only hear the horns and not the recorded slogans being spewed via the amplifiers.

He lifted his glasses to rub at his eyes. Just looking at the smog pressing into the glass of his fifth floor window made him feel ill. Was it better up on the eighth floor where Dad's office was? And Pratish? Three years younger, but given an office on the sixth floor, one floor above Monish. His Dad probably had wanted to see him kick up a fuss; show how invested he was in his status as first-born son; but Monish had contrarily refused to protest. He'd fumed, but not to Dad or the Prat. Had he been vociferous he might be sitting pretty on the seventh floor.

He returned to his desk, his eyes smarting. This election had caught people unawares. Fewer candidates were in contest than at the last election, where there'd been a normal lead-in, and time to contemplate and prepare. Only half as many nominations had been received than at the previous election. Still the statistics were boggling: in the contest there were seven national parties, thirty state parties, another 139 small local parties (like NPF) and a handful of independents. Six hundred million people were eligible to vote. He'd been checking the goings-on in Dhoonpur, which was one of sixty-seven constituencies in U.P. Twelve candidates were in the fray there. Waheeda was the only woman. Overall in the state there seemed to be just thirty-eight women standing, and if the past was any guide, most of them would forfeit their deposit.

He wondered where Waheeda was this afternoon. What mad seething place was she making herself hoarse in? Why did she do it?

His direct line buzzed. It was the Vice President of Retail Decorative Paints. He was an excitable man with fantastic ideas. He launched into a new concept that he was sure would be an absolute hit for the year.

'Tell me.' Monish was intrigued. 'Explain it slowly.'

'Colour Horoscope, sir.' The VP spoke at a less hurried pace. 'It will make people consider paints they hadn't thought of. They are given their lucky colour choices according to their birth dates. We'll mention the system on all the colour charts and they'll come to the store to choose. Or they can phone a branch for advice. It will work well for homes and offices. Everyone wants to invite in Luck. Am also thinking a round colour chart can be produced for distribution, one in which you can rotate one needle for your birth month and another for the date. A spectrum of lucky colours will line up. It might be tricky to produce but—'

Pratish appeared in his doorway with Chanda hovering behind him. He felt a flash of irritation at his brother. He should wait outside until she'd checked Monish was free and wanted to see him and let her usher him in. Why was he gaining all the bad habits of his father? Barging into Monish's office as if it belonged to him?

He nodded at Chanda and motioned to the Prat to take a seat.

'Maybe you should fly to Delhi for a meeting with me?' he suggested to the VP, wrapping the call. 'Let's speak tomorrow. I'll see if we can get the print production people in at the same time, so you can explain the concept to them directly.'

•

'COME TO VISIT, bro?' He felt himself sneering. The only time their paths crossed was in the boardroom on the eight floor or at family gatherings. 'Are you well?' He looked closely at his brother, 'four inches shorter than me, and ten inches wider' as he'd once described him to Waheeda. Pratish's forehead, with its three creases, glistened. Oh, the effort of coming down to Monish's floor!

'We've got to talk,' Pratish said.

'Oh? You've developed an interest in the paint business now? Not happy with your lot?'

Pratish waved his fat little hand impatiently. 'Cut the crap, bro. I'm not here to talk business. I want to get married.'

Laughter spurted out of Monish. 'Fallen in love? So get hitched, if that's what you want. Anyone stopping you?'

Pratish stood and banged his hand on the table. 'Yes, fucking hell. You. You bloody oaf.'

Me, oaf? If me oaf, you lout. Monish hurried across to shut the door to his office.

Pratish shouted again. 'Why don't you just do as you're told?'

'What's the problem?' Monish asked quietly. 'Sit down; let's talk. But don't scream at me or I'll have to make you leave.' Pratish looked unimpressed. 'Or I'll walk out of here myself. That's not going to solve anything is it?'

Pratish pulled at a chair with force and lowered himself into it.

'Are you in love?' Monish couldn't help his curiosity. Which poor woman had agreed to tie herself to this specimen?

'No!' his brother responded abruptly. 'It's time for me to get married. I want it. The parentals will put an ad in the papers and tell the classy families.'

'I see.' Monish deduced that the Prat was broken-hearted. An affair gone wrong. So now he wanted to swan about at viewings and select a girl to marry. Yes, he could totally see that happening and how much Pratish would enjoy the attention. Salve to the cracked heart.

'You have my blessing,' he said. 'Is that what you came for?'

Pratish visibly ground his teeth. 'You fucker. You know the deal. *You* have to get married first. It's tradition. Dad and Ma are set on that. Older son gets married first.'

Monish put his elbows on the desk and his head in his hands. 'Have you tried telling them that there's no *rule*; nobody's going to *die* if the younger son marries first? It's just a tradition; they don't have to follow it.'

'They aren't listening to me. Ma said, "The two of you can get married at the same time. That'll be fine. We can live with that."'

Monish sat up. He looked at the babyish round cheeks of his brother. He raised his hands, palms up. 'What can we do?' It was dawning on him that he would need to deploy the strategy that Waheeda had once come up with for him. He'd hoped the day wouldn't arrive, but now it had, and he hadn't thought of a better plan than hers.

'Do?' Pratish asked. 'You get married. Pick one of your girlfriends. Then get divorced; what do I care?'

'What a nice boy you are.'

'A little tip: don't pick Kriti. She's already divorced, so she's out. Dad can't stand her. He says she brings huge dishonour to her family with her playgirl behaviour. He is not having *her* cross the threshold into his home.'

'Thanks. Thanks for sorting out who I can and can't marry. Much obliged, bro.'

Pratish shot him a look. 'Don't get hoity-toity with me.'

He sounded just like Dad!

Monish leaned forward. He took a deep breath. 'Listen, there's something I have to tell you. I've never told anyone before. There's a reason I can't get married.'

Pratish's body inclined itself over the desk of its own accord. His deep-set eyes gleamed eagerly. His stomach rolled over the top of his trousers.

'Best not to speak here,' Monish said. He needed a bit of time to get his story straight. 'How about one evening? We'll go out for dinner. I'll tell you what's going on with me and we'll resolve your marriage situation. It'll work out; and you'll be married before you know what's hit you!'

'Tonight. Let's have dinner tonight.'

'Well I…' Monish opened his diary. He made a show of checking his PalmPilot. He knew he had nothing planned.

'Call in Chanda,' Pratish said, 'and she can book that place we used to go to as kids.' His face was bright and hopeful.

'You mean the Chinese restaurant.'

'Yup. Call in Chanda—'

'We don't need her to make the reservation—'

'Call her in—'

Oh hell, the bastard wanted to ogle her. Could his day get any worse? Monish pressed the buzzer.

Yellow bangles. He said, 'Could you make a reservation at that Chinese restaurant—'

The Prat butted in, 'Mountain Dragon.'

'…for this evening,' Monish went on, 'eight-thirty.'

'Table for how many, sir?'

'Just two.'

'Two of us,' Pratish said to her in a complacent tone. She looked startled.

'Thanks, that's all,' Monish said quickly, before the Prat could find something more to say to her.

·

WHEN HIS BROTHER had gone he laid his head down on his desk. What had Waheeda said? The power of religion would silence his father, at least temporarily. He remembered that evening: he'd been complaining as usual, and she'd just cut into him. 'Stop moaning, Monish. Take control. If the pressure from your parents is unbearable, then instead of all of you being stubborn and everyone being unhappy all of the time, you should find a solution.'

'Oh, you're so very wise.' He was scathing. 'What do you suggest?'

'You want me to come up with the solution?'

'You're the strategist. Or so you tell me.'

He could tell she was thinking. 'Get Pratish on your side,' she began. 'Tell him you know he wants to get married and have heirs and safeguard the family business. He knows how obstinate you are. Tell him he should persuade your parents to let him go ahead with his life plans, while you continue with your head in the sand.'

'That's what you call a solution?' Monish had been incredulous at first. 'I tell Pratish to birth my competition?'

They were lying down, talking to the ceiling, but at his tone she turned on her side to look at him. Then she'd lain on her back again and gazed upwards. 'You don't mean to block him forever, do you?'

'I hadn't thought about it,' he said slowly. 'I was thinking of my life and what I want. But now that you mention it, the thought of him having progeny and me none will get Pratish going like nothing else. No doubt about it.' He grimaced. 'Mind you, I don't like the thought. But if anyone can get my *baap* off my case, it'll be him, favoured son.'

He sat up then, the shock of having to deal with competing nephews and nieces in the future getting to him. 'Wija, it's not enough. What's my excuse for not marrying?' He placed two pillows behind his back.

Her eyes were half-closed. 'I'm thinking…'

She pulled the sheet over herself and sat up, too.

'You made a pilgrimage to Badrinath when you were twenty,' she said. 'There was something you wanted. You prayed for it there and you vowed in return that if your wish was granted you would not marry for twenty years. *If* you're believed, then you've freed yourself from pestering for another ten years. By which time you may well have changed your mind, you may want children—'

'I won't. I have no intention of changing my mind on this.'

'All right.' She soothed him like he was a heedless brat.

He laughed and kissed her bare shoulder. 'Don't people make vows to be celibate?'

'I would've suggested that, but it's not credible in your case, is it?'

'I think you're right,' he said. 'Dad would rather believe this outlandish tale of why I won't marry than the truth that I can't inflict marriage on myself or anyone else.'

She smiled. 'Tell me if it works.'

He put his hand on her knee. 'I haven't been to Badrinath. But you know where I have visited? Chishti's *dargah* in Ajmer. I've offered a *chadder* there. We all did—the whole group of us who went. Shall I say I made my wish and vow there?'

Waheeda closed her eyes for two seconds. She almost looked like she was praying. She opened her eyes. 'I have a feeling that Badrinath, being a Hindu *char dham* shrine, will hold much more sway for your parents than a Muslim Sufi shrine.'

'I think you're right, Waheeda Rela.'

•

HE LIFTED HIS head from his desk to scribble little notes to himself: 'buy a book on Badrinath so I can talk plausibly about it; tell Pratish that on no account should he share my confession with Dad, because then that's exactly what he'll do; find a date to helicopter to Badrinath for a quick pilgrimage?' Yes, he would, as a thank you to God, when Pratish was safely married.

Chanda knocked on his door and came in. 'I'm leaving for the day, Mr Monish. Is there anything else?'

He looked at his watch. Six o' clock. He was about to say 'Nothing more, go home,' but changed his mind. The way the Prat had regarded her disturbed him. 'Has my brother asked you out? For dinner?'

She bent her neck at once. 'I am not that kind of girl, sir.'

Something niggled. 'Has he asked you out for coffee?'

Her head stayed bent. Damn, why hadn't she told him she was being bothered. 'Have you actually gone for a coffee with him?'

'No, sir, not with Mr Pratish. I am not that kind of—'

'Yes, yes, I know. But you need to tell me if—' He paused. He wasn't sure what he was asking her to tell him. How to make it clear that he just wanted to protect her from unwanted attention? From being taken advantage of in case she was scared to stand up to a boss.

He wanted to knock her parents' heads together. Why hadn't they managed to get her married as yet? She was only a year younger than him, and he was sure she was a virgin. She took pride in being a good girl, fending off advances, but really, her folks needed to get a grip and find her a suitable husband.

'Pratish is getting married soon,' he said instead. That would give her an excuse to decline if he asked her out again.

'Congratulations, sir.' She raised her head. 'He's engaged?'

'Well…not yet. But soon.' As far as Monish was concerned, it could be her scoop for the gossip vine in the office.

'Chanda…' She wasn't looking at him but somewhere to the right of his face. 'If anyone in this building bothers you and I mean *anyone*, don't be shy, don't be intimidated. Tell them to…' to fuck off, 'to get lost. Don't worry about it. But you have to let me know so that I can stand by you and protect you.' *I'm not having my brother get his chubby paws on you.* 'Do you understand what I'm saying?'

She looked into his eyes then. 'Yes, Mr Monish, I understand. Thank you.'

'All right.' He felt his face relax. 'See you tomorrow.'

NINETEEN

WITH THE DISINTERESTED expression he'd cultivated, Monish watched the girl on stage disrobing. He'd become quite the socialite in January, reconnecting with friends. In truth he'd been out six times perhaps, but that was more than he'd been out in the last six months.

He'd had two outings with the Ranjan sisters; their boy-friend lived in Hyderabad, and they were in rehearsals for a new production during the day, so it suited them and him to go to the theatre together—there was always something they wanted to see and he liked their company for dinner and discussion afterwards.

This evening he'd invited over an old school-friend and somehow it had been decided it was a boys' night out; they'd been joined by a few others, and here they were at a striptease. Monish couldn't remember whose bright idea this was. He struggled with that same hollow feeling he'd had on New Year's Eve, like he was going through the motions of the good times he used to have, but enjoying nothing.

The three guys nearest him were staring at the podium, waiting for the next item of clothing to come off. One of them was joining in the hooting that came from other parts of the dim room. They were calling out 'Bra off, take your bra off.' The room was full; eighteen round tables with stained red tablecloths and brash groups of men at each. Some women were scattered among them; he wasn't sure what they were doing there. He caught the glance of two friends sitting across him. He could see they were bored, too. One mouthed '*Chalo?*' indicating the exit with his head. Monish mouthed back, 'Soon.' He gulped his drink and began a mumble of excuses to the man beside him, who paid no attention. He was too busy cheering the slim woman on stage who was prancing back and forth on her shiny high heels. She was nude now, except for a large square watch with a broad suede strap on her right wrist. It looked incongruous and Monish wanted her to remove it. He twisted his lips, amused at himself. Should he stand up and yell 'Take your watch off, watch off'?

He nodded at the two who wanted to leave. The three of them slipped away as a thick-set man wearing only a *lungi* emerged from behind the stage to join the act.

Outside, one of his friends commented, 'We've seen better shows than that, *yaar*, it was pretty hopeless.' The other defended the act: 'They're just warming up now.'

'Anyway,' said the first one, 'let's go to the Kitty Bar.'

'The Kitty Bar?' Monish was astonished. 'It's a—'

He broke off. It was the sleaziest joint and he wouldn't step foot in there.

A slow drunk smile from his friend who patted his arm. 'I know it's a dive but that's where we're heading.'

'You go on,' Monish said. These two were married; they were looking for quick fun this evening; of course they wanted to go where they were unlikely to meet anyone they knew. 'I think I'll call it a night.'

'Already?' One of them elbowed him. 'Got a cat waiting at home? Waiting in your bed?'

'No,' he said. Then he laughed to appear less morose. 'I'm not set up tonight *yaar*, but I'm happy to get an early night.'

They began to walk towards their cars. The drunken one said, 'We hardly see you around these days. Seems like you're often having an early night. Staying in lonely lonely, like. Or pretending to. You know what they're saying about you, right? My wife told me.'

'What?' Monish said, although he wasn't sure he really wanted to know. Every rumour that had ever been repeated to him had been hurtful.

'They're saying you're AC/DC.' He slurred his words, perhaps deliberately. 'Shwings both ways.'

Monish shrugged, they all laughed, he shook their hands in strong tight handshakes and got into his car. They drove off and he was still sitting there, his fingers holding the car key, the key in the ignition. His head throbbed. He'd ordered decent whisky at the strip-show, but in that kind of place they probably cut it with something else, figuring no one had come there to savour their drinks.

AC/DC indeed. Just because he'd not been seen wining and dining a girl for a few months. Dammit, Waheeda. If I date someone too often, Naaz will hear that I have a girlfriend and she'll be reporting that to you double-quick in some secret code. If I limit myself, I'm a 'homo.' Not that I should care, if it wasn't for Dad.

He had no problem with anyone's sexual preferences. People should live and let live. But if that's what was being said about him, AC/DC, and his Dad heard that, he would be in deep shit. Another reason to pass him over for succession in favour of the younger son. Just because Pratish was a fucking *poonch*, smugly tailing Dad around everywhere, morphing into mini-Arun, complete with creased forehead and swagger.

Monish punched the steering wheel till the pain from his bruised knuckles matched the pain in his head. He started the car.

February 1998

IT WAS THE penultimate day of campaigning. For the last week Aseem had decided that Waheeda would travel separately from the campaign bus. She was in a car, sitting in the back, hidden by tinted windows. Habib drove with Shakeel in the front passenger seat. NPF cars hemmed them in, front and behind. Sometimes their little convoy travelled ahead of the campaign bus; other times, half an hour behind.

Today Waheeda would visit three villages for short meetings and finally speak at a rally in a small town at the western edge of the constituency; the last stop before returning home. Shakeel scanned the cloudy sky and turned round: 'Looks like rain; I'm sure that's good luck.'

The straight gaze of his light brown eyes reminded her of Nafis. 'Good luck for the low-life,' she said. She didn't know why she was suddenly upset; upset with them all.

'What?' He was puzzled.

'You don't know? You haven't been referred to as "low-life"? Would he have dared to say that to your father?'

A flash of amusement in Shakeel's eyes. 'Nafis? You're referring to something Nafis said? His bark is worse than his bite, you know.'

'Would he say such a thing to you? Could he have said it to your father?'

'No…but you're his wife…'

'So he can be disrespectful to me? That's OK?'

A small sigh escaped Shakeel. 'He's worried about you, Wija. He told me it's my responsibility to keep the mother of his daughter safe. I don't want to get stuck in this argument between you two, about some throwaway line of his. Keep me out of it, please.'

Easily said, she thought. In reality, Shakeel could not escape family arguments, whether they were between Nafis and her, or Nafis and Aseem. He became embroiled in them because his own career was tied up with Nulkazim Peace Forum.

Had Nafis really said 'mother of my daughter?' That was the reason he wanted her protected? So she could carry out her primary function in life? Get a grip. It was still early in the morning, she would fray by the evening if she lost her cool now.

Shakeel gazed through the windshield once more, first at the pot-holed road ahead, then up at the darkening sky. If she told him he was responsible for the disintegration of her marriage, what would he say? In retrospect she could pinpoint the actual day that her life in Delhi had begun to unravel. Shakeel had come to visit, and it was his requests and his then-fiancée Parveen's demands that had sparked Nafis's dreams of living a secluded life in the hills.

Through how many degrees of separation could blame be spread? Could she really fault these unwitting actors in her story?

The first drops of rain hit the windows, dampening the dust and streaking it downwards.

•

SHE REMEMBERED EVERY detail of the second weekend in September 1993. Setting up a spare bed for Shakeel in Nafis's studio room on that Friday evening. Shakeel going for a short walk in Malviya Nagar before they sat down to dinner. Announcing that his girlfriend Parveen had accepted his marriage proposal. He wanted to fix a date for the wedding so that his brother and sister-in-law could attend; and he needed to talk about some other things, to do with his new life. Waheeda initially had enjoyed dinner that evening—the two brothers joshing about the happy news. Hira, just one, normally wailed through dinner, so that they had to take it in turns to eat, but this evening she was content on Shakeel's lap, pulling at his kurta buttons, and giggling at the unfamiliar faces he was pulling. Waheeda had tried to stop her tugging at his buttons. Shakeel wore a long raw-cotton kurta, with beige and burgundy stripes, the buttons covered in burgundy fabric. 'Don't worry.' He'd waved his hand. 'I never do up these buttons. If Zahira pulls them off, it won't matter.'

Then he'd let fly the arrow. 'Parveen wants to live in a new up-to-date flat.' He'd looked at Nafis, as if expecting trouble. 'We'll have to decide what to do about the house.'

'You're going to follow her?' Nafis asked. 'With your tail wagging? To a modern block. To live in a flat? In another part of Lucknow?'

Shakeel threw a cheeky glance at Waheeda. 'That's what the Rela men do,' he said. 'They follow their wives. Wherever their wives want to live, that's where the Rela men go.' He waved his hand again. 'That's why you live in Delhi, Nafis.'

Nafis grunted.

Waheeda took Hira from Shakeel's lap. 'I'll put her to bed,' she said. 'You two brothers talk.'

When Nafis came into their bedroom later, she asked, 'What will happen to the house?'

He shrugged. She could tell he was unhappy.

'Can they renovate the house?' she suggested. 'You've met Parveen and I haven't; you know what she's like. If she's got artistic vision, perhaps they can turn it into two flats with modern conveniences…one theirs, one ours…'

He snorted. 'That's a lot of hassle. The lady wants not just mod-cons, but to be boss of her own home; who can blame her?'

'If we let them have the house, then she could do what she liked; and it would still be there, still be in the family…'

Nafis glared at her like everything was her fault. 'I'm not giving it away! Do you know how much it's worth? And I think Parveen doesn't want to live in the old Rela home. She wants to start a new life with Shakeel in a new flat. She doesn't care about old things…'

'What's she like?' Nafis had met her a couple of times on his visits to Lucknow.

'She's fine. She's a nice-enough person. It's just Shakeel…'

He gritted his teeth. 'He's besotted. He wants to fulfil his ladylove's every wish.'

Waheeda suppressed a smile. Long back, or at least it felt long back, that's what Shakeel had said about Nafis, when he'd proclaimed to his father that he was marrying Waheeda and moving to Delhi because Waheeda had made it clear that she would live in Delhi and nowhere else.

'Our house will have to be *sold*.' Nafis spoke with heavy emphasis. 'There's no other way.'

'Can we buy him out?'

'Are you crazy? The value of property has shot up. It far outstrips our other investments. We don't have the money to buy him out.' He frowned at her. 'Unless you've been growing a money tree in the back garden from which I can pluck as much cash as I need…. Ha-ha,' he added, mirthlessly.

Waheeda heard Hira crying in her room. She got up from the bed to go to her and bumped into Shakeel in the hall. He'd heard Hira, too. 'Do you want me to hold Zahira for a while?'

'No, it's OK. I'm going to walk with her for a bit and then lie down with her until she sleeps again. This is her regular routine.'

'That's what I heard.' Shakeel's face was full of pity. 'Nafis is tormented by the noise.'

'Is that what he says?' Her face grew tight. He'd been saying that to her daily lately, so she knew it was true. She settled Hira on her left shoulder and took her into the sitting room. She put on the fusion music of Ananda Shankar and paced round the room, rubbing Hira's back. Shakeel had followed her. 'Have you got a diagnosis?' he asked.

Hadn't Nafis filled him in on that bit? 'It's just that she's had ongoing ear infections…from when she was born,' Waheeda said. 'It's a torment for her, too, poor little mite. We can only give her antibiotics or other strong medicines so many times. I've tried alternative suggestions....I've tried everything! I've been to an ENT specialist just recently. He was very reassuring.'

'Oh?'

'Well, he said he's seen other cases like this. As soon as her organs get a little bigger, she'll be a different child. I know it sounds strange, but he said she'll just grow out of this. We have to be a little patient. And I believe him.'

Shakeel nodded. 'That's good. Florrie is very serene with her. It's good you have her to look after Zahira when you're at work.' But she could see him thinking. Perhaps he'd heard more of Nafis's complaints than she knew.

Nafis was at the end of his tether, even though he barely looked after Hira. Lately he'd been shouting at Waheeda as soon as she came in the door in the late afternoon. 'Incessant clamour, do you hear me? Incessant. She's a little thing but do you know I can hear that crying everywhere I go? Even sitting out at the end of the garden. When she starts up, I can't breathe. I can't bear it. The roads are choked in this city, choked with cars, with people, with honking, with hollering. And now at home, we have this. There has to be a room of peace somewhere, I'm telling you, I can't stand it, Wija.' And he'd place his hands over his ears in frustration as she went to take over Hira from Florrie.

•

BLACK CLOUDS ABOVE them, pelting them with driving rain, but already in the distance, the sky was clear in the direction they were heading. Habib and Shakeel were both concentrating on the road conditions. 'Another half hour,' Shakeel said to her.

Waheeda returned to her ruminations. On that Saturday in September the brothers had discussed plans for the wedding and made some tentative decisions about their father's old house. On Sunday Nafis had spoken for the first time about living in Theog. Waheeda pinpointed that as the moment. The beginning of the end.

Shakeel had gone out on an NPF errand in the morning and returned after lunch. He would leave for Lucknow in the evening; he preferred driving late when the roads were quiet. Hira was in a good mood and Waheeda brought a big bouncy ball into the garden for her and spread out a thick picnic mat on the sparse lawn. Shakeel sat down with a cold glass of the *shikanji* that he'd made for all of them. Waheeda went to knock on the window of Nafis's studio to tell him to join them. She was surprised to find that the window was open; Nafis was sitting on the ledge with his legs hanging out and a cigarette in his hand. He was staring moodily at the low wall that separated their garden from their neighbour's. Waheeda and Shakeel had thought he was working on a painting.

Nafis raised his eyebrows at her. She said, 'We're in the garden. Come and join us.' She decided not to mention the cigarette. Was he smoking every day? He wasn't in the habit, as far as she knew. But then, she thought, he wasn't in the habit of weeping either, yet as she'd stepped towards him she'd caught a glisten in the light; she was sure it was wetness on his cheeks.

Hira was bouncing along with the ball and laughing. It was such a glorious sound, her laughter, so rare that whenever she heard Hira laugh, Waheeda would be overcome by relief and happiness and start laughing, too. Shakeel held his arms out to the toddler, cooing, 'Zahira...Zahira...'

Nafis smiled as he sat down by them. Waheeda looked up at the sun. Bless this moment, my family is happy. Her insides shook with sweetness and for some reason, dread.
'I'm wondering what Hira should wear for your wedding,' she said to Shakeel. 'This is so exciting, to get her dressed up for her uncle's wedding. A *ghaghara-choli*...'

'Can we discuss Hira's outfit another time? You don't need

to bore Shakeel with it.' Nafis squinted into the sun. He was wearing the sweater his mother had knitted for him a year or two before she'd died. It was in rough wool, loose-knit, with horizontal black and white stripes. Waheeda had made the mistake of telling him it was the kind of sweater a small-town man would wear to dissuade him from wearing it and now he wore it often, especially at the weekends when she was home.

'We could get an architect.' He addressed Shakeel. 'See if it could be made into a grand property again. With landscaped gardens. Just an idea.'

'Who would live there? Would it be affordable?'

'I would.'

Waheeda couldn't quite believe what Nafis had just said. 'You really want to live in Lucknow?' Shakeel seemed astonished, too.

'What I've realised is that I want to go to somewhere small and peaceful,' Nafis said. 'Somewhere quiet. Where you can appreciate Nature's beauty everyday instead of mankind's mad ingenuity.'

'*Lucknow*? Nature's beauty? Peaceful? *Lucknow*?'

'Not Lucknow, not really. I was thinking more of the kind of places we passed when we went up to Himachal that time, you know the small hamlets, a bit isolated…'

He was shading his eyes. If he hadn't got his hand on his brows, she would have been able to look into his eyes to see what he was thinking. Whatever he was dreaming up, she would have read it in his eyes. What were these sudden shifts of thought? Did he want to live in his father's old house once it was made grand; or did he want to live in a cottage in a hilly hamlet?

'Those sorts of places look good,' she said, 'but it's hard work to survive there.'

'Not if you have a comfortable home to live in. If we sell

our family home and Shakeel and I split the profits, we'll have enough to buy a cottage somewhere special.'

He sounded so sure that it was unsettling. 'Have you got somewhere in mind?' She strove to speak neutrally. How had they segued from Shakeel's wedding plans to bulldozing their own life?

Hira had had enough of the ball and returned to Waheeda's lap for an instant. Waheeda handed her a toy piano that played the tunes of popular nursery rhymes at the press of a button. Hira very deliberately set it down on the grass, then sat herself on the grass and began methodically tugging the fringed corner of the picnic mat. This engrossed her.

Nafis didn't answer and Shakeel stayed diplomatically silent, although he seemed as dazed and dismayed as she was by the turn the conversation had taken.

'Are you serious?' she asked the husband-stranger sitting next to her with his eyes carefully shaded. 'You want to live in some godforsaken village?'

Nafis removed his hand from his eyes. 'I'm going mad.' He stated this matter-of-factly.

He stood up and Hira began to sob at once, her face puckering. He ignored her, speaking louder so that Waheeda could hear him. 'All of this…I can't bear it.' He swept his arms from side-to-side. Hira's arms began to beat on the ground and she cried harder. He let out a deep sigh and then bent to pick her up, uttering '*Shh… shh…*'

Waheeda held out her arms. 'Give her to me,' she said grimly.

•

IT WAS SPITTING down dirty drops when they pulled up at the first village. Waheeda covered her head with her sari pallu. She didn't mind getting wet but she hated her feet becoming damp and muddy. Today they would. She stepped out into a puddle and her toes curled into the insteps of her black leather sandals. She was escorted to the home of their local representative. He seemed to have the respect of many people. Why had he turned against those he'd supported in the past? Why had he agreed to throw his weight behind NPF? Annoyance with his previous alliance? Had he not been rewarded appropriately? Or could he tell which way the wind was blowing? She hoped it was the latter.

Nita, who had been travelling in the car behind, joined her. A group of women were awaiting her speech in the front room of the man's home. Shakeel and Habib stayed outside, standing by the door. She told the women about her plans for toilets in every village in Dhoonpur and for ensuring education was available to all girls. In this particular vicinity, she could tell they were not impressed. 'Running water in my home would be better,' one woman said as others around her nodded.

'It's on the list, too,' Waheeda said. Of course it was. Who wouldn't want running water all day? And fridges. And ceiling fans. And cell phones. And all those things they could see on the TV nowadays. There was a TV in their local representative's home. He probably had his own generator. And his own well for water. Perhaps he let families from the village gather here to watch the popular shows. Those whom he allowed.

Later she would walk through some of the outer lanes of the village and greet the half-hidden people who weren't considered worthy enough to mix with the mainstream.

'Education has done nothing for me,' one woman said. Waheeda wondered if she'd somehow been bribed along to this meeting and was determined to be difficult, despite taking whatever had been offered. 'I still have to work in the fields, raise my children, cook, serve my in-laws, and pamper my husband.'

But you know your rights,' Waheeda pointed out. 'Because you have an education you know what's best for your children. You know your options.'

'I don't have any,' the woman said simply. Her sari was tied short, the hem falling just above her ankles. Her black hair was scraped back in a severe bun. It was hard to tell her age. She could be twenty or thirty; there was no youthfulness left in her.

'It's because you're educated you know that, too.' Waheeda spoke gently, with a slight smile to hide her own sadness at this woman's predicament and to remove any sting from her words. 'If you want to talk to me separately,' she offered, 'if there's any particular problem that I can help with, come to me later. Please. I would like to help you if I can.' She raised her chin at Nita, a signal to make a note about the woman.

•

ON THE WAY to the second village of the day, she studied the file she'd requested from Shakeel. A map of the constituency and a list of all 638 villages, with her past excursions noted. There were zones shaded out that she could see she had never visited. 'Shakeel,' she said. 'I know Umair-ji crossed out these zones.' She lifted the folder and pointed at them. 'But shouldn't I visit one or two villages in this area?'

'You know why he crossed them out.'

'Yes, but there might be one or two places that may not be so hostile…have *you* been? Have you seen?'

'Yes.'

'And what do you think?' she persisted. 'Shouldn't we try?'

'No. Hostile is not the word. WW Singh's henchmen have a *kabza* on those villages. Not only is it dangerous, but there's absolutely no point.'

'What about the women there? And surely some constituents must feel differently? Not everyone can blindly support the thugs. They must have made so many enemies with their arrogant conduct.'

'When WW's out of the picture, and the two rival successors are sabotaging each other, that's when you should appear there. You might win some people over. Now? No way.'

Waheeda set down the folder as she sat back in her seat. It was all so rushed this time. Jehangir Wazan had remained true to his word at least. No candidate from his party in Dhoonpur. But there were still eleven other candidates ranged against her, of which only three were serious contenders. Did anyone think of her as a heavyweight challenger? She doubted it.

•

THAT EVENING AS they drove back to Nulkazim the sky was dazzling: pink, amber, orange. The horizon was vast over the just-sown *arhar* fields. She rolled up the window—the breeze had abruptly turned chilly as the sun went down. She lifted a newspaper again, but after peering at a few lines, she set it down and pushed them all aside. There was a pile of local papers on the seat beside her. She'd skimmed most of them earlier, pausing to read the paragraphs where she was mentioned. Someone had kindly circled the relevant bits for her.

How had she ever believed what was written in the papers? These local dailies were full of bullshit. A couple of them were owned by supporters of the two main parties, so their agenda was understandable. Knock down and slander all the candidates, bar one. The truth was but a small rock to be kicked aside. Some papers were offshoots of the national papers and although they tried to be fair, they reported the stories that were run in the other broadsheets. They didn't point out these stories were false.

According to the papers: Waheeda was a dreadful wife who had abandoned her husband and child so that she could take over the mantle from her dead brothers. Nafis and little Zahira lived in the hills, while uncaring Waheeda resided in Nulkazim with her over-ambitious father. Sometimes she forced her husband and child to make an appearance on the campaign trail. She was unfaithful to her husband. (Naturally.) Moreover, the toilet scheme was just a whitewash. No one used the actual toilets that had been built. The success of the scheme was exaggerated. Not only that, setting up the Golden Oriole charity was the cover Waheeda used for visiting her lovers. They seemed to be a diverse lot, spread all across the state. This, apparently, from a 'source' within her own party.

How could the papers even print this stuff? But they did. Umair had warned her early on to build a tough carapace. At the start of the election he'd said, 'Now the knives will really come out.' So they had.

The local newspapers in Nulkazim were more sympathetic. They all had connections to Aseem, and he could point out discrepancies which would be fairly efficiently corrected. These papers had their own slant. She was a 'daughter of Nulkazim.' They pointed out that she'd abandoned the fight in Patharghat, although at the last election that was where NPF had come second. That was the only place NPF had fielded a candidate at the last election. It was her best chance. 'Shuns Patharghat' had been an early headline. Long articles on the fact that she'd chosen Dhoonpur to stand. It was much further away. A reasonably kind analysis that perhaps she was running scared, and that it was better to fight it out in a new location.

Which would be the truth. She had no desire to be killed.

TWENTY

MONISH TOSSED THE newspapers he didn't want to read into a pile behind his chair. He retrieved an opaque plastic bag from a drawer, shoved in the discarded papers and left the bag under the grey bin by his desk. He placed the newspapers that he did want to peruse—those from Dhoonpur and Nulkazim—in another plastic bag and slid it into his soft leather briefcase.

He began to tidy his desk-top; he liked to leave it neat for the next day, all the files in the order he wanted to tackle them. Everything in straight lines if possible. His office door was shut but he heard it open, and looked up. There had been no knock. His father strode in, Chanda mousing behind him.

'Dad.' He stood up and nodded at Chanda who melted away, shutting the door behind her.

Arun Selvani came round to Monish's side of the desk. He took a moment to look around the office. Then he did that nasty thing, where he looked right through your clothes, as if he was appraising the naked person beneath, so he could see how far he could push, how tough or vulnerable the exposed person was.

'Dad?'

'Yes?'

'You want something?'

'I came to ask you that.'

'What?' Monish frowned at his father, who bounced on

the balls of his feet and swayed forward towards Monish.

'If I told you I would give you anything you wanted, anything that was in my power to give, what would you wish for?'

Monish gaped at him. He couldn't help it. 'What would *I* ask *you* for?'

'Yes, son.'

'The farmhouse.' Monish knew what he coveted, what he wanted to be solely his. The place that he liked spending time in, by himself. 'I'd want that in my name.'

Arun Selvani repeated 'The *farmhouse*?' in a tone of intense surprise. He pulled up a chair so that he was sitting opposite Monish. 'Well, well…'

He bounced once on the chair and leaned forward. 'So this is your chance. Pratish is looking for a bride. If you also decide to get married now, at the same time, I'll give you the farmhouse. I'll put it in your name.'

Monish's jaw dropped again. He remembered the conversation he'd had with his mother at lunch the day before. She'd told him about the moment that Arun Selvani had trotted forth the Badrinath pilgrimage story for public consumption. It had happened at the Mathur family's house where Pratish and the parents were meeting one of the Mathur daughters.

'Dad,' he spoke slowly, 'I can't get married. You know I made a vow…'

'Everyone has their price, boy, and I've just found out yours.'

'I made a pledge to God. You can't bribe God. Or can you? Can Arun Selvani hand God a sweetener; a kickback for breaking the statute?'

His father's eyes bored into his face. 'You don't build a conglomerate like this,'—he twirled his small chubby hands around him, the rings on his two little fingers catching Monish's eye—'by being a fool.'

'Meaning?' Monish looked at his father's rings—gemstones set solidly in gold. The right hand still sported an emerald, but the coral that his father had worn on his left hand had been replaced by a bulbous white pearl.

'Meaning this, sonny boy; I might know God better than you do. Let me get this straight: you trek to Badrinath to make some special wish for your juvenile heart. You promise Vishnu-ji that if you get your wish, you won't marry for twenty years. So what did the deity do then, eh? Did the deity bend down to you and whisper in your ear: "Monny boy, I'll take care of your wish. I'll accept your pledge. Off you go back to the plains and screw all the chicks you want." Because that's what you've been doing the last eight years.' His small eyes tapered as he glowered at Monish.

·

MONISH GAZED AT the geometry of his parquet floor. He thought back to the lunch with his mother the previous day. She'd said that Dad had mentioned the Badrinath pilgrimage and vow in irritation, because he was getting upset at the line of questioning taken by Mr Mathur. Mr Mathur had two daughters and he was keen to know if Monish was also looking for a bride. When Pratish and one daughter had been escorted to the dining room and left alone so they could chat a bit to each other, Mr Mathur had launched into a dialogue about Monish. Arun had told him tersely that Monish was not in the market; he wasn't going to get married. As yet.

'That child does his own thing, doesn't he?' Mr Mathur asked. Ma and Dad had nodded assent.

'I heard he barely comes home. Everything separate...'

'Not at work,' Arun said. 'We're a family-owned firm. And we all work together. We see each other every day.'

'He's still your heir, Arun? As the older son?'

Dad had clarified. 'Both my sons are equal heirs. I treat them equally.'

'But he's the older one, so why won't he marry first, like

he should?' Mr Mathur seemed to have his own agenda, according to Ma. 'You should let him choose his own type of bride,' he'd said. 'If you like, we can introduce him to our other daughter; she's the independent sort, too; they can see if they get along or not.'

Ma had waded in. 'It's not about this or that type of girl. He's free to choose his own wife. He will *not* marry…or not yet, anyhow.'

'Something wrong with him?' Mr Mathur asked slyly. 'He has a health problem?'

'He's very healthy,' she responded.

'Something abnormal about him?' Mr Mathur persisted.

'He's perfectly normal,' Ma snapped.

'Listen, because you're a close friend, I can tell you this in confidence,' Dad had said, unable to contain himself. 'Only our family knows. Monish, when he was young and perhaps foolish, made a pilgrimage to Badrinath…'

•

'LAST CHANCE,' DAD said, breaking into his reverie. 'If you want the farmhouse…'

Monish swivelled in his chair towards the louvered window, his back to his father. He was tempted. He could marry someone that his mother selected for him; all he had to do was give the nod. She would choose well. Or like Pratish was doing, he could pick someone he found immensely fanciable. Someone with whom he would actually enjoy a long honeymoon period. When the Mehrauli farmhouse and its surrounding acres belonged to him, legally so, he could ignore his wife. Or do a deal with her so that they lived separately. She would have money to console her.

He swivelled back to face his father. 'No.'

He couldn't do it. He couldn't put himself through that misery and guilt.

Arun was out of the chair. For a heavy rotund man, he was

quick with his movements. He bounced twice on the balls of his feet. He came to stand by Monish. 'Just one question.'

'Yes?' Monish was wary.

'What did you wish for? When you were twenty? What drove you to go there?'

Monish couldn't look him in the eyes. He put his fingers on the edge of his desk and checked his nails. He needed to trim them; he must remember when he got home.

'That's too personal, Dad. I can't tell you.'

•

WHEN HIS FATHER had left, Monish swivelled in his chair to face the wall to his right. There was a large map tacked on the wall, marked with the offices, retail stores, and manufacturing units of his paint business. Monish wasn't focusing on the map. His mother had asked him the same question yesterday.

After lunch they'd settled themselves in the sitting room that opened out into a section of the back garden. They often sat there for coffee together. But even before he'd had a sip from his cup, she'd begun probing. '*Beta*, what did you wish for?'

'Huh?'

'At Badrinath?'

Monish stared down at the fine-grained wood of her antique coffee table.

This is a sham, Ma, you and I both know it. I had everything I could want at twenty. At least as far as my youthful heart knew. I was making out with the most beautiful girl in the world, I had all the money I needed. Why in heck would I need to go to Badrinath with a begging bowl? Even Pratish was not a thorn in my side; he was still at school, and the days that I came into the office for work experience were happy days. Then.

How is it that you prefer to believe this lie about a pilgrimage and a pledge? What is so distressing about the simple truth that I don't want to go down the route of marriage and kids? You didn't do anything wrong in bringing me up, or put me off holy matrimony. Some people decide what suits them is a solo life. Look at Ratan Tata. He's over fifty, and single. For me, other people can be like clutter. If you're not committed, if you've not made promises, or endured religious ceremonies tying you together, you can move on and clear your life of unwanted stuff.

He was unable to answer her or speak. A sham, Ma, a sham.

It was amazing that Waheeda, who didn't know his parents, had the psychological measure of them. They were worried now that they had somehow failed him and been unaware that he was a sad-sack twenty-year-old. They wanted to believe this fiction about Badrinath. Only Pratish had taken him at face value, uncaring if it was true or false. He had cottoned on immediately that he could get on with his life, without having to hear about Monish this and Monish that.

After a few minutes of silence his mother had looked out towards her precious yellow roses and taken a sip of her coffee. He'd felt able to drink his, too. The tall old-rose bushes were in spectacular full bloom, positively toppling with lush blooms.

'Are you happy now, *beta*?' she'd asked eventually.

'Yes, Ma.'

'You have a steady girlfriend?'

That's not quite how he would describe his current relationship. But…keep it simple. 'Yes, Ma.'

'That's good…'

He set down his cup. Something was coming.

'I was just thinking, you don't want to harm other people…'

'No,' he agreed.

'If your girlfriend is your age, she may not realise that she's missing her chance to have children, because she's with you. You should not be so selfish. You should not hold back other people.'

'My girlfriend is a strong, autonomous woman. I'm not holding her back in any way, I assure you.'

'It could be too late for her in a few years if she wants to have children—'

'You really need to mind your own business, Ma. But thanks for thinking ahead for my girlfriend. It's not required. She has a child. I'm not holding her back from *anything*.'

He regretted it as soon as he'd said it. He could bite off his tongue and toss it away. He'd stop the tide of his mother's homilies but his remark would lead to something worse—her insatiable curiosity.

'I haven't been to your flat for a long time,' she said.

'Come any time you like. Just let me know.'

'How about Sunday?'

'This Sunday? Fine. Not before noon.'

'I'll come at noon,' she said.

He knew from past experience that she would arrive earlier than she'd said she would. She'd hope to 'accidentally' meet whoever happened to be in his flat that morning. Well, she could come by anytime she liked on Sunday; she would find him on his own.

The bombshell had come when he was leaving to return to the office. 'I'd like to meet her. I really would.'

'Not possible.'

He'd lost the argument. He always found it difficult to hold out against his mother. The only thing he'd managed was to swear her to secrecy.

•

HE SPUN IN his chair, round and round, stopping on the fifth spin, arms on desk, palms pressed together. His mother had taught him to pray. Every night, sitting up in bed, he had to clasp his hands together, bend his neck, and speak to God. He could say anything he liked, aloud or in his head, sing *bhajans*, or speak prayer words he didn't really understand, as long as he always started and ended with giving thanks for everything he had. Because he had so much.

It was a habit that had stayed with him. He gave thanks to God daily, at different times of the day, depending on the day. Usually it was in the morning, when he had his first cup of tea. That hot sweetness in his throat, those moments of sitting by himself at his dining table, contemplating the world; that was often the instant of his private communion with God. Other times it was fifteen minutes later, after the tea had sent him to the bathroom. Pleased with the fact of his bowel movement, pleased that his digestion was working as it should, that his body was whole, his limbs were lithe, his brain was alert, that he was good to go; he would give his thanks, for all of that and everything else.

Occasionally, he spoke to God via the moon. When he sighted the moon his spirits became lighter and if he hadn't yet prayed that day, he would rectify his omission. The moon often mocked him, of course, but it was still a handy messenger to God. The moon liked a chat. It was a coincidence, a good one, that his trusted secretary was named Chanda. It may even be why he trusted her above his other staff.

Monish didn't know for sure, but he guessed that all wealthy people gave thanks for their lot every day. There were enough daily reminders in their path of what life was like if someone up there was not looking out for you. If you had not been born in a well-off household. Or been lucky and made it. He switched off the lights in his office. His communion with God was always personal, but he would be happy to make an exception and visit Badrinath to give thanks and make a large public donation once Pratish was married.

Vishnu, the Preserver of the Universe. Vishnu, the preserver of Monish Selvani's lifestyle. Thank you God.

February 1998

IT WAS A pleasant evening, about twenty-two degrees centigrade, the sun dipping as Waheeda started on the rounds of the
polling booths. The end of polling day in Dhoonpur. She was
in a seven-seater van, with Nita and another woman, Habib
as bodyguard, Umair as her escort, and one local man from
this northern area of the constituency. Aseem was checking
the booths in the western area, Shakeel in the eastern. She'd
been given a list of sixty booths and picked six random ones
to visit. The local man jotted down the locations of the booth
numbers she'd chosen and he began issuing instructions to
the van driver.

Umair's shock of white hair glowed in the gentle red rays
of the sun and the lines on his long face were deeper and
more solemn in this light. 'You will see things you've not seen
before,' he said. 'Don't let it wound you.' What did he mean?
That she was still an innocent in this world?

She knew Aseem and Umair shielded her from anything
they thought too unsavoury. They were aware of her quea-
siness about many aspects of politics although they must've
noticed how her perceptions and sensibilities had shifted in
the last year. When you can't beat them, join them. She had
almost begun to believe in that, almost, but not quite. Could
she really condone murder as a means to destroying her opposition? Never. Would she ever let her second-in-command be
like the thuggish henchmen of the Dhoonpur front-runner?
She didn't think so. Would she turn a blind eye to arrange-
ments that she didn't care to delve further into? Possibly, yes.
The two elders, Aseem and Umair, ran the funding of her
campaign and one of the things they shielded her from was
the worry of the financing and the sources of their income.
She had never been told to be nice to so-and-so because they
were a donor to the party. She had deliberately not asked to

see a donor list, fearing it would put her off her stride if she found people she knew on it and then felt awkward with them instead of behaving normally. That would change one day, but now she was a dark horse in the race, a blind dark horse, that some people were willing to bet on. Any blinkers she'd donned would forcibly come off the day she became a favourite to win.

•

BOOTH 32 WAS a small, ramshackle school building at the end of the lane. A large crowd surrounded it. Their driver stopped at a distance and gestured for them to dismount. Waheeda could tell he'd seen something through his windscreen that made him wary of driving any closer. She stepped down from the bus, one end of her mauve cotton *dupatta* trailing on the steps, sweeping down the dust. She adjusted her *dupatta* over her head and shoulders and peered towards the men now bearing down towards her. Guns. They had what looked like rifles in their hands, she didn't really know anything about what type of gun it could be. Habib was by her side; Umair stepped in front of her. 'We've come to speak to our polling agents,' he called out.

The men halted. One of them came forward. He was very young and smartly dressed in a long-sleeved shirt and trousers. His clothes were crisp, seemingly fresh-ironed. Up close he would smell of expensive cologne. The whiff of manure that surrounded them would not touch him. He reminded her of her brothers. His hands empty, weaponless. He must be the boss of the armed group. He didn't belong in this backwater any more than she did. 'They've gone home.' The youngster with the city-gleam spoke calmly.

'Our agents have left?' Umair's tone mild. 'They've just got up and gone?'

The man shrugged.

'I'd like to speak to the election observers.' Umair's request soft.

'None here.'

'Can we look at the ballot box?'

'No.'

'I just want to inspect it, on behalf of Nulkazim Peace Forum.'

'The candidate is not allowed in.'

'I am not the candidate.'

The man shook his head and his armed posse took a step forward. 'No one is allowed in.'

'All right, we're going.' Umair held up an appeasing hand. His white kurta-pyjama flapped around his lean frame as he retreated.

Waheeda felt intensely foolish as they all climbed back into the van. She hadn't intervened or said a word. She would speak up if the situation was the same at another booth.

This booth had been completely taken over by WW Singh's people. That was an easy guess, his party flag was plastered on placards held by some, although no party symbols were meant to be displayed at polling stations. Her tri-leaf was nowhere in sight.

'They're probably emptying out the ballot box and re-stuffing it with ballots they're filling in themselves,' Umair said. He wrote a note alongside *Booth 32* on the list he held.

He sounded so tired that it shocked her, as much as the scene at the polling station. This was only their first stop. What was she going to think of democracy and its processes in this country at the end of the evening?

She regained her equilibrium at Booth 36, their next stop. NPF polling agents were inside, where they were meant to be, and they seemed to be a general air of cordiality between the agents of all the parties. The ballot box was being guarded by the polling officer-in-charge. Umair and she spoke to their agents who seemed to think that fifty percent of voters in the area had made the effort to show up and that NPF had garnered a reasonable number of votes. They based their assessments on chats they had had, but many people tended to fib on election day, so as not to be pressured or fall out with friends and relatives.

Dusk had fallen when they arrived at Booth 42. Waheeda's insides had been uncomfortably jolted on the bumpy path to what seemed to be just a hut in the distance. Again the driver stopped because of what he'd seen through the windscreen. He pointed, then parked on the side of the path, keeping the engine running. Waheeda twisted her neck to look outside her window but could see nothing other than a thick forest of trees to the right of the van.

Habib and Umair stood up and looked ahead.

Habib said, 'We should reverse. *Reverse*. We should not even step out here. I recognise some of these men. This is a bad lot.'

Waheeda stood up, too, and squinted ahead in the dimness. She couldn't discern any faces but she could see the silhouettes of stocky men and the *lathis* they held.

'We should get out of here—' she heard Habib repeat as she opened the door of the van and stepped down before Umair and Habib could stop her. She walked towards the group slowly, holding her arms stiffly away from her sides, to show she held nothing in her hands. She swallowed down the trepidation that filled her mouth with sour saliva. The men would see she was not a threat; they wouldn't do anything rushed or silly. Three *lathi*-yielding men approached her. A large group massed behind them. She looked beyond; the voting booth was obscured by all those bodies. She couldn't see, what, if anything, was going on there. Umair, hurrying behind her, took her arm. '*Stop.*'

She looked around. Habib was behind her. Strange, shouldn't he move in front? Nita was standing uncertainly by the van's open door. The others remained inside.

Waheeda used Umair's tactic, calling out to the men

striding towards her, 'I've come to inspect the ballot box.'

The three men stepped up to her. The one in the middle addressed Umair. '*Bhaisaab*, take her away. We don't want to hurt a lady.' His face was familiar. The moustache. The shaven head. Waheeda tried to place him, but couldn't at that moment. Wasn't he a distant relative of the Relas?

'It's every party's right to observe at the poll booth,' she insisted. 'If my agents are here I want to speak to them. If they're not here, I'd like to observe the box being taken to the counting station.'

The man ignored her, addressing himself to Umair. 'I don't want to hit you either, *Bhaisaab*. *Aap buzurg ho*.' You're an aged man. 'Take her away. Now. Or it will be too late.'

She looked past them at the men pressing up behind and felt fearful and weak. No women here. Not one. There was one face that caught her attention. It was a bearded man with a broad forehead she'd seen somewhere before, but she couldn't remember where—she was spun around by Umair, and he pulled her to the van. The three men had raised their *lathis* ready to strike if she persisted in talking.

The driver was already turning the van around. When she climbed in, he said, 'Madam, why are you going there, asking for trouble? They will kill us all and have no care. They will throw us in this forest and leave us to rot.' He sounded as scared as she felt.

'They can't do that.' She hoped she appeared brave. She couldn't let them all croak from fear when nothing had happened to them. Yet.

'They can and they will,' Habib said. '*Didi*, we must return to Nulkazim now. It is dark and it will become even more dangerous.'

She looked at Umair. 'We were going to check on a few more polling stations…What do you think, Umair-ji?'

'We've seen enough,' he replied. 'It's worse than I expected.

We tried to choose the safer region of the constituency for you to observe this evening, but perhaps all over Dhoonpur, one party or another has captured as many booths as they can. WW has a big army of people he can mobilise and he's sent his strong-men to places I didn't expect. He must really be feeling the BJP at his heels!' He rubbed at his cheek, thinking. 'We should head home.' He glanced at the driver, 'To Nulkazim. But drop him off first.' He nodded at the local man. He murmured to Waheeda, 'Yes, I'd like to get you home safely.'

Waheeda put her head back on the seat and squeezed shut her eyes. 'Does this mean he'll stuff every single ballot box with his own votes and all 280 polling booths will show him as the clear winner?'

'Don't be disheartened, Waheeda. WW is not in possession of every single booth. So many *netas* have switched allegiance this time; and their people will be briefed to do what they did before; except in favour of the BJP this time. Unlikely though it seems, many polling stations will remain securely independent and the officials will follow due process. But from what we've seen tonight, the Dhoonpur election is rigged one way or another; and the shame is *our* real vote-count will not be known.'

'Some of those people were convicted criminals,' she said. 'That *lathi* front-man who spoke to us, he's from Lucknow, isn't he? His family is known to the Rela family. He's a goon, however politely he may speak. How is he allowed near a polling station?'

Umair responded with something close to a giggle. 'If criminals can stand for election; if most of the candidates are criminals, or would be if their deeds were known; how can you stop felons and delinquents from surrounding them and doing their bidding? The only way to keep the polling booths secure is more policing, but in a system where only money talks or the quid-pro-quo...' he tailed off.

She giggled, too. It must be from fear and from relief, she thought. They'd not been bloodied and broken by someone who had no compunction about smashing them with his *lathi*. She giggled again. She'd been foolish, she could tell from the vibes of the others in the van. They did not want to confront groups intent on capturing polling booths. They'd seen the *lathis* in the dim light and decided it was enough; it was time to turn tail. Her bravado was unlikely to win her friends. But at least they would say she wasn't scared.

She turned to Nita who was in the seat opposite. 'Do you want to choose a cassette? We can all listen to some songs and sing along?'

She knew Nita liked to do that to unwind; well, they would say later that Waheeda had been relaxed enough to sing despite being threatened by *lathis*. Despite realising she had lost this election. Despite realising that she wouldn't even know how many votes she had actually received. She'd been cool as a cucumber. That was what she wanted the whole of NPF to hear. Her stomach was molten, and it turned over with each bump of the van, but as the songs began to play, she sang.

TWENTY-ONE

March 1998

THEY WERE ARRANGED in a semi-circle around the television in the drawing room. Waheeda at one end, the space on the sofa beside her saved for her mother, who flitted in and out of the room, bringing refreshments; three chairs curving in, with Shakeel, Aseem, and Umair occupying them. A small low table by Umair had two phones placed on it, one whose cable extended to the study where the socket was. The other phone was plugged in behind the sofa. Aseem fiddled with his mobile phone, which buzzed regularly in his hand. His grey eyes moved constantly from the screen to the faces of those in the room. Occasionally, he went into his study to speak on his phone, to congratulate or console the candidates who were his acquaintances. The results from the counting of the votes were coming in. At each update their necks craned towards the TV and then rested back. It was nine-thirty in the evening and the results for the constituency of Dhoonpur had not yet been announced. *Any moment now.*

There had been a rout in U.P. by the BJP. The Congress (I) party was pretty much annihilated. They were a close second in many constituencies, but had been definitively pipped at the post. Mayawati's BSP and Mulayam Singh Yadav's SP parties had also not done as well as expected. The rout wasn't confined to the state of U.P., thought Waheeda, it seemed like the entire country had suddenly swung to the right, to the might of Hindutva. The population of the nation was sick of one lot of politicians, so they'd gone over to another lot.

249

That could be read as a hopeful sign. If she held her nerve and stayed in the game, the arc could turn towards her. Yet it also made her despondent that such a divisive party could win over voters in bulk. Their breakthrough strategy had been simple: 'the clever use of caste equation,' as one of their spokesmen put it. 'Analyse the constituency, and field the candidate most likely to appeal to the disaffected.' So, if Party A's nominee was a high-caste person and the constituency included enough non-high-caste voters, then Party B fielded an opposing low-caste person. The votes got divided mainly between the two. What were the little parties to do? Find their own disaffected vote-bloc somehow.

'Dhoonpur.' The announcer read out the outcome in her practised dispassionate tone. Waheeda held fast to her neutral expression, but hardly had the presenter delivered the results than she felt the sting of tears. She excused herself, set her jaw in the bathroom mirror, wiped her eyes, and returned to the drawing room. WW Singh had won, scraped through, seemingly the only Congress nominee in the state to hold his seat. 53,000 votes. Only five thousand votes behind him was the BJP contender. The SP candidate in third place. Followed by Waheeda Rela, Nulkazim Peace Forum, in fourth. She'd garnered nine thousand votes. Her mother was squeezing her hand and her arm; Shakeel's face was animated with pleasure; why? Umair and Aseem were both on the phone but were beaming at her. Out of kindness? She took in a quivering breath.

'It's a good result,' Shakeel said.

'What?'

'Nine thousand unspoiled ballots. For you. There must've been more. It's a good placing.'

She nodded at him, but didn't risk a fake smile. She was still concentrating on keeping her jaw strong and her eyes clear. She only half-noticed the hugs and pats from Aseem. She half-listened to the longish lecture from Umair about how this was a dry run, a useful exercise, a great experience for her, and how they now understood the local strategy of all the parties in Dhoonpur. She didn't feel able to respond to her mother's comforting words or return her little squeezes. She needed to be alone. Alone, alone, alone. A loser.

She stumbled to Hira's room and sat on her bed. Why had she sent her daughter away to be with Nafis? If she was a failure in every which way, at least she could have cuddled her daughter and felt better. A good mother. Not a completely botched-up life. Her daughter loved her and she loved her daughter and that was all that mattered. Hira would have been of comfort to her.

She smoothed Hira's violet eiderdown. Why did I send you away? She knew why. Even though she'd been a seven-year-old child in 1971, Waheeda could still remember the bitter taste of Aseem's electoral defeat. It had permeated the house for days. She remembered the evening of the election results and how very upset he had been. She held the photo of Hira to her chest. 'Just saying goodnight, my baby.' She would go to her own room. Alone. She needed to be alone, where no one would see her.

She knelt on the floor of her room, let her head fall on the bed, and wept.

She ignored the continual burrs of her phone. There was a knock on her door. Ammi. Spoke through the closed door. 'Just passing on messages. Naaz called. Lara called. Nafis called. I told them you didn't want to come to the phone now, but they could contact you on your cell?'

'Yes, OK, Ammi, thank you.'

She drew a thin cotton quilt towards her and used it to soak up her steadily falling tears.

After a while she checked the messages on her phone. She texted Nafis first—she would speak to him in the morning, but could he bring Hira back as soon as possible? Tomorrow, if possible? All was well; she was fine. Absolutely fine. She texted Naaz and Lara: 'thank you for your support and kind messages.' Too formal, but that's all she could muster. (Heaven knew what time it was in Singapore, and how did Lara know the results?) There was a one-word message from Manisha Doctorwala. 'Sorry.' Some minutes later a second one. 'You can tell me what it was like when we catch up.' A hint. She deleted Monish's messages. She would call him in a day or so and fix a date. She removed the double-strapped watch from her wrist, fondled it absent-mindedly, and set it on her bedside table. She wrote brief responses to all the people who were important enough to know her mobile number and who had sent her direct messages. Aseem would be collating the rest; the phones were ringing off the hook as expected and she was glad she was not downstairs.

There was another knock on her door. Ammi again. 'Shakeel's leaving; do you want to speak to him before he goes?'

She washed her face quickly and went to the hall. Thankfully, only Shakeel waited there. He would pretend not to notice her red-rimmed puffy eyes. 'Why aren't you staying?' she asked. 'A bed is made up for you…'

'I know. But I want to return to Lucknow. The roads will be quieter than in the morning…'

'It'll take you three hours to drive there. And you haven't eaten.'

'I'll be fine; Parveen's waiting for me. She'd rather I returned immediately. And now that it's all over…'

'…you can go home and spend time with her.' There were no jubilations to attend at party HQ the next day. 'Of course. I understand.' She didn't attempt a smile. She would crack if she did. But she said sombrely, 'Give Parveen my love. Tell her how grateful I am to her, for her patience. You should take a holiday. The two of you. Don't ask Abba for permission. Just go.'

He laughed. It was a sound she hadn't heard in weeks. How

wound up he must have been. As he said, it was all over, now, for the time being, and he could enjoy himself with his wife.

'*Khuda Hafiz*, Wija.'

'*Khuda Hafiz*, Shakeel.'

She returned to her room. Under a searing hot shower she felt human again, more like herself. She sat on her bed in her white cotton nightgown. She wanted to be alone. She didn't really want to be alone. She wanted one person that she could love and trust to be with her through this night. Instead, she had herself to talk to. Or she could weep some more. She could feel that coming on.

She knew that tomorrow Abba and Umair would want to have in-depth discussions.

She would be ready. She would be stronger than they anticipated. Her trajectory and temperament were different from Aseem's.

•

ASEEM ZAFAR HAD meant to found a fair-minded political party in 1970, one that could represent people like him as well as those who were not well-off. He would battle for those people in his cultural and religious community who were not well-connected and not well-educated. The first year went well. NPF was a small but capable organisation and his ambitions seemed to be on track until he stood for election as an independent candidate in Nulkazim. He came third. He was told by the wise heads of the town that this was a good showing. The Royals always came first. And if there were two erstwhile Royals in the fray against each other, then you couldn't expect anything more than coming third. No one even believed an independent was truly independent. They looked for your affiliations, your back-up team. The Royals, after all, belonged to proper national-sized political parties.

That first election defeat was where Aseem learnt his vital lessons. People who had been your friends became your enemies. He was connected to the Royals, too, but now they viewed him as opposition to be squashed. In addition, money was required to flow like water. Aseem didn't like waste, even for his own ambitions. The machinery of the established national parties would overwhelm anything he could muster. He changed tactics. It was better to wield influence behind the scenes. Do what you said you would do. Build a community that turned to you for favours. Keep up the cosy connection to the royal contenders. Maintain the loyalty and respect of your staff and of the villagers in the areas that spread beyond Nulkazim. He had never put his own head on the block again at election time, but every year his influence had grown manifold. NPF had offices in Delhi, Lucknow and Bareilly. In Nulkazim and all the ten state legislative seats that came under this territory Aseem was involved in the choice of the MLAs. NPF had taken the step of fielding candidates under its own banner for the local elections and been rewarded with three seats in the State Legislative Assembly.

Twenty-five years after his own defeat, he had put up Bir Sultan as candidate for MP in Pattharghat at the last elections. Bir had been declared runner-up. That was close, so close. NPF was gaining ground.

Waheeda wiped away tears. Her brothers—Aseem had been preparing them, too. She slipped under her sheets. She would not duck down. They would find her resilient, ready to move on. If the other parties thought she was finished, they were wrong.

•

MONISH HEARD THE lift judder and stop at the floor below and her soft footfall on the stairs. He opened his door as she came up. He shut the door and let her drop her bag on a chair before he took her in his arms.

'I lost.' Her voice quivered. He held her tighter. 'I'm a laughing stock,' she said into his chest.

He had never heard her sound so sad. 'Stop. Let it go. You're with me now.' He wrapped his long arms around her in a way that left no space between their bodies. Her face was squashed into his chest, her arms were snug around him, his knees were knocking into her thighs, and he felt atoms transfer upwards from her breast to his. If he hadn't felt this himself, he wouldn't have believed such a thing possible. He leant his neck to the side, resting it on the top of her head. Memories, not his, were crowding his mind. He closed his eyes. He didn't believe in the supernatural, but to prove him wrong, something was happening to him. His arms around her trembled. He could see her on the evening of the vote count. Chin strong, neck taut, no words, as she sat with her family circle. Then he saw her in her room, kneeling on the floor, weeping. A glass dome enclosed the two of them as they stood in their tight embrace and in it they were transported to a wild beach. Salt spray in his nostrils; crashing waves, huge, dangerous, and unseen in the dark; their clothes tearing away in the wind. He opened his eyes and looked up. The southern cross in the black sky.

He opened his eyes and looked up. His off-white ceiling. The light diffusing from the cream shades on the central light-fixture. They were just a man and a woman in a claustrophobic flat where all the drapes had been closed. They were a man and a woman who understood each other. They were a man and a woman who spoke the truth to each other. (Mostly). He was a man with the ability to look into this woman's head. He hadn't imagined what had just happened to him. He drew her to the bedroom without asking her if she wanted a drink. It wasn't until two hours later that he asked her if she was thirsty—did she want water or a Limca? Both, she wanted a glass of each and she would come out to the sitting room.

•

He set their drinks down on the side tables. It was now too cold in the living area and he switched off the air conditioner. Its loud hum ceased and he could hear the shower running. He smiled. She needed that shower, she would be sticky all over. He had splashed his semen not just between her legs but across her breasts and on her feet. He had made her say words she didn't normally like to say. 'Tell me that you want me,' he'd demanded.

She'd looked down the length of their bodies, at the space between them as he hovered above. Her nails in the backs of his thighs. 'Can't you see?'

'I need to hear it. Tell me how you want me.'

•

When she'd sat down on the sofa and run her fingers through her wet hair—that was new, too, he hadn't seen her with her hair wet before—he reached to the lower shelf of the side table. Under the ashtray there he'd saved the newspaper clipping of the advertisement for a bride for Pratish. 'My auntie organised this,' he said, handing it to her. 'Your plan is working beautifully.'

He wanted to keep her mind off the campaign and its aftermath for a little bit more. In a while he would ask questions and listen; he was prepared to listen, and to understand, but their mood would become gloomy. It could wait. They had a few more hours before he had to drop her back at Naaz's at three a.m. 'Fat Prat is getting married.'

'So soon?' she blurted. 'To whom?'

'No, no, I mean, not yet. But soon. *Your* plan worked. Look at this advert that my *bua* put in the paper.' He jabbed at it. 'See what you've saved me from?'

He grinned; she knew he wanted to keep things light. But already, for no reason, she was growing heavy-hearted. She skimmed the advertisement that he'd circled with ballpoint: it was in *The Hindustan Times*, one of the longer ones in the

`'Matrimonials' section, in bold and in its own bordered box.

> **Bride sought for a good-looking Hindu boy, 25, who works in his own business and comes from an excellent and well-connected family. The girl must be fair-complexioned, beautiful, slim, convent-educated, sophisticated, well-mannered and from a status family. Families of girls aged 18-22, height 160–170 cms, who meet the requirements are advised to write to the PO box below. Please send full particulars in the first instance, including a photograph of the girl. Please note we are advertising for wider choice only.**

•

See what you've saved me from. It was disingenuous of him to say that. Reading the advert made her suddenly aware that she was dark and not exactly in the beautiful category. She was slim, though, and convent-educated. As for being well-mannered and from a 'status' family, that was a matter of perception. The Zafars hailed from nobility; her real father's family didn't; but not being a Hindu, in this instance she was cancelled out anyway. It was very convenient for Monish to have a lover he didn't have to marry. He could continue on his own way safe from the farcical shenanigans that he disliked. After her time with him was over, he could grow old playing the field, if he wasn't already doing so behind her back. Then one day it would happen to him. He would be fifty, and he would think: I want to settle down. I want a sweet wife and I want my sweet wife to look after a sweet baby. Yes, all that sounds very nice. I'm ready now.

She expected that to happen, but not for two or three decades yet. 'You're staring into space, Wija. It doesn't take that long to read those lines, does it?'

She set down the clipping. The black newsprint had rubbed off on her damp fingers.

'Advertising for wider choice only.' Monish folded the clipping and returned it under the ashtray. 'So he can see if there's some beauty queen heiress he doesn't already know about! *Good looking boy*. That's Pratish they're talking about. You don't think it's hilarious?'

And then he said very quietly, 'No, I can see you don't think it's funny. I've made you sad.' His eyes were suddenly anxious. 'I don't know why…I thought…What have I said to hurt you?'

'Nothing. I was just thinking about the future. I mean, *yours*.'

He sat by her and held her hand. 'Mine?'

'I was thinking that you might regret this one day. Not doing what's expected of you. I don't know if your Kritis and Sashas will be hanging around lonely, too, years from now, or whether they'll be ensconced in families. You might be shut out.'

'Let that day come,' Monish said gently. 'I'll worry about it when it happens.'

He put his arm around her waist and downed a third of his drink, waiting patiently with the upturned glass as the amber liquid slid past the ice he'd filled to the brim of his tumbler.

He set down his glass and jumped to his feet. 'Talking about the future, let me show you something more scenic than a matrimonial ad.' He pulled out a photograph album from the shelf under the CD player. It had a black silk cover decorated with a Chinese medallion. He opened it to show her photographs of a big empty beach and rolling waves. He turned a few pages. More pictures of empty sandy beaches, tangled seaweed and big waves. She spotted dogs and their human companions in the corner of some of the shots. Monish turned another page. Three photos of what seemed to be a plot of land. He pointed to the picture of the ground—dry brown earth under a blue sky—which could have been anywhere. 'Mine,' he said.

'What, this piece of land?'

'Yes.'

'Outside India?'

'Yup. When I've got access to my own money and my freedom, you know, when dad decides to give up some control,' he paused, 'or dies, more like; anyway, this is where I'll build a house. And spend a few months a year. In complete peace.'

'Where is it?' she asked curiously.

'Guess.'

Waheeda felt the old small-town complex come over her. 'You know I've never travelled outside India,' she said in a low voice, trying not to show her embarrassment; trying in fact, not to be embarrassed at all. There was no reason to be. She studied the patch of brown earth and blue sky for a few more seconds, thinking that the key word was *peace*. Was Monish turning into Nafis? Had he always been like this?

'This could be anywhere. Hawaii?' she hazarded.

'Australia,' he said. 'Near Coolum.' He tightened his arm around her. 'I know you don't know where that is. But you can see the area next month if you like.'

'Oh?'

'I'm thinking it's time for a holiday. Away from the heat. There's a quiet hotel in the hilly area there; away from the crowds. Come with me next month.'

'You know I can't.'

'You mean you won't.'

'I can't, Monish. I can't be seen with you. I can't leave my daughter behind. So many reasons...' she shook her head. 'Must we argue? You go. Enjoy yourself.' She forced a smile. 'Surround yourself with pretty women in bikinis. I don't do the bikini thing. What will you do with me there?'

He was silent, looking intently at his three photos of the plot. He shut the album.

'Well, now you know this is a place I like. If you ever need to get away, *with* Hira, with a friend, I'll arrange it for you. You just have to ask me once.'

'I don't need to go anywhere. Thank you, anyway.'

'If you need a break…if you decide that you're *not* going to pursue…'

'But I am. I *am* going to pursue my career in politics.'

•

SHE STOOD AT the sink in his bathroom smoothing out her hair with her fingers. She raised her arm to fasten a section of her hair with a clip. Monish spoke to her, into the mirror. 'Ma wants to meet you. She's invited you for lunch.'

Waheeda turned. Her elbow went into him and the clip dropped to the floor. He bent at once to retrieve it. 'I misheard you,' she said, disbelievingly. 'Please tell me I misheard you.'

He straightened up and set the clip on the vanity surface by the sink. 'It was a mistake. I didn't mean to. She got it out of me. I can explain. She's sworn to secrecy.'

'Did you say your *mother*? Wants to have lunch with *me*? She knows? You told her?'

She pushed him hard and he staggered backwards. He put his hand out to the door-frame for balance and stepped out backwards into the bedroom. She followed, punching his shoulder twice. He fell to sitting on the bed. '*You bloody idiot.*' She sliced at his neck with the side of her palm. 'Do you know what you've done? How could you be so *stupid*?'

'Monish, are you laughing? Are you *laughing*?' He was, his eyes crinkled, his shoulders shaking. She aimed a boxing blow at his ribs, but her own wrist got bent. 'This isn't funny.' She held her hurting wrist in her left hand. Her brow and palms were hot.

'You've lost it,' he said. 'Finally. This is what it's like when you lose control.'

She sat beside him on the mussed-up sheets. 'This isn't the

first time I've lost control.' She was thinking of just two hours ago, on this bed.

'Oh, it is. I always knew there was a tigress lurking in you. I thought she would leap out when…' he turned away, not finishing his sentence, his shoulders shaking.

Had she disappointed him? Well, she didn't care. He was history. 'You have no idea what this means. It's almost like you *want* me to have a heart attack.'

He turned back to her and took both her hands in his. 'Wija, please. Before you get melodramatic, just hear me out. It was a huge mistake. You're right, I'm stupid. But it's all under control.'

'Is it now?' The iciness of her own voice made her feel bad. Oh, for godsakes she was entitled to be mad at him; he was nothing but a fool; why was she feeling sorry about being livid? Because he'd shown her love earlier in the evening, even if neither of them went in for stock phrases? Until a minute ago she'd been sated, comforted, happy, dizzy.

'Let me explain,' he began. 'Ma was bugging me about something and it just slipped out that my girlfriend had a child and then she began to dig—'

She held up her hand to stop him. 'I'm your *girlfriend*? Is that what you said?'

'Do you have a better term?'

'Forget it.' She dropped her hand. 'Go on. I need to know what you've been saying. Although I can't believe this, I just can't—'

'If you could just listen for a few minutes.' He explained how he'd tried to hold off naming her but had given in at his mother's persistence on inviting over his 'steady girlfriend.' He'd tried to tell her it wasn't possible and why. Huge mistake, yes he knew he'd been a dupe. But his mother wouldn't breathe a word to anyone. She understood completely the reasons for secrecy. And he'd come up with a great idea. 'You can put it in your diary as a meeting where Mrs Selvani is picking your brains on women's education. You will find out more about her charity for possible future collaboration. You know Ma runs this pickle factory where she employs widows, young and old, at reasonable wages, so that they are not seen as a burden for their families and are less vulnerable to exploitation.

'I didn't know what her charity was, exactly, but in any case, this is not going to happen. I'm not meeting her. There is no way I'm putting myself in that—'

'She loves me.'

'Who? Your mother? Of course she does.'

'Well, she's the only one who does. In my family. She won't do anything to hurt us. Either of us. She's a sensible woman, she understands the situation. It's just lunch, for chrissakes.'

'No, Monish, no.' Waheeda placed her arms behind her and leant back on her hands. The sheets were soft under her palms. She took a fold in her fingers. A lingering memory at the back of her head of the time earlier in the evening. She looked into his pleading face. Her eyes were drawn to his lips, to the tiny black mark just underneath.

He lay back on the bed, his knees jutting out at the edge, his feet on the floor. She had a feeling he knew that she wanted to kiss him, to take his lower lip in her mouth. She wondered if she'd injured him at all. She checked his neck. His pale skin was red where she'd struck him. She lifted his T-shirt. No obvious damage to his shoulders or ribs. Her own hand throbbed. She stroked the narrow strip of dark hair that ran down from his chest to his belly. He murmured dreamily, 'You know you were asking what you could get me for my birthday…'

She wasn't fooled so easily. 'No.'

'It's something you can do for me. For my birthday. Seriously, it's all I want.'

'You mean it's what your mother wants. I'd like to give a gift to *you*, not her.'

'It will be a very sweet present from you to me. And it will be my present to her. So what? She loves me, you know.'

'You keep saying that. It's not rocket science. She's your mother.' Waheeda straightened up. 'We should get going now.'

'You can kiss me first. If you want to.' And then, when she sat up again, he said, 'So, you'll meet her for lunch, yes? On my birthday?'

'Your birthday is on the thirtieth, isn't it? I can't organise it this month.' *If at all*, she thought.

'It can be a belated gift. That's all right with me. Let's set it up for April.'

'How old will you be this month?' she asked, patting down her hair. 'Remind me.'

He sat up and pulled his T-shirt down. 'Twenty-nine.'

'Hmmn.' She returned to the bathroom mirror to fasten her clip.

He followed her. 'You don't seem surprised.'

'I saw your passport a few months ago. You'd left it on the dining table, when you returned from Singapore, I think. You lied to me about your age when we met.'

'Only at the beginning. That first time. Because…I knew if I didn't say I was thirty you wouldn't come back the next day.'

'What else have you lied to me about, Monish?' She looked into his eyes in the mirror.

'Nothing.'

•

SHE SCANNED THE bedroom to see if she'd left anything lying around. There'd been a split-second hesitation before he'd said 'Nothing.' He must be concealing something from her but she didn't have a clue what it was. She went through to the sitting room. Maybe he was seeing another woman. But he'd told his mother Waheeda was his girlfriend. That was amusing. She had not been anyone's girlfriend since 1985. But what did all this mean? To name her as the steady one. And how could he have been so very stupid?

If she confronted him now, asking whether there was another lie, he would deny it. He'd already responded with 'Nothing.' She watched him put on his disguise. A new firmly-tied turban from Choppy. The previous one had become loose and started slipping off his head, but Monish hadn't known how to re-tie it and nor had she. They'd stuck pins here and there. Obviously, in their enforced break, he'd found an excuse to get another turban off his neighbour.

TWENTY-TWO

March 1998

'THEY WANT OUR support. They want us to join them. To fit under their umbrella.' Aseem's high-ceilinged office was shady and cool after the heat outside, even though the old black ceiling fan revolved at a glacial pace, hardly seeming to ruffle the air. He was filling in Waheeda about the calls he'd had while she was away in Delhi.

'What do we have to offer them?' she mused. 'It's not like we have MPs in the Lok Sabha who they can muster to prop up their numbers.'

The BJP had formed the government in Delhi. Surprisingly, to her, it was the local offices of the BJP and the BSP who had made overtures to NPF. They were already organising themselves for the future, for the next elections, although there were five years to go.

She had been thinking about her education programmes and toilet-building schemes, but she should've been drawing up a strategy for the next elections. Five years away. She would be nearly forty by then.

'You must be a threat to them,' Umair said, 'In Dhoonpur.' He and Aseem sat across from her in the heavy old wooden chairs. She had been allotted the 1970s sofa. 'By asking us to join with them in Nulkazim and Patharghat, they will hope to neutralise you there.'

'What good will it be to us?'

Aseem let Umair answer.

'Depends what we want to achieve. Continue to be a force

in the background? Using our goodwill and people on their behalf and reaping influence in return?' Umair paused, looking down at his bony knuckles. He cracked them on one hand. Then he glanced at Aseem. 'That was the old NPF style.' She could tell he was trying not to rile Aseem. 'Until we fielded Bir Sultan in Patharghat and realised how the time was ripe.' Aseem's face was impassive.

Ripe for what? Waheeda thought. For having ourselves murdered? Or blackmailed, like Bir had been?

She looked at Umair, his shrewd long face familiar to her from childhood, but only recently had she come to respect and admire him. Not just his rhetoric and his style with words, but his ability to negotiate and placate, as required.

He leaned forward. 'Do you want to fight in Dhoonpur, Waheeda?'

'Yes.'

She heard the sigh that escaped from Aseem; she thought it held a note of relief. And pride.

She picked up her pen and notebook from the rectangular coffee table. 'Who did you say called? Because I should set up meetings with them.'

'To say what?' Aseem's grey eyes gleamed both with mischief and wariness.

'The same as they've said to us. Last time, in Dhoonpur, when Jehangir-ji didn't cut into one of our vote blocs, we probably stood a good chance. But we'll never know. We didn't have the manpower, the strength, the machinery, the money to feed and monitor it all. I don't want to be under their umbrella, I want their support for us! It's their turn to do something to get something.'

'I'm not sure this is going to work. I see your point, but—'

'We've got time,' she said. 'Let's start talking and see what happens.'

•

'Not giving up?' She heard the smile in Lara's voice.

'To do what?' Waheeda asked, with a laugh. 'Run to the hills like Nafis and begin to paint?' She held the phone tight. 'Return to my old job? Disrupt Hira's life again? She's happy in the school here.' She lowered her voice. 'More than I ever was.'

'You always liked a challenge,' Lara said dryly.

'When am I going to see you?'

'Ah, about that, in a couple of months I might have a conference in Delhi; and a couple of days free after that; I'll call again with the dates. I was thinking...'

'Yes, what?'

'I would like to meet old and new friends.' She put a naughty emphasis on new, and Waheeda guessed she meant Monish.

'Let's see nearer the time,' she said. She was about to hang up when she heard Lara exclaim, 'Oh, I almost forgot. Fal!'

'Falguni? What about her?'

'You've upset her big time. Apparently you don't call her, or tell her what's going on. You're too big for your boots. You think you're very important. You go and stay with boring Naaz and her boring baby. You don't even *ring* Fal when you're in Delhi.'

'She complained to you?'

'She certainly did. I would call her, Wija. Visit her once in a while. You know what Hyper can be like when she feels snubbed. I'm surprised you're not asking her to bankroll you.'

'What? Lord, No!'

'You can't be scrupulous and a politician.'

'Thanks. You sound just like Nafis.'

'Oh dear. Sorry.' But Waheeda knew Lara was grinning. 'Bye, see you later in the year, I hope.'

April 1998

MONISH ENTERED HIS flat, placed his briefcase on the dining table, switched off the air conditioner that Malti had left running, threw open the balcony doors, removed his shoes and socks, splashed water on his eyes and face, scrubbed his hands and poured himself a drink. He selected a disc to play, the songs from the film 'Aradhana,' a Rajesh Khanna starrer from the year of his birth, 1969. He hadn't seen the movie, but the songs were fabulous.

He was belting out *'Roop Tera Mastana'* in sync with Kishore Kumar when his doorbell rang. Kriti wafted in. 'Hello, stranger,' he said hugging her lightly. 'Thanks for your card.' She'd slipped a birthday card under his door the previous week.

'Hello stranger, you, too. We haven't talked for a while.'

'Can I get you a drink?'

'Whatever you're having. I'm sure it'll be fine Scotch.'

'You won't like this one; it's peaty and smoky. I'll pour you a lowland whisky.'

The heat from outside drizzled into the cool room. The sky was dark grey, coated in smog. He turned down the volume of the music. 'What's up?' he asked, sprawling on an armchair. She'd snuggled herself into the sofa.

'Monish, there's something weird going on and I wondered…I've seen some peculiar things…'

She peered at him. He looked blankly back at her.

'Are you being blackmailed?' Her expression was very earnest.

He sat up straight, alert suddenly. 'Me, blackmailed? No. Why're you asking me this, babe?'

'I've seen a strange man drive off in your car sometimes, in the evening. For some reason your car's been in the back alleyway. And at least twice, recently, this man, a Sird, he's been carrying the same large plastic bag—'

Monish nodded. 'Yes, I know all about it. I gave him my keys. I lent him my car.'

'What's happening?'

How could he explain it to her? His last two dates with Waheeda. 'It's business-related surveillance.' He waved a hand. 'Not for me; for someone else. I can't talk about it.'

Kriti blinked once. She curled her legs under her. She sipped slowly at her whisky, pausing to inhale the aroma each time. She must have got this habit from him, he thought. From when he drank more moderately. She scrunched her eyes up at him. 'You can ask me for help if you need anything,' she said.

'I know.' He whistled in a breath. She wasn't convinced that he was absolutely fine. 'The man is Choppy's friend,' he added, hoping she wouldn't now bring it up with his neighbour. 'I'm just doing him a favour. Don't mention it.' He pressed the air downwards with his palms. 'It's all hush-hush.'

'But why is your car in the alley instead of the carpark?'

Monish tapped his bare foot. He couldn't immediately come up with a plausible reason. He deliberately parked there for the start and end of the evening's manoeuvres. He hadn't wanted people in the building noticing an unfamiliar person enter his car. His driver was the only other person who normally used it. If they saw a stranger, they might think they ought to report it to his driver, or to him, or else, they'd rumble his disguise.

What had Kriti been doing anyway to detect it twice?

'Are you spending your evenings sitting on your balcony?' he asked. That was the only spot from where you could gaze down into the cul-de-sac.

She lowered her eyes. He'd missed the signs. She was in a low spiral again.

'Just smoking,' she said.

'Regularly?' he asked. 'Just smoking, sitting in your balcony? Smoking shit?'

269

'Yup.' She took a big swallow of whisky.

'You should have told me. I would've joined you. We could've been miserable together.'

She looked at him anxiously, and he backpedalled. 'Not that I'm unhappy. I'm ecstatic. Pratish is making wedding plans.' He got up to retrieve the clipping that was still under the ashtray. 'Look at this.' He handed it to her.

She skimmed it and didn't laugh. The expression on her face was unreadable.

'Isn't it funny?' he demanded. 'Fat Prat swanning about... Someone ditched him and he wants to show her he can scoop up another shimmering fish from the same pond...'

'The ad *is* funny,' she conceded slowly, but there was no accompanying smile. She set aside the piece of paper. He balled it up and threw it into a corner. He wouldn't understand women!

'That's another thing I wanted to ask you,' she said. 'Badrinath?'

'Ah, you've heard? About my pilgrimage.'

'When you were twenty.'

'Yes,' he agreed.

'Look at me, Monish. That's the year we went out.'

'I know that, babe.'

'We went to Europe that May and June.'

'I *know* that.'

'When did you go to Badrinath? You never spoke of it. You told me everything. But not this?'

'It was too personal. And I went on a sudden whim...ah... later that year.' He tapped his foot.

'Later, when?'

'What is this inquisition in aid of?'

Kriti blinked. Twice. 'Badrinath is only open in the summer and autumn. I'm sure you know. I don't remember you bunking your course...'

'I didn't tell you every single thing, Kriti,' he said in irritation.

She stretched out her legs. Her blue jeans were cut-offs, ending at her lower calves. Her toenails were painted silver. She held out her glass. 'Refill, please.'

He came back with savoury crackers and cheeselets that he set on the side table. He lifted the table onto the silk rug so it was in front of her and they could both reach the bowls.

'So, your parents have swallowed your Badrinath vow,' she said, 'and you're off the hook.'

He nodded, throwing cheeselets into his mouth.

She raised her glass. 'Congratulations. Cheers.' They clinked. 'Clever man.'

She brought the other side table onto the rug in front of her. She opened her orange pouch-bag and laid out her little accoutrements. Cigarette papers, a small box of tobacco, a purple lighter, a dark-velvet jewellery pouch from which she drew out a piece of hash. 'There's another thing I wanted to ask,' she said. 'So many rumours, I don't know which to choose.'

'What do you mean?'

'AC/DC. Mean anything to you? Other than the band?'

'Oh God.' He put his hands in his hair. 'I hope you nipped that one in the bud.'

She'd spread out a cigarette paper and picked up her lighter but she set it back down.

Monish stared. 'No,' he said. 'For fuck's sake, No. You put fuel on the fire. Why, Kriti? What did I do to you?'

'You were rude to me.'

'Aren't we over that? Seriously, you've encouraged these rumours?

She shrugged. 'I thought you might be finding yourself.'

'You didn't really think that at all. For the record, just between you and me, I haven't yet felt attracted to a man. But even if I were...Do you know what you've *done*?'

She looked into his eyes at his tone.

'You want me to be a poor man, is that it?' He shook his head. He wanted to shout but his voice came out a whisper. 'If Dad hears this, he could disown me. I mean, *properly* disown me. And if it affects Pratish's marriage—oh, hell, I don't even want to think about it.' He put his hands over his eyes. 'What if the Prat's newly-chosen fiancée starts telling my folks that their older son is gay? Is bisexual.' He mimicked a high girlish sound: '"Did you know, Arun Papa, your son Monish…" How do *you* think he'll react?'

Her lips closed into themselves. She grimaced in sympathy. Then she said, 'Sorry.'

'Sorry won't cut it. You'd better help me close down this thing.'

She put the hash back in its pouch and rolled a quick cigarette. 'What do you want me to do?' She lit up.

'I want you to…'—he thought for a moment—'spread a different story. "Monish is deflowering every pretty new bird in town." Yes…that will do nicely. The folks won't like that either, but needs must.'

Kriti's whole body went into a giggle. She was bent over, head to knees, eyes squeezed in glee, hee-hee-hee-hee-hee. He watched her hands dangling down, the ash from her roll-up shaking. He worried it would drop with an ember and set his carpet ablaze.

She sat up and leaned down to get the ashtray. She tapped out the ash. 'You hardly go out anymore. When you do it's with the Ranjan sisters, as far as I can tell. Where exactly are you meeting these fresh young things?'

He jerked a thumb outwards and left. 'The hostel.'

A glint in her eyes. 'That's good. Clever Monish.'

'I mean it. I can count on you to tell everyone, any opportunity you get, right? Especially any aunties.'

She giggled again, smoke billowing from her mouth and

nostrils. 'Every. New. Bird. In. Town.' Hee-hee-hee. 'Deflow-ered. By. Monish.' She stubbed out her cigarette. 'Consider it done.'

'Thanks. I'm holding you to it.'

She munched on a cracker, eyeing him speculatively.

'What?' he asked.

'If that's really what's floating your boat, I can introduce you. I know some of the young women in the hostel. Two of them work for me—one full-time at the boutique. The other one, she works for an academic publisher, and models for me part-time. I'm using her for my trunk shows when the new stock comes in, not that you care to attend anything anymore. She's a beauty, very tall, very short hair, face like Audrey Hep-burn—an extremely tanned, sexy Audrey I mean—and she's got a crush on you. Oh, and she's a virgin.'

'She doesn't know me, Kriti, how can she have a crush on me?'

'She's noticed you. Driving out of the building to work in the mornings. She asks about you. She likes the look of you, who knows why? She says that sometimes when she's hang-ing out there'—she pointed out the balcony and down to the cul-de-sac—'she waves at you, and you smile back.'

'I do not! How can she see me smile in the dark and at this distance? I've never even noticed anyone wave at me. She's fantasising.'

'Yes, she is. About you.'

He took a sip of his drink. It was all watery. He would fix himself another drink in a minute.

'You'll like her,' Kriti continued. 'She's the fiery, intellectual type. And so young. Just nineteen. She got double promo-tions all the way through school and she's finished her degree and in her first job! It pays peanuts, so she models part-time. Parents have no money. Come for dinner one evening and I'll invite her, too. She'll be thrilled to meet you.'

'Not just at the moment,' he said. 'My head is full of…uh, troubles. I seem to crave solitude in the evenings. Every day at work, something blows up…and I've been very distracted—'

'I've noticed,' she said, her exuberance dissipating. 'When the girls ask me about you at the boutique, I tell them that you used to drop by on Saturdays with pastries and charm the customers into buying additional accessories. "*We've* never seen him here," they said.' Tears formed in Kriti's large eyes. 'I tell them you haven't been round for a year, at least. You don't even come to the seasonal events, although you must see all the invitations.' Her tears plopped onto her knee.

He'd been oblivious. He hadn't done his duty as her best friend. He couldn't even say to her that he didn't feel it mattered, that he was in a state of ennui where all his responsibilities were concerned, and that he dedicated his efforts to his secret affair. He hadn't even asked about her life, but clearly the romantic side of things wasn't going well.

He stood up and held out his arms. 'Come here, babe.'

She sobbed into his chest. He could smell, almost taste, her perfume—Samsara. It took him back to being twenty years old and their travels together. The perfume had just been launched in Paris that year. She'd liked the red bottle. The perfume's notes were Indian, and perhaps they were both slightly homesick, because they'd loved the smell. Kriti had dabbled with other fragrances over the years, but this was her longstanding favourite. Her hot tears drenched his shirt. He would find black mascara stains on it later. It was like old times. Her chest, encased in a pristine white tee, heaved against him. He felt himself getting aroused and pushed her away to arm's length, then dropped his hands.

Kriti wiped her eyes and face with her fingers. 'Tissues,' she muttered, going to his bedroom. He followed her. 'Shall we go out for dinner?' he asked, as she blew her nose.

Her face brightened.

He unbuttoned his shirt, hanging it on a hook behind the door to dry. He pulled on a T-shirt. 'Give me a sec,' he said, heading into the bathroom with a pair of jeans.

'Monish, I need to go down to my flat for a few minutes first. I need to do my make-up. Look at me.'

Her eyes were puffy and red and so was her nose, but she was still beautiful, what with her curly wet lashes and her tremulous mouth. He had not had that mouth on him for a long while. He tried to push away that thought while at the same time thinking that perhaps this was going to be one of those evenings when they used each other. Stop, stop, he thought.

'You don't need make-up,' he said, out of habit to her.

'I have to put some on,' she insisted. 'See you in the lobby in ten minutes.'

She reached out her hand to squeeze his. 'I want to go dancing after dinner. Please?'

'Sure.'

TWENTY-THREE

May 1998

IT WOULD BE torrid in two hours. Just gone eight in the morning but the heat was perceptible in the garden. Sunlight glimmered on the shrubbery, highlighting the variegated leaves Ammi liked to cultivate. Waheeda was glad that the forecast was for light rain in the afternoon. Falguni was coming to visit, staying over for just one night. Waheeda stared out of her bedroom window, forgetting to sip from the mug of tea in her hand. Their friendship had dissolved, but Fal wasn't going to admit it, or let it go. Waheeda couldn't bear to have an outright confrontation; it would be too painful. It would be like a relationship break-up, and Fal would be vengeful. That's just how she was. Waheeda had rung her and elucidated on her lack of time in Delhi. Fal decided *she* would come out instead to get the full report on Waheeda's electoral failure and future plans.

When had Falguni last been in Nulkazim? Years ago, at Waheeda's wedding. January 1989. On the evening before the nikah ceremony the four of them—she, Fal, Lara, and Naaz—had squeezed themselves on the swing seat at the far end of the garden, laughing late into the night. After that Waheeda had not had time to chat again during the wedding, what with the big reception and the *vidai* ceremony, after which she'd left for Lucknow to spend a few days in Nafis's family home.

She gazed at the swing seat, static and silent in the blazing morning. Eighteen months ago she'd imagined that when she moved here she would sit idly on it reading to Hira, like she had with her brothers. But she hadn't done that. Hira used it occasionally with her friends. Decorously. When Waheeda's brothers were young, they would leap and jump on to the seat, making the metal joints creak threateningly. The swing was big and sturdy enough to hold three people. Waheeda would sometimes sit there with a magazine, hoping for solitude. Rohail and Irfan would come running out as soon as they spotted her. 'Read to us, read to us, Wija.' And Rohail, who was the more energetic of the two, would dash back into the house, returning with a stack of books. *The Hardy Boys. The Secret Seven*. Waheeda would read aloud knowing that they were paying no attention, because already they were distracted into a game of seeing how high they could make the seat swing when there were three of them sitting on it. And how loud could the grating and gnashing of the chains become before their mother came out of the house to scold them.

•

'REHANA AUNTIE, LUNCH was delicious.' Fal flashed her charming smile, her top row teeth perfectly square and white. She tossed her head like a horse, her long brown hair moving about her face. The ends of her hair were very light, very dry and ragged. They'd always been like that and Fal didn't like to cut her hair that often because she liked it long. But there seemed to be no hair product in the world that could deal with her desiccated split ends. 'Let's take our coffee to your room,' Fal said to Waheeda. Clearly, she was chafing at being on best behaviour already and wanted private time with Waheeda.

In the bedroom she prowled about in the space between the large window and the closed door. 'What time will Hira be home from school?'

'In another hour.'

'How old is she now?' Fal's brow wrinkled as she worked out the number of years since Hira's birth.

'She'll be seven in August.'

'Time flies.' Fal tossed her head and curled a tendril of hair around her middle finger. The huge oval diamond on her forefinger caught Waheeda's eye. It matched the ones in her ears. 'So, you should fill me in now on *everything*. Presumably we can't talk openly in front of Hira.'

'Depends what you're talking about,' Waheeda said. Falguni's child tolerance was low. It was perhaps for the best she didn't have children. She'd decided at seventeen years, if Waheeda remembered correctly, that no one in India should have children. That would solve the population explosion. A somewhat extreme position to take, and her opinion may have softened over the years, but not Fal's general attitude to kids. Waheeda wondered if there were still all those Post-it notes on Fal's bathroom mirror and dressing-table mirror reminding her to take the pill. So many prompts to herself, all scrawled with one word: *Pill. Pill. Pill.*

Waheeda began to tell her of how she was being courted by the large parties active in the area. 'But I've decided, this strategy needs to work in the opposite direction,' she said. 'I need to forge alliances with the parties in Dhoonpur, who may agree to support me if I cut a deal with them here in Nulkazim. They could use Abba's power here, especially for State MLA elections. Also, if I could gain some influence in the neighbouring constituencies, that might spill over onto the outer villages of Dhoonpur.'

'Who are the next-door MPs currently?' Fal stopped pacing and sat on the bed.

'Well, in Tebilly, it's the young Maharaja. First the subjects voted for his father, and now him; they don't even care which party he switches to. *He* has no compunction about transferring when it takes his fancy. And the people! No better. As long as they vote for the king, even if he's no longer the king, they seem to be in ignorant bliss! I mean, can anyone tell them that the royals are *not* royal anymore? They are just people who've inherited a different stratosphere to live in compared to their toiling subjects.'

'My, my.' Fal's green eyes had a wicked twinkle. 'A little rant there, Wija. And if I may say so, to the wrong person. Very unlike you to make that mistake.'

'Oh?'

'I know him,' Fal said, 'Binty is my friend.'

The mini-maharaja's nickname was Binty? She wouldn't giggle, it would annoy Fal. Oh dear, he was Fal's *friend*. What did that mean? An ex-lover? She gulped. 'How friendly are you with him?'

'Good friends. No, I haven't slept with him. Yet. But I see him quite a bit in Delhi; the same gatherings, etc. Look, when you're next in town, I'll introduce you to him. You should ask him directly for his support. He won't be able to wriggle away at a social bash.'

But he might just lie, Waheeda thought. Although that would be true of anyone. Even so, her own preference was to set up a formal meeting. 'I'll tell you when I have a day free, but Fal, he might take it amiss to be approached about politicking at a—'

'Wija. Everyone in Delhi talks politics all the time. You know that. You can't get away from it. Maybe Nafis could, but no one else. Everyone has a handle or an agenda. Trust me, meet Binty at *dinner* at my place; discuss a pact with him when he's had a couple of drinks and he won't be able to go back on his word in the morning. Plus, I'll tell him you're my close friend from school and it's the right thing to do.'

'Yes, OK. Not sure if it will work…' Waheeda disliked the thought of ambushing Binty at the point when Fal brought out her cognac and slim cigars, but an introduction from her would count. 'I suppose there's no harm trying.'

'Exactly. Speaking of Nafis, when he visits Nulkazim, does he sleep in here with you?'

Waheeda felt herself blanch. 'I…no…he stays in Rohail's old room. He's only ever here for a night or two anyway, and barely seems to sleep—'

Fal stood up and prowled again. 'What's it like?' she asked. 'To be back here in your childhood bedroom, alone, night after night after night, and never a man in your bed?'

A hard lump lodged in Waheeda's throat. 'What a question.'

'Don't answer. I've seen what it's like in your eyes.'

She sat down beside Waheeda again and put an arm around her shoulder. 'Don't you think now, Pious, that you wasted all those years? All that time you saved yourself for your marriage. Remember that wonderful guy who you broke up with in… when was it…1985? He got fed up of you not making up your mind whether you would have sex with him or not.'

'That's not why I broke up with him,' Waheeda snapped. 'Hanif wasn't as wonderful as he appeared. He was insulting to Sikhs and to Lara's family; he had a rabid view of other religions generally, and *I* got fed up with his outlook on life.' She wanted to shake off Fal's arm. It felt heavy and insincere on her shoulders. 'I regret nothing.'

Fal put her hands in her lap. 'You know what they say: be careful what you wish for.' A sigh emanated from her, startling Waheeda. 'You got what you wished for. Remember: "a handsome man who didn't care about money or politics, who would woo you and marry you." Well, here you are, Pious.'

'So I am.' Waheeda wondered whether Fal felt she'd wished for the wrong things. She'd said: 'I want to live like a man.' And so she had. *Well, here you are, Hyper.*

Delhi

MISS CHANG BROUGHT the hairdryer too close to Waheeda's scalp and her round brush pulled at her hair. Waheeda winced and moved her head away.

'You said you want glamorous, na?' Miss Chang said. 'Beautiful waves I'm doing for you. Be still.'

She had not been to the hair salon for a year. Miss Chang had something to say on the subject. 'Forgotten us?'

'No, you know I don't live in Delhi anymore. A lack of time…'

'I know. You're somewhat famous now.'

'Somewhat.'

Miss Chang looked just the same. Her own sharp bob was immaculate and there were the same fine lines around her eyes and mouth. Dry powdery cheeks. Black eyeliner. Every time Waheeda had asked her age in the past she'd become younger at each query.

'You won't believe this,' Miss Chang said as she twisted the brush in Waheeda's hair, 'but just yesterday I was thinking that I hadn't seen you for so long. And this morning, out of the blue, you turn up.' Expertly, she let out a curl from the brush and her hairdryer pointed at the ceiling for a second as she mused aloud. 'I should have made a wish to see one of my more famous clients, like film-star Sarika. Then *she* might have walked in unexpectedly today.'

'Mm-hmm.' Waheeda smiled, flummoxed at what response she could make. She shook out her hair and checked the back of her head in the mirror that Miss Chang was holding up. Her hair looked great, but oddly, now her face seemed washed-out. She needed a darker lipstick. Heavens, she was as nervous as if preparing for a first date. All of this effort for lunch with Monish's mother. Miss Chang offered her a dark pink lipstick and Waheeda rubbed some of it onto her fingers and then her lips.

Butterflies fluttered in her tummy as she instructed Habib to drive to the Selvani residence. In her diary the appointment was in capitals. NN Foundation. Underneath she'd written: 'Charitable Organisation—Pickle Factory. Meeting to discuss further education for young widows.' She'd already prepared a folder with useful materials to be copied and disseminated to the employees. Depending on their previous education levels she'd included sections of the law that pertained to women's rights, to family law and inheritance. Some of them would not have been told they were inheritors of their husband's property. She'd listed details of useful further education courses that could be done by correspondence, recognising that these women were working part-time or full-time at the pickle factory and being paid wages directly into their own bank accounts. She'd included basic finance courses in Hindi and English. She knew there wouldn't really be time to discuss any of this, that Monish's mother wanted a social visit, but at least she'd leave behind the materials.

She was tense about being scrutinised. She just didn't feel glamorous enough. Visions of Kriti, that one time she'd seen her, flickered in her mind. And Sasha's cool style: the green-framed specs and husky drawling speech. Oh, why, oh why, had Monish insisted? He'd not let her forget this 'promise,' although she hadn't actually promised. Coerced, more like. 'Have you found a lunch date yet? Have you put it in your diary? Don't worry, I'll be there; it'll be fine.'

Waheeda was suddenly reminded of her visit to the town of Makeri the previous week. One of the voluble ladies had interrupted her while she expounded on her girls' toilet scheme and said, 'Waheedaji, why aren't you wearing sunglasses? Waheeda had squinted at her in surprise. 'I never do,' she'd replied.

'Sonia Gandhi comes here wearing enormous sunglasses. She's stylish. And some of those ladies who came from the city to campaign at the last election kept their sunglasses in their hair day and night. You could do that at least.'

'I'll consider it,' Waheeda had said, while thinking, 'But that's not me. I don't wear sunglasses.' She'd carried on speaking, but the woman had interjected again. 'I think you *should* wear sunglasses. *And* silk saris. And larger pearl tops in your ears.' She tapped her own ears, which sported small gold *jhumkas*. Waheeda gave her a searching look. She was Waheeda's height, with a similar complexion, but dressed in a crushed cotton sari. On her forehead were three tiny black *bindis* in a triangle. Her hair was oiled and tied back in a plait that had been rolled into a bun, but it frizzed up over her head. Her creased and chapped feet were thrust into old slippers. She was perhaps forty-five. Waheeda had not forgotten her. Shabbily dressed, for reasons of poverty or otherwise, but certainly not reticent with her advice.

•

SHE COULD DO with a pair of designer sunglasses for this moment; something to hide behind; something to up the glamour quotient. She directed Habib to park outside the main gates of the house. 'Have your lunch,' she said, 'We'll leave by three.'

She walked up the driveway, the folder in her hands, a small bag slung on her shoulder. There were no cars on the drive, but a vintage Bentley was parked under a roofed space to the right. She turned left to the front door and just as she rang the doorbell Monish's royal-blue BMW rolled up. She glimpsed Monish in the back seat and hurriedly looked away so his driver would not see her face.

Mrs Selvani opened the door, greeting her effusively, 'Hello, Waheeda, come in, come in…oh, I see Monish is here, too, you've arrived together, I thought I would get some time alone with you first…anyway, I'm so pleased you could come for lunch, I hope you like *rajma*, because that's what Monish requested…'

'Hello,' Monish said behind her. She turned and smiled and then tried not to stare. He was in a pinstriped suit, a lavender shirt and a silver-grey tie. Wasn't he sweltering in that get-up? He was unstubbled. His hair was brushed neatly.

Funny, she was all in lilac, too. And he must be internally remarking on her hair. Mrs Selvani led them into a room that Waheeda hadn't been in before. A cosy sitting room at the back of the house with French doors that led on to a narrow private patio, beyond which were flower beds enclosed by tall hedges, separating the area from the rest of the garden. Waheeda remembered the broader patio that the kitchen opened onto; that was where she'd bumped into Monish. A year ago, as he'd reminded her in a text. The date was imprinted in her, but she hadn't had the chance to tell him.

She took a chair by the tiny fireplace noting the Portuguese-looking tiles in the surround. From what Monish had told her about his mother's art interests, she guessed these were Goan antiques. She accepted the offer of fresh minty lemonade and Mrs Selvani left the room with a flutter of the lime-green chiffon scarf she wore with her beige *churidar* and short kurta. She was so pretty, and Monish was lucky to have inherited her looks and litheness. According to Monish, his younger brother Pratish had the misfortune of resembling his father. Waheeda supposed Monish was exaggerating whenever he described Pratish to her—his weight, his shortness, his manners, his intense jealousy.

Monish came to stand by her. She was about to comment on this unfamiliar incarnation of him when he spoke very fast: 'Ma wants to spend some time alone with you.' He lifted a palm up. 'I don't know what she wants to say, must be usual mother-type stuff, nothing you can't handle.'

'Oh, Wija, don't look so worried. I'm here. I won't leave you alone for too long. But since she's requested—'

He broke off when his mother re-entered the room and returned to his seat across from them. He removed his jacket and tie, draping them on the chair. 'I had a meeting at an embassy,' he said to Waheeda, answering her unspoken question.

•

It seemed to Waheeda that over lunch she and Mrs Selvani were playing a game of darting gazes. Waheeda would notice from the corner of her eye that Mrs Selvani ('please call me Nikki') was studying her but when she flicked her own eyes up Mrs Selvani would be staring at Monish. Then back to her. Waheeda herself couldn't help but keep catching Mrs Selvani's gaze. What opinions were forming behind those mascara-brushed lashes? Short thick lashes like Monish's.

There was much more than *rajma* on offer, there was chicken, cauliflower, *mattar-paneer*, *jeera aloo*, plain rice, saffron *pulao*, chapati, grated carrot salad, long sticks of cucumber, and *boondi* raita. Waheeda found herself filling up too quickly. Her nerves were still unsettled, compounded by the information that his mother wanted to speak to her in private.

'What are your plans now?' Mrs Selvani asked her. 'For the next few years. Are you continuing to campaign?'

'Yes, I intend to stand for the Lok Sabha again—'

'We've just had general elections. So your plans have shifted five years hence?'

'Yes, I suppose so. But also…if there is a need for a by-election…'

A muffled snigger from Monish. 'Tell the truth, Wija,' he said. He addressed his mother. 'She's waiting for WW Singh to die. This is how calculating—'

Waheeda cast an amazed wide-eyed glance at him and he received a reproving look from his mother, too.

'Who is WW Singh?' she asked.

'He is the sitting MP for Dhoonpur,' Waheeda explained. 'That's the constituency I stood in. And probably where I will stand again.'

'And what will happen to WW Singh? Which party is he from?'

Waheeda shot another dismayed glance at Monish. 'He's a Congress MP. It's a sad story. He's been suffering from cancer for a few years and spends most of his time at the cancer institutes in Bombay…he's hardly ever in Dhoonpur. At the moment we've heard he's very ill again, but he does seem to have the will to go on and battle through. Good for him. But you know, support for Congress has eroded. If a by-election were to be called the contest would be wide open…'

'Hmm,' was all Mrs Selvani said. And then, 'Are you going to stand from one or two constituencies?'

Waheeda knew that in certain circles in Delhi everyone was well-versed in politics, but it still surprised her when she was asked questions that displayed more knowledge than she had assumed. She was non-committal in her reply. 'I haven't decided. It depends on whether it's a general election or a by-election.'

Mrs Selvani pushed back her chair. 'You two are hardly eating anything. Would you like a break before I bring in the fruit salad?'

'Yes,' Monish said.

'Waheeda, why don't you come out with me into the garden for a while?' She looked meaningfully at Monish, who scraped back his chair and said, 'I want to find some of my old CDs to take to the flat. I'll join you in a few minutes.'

He paused behind Waheeda's chair to squeeze her hand reassuringly before he went upstairs. Waheeda was very aware of his mother's eyes on them. Did her hand look sun-burned and dry in his light-skinned smooth one?

•

MRS SELVANI OPENED the French doors of her sitting room and Waheeda followed her into the weak sunshine. A gloom hung over Delhi, the air thick with unseen pollutants. It was too hot and sticky to be outside, but Mrs Selvani pointed to her roses, and Waheeda said they were lovely. She followed Monish's mother as she walked on to the two tallest topiary hedges beyond the flowerbeds. These had been shaped like cones, rising high above them, offering shade and privacy. Waheeda enjoyed the fragrance of being so close to cool, clean, green plants. These bushes smelt like they'd been freshly watered, leaf by leaf. Perhaps they had.

'When I met you at our party,' Mrs Selvani said, '*upstairs*, I thought you were Monish's friend.'

'Yes, I remember. But I didn't really know him then.'

'He said that was when you first met.'

Waheeda bobbed her head in agreement.

'Imagine,' said Mrs Selvani. 'You met here.' Waheeda didn't know what Mrs Selvani was imagining; whatever it was, she couldn't see Monish's mother being over-the-moon at the outcome of that meeting.

His mother's eyes seemed to sink into Waheeda's face. She had adopted a confiding tone. 'Monish says,' she began...and then paused. Her speech patterns were quite similar to her son's. 'He says that you've been his girlfriend since that time.'

Waheeda looked intently at the tall shrub. It had bright green leaves and minute needle-fine thorns. Nestled in the needles were two little birds. It was only because she was gazing right into the shrub that Waheeda had been able to discern them amid the greenery and the slim branches.

She gave a soft blink of acknowledgement; unsure how much disclosure was required on her part. She wished Monish would join them now.

'That's a year,' Mrs Selvani mused. 'Steady for a year.'

She was on the brink of saying something important. Waheeda felt that heavy vibe in the air, Mrs Selvani's thoughts churning, a request being formulated.

She kept her eyes studiedly on the shrub. The two birds were scuffling, tiny wings beating in consternation. One bird flew out of the foliage, leaving the other twittering to itself.

'I can't help you,' Waheeda wanted to say to Monish's

mother, but couldn't, not until she'd actually been asked to do something by this pretty but anxious lady, this lady who was yearning to say something to her. *Don't imagine that I have any influence on your son.*

'I worry about his liver,' Mrs Selvani said.

'What?'

'He drinks too much. He's doing so much damage to himself. He's young now, but…if you could—'

Monish came out on the patio. 'Why are you just standing there?'

'We were chatting,' Mrs Selvani said.

'Did you find the CDs you were looking for?' Waheeda enquired.

He nodded. 'Shall we go in, Ma, and have that fruit salad you promised?'

The sound of car doors shutting reached them. Waheeda heard a male voice and an instantaneous sharp intake of breath from Mrs Selvani. She saw the killer look Monish cast at his mother before he practically ran into the house. Mrs Selvani hurried after him. Waheeda trailed behind, dread rising in her like bile. She felt faint. That must be Arun Selvani's voice.

She entered the sitting room and heard that voice again, in the hall, barking at Monish. 'You are supposed to be in a meeting.'

'I have been. I just stopped in to see Ma for lunch.'

'It's a work day.'

'Dad,' Monish's voice was filled with derision, 'I'm going back to clock in now and don't you worry I'll do my full quota of hours before I leave in the evening.'

Waheeda picked up her bag from the chair and walked slowly into the hallway, her limbs numbed by fear, just as Monish seethed at his father: 'Why are *you* here?'

Arun's eyes alighted on her. 'I, too, want to see the company you keep.' He looked her up and down slowly, offensively. Waheeda saw the bolt of colour rush from Monish's jaw to his cheek. She was too shocked at the feeling of being stripped to be able to move.

Arun's eyes moved to his wife. 'Nikki, you didn't tell me—'

'I thought I'd mentioned I had guests for lunch…'

'Guests.' He mocked the word. Behind him, Pratish leered at her with open curiosity. He was quite like Monish had described.

Monish gripped her elbow. 'We were just leaving.' His lips had gone thin and white. He steered her past his father and brother, his hands very tight on her arm, bruising her, 'I'm sorry. I'm sorry. I don't know *how*…'

'Don't touch me,' she said, as they stepped onto the drive. He dropped his hand immediately and hung back as she walked out of the gates. It wasn't three o'clock yet but she was relieved to see her car was outside. Habib was standing by it, talking into his phone. He put it in his shirt pocket when he spotted her and showed her into the back seat. Just as he started the ignition, there was a knocking at her tinted window. Waheeda opened it half-way. Mrs Selvani's face was composed. 'Thank you so much for coming,' she said formally. 'Your recommendations are really helpful. I hope we'll meet again to discuss this further.' Waheeda couldn't speak. Her jaw was jammed in fury. She lifted a hand in a feeble wave, not for politeness, but because Habib was witnessing this exchange.

As they drove off, she closed her eyes and was tempted to bury her head in her hands, but knew that Habib must have already noticed how agitated she was. She sat up straight and looked out of the window. She would strive to keep a neutral expression until they got to Sangeet Vihar. In her own room she could have a fit.

TWENTY-FOUR

June 1998

'He's called several times to say it's under control, it's resolved; not to feel any apprehension about anyone else knowing; he's extremely sorry; his mother is *tremendously* sorry; he needs to see you and explain what happened…and Wija, *I'm* sorry, but he's almost becoming a nuisance the number of times he's called on my cell, so I think you better speak to him.'

Naaz fixed Waheeda with her strict teacher look before she dunked her biscuit in her coffee and nibbled at it. Her six-month-old son, Kabir, was having his afternoon doze in his cot. Naaz and Waheeda were in the guest suite on the ground floor, where Waheeda often stayed. Naaz had settled herself on the black chair at the narrow wooden desk, arraying the baby monitor, her phone and her coffee on the desk. Waheeda perched herself on the upholstered stool by the bed.

'I never want to see Monish again,' she said, not very convincingly.

'It's not my business to tell him that. You have to.' The airconditioner was on full blast, giving Waheeda a headache, but Naaz was gently perspiring at her temples. Outside, the temperature was forty-five degrees centigrade. Naaz offered Waheeda her phone. 'Call him now if you like. He says you haven't responded to his texts and calls although he's tried to tell you in code that he's done everything he can.'

Waheeda ran her finger round the gold-edged rim of her cup. 'Can't you tell him not to ring either you or me? It's over.'

She saw how Naaz cringed at that. 'I'm fond of him…he's

my friend, too…and no, I can't do your breaking up for you.'
She placed her half-eaten biscuit on her saucer. 'Besides, if it's
all sorted as he says, if Selvani senior is going to keep the lid
on it forever, as Monish assures me—'

'Then what? Risk it again? Do I look like a fool to you?'

'Yes,' Naaz half-laughed, half-snorted. 'You've already been
a fool; you could carry on being one. Or you can be glum the
whole time. The decision is yours once you know the facts.'

Waheeda put her coffee cup on the floor. 'I'm not glum. I'm
freaked. I do need to know what's going on. Am I finished or
not? Is my reputation already tattered and I don't yet know?'

Naaz shook her head.

Waheeda picked up her own phone and texted Manisha
Doctorwala. 'Lunch tomorrow? At your college? I only have a
half-hour, but want to hear how it's going in the department.
What did the Head of history have to say?'

•

AT HIS APARTMENT she shook him off when he tried to
embrace her in greeting. She took the armchair nearest the
door. He stood above her, in his office apparel, blue shirt and
dark trousers, his shoes and socks on. The false yellow of electric light played on his shiny hair. Outside, the sun was fierce
at its pinnacle in the sky and hot winds were blowing through
the city. 'You want to know what the head of department
says? Or can I first apologise and also pass on apologies from-'

She waved her hand brusquely to dismiss that stuff.

'Dad has promised he's not going to breathe a word.
Pratish has just got engaged. The family is busy with that and
with keeping up appearances more fully than before. Dad is
not going to share news of our relationship with anyone. At
this point. Or ever. He won't be conferring with anyone in
Nulkazim, or Lucknow, or passing on the info. He *promised*.'

'Like your mother did.' Of course, she understood that this
liaison was nothing to brag about at this juncture for Arun

Selvani. Younger son engaged into some carefully chosen family and older son dallying with a married woman. No, no.

Monish sat down on the rug beside her. He looked up into her face. 'She *didn't* tell anyone.'

He gave a little groan. 'I don't even know how to tell you this, I'm so livid. The cook was spying for Dad. When he saw you and me there for lunch and noticed that we knew each other well, he rang Dad to tell him, thinking it may be of interest. And it was. Dad realised that Ma must've arranged to meet whoever I was seeing…'

He put his hands on her knees. 'You don't know how sorry she is.'

Waheeda was silent, wanting to brush his hands off, but not trusting her own hands to touch his.

'My mother knows I'm furious with her, in so many ways. I told her to walk out on her bastard husband, but she won't.' He sighed, his fingers tightening on her knees. 'Naturally, we all have to play happy families now. Anyway, you don't need to hear what's going on there. *I'll* never tell her anything confidential again.'

'That's nothing to do with me.'

He pushed her knees slightly apart, his touch feeling warm through her thin silk *salwar*. 'I told her it's over between us. Obviously. She's dying of guilt. And I'm going to let her. I've told Dad it's over, thanks to him. I've even told Pratish it's over. And if he mentions it as a past affair, to anyone, I will *kill* him. He won't though, because as brothers, we *have* to keep each other's family confidences. I have kept plenty of things quiet for him. And there's all the drama of a wedding to come.'

'OK.' She drew a proper breath and let it out. It did seem that for the moment the spill was under control. She had been in near-mortal panic for the past two weeks. 'Monish, take your hands off me.'

'Everyone thinks it's over.' He extended his thumbs so they pressed into the insides of her thighs.

'It *is* over,' she said even as she felt instant arousal.

'Do you want me, Waheeda?' He thrust his head between her legs and kissed her through her *salwar*. His mouth was hot. His tongue flicked. She felt the thin silk wet where his mouth was. Outside, inside.

'Do you want me?'

Yes. Right here. Right now.

No. Where were all those rehearsed words? She'd planned on being Gracious. With a capital G. Unwavering. Thank you, goodbye, you are an *idiot* and could have *ruined* me.

Why had her hips slipped off the chair with his hands under them?

'Here?' he asked. 'Right here?'

September 1998

'OH, MY CHWEET-CHWEET Hira.' Large tears rolled down Naaz's cheeks as she hugged Hira. 'I haven't seen you for *months*. I've *missed* you.'

'I know, Naaz *masi*,' Hira said, only slightly bewildered by the tears. 'Everytime you told me on the phone, I said to Ammi to bring me to Delhi, but she never did.'

Waheeda decided that she might as well get used to being painted as the villain. No doubt this *khus-pus* between Hira and Naaz would continue through the weekend.

'Let me introduce you to Kabir.' Naaz pulled Hira upstairs, leaving Waheeda in the hall with the luggage–two small holdalls. Deepak came out of the dining room on cue to greet her and pick up the bags. He deposited them in the guest suite.

'Thank you. I haven't seen you for a while,' Waheeda said.

'You seem to be here a lot when I'm away.' The white mark

on his forehead from his morning *puja* was mostly smeared off. Only a tiny downward arc of the ash was left. He was looking well.

She nodded. 'Yes, I do stay here every few weeks. You're right, we don't seem to coincide.' *Deliberately.*

'It's good; Naaz has company when I'm travelling. Of course, she's always happy to spend time with you.'

'I've enjoyed watching Kabir grow. He's just the cutest thing; I love his mop of curls. I hope Naaz never cuts his hair.'

Deepak swelled with pride. 'I know what you mean. But in a few months it'll be time to shave his head, for the *mundan* ceremony.'

Oh no. Those fab curly locks. But Deepak did like to follow all the Hindu ceremonies to the letter, just like Naaz liked to follow the Muslim ones. Kabir was going to be one inculcated little boy—circumcised, *mundan*. Waheeda herself disagreed with both of those. No son of hers would have to undergo such traditions. She followed Deepak to the sitting room. She was not going to have a son, so she could think up any rules she liked; how did it matter?

That evening Hira posed with Kabir on her lap while Naaz clicked away with her camera. Kabir was gurgling and smiling into Hira's face and she was clutching at him too tightly, so he wouldn't fall, but Kabir didn't seem to mind.

'I wish I wasn't going out,' Waheeda said to Naaz. She'd rung Falguni some days ago to see if it might be possible to meet the Maharaja of Tebilly for lunch. Fal had said he wasn't in town this week, but Waheeda should accompany her to the theatre. Waheeda had tried to refuse. 'I'm bringing Hira for the weekend,' she'd said. 'I can't just leave Naaz to babysit her.'

'You were going to leave her at lunch-time,' Fal pointed out. 'Instead, I'm asking you to come out in the evening. To see a Hindi adaptation of Chekhov's *Uncle Vanya*. There's an important moment in it that I've heard about. I want to see it. If you're in town, I want you to come with me to this.'

•

OUTSIDE THE THEATRE, Waheeda pointed out the banner of the play to Fal. *Vanya, Sonia, aur Doctor Saab.* 'It sounds more racy like that,' she said, making Fal laugh. She meandered up the old mosaic staircase behind Fal. 'Is it going to be very melancholy?'

'It is Chekhov, after all, you can't expect it to be frothy. But in the first act there's an important speech about the preservation of our forests. That's something both you and I believe in. *Strongly*. I thought it would be good to hear how they've updated the speech to point fingers at the politicians who are selling our forests and those who are smuggling timber for personal profit.'

They stood by the brown-tinted rectangular windows in the hall waiting for the auditorium doors to open. 'All this *bak-bak* about conservation and next thing you hear, it's the ministers themselves who've sanctioned the cutting down of trees.' Fal was on a roll. 'If there's *one* thing in this world that I'm passionate about, it's keeping the natural beauty of our land. Preventing the populace encroaching everywhere. Wrecking everything.'

There was no point telling her that natural beauty was something appreciated and enjoyed more by the rich than the poor. If you needed money to eat you would loot Nature's resources if you could. Although poverty was not an excuse the ministers could use. In their case, it was plain greed. Short term gain for some families; long term pain for the nation.

'Shall I get you a drink or a snack?' Fal asked her.

'No thanks, I'm fine.'

Fal's eyes skimmed the hall while Waheeda regarded her. She was in a turquoise jumpsuit, belted at the waist with a purple cord. A soft leather bag in mustard was slung on her shoulder. It was fringed at the bottom. Her high heels were purple and with them on, she towered over Waheeda.

'What're you looking at?' Fal asked.

'You're brightly dressed. Nice!'

'Intentionally. So many of the arty-farty types here will be wearing black *kurtis* with heavy silver earrings, or that other uniform,' she pointed down the hall to the far end, 'white shirts with torn jeans.' Waheeda turned to look.

'Those two women,' Fal said. 'In the left corner.' She peered. 'Actually, it's the Ranjan sisters. Oh, they're with Monish!'

Waheeda looked again carefully, an 'Oh!' escaping her.

'You know them?

'No…I know him…I've met him…'

'They're actresses. He went out with them a couple of years ago.' Fal put on her gossip-voice. 'Both of them. Together. Used to sleep like a baby between them.'

Waheeda choked. How would Fal know this? Who had told whom such a thing? How did these intimate details, if true, get around?

'I wonder if he's back with them?' Fal raised her hand to wave at their cluster. To Waheeda's horror they noticed and began walking towards them.

Fal spoke in a quick low tone. 'Hey, he has a breast fixation. He won't pay any attention to me, because I'm flat as a pancake, and he already knows that, but I bet he'll check out *your* boobs. Just watch, that's the first thing—'

'I *have* met him before,' Waheeda snapped. She wanted to add: I don't think he has a breast fixation. He has a normal healthy interest; he's a man, what d'you expect?

Fal wasn't listening anyway; as Monish approached she flung herself on to him like he was her long lost brother. He responded with a loose hug. Fal was more distant with the women, proffering her hand to them. They shook her hand, and each put a hand on her shoulder in a pretence at a hug, then withdrew to stand at a slight distance, as if she was toxic.

'This is my friend Waheeda Rela,' Fal introduced her. 'Seema and Neha,' Fal gestured to each in turn, and Waheeda struggled to say 'Hi' and smile a greeting. She couldn't breathe. 'This is Monish Selvani,' Fal said.

'Yes, we've met before,' Waheeda interjected. She could see him looking at her for cues.

He nodded. 'Yes, of course, hello Waheeda, how nice to see you again. How are you?'

'I'm…fine…'

He'd spoken with disarming ease but his expression was quizzical. A hurt question in his eyes. She hadn't told him she would be in Delhi this weekend. She regretted it now. But who could've thought that—

'You two know each other?' Fal broke in, green eyes illuminated in curiosity.

'I just told you,' Waheeda said. 'We've met once or twice.'

'Where did you meet?'

'It was at my parents' house,' Monish replied. 'At a dinner party they had. A couple of years ago. Weren't you there with your family, Waheeda? With your parents?'

'Just my father, I think. I'd accompanied him that evening.'

'And the second time? When did you meet again?' Fal must've scented Waheeda's embarrassment. A true friend would've changed the subject, but Fal would probe and probe. Waheeda faltered, unable to think what to say.

'Wasn't it lunch at my friend's home?' Monish said. He was smooth, she thought. He spoke unhurriedly. 'She's a journalist and you were there giving a talk about a charity scheme.' He furrowed his brow at her. 'Toilets?' he asked.

She smiled. 'Yes.'

Monish turned to Fal. 'We're meeting some other friends here. We should go find them. But how fantastic to see you,

Fal.' He beamed flirtatiously at her. 'It's been too long.' He inclined his head at Waheeda. 'Good to see you again.'

'You, too.' Despite feeling a shortness of breath she was able to squeeze out a few words. 'Bye, nice to meet you,' she said to Seema and Neha, who lightly touched Fal again on her shoulders before they flanked Monish as if they were his bodyguards. The three of them walked away. She hadn't had a chance to inspect them. Just her first impressions of two attractive, confident women, one harder than the other. His ex-lovers. Current lovers? Was this what he was hiding from her? Waheeda stared after them. Their loose long plaits snaked seductively down their backs.

'How *interesting*.' Fal took a step towards Waheeda. 'He didn't even look at your boobs.' She took another step forward, uncomfortably into Waheeda's space. 'And I've never seen that expression on your face before. It can only mean one thing.' Fal leaned down to speak in her ear, her mustard bag bumping into Waheeda. 'You've fucked him, haven't you?'

Waheeda stood stock still.

'What I want to know is how in the world did he mange it? What did he *do* that got him into your knickers, Pious?'

Waheeda took a step back and shook her head to get out of the spell. 'Nothing. He did not get into—You're *wrong*,' she said. The auditorium doors had opened. 'Let's go inside, shall we?'

'When did it happen? How? C'mon, Pious, tell me.'

'You've got the wrong end of the stick, Fal. You're being ridiculous.' Her breath was still short, perhaps Fal could hear and see that.

Waheeda marched to the queue. Fal was quiet until they'd taken their seats. The seats were very old and hard metal, famously uncomfortable. Fal's long neck moved left to right scanning all the rows behind and in front of them. Waheeda kept her eyes on the stage. The backdrop was painted with ripe fields of wheat, seen through large windows. The foreground was dotted with heavy wooden furniture, ornately carved, a period sitting room of a wealthy landlord in the Indian countryside.

Fal muttered 'There,' and settled back. She'd probably spotted where Monish and his angels were sitting but Waheeda didn't want to know.

Fal whispered in her ear. 'How many times? How long did this thing last? I am *shocked* at you, Pious.'

'Fal, please stop. This is getting ridiculous. You're *wrong*.' She hissed at Fal. 'If you persist with this, I'll just have to stop talking to you.'

'OK, don't throw a tantrum…I'm dropping it.'

The lights dimmed as the actors took their positions. Waheeda heard not a word they said. Her heart thumped; its frantic thrum filled her ears. When she returned to Naaz's she would have to call Monish. Tell him to deny any liaison no matter how resolutely Fal questioned him. She would explain that she was in Delhi with Hira and that was why she hadn't told him of her visit.

Could her luck be any worse? How had Fal guessed? What did her face show? Could she not conceal this one thing?

TWENTY-FIVE

October 1998

CHANDA'S BLUE AND white bangles clinked as she typed away efficiently, ending each email with 'from CJ (on behalf of MTS).' Monish always found it funny when they did this exercise of clearing his email backlog, because she sat at his desk, on his chair, at his computer, and he sat opposite, telling her what to say on his behalf. He still didn't like to respond to work emails himself. Every couple of weeks on a Friday, Chanda would force him to respond to the pile-up on his work computer. Sometimes she'd read out an email and he'd think: 'That's a conversation I need to have there; I can't be bothered with this'; and he'd tell her to reply: 'Telephone me.'

Computers were meant to give you more time, but sticking one in his office had just brought him a load of junk mail and notes from people he didn't want to respond to. He should have left all this to Chanda, sitting at her own desk, but he had given in to peer pressure. He'd got sick of the you-don't-use-a-computer-at-work? amazed faces. 'Fuddy-duddy' one friend had called him. Monish had winced and been defensive. 'I do use email, at home, on my own; and no, my email address is private.' He was bent on keeping himself accessible by personal email only to a handful of friends. Already, he was sick of the long joke messages that he received as a regular occurrence from Gaurav. 'I employ staff here,' he'd said to the cutting-edge friend, 'why should I be tied to that machine?' But here he was, tied to it, albeit using Chanda as the channel.

'Ignore,' he said for the umpteenth time that afternoon.

'But, sir, delete or keep?' she asked.

'You decide.' She tapped a key; he didn't care which one it was. Pratish had given him a talk when Monish had the computer installed. The IT guy could read all the emails, if he so wanted. Dad had decreed that money was never discussed in an email; whether it was about something within the firm or out of it. And a couple of other rules, so that even if their trusty secretaries had access to their accounts, they were not reading anything hugely confidential. Someone walked into the room behind him. Chanda froze. There had been no knock, no diffident 'Excuse me, sir,' so Monish could guess. He turned his head to the door just as his father came to stand by him. He stood and so did Chanda.

'Exchanged places?' Arun Selvani asked. 'Made her the boss?'

'This is how I work some afternoons.'

Arun bounced on his toes. 'Oh?' His black shoes were well-shined. He was holding a folder.

'Chanda's whittling down my email backlog.' Monish looked at her, his expression giving her permission to leave. She bent over the computer to finish typing, closed the programme, and left them. Monish went over to occupy the seat she'd vacated. Arun walked to the window, so Monish had to swivel round to him.

'I've left some boxes of wedding cards on the table outside,' Arun said. 'Here's the list of people you need to visit to invite to the wedding.' He handed the folder to Monish. 'The cases of special *pista gajak* are stored in the cold room. Have them loaded in the car when you head out to deliver the invitations. *Don't forget* to give one box at each home and to convey our sincere entreaty to attend Pratish's wedding.'

Oh, hell. What a task. Monish leafed through the pages in the folder. Names and addresses, alphabetically. It would take him a week. 'Am I doing them all?'

'All of these, yes. This is only a third of the invitations. I've left a copy of this list on Chanda's desk, so she can keep you organised.'

There was a large red and gold envelope in the folder. Monish pulled it out. *Pratish weds Shobana* artistically inscribed. He opened the envelope to check the contents. Six different cards inside, each one starting "You are invited to…" blah blah blah. *Seven* ceremonies across six days. More hell. 'Dad, I don't have to attend *all* of these, do I?'

He got a look that told him he was being tiresome. 'What do *you* think, only brother of the groom?'

'I'll be bored out of my mind.'

'You'll behave.'

'Yeah…'

'You can invite a friend if you like,' Arun said magnanimously. 'To all the events.'

'Good; I'll invite Kriti. She'll keep me amused.'

Arun's face fell at once. 'I will *not* have that woman in my family line-up. Standing with us. Never. Do you not have any *decent* friends?'

'She is more decent than you.'

Arun walked round the desk and took a chair. Monish swivelled back to face him. 'She's a woman or a sofa?' Arun asked, in silk-voiced anger. 'How many men have sat on her? That's your definition of decent? I'd say she's soiled goods. Filthy. I don't even understand how you can be her—'

'Dad, don't talk like that. Please. If you were toting me around town looking for a bride, I'd be labelled all wonderful and sparkling clean. She and I have probably had the same number of lovers. So—'

'Grow up, son, and join the real world. You're a man. She's a woman.' He pressed the tips of his fingers together, creating a chunky webbed diamond.

'I can't talk to you,' Monish whispered.

'I said you can invite a friend, but you clear it with me first. Understood? And don't bring along a darkie like that last one.'

'Who?' Monish stared.

'The Nulkazim *laundiya*.'

Monish leapt to his feet. 'She's the same colour as *you…*' *fuckface*, he wanted to say. 'And don't call her *laundiya*—'

'It's not a *gaali*.'

'No, but the way *you* say it is coarse. You're crude and…just go.' He raised his arm to the door.

'Why're you so het up? I thought it was *khatm*. Fully *khatm*.'

'You're right, I'm not in touch with her anymore. But still—I don't want you to speak ill of her.'

'I never would.' Arun raised his eyes to the ceiling in exasperation. 'I've heard good reports about her from the Dhoonpur area. Apparently she really is building influence. Becoming an authority.' He laughed. 'They say Nulkazim Peace Forum has the say-so in appointing some high officials. Well, you never know, one day, if we have a project there, we'll send you to sort out the clearances.'

Monish harrumphed through his nose. 'She's not going to blindly sign papers,' he said. 'She's not like that.'

'Who said blindly? She only has to see you to remember what you know about her. She will do *whatever* you ask.'

Monish's stomach cramped. At the window he swung aside the louvres to open the window a sliver, pushing until it got caught on the safety latch. It was a rare clear day and the sky was a burning blue. He breathed in, his nose as close to outdoors as it could be. He swallowed down his sick. Behind him he heard the chair creak as his father stood and then the heaviness had gone from the room. Monish turned to check. Yes, he was alone. He shut the door and sat at his desk, his hands clasped in prayer and his forehead bowed into his hands. I never ask for anything, God, but today, two things, please. One, don't let me turn into my father. Ever. I know it happens to people, that's what they say. Please don't let it happen to me. Never could I be so boorish, so vulgar.…I haven't the words, but you know what I mean. Second, please never let it happen that I'm sent to cajole/bribe/blackmail Waheeda. Never may there be a Selvani project in her area. Please God.

His office door opened again. He straightened but not before Arun had glimpsed his posture. 'Praying?' he asked, in silken anger. 'Praying to not be like your father?' The man knew everything. Monish clamped his lips. 'Praying to be like your mother?' Arun goaded him. 'Cultured person. Don't forget, Monish, on which side your bread is buttered. Who is the money man here? Who earns? Nikki Selvani may be very refined and cultivated, but she is not a profit centre. She will never be able to save you from anything.' He sat down. 'If you try to stir up anarchy in *my* home, you will pay. Get it?' Monish nodded.

'But that's not what I came back to say.' Arun gave a small bounce in his chair. 'There's something I forgot to tell you earlier, because you were so intent on showing me the door.' He leaned forward. 'I was offering wedding presents to sons of mine who would get married, remember? We had a talk about it months ago.'

Monish remained silent.

'Pratish wants a sports car. I don't think he's decided which one yet. But guess what? Girls are so smart these days. Shobana said to me, 'How come I don't get a car from you, too?''

Monish stared. She *was* smart. She'd already wrapped Arun around her little finger, with her saccharine ways, and wheedled him round to her way of thinking on certain ceremonies. But Monish had to concede that she was genuinely sweet-natured, too. She'd agreed that Dad and Ma could go on safari along with Pratish and her. This was their *honeymoon*. She didn't seem to mind as long as they picked the luxury lodges and the private flights. Well, she was going to live with them after all; he supposed she would have to get used to having them around.

Arun said: 'I told Shobana she could have a car, too. A Porsche Boxster? She said: "Perhaps. Why does that car get offered to women? I might choose something else." So smart, don't you think?'

In the old days, *her* father would be buying Pratish a car. Maybe he was buying him something else instead. Some other material desire of Pratish would be fulfilled by his pa-in-law.

'Just thought I'd tell you about the cars,' Arun said. He looked closely into Monish's face and walked out, leaving the door open.

Monish removed his glasses and put his palms over his face. He was a grown man. He would not cry because he hadn't been given a toy. He would not cry. He heard Chanda's soft knock on the door and placed his hands on his desk. She came in and laid out three pages. 'I looked at the invitation list very quickly,' she said. 'I've divided it into South, West and East Delhi for now. I'll prepare a full list for each area for the driver with the correct addresses. It'll save you time if you make the visits by area. If you agree, I'll prepare accordingly.'

'Yes, Chanda,' he said, and his voice was hoarse. 'Thank you.'

Her gaze was on the red and gold envelope. 'Mr Pratish is really getting married...'

'Yes.'

'Before you, sir?'

There was such concern in her voice that it made him want to laugh and weep at the same time. Her unease would be about the breaking of tradition, of how it would look, of what people would say about him, her Mr Monish. But deeper than that she was feeling bad on his behalf, even though she didn't know the background. Tears stung at his eyes and he lowered his gaze to the desk.

'Yes. Before me.' His voice was still hoarse. 'It's how I want it, Chanda.'

She collected up her three pages. 'I'll see you on Tuesday, sir. Happy Diwali.'

'Oh, yes.' Monday was a holiday. 'Happy Diwali.' He smiled till she turned away but then grimaced at himself. He'd arranged a big bonus for her, but he'd meant to buy her a personal gift, too. Well, it was too late for Diwali, but never mind. He would buy something in old silver; something that would keep its value, something she could cherish and take with her to her new home when she got married. He was tempted to lecture her: 'Don't leave it another year. Are your parents doing what they should? Feel free to take time off to meet men who are looking for a wife.' But he wasn't setting the best example himself.

He placed the files on his desk in neat piles and turned off the computer. He'd just switched the lights off when his direct line rang. He picked up. 'Fal? Hello! What a surprise! A meeting? Next week? No, not really. No day free. Would you rather go out for lunch instead? The following week. I see. An official meeting. Well…yes…sure. What with Diwali holidays and then a week delivering Pratish's wedding cards, I can't really fix anything before next month…yes, of course, I'll see you at the wedding, your parents will be invited no doubt and you're welcome to come along, as you know; everyone's family is welcome; no, I haven't done my own list; no, not at all, The Prat and I don't have mutual friends; yes, that's normal for siblings, I know you don't know, being an only child.…Yes, I understand, official meeting, I'm putting it in the diary, first Wednesday in November.'

He switched on a lamp and made a note. Then he texted Moonraker. 'Miss Lava has been in touch.'

•

November 1998

HE ESCORTED FALGUNI to the small conference room. It had a round table and they could sit adjacent to one another, so that the meeting wouldn't seem too formal. Chanda brought in black tea for Fal and a coffee for him along with a plate of wafers and cream biscuits.

'How're things with you?' he asked.

She'd seemed taller than normal when she'd arrived, standing almost level with him. As she sat, he noticed her high heeled grey suede boots. They'd accidently kicked against his shoe. She was wearing black jeans and a pink jacket. Rubies in her ears and on her right index finger. She tossed her head and swept her hair down her right shoulder, bringing it to the front so it fell to under her breast.

'All good,' she said, her eyes sparking. He knew that look. He was in for a grilling. He was ready. 'Didn't know you knew my school friend.'

He hesitated. 'Who?' he asked. Tricky. He'd almost said, 'I didn't know she was your friend.' That would've been an immediate giveaway. Damn, he'd have to stop and think carefully every single time before he opened his mouth.

'Waheeda,' Fal said.

'Oh yes. The one you were with at the theatre. The politician. She's your school friend?'

'We had the best years of our lives together. You know those years: 16, 17, 18, 19, 20, 21. Then it all becomes a blur. Life becomes over-wrought and nothing is simple anymore. And time is not slow slow slow…and your old friends are not the most important people in your life anymore…'

'Right.'

'So tell me about her.'

'I'm sorry.' He shook his head in puzzlement. 'You want *me* to tell you about your friend?'

Fal narrowed her eyes. 'Don't be coy. She told me you've done it.'

He laughed at her brazen cheek; he couldn't help himself. 'Good God,' he said, 'you women certainly know how to make up things. I'm sorry to disappoint you, Fal, but…No, that isn't true. Ask your friend to check her facts again.'

Fal opened her mouth to speak, but he carried on. 'You wanted an official meeting to talk about…what exactly?'

'I'm coming to that.'

'OK.'

'How's life with you? How come you're not getting married?' she asked.

'Probably the same reasons as you. I follow where you lead, Fal.'

She grinned and her eyes lost that dangerous spark. She would drop the questions about Waheeda even if she didn't believe him. He hoped.

'Who're you seeing?' she asked.

'Who're *you* seeing?' he asked.

'None of your business,' she said.

'Same to you.'

'Oh, Monish, I don't understand why you're being so combative. I'm just asking who you're seeing. I don't care if it's one person or twenty.'

Then why ask. Because you think you can get away with behaving like a snooping bossy older sister? 'A mixture,' he shrugged.

'A mixture of what? Men and women?'

He closed his eyes in annoyance. 'How long have you known me?'

'Since you were a brainless ten-year-old. You tried to smoke at the back of my house, remember? You rolled up a page of paper and lit it. You almost set fire to your nose! Idiot.'

'Right. Since I was ten. So what do you think about my

sexuality? Just by instinct. Not even because Nikhil is your best friend.' Nikhil was one of the few openly gay men in Delhi. Fal and he were childhood friends. She'd told Monish that Nikhil had stolen all her dinky cars, and even though he was a thief, she'd loved him, and pretended not to notice that her dinky toys went missing whenever he'd been round to play. 'You think Nikhil wouldn't sniff out—'

'I'm pulling your leg.' She sipped her black tea. '*Your* best friend Kriti seems to spout the most incredible rumours about you. I'd discard her.'

'You've seen her lately?'

'No, but I hear from X, who's heard from Y, who's heard from the horse's mouth; or Kriti's mouth, so to speak…'

He raised up his palms. 'Hazards of life in Delhi,' he said.

Fal, of course, saved her longer and more serious trysts for her holidays in Goa, well away from Delhi folks. She was somewhat successful in keeping her private life private, in that he didn't know until much later who she'd been having an affair with. By that time, she'd usually moved on, so although there was always gossip swirling about her, unless you tracked her to her remote bungalow in Goa you wouldn't know whom she was currently dating.

Fal leaned forward to flick something off his shirt. 'You know Waheeda's husband Nafis is an artist. Have you seen any of his paintings?'

'No, I haven't. Should I have? Is he well-known?' Monish looked at his watch. 'And if you just wanted to chat we could've had lunch as I suggested. But you said you preferred—'

Fal pushed away her empty tea cup. 'On behalf of the agency, I wanted to fix a date to do a pitch. For all the advertising business for Vani Paints.'

Monish almost gasped. *All* the advertising? Thankfully, he'd thought of what to do in this scenario.

'You're very welcome to do a pitch, Fal. You'll have to pitch to Dad. I'll arrange it with his secretary so she can fit you in whenever he next has a free slot. He's pretty occupied as you know, what with the wedding…'

'You're the boss of the paints business, Monish. We'll make our pitch to you.'

'I'm not the one who chose our agency. Dad did. And he still makes the big decisions.' Not strictly true, but Monish had worked out that if he kicked the problem upwards, it would stall for a while. When Dad did meet her, he wouldn't feel the same obligations as Monish did. She might charm him, but if Monish filled Dad in on the fact that she was being overly insistent, he would dislike that approach. He might think his son a wimp for not standing up to her, but he would help out. Depending on how good the pitch was, perhaps Dad would *want* to give her a slice of the biz; then the problem would be back with Monish. But he'd bought time.

'Is that true?' Fal tossed her head. 'You're a bloody nobody in your own company.'

Monish breathed in. He removed his glasses.

'You're telling me you're not the person who signed off on that last campaign? I've heard you take credit for those ads!' She glared at him. 'You're a useless fake.'

He breathed out on his glasses. He waved them in the air to dry. He'd asked Waheeda what he should do—should he give Fal some business when she came in or not? Waheeda had said, very firmly, so firmly that it had amused him, that she didn't want Fal to have an excuse to spend time with Monish. She would dig for dirt and Monish might slip up. If he wanted to keep seeing Waheeda, no advertising business to Falguni. That was the deal.

'Do you want some more tea, Fal?'

She pursed her lips and scowled at the floor. He buzzed Chanda and asked for another tea and coffee. 'You didn't like the biscuits?' he asked. Fal looked at the plate disdainfully.

Monish caught Chanda's eye. 'Get us cakes from the bakery downstairs,' he said.

'Which cake, sir?'

'A slice of each.' He turned to Fal. 'They're very good. You can see them all and choose what you like. Although I think the carrot cake will go well with your black tea.'

TWENTY-SIX

November 1998

'WELL, THEN, FAL ate the carrot cake, and called me a phoney tycoon and a puppet and departed.' Monish put on a hang-dog look, waiting for her sympathy and her gratitude at his acceptance of Fal's barbs. 'She was trying to make me retract and tell her I was the proper managing director; that, yes, I made all the decisions for Vani Paints.'

Waheeda hugged his wiry arm to her body. They were waiting for Lara to arrive at Monish's flat. Then he would drive them to the farmhouse in Mehrauli. For the first time, Waheeda didn't mind going out with him in public, because she was tagging along as Lara's friend. It was Lara who wanted to see Monish's farmhouse; he'd told her it was where he spent his quiet weekends. Anyway, this outing wasn't really public, other than sitting in the back seat of his car, most of the visit was secluded.

'Fal spoke about Nafis at the end,' Monish said.

'Nafis?'

'Yes, your husband?' Waheeda felt his arm stiffen against her. He seemed upset.

'What did she say?'

'Just asking if I'd seen his paintings…I saw a picture of you two last week.'

It took Waheeda a moment to register what he meant. 'Me and Nafis?' she asked, 'or Fal and me?'

'You and your husband. In the Nulkazim edition of the Express.'

'I didn't realise you read the Nulkazim papers.' She looked keenly at him. 'Shakeel includes photos of Nafis and me in the media packs. They are old photos—'

'Not this one. It was recent. You're both looking cosy in Theog—'

Was he jealous? 'Oh, that one. I'd gone to pick up Hira. Shakeel had called Nafis and requested a new photo, so we posed quickly early in the morning before Hira and I drove down.'

'You spent the night there? You never told me. In the same bedroom?'

She hugged his arm to her tighter. 'No, Monish. Not in the same room. There is a small room that Hira sleeps in. I did sleep in the main bedroom. But Nafis was on the couch in his living room.' Her voice shook slightly. She wasn't yet used to Nafis's implacable renunciation. She couldn't speak of it to Monish.

'The man's an idiot. He's inept, impractical, selfish, a moron.'

'Don't say that…'

'He is.' Monish jabbed his forefinger on his thigh. 'He left you so that he could live in a hovel in the hills. Worse, how could he not be there for his daughter? What sort of man—'

'Don't judge him. Not till you've been in the same position yourself.'

'What position? Spending my days rubbing paint on canvas? With a hard-working wife and a beautiful child? That situation of extreme duress?'

It's a situation you may not be able to handle. But you're clever enough not to place yourself in that position. 'Monish…have pity…he was depressed. He was living in a city he'd come to hate. He was losing his sensibility of being an artist, his sense of self. He hadn't known these responsibilities would make him feel trapped. In one way, he was just like you—he needed his freedom. That you can understand.'

Monish made a *pfft* sound. '*You* don't get your freedom.'

'I'm not that needy.'

He laughed but it had a grim undertone. 'The tigress leaps out again,' he said. 'She attacks when you threaten her *husband*.' He pulled his arm away. 'It's kind of you to continue to defend Nafis. Or is it love? You wouldn't do it for me.'

'I would.' Immediately she regretted saying that.

He pounced. 'Let's see. You're at someone's home for dinner, or a gathering, whatever; and the talk turns to the Selvani's, say, and someone rubbishes Monish. He's a rotten egg. You would defend me, would you? You would say: He's a decent guy. I know him. I have put my trust in him. He may suffer from poor-little-rich-boy syndrome, but he's not a bad human being. You have to put yourself in his position before you judge him.'

'I can't speak up for you.' She stroked his arm. 'You know that.' She put her hand on his thigh, high up.

'There's plenty you can't do for me.'

Waheeda bit her lip and interlaced her hands in her lap. If he'd wanted to hurt her, he'd succeeded.

•

SHE JUMPED UP when the bell rang and stood in the bedroom until she heard Lara's voice, at which point she rushed out to embrace her.

'The traffic!' Lara exclaimed. 'It's not even rush hour. Eleven a.m. on a weekday. It took me an hour to get here. I'm sorry I'm late.'

'It's all right,' Waheeda said. 'I'm used to the time it takes to get across from South Delhi and I should've warned you. When we have the metro, travelling around Delhi might be easier.' She smacked her forehead. 'How silly, we should have all met in south Delhi.'

'But then I wouldn't have seen Monish's apartment.' Lara looked around curiously. 'Are all the curtains closed because of you?'

'Yes.'

'Shall we head off to the farm?' Monish asked.

'I'd like to see a bit of your home, if you don't mind.' Lara turned to Waheeda and spoke in a stage whisper. 'The scene of your assignations.'

Waheeda looked at the floor.

'Oops, sorry,' Lara said, but when that didn't raise a smile, she asked, 'Have I come at a bad time?' There was no response and she added, 'I think I've said something really crass and stupid. I apologise.'

'No, no.' Monish spoke up. 'I've been impatient and insensitive...before you arrived...Lara, if you don't mind finding your way to the kitchen, it's through there.' He pointed. 'See if there's something for you to do for a minute...Help yourself to a drink...'

'All right,' Lara's eyes danced at him as she disappeared into the kitchen.

Monish took Waheeda's hands in his. 'Let's not spoil our day out, Wija. I get irritable, I know I do, and it's only because we can't do anything normal; you won't even have a meal out with me or meet my friends...I don't expect it of you, I'm not saying I do, it's just that your husband has spent the entire night with you, many times, and we've not had even one night...and you love him more.'

'No. That's not true. That last bit.'

He pressed his lips on hers and she felt his relief, his sudden joy at her words, she felt it through the clasp of his hands on her shoulders. He kissed her closed eyelids and straightened up. 'You can come out, Lara,' he called.

•

IT TOOK THEM over an hour to weave across to Mehrauli. Waheeda sat at the back, her light-green *dupatta* partly obscuring her face, and she was content to let Monish and Lara jabber to each other in the front. Occasionally, she would catch Monish looking at her in the rearview mirror, or Lara would turn to ask her a question, but she was happy to make brief responses. Today she wanted to observe and not be observed. Monish would love to own the farmhouse outright, she knew that. As it was, he had to check with his mother when he could use it for himself, without the rest of the family piling in. She expected there to be no staff at the property today, or she wouldn't have agreed to the expedition. Monish had told her that he'd arranged for the caretaker and his wife, who was disabled, to visit their home village. Some of the ceremonies and parties for Pratish's wedding were to be held at the farm, so he'd made that the excuse for them to take a short break before the busy period.

'The caretaker at the farmhouse, Ashwin, is my man,' he was telling Lara. 'He used to be my office driver. Then his wife had an accident. She lost a leg. He needed to be home a lot more than he could be with a regular driver's job. So I suggested that they move to the farm. He's intensely loyal to me. When I'm there, he cooks and looks after me very well. For the others, he's just the caretaker. Mom brings her own staff when she uses the house.'

'I'm getting hungry,' Lara said. 'Is Ashwin cooking us lunch?'

'He's away for a few days. We're getting a takeaway from the best restaurant in the area. I've ordered. It'll be waiting for us to pick up.'

'You're very organised.'

'I try to be.'

He sent Lara in to collect the takeaway. She came back weighed down by two large plastic bags, which were stuffed with several white boxes. How much did he think two women would eat? 'That aroma is making my tummy rumble.' Lara set the bags down on the floor of the back seat.

A few minutes later they halted at a high black gate. Monish hopped out to open it. A winding drive through woods brought them to an open expanse dominated by the villa. It was yellow and white, Mediterranean in architecture and style.

'The plot is six acres,' Monish told Lara as they ate. 'Dad bought it aeons ago, in 1980, when the area was first becoming fashionable for "country homes." The house and gardens are my mom's ongoing projects; there's always something she's planning or renovating.'

He showed them around the two-storey house after lunch. Five bedrooms upstairs, the largest being the master bedroom, the next biggest for the two brothers, and three smaller rooms. Each room had an attached bathroom sized as the rooms. Monish's room was furnished with a four-poster bed. The dark wooden posts had elaborately-carved finials. The bedspread was tie-dyed indigo and white cotton, with indigo tassels. Waheeda stood looking at his bed. If she turned down the cover, would there be plump white-clad pillows? Soft white sheets? Blue?

'All the rooms have verandas. I *adore* that.' Lara bounced about. 'I'm going to have a look at the different views from the other rooms.' She left them.

Monish came closer to Waheeda, in her space, at her back. 'Seeing you and Lara together has reminded me of that first evening we met. It's made me think of something I want to do with you,' he said, into her ear.

'What?' She rested her hand on the post so that if he leaned into her she could take his weight. She would feel his warmth all the way up her spine.

'Remember those *gajras* you brought to my room? I want to buy *gajras* and bring you here. I'll tie them to your ankles. Put your ankles on my shoulders. I'll have the fragrance and the touch of jasmine, right on my face, when I—'

He broke off at Lara's returning footsteps.

They went into a large atrium downstairs. 'Party place,' Monish said.

'How many people can you have here?'

'Hundreds.'

'Really?'

'Well, for one of the parties for Pratish's wedding, we have four hundred guests. That'll be here. "Not a big event" according to my parents, you understand.' A grin appeared. 'I think they're squeezing out what they can from this wedding. They're not due another huge event for a while.' His face darkened. 'Unless they decide to have an anniversary bash for themselves. They could have six hundred or more people for that. In which case, it'll be outside; let me show you.'

He led them through meandering paths that led to different end points. A Mughal-style fountain. A secret enclosed garden with high topiary which made Waheeda think of Nikki Selvani straightaway and her request to Waheeda. Through a small wood to a massive round clearing. 'Here,' Monish said. 'Party location.'

'Does your Ashwin look after all this?' she asked.

'Oh no. Mom has two gardeners. They come in every couple of days.' He looked at Waheeda. 'They won't be here today. Everyone knows I hate them being around when I'm here.'

'What do you do when you're here, Monish?' Lara asked. 'It sounds like you don't want to see anyone.'

'I walk, I listen to music. I read. I ruminate. Most of all, I enjoy the silence. And the weight of expectations dropping off me.'

Waheeda noted that he was careful to exclude 'women' from the list. She had no doubt that in the past his girlfriends would have spent time with him here; weekends perhaps, when it was his turn to have the farmhouse to himself.

Lara was sniffing at bitter-orange-blossom. *Kinu* bushes with their delicate white flowers encircled the clearing. 'I have a name for you,' she said to Monish, 'The Luxurious Hermit. That's what I'm going to call you from now on.'

December 1998

'Finally, I get to see the little one.' Monish wasn't sure what the form was with babies. He patted the soft curls on Kabir's head. Kabir immediately began yelping. Naaz, who had him tucked into her hip, laughed.

Monish felt hurt. Didn't the baby like him? He'd smiled into its face. Even dogs were easier to read than babies. Some of his friends had small children, and he enjoyed joshing with them, and being the chocolate-distributor-uncle, but when he'd met them as newborns, their mothers had giggled at his nervousness and incompetence. But no one had actually helped him or shown him what to do. Anyway, Kabir was a year old. He shouldn't be afraid of Monish.

Naaz wiped Kabir's mouth with a square of cloth and placed him on the rug. He stopped whining and began crawling. He reached out for the armchair and tried to use it to stand up. Naaz sat down keeping her eyes trained on her child as she spoke to Monish. 'Wija insisted I bring him before the *mundan*. She's afraid he won't be so cute after his head has been shaved.'

'He will be,' Monish said. 'Plus his hair will grow back. It's no big deal.'

Kabir pulled himself up to standing by Naaz. She bent down and hovered her arm protectively around him. He was unsteady on his feet.

'Yes, but Wija says his baby curls will be lost. She says his hair will be fine and silky like Deepak's but no more glorious curls!'

'She's probably right about that. I wouldn't know. Tea?'

'Yes, please.'

The little boy stared at Monish with his mouth agape. His eyes were huge and black.

Monish handed over the present he'd bought for Kabir

before he went into the kitchen. An antique silver baby's rattle. Hopefully it would keep the toddler amused while his mom drank tea and chatted. He laid out a teapot, two mugs, a strainer, teaspoons, milk and sugar on the glass dining table. Brownies and fresh ginger biscuits from his favourite bakery. Side plates. Paper napkins. He knew about Naaz's sweet tooth.

Naaz had taken out some plastic toys and placed them on the rug. She came to the table, an eye still on her son. He crawled to her and squealed for attention. She handed him a teaspoon and he banged it on the marble column base of the table. *Tak tak tak tak tak.*

Monish tried to speak above the noise. That was one very irritating thing about mothers. You only ever had half their attention when their child was around. 'Why don't you open his present?' The rattle chimes had to be better than this *tak tak tak.*

'It's not something fragile?' Naaz asked.

'No, no. It's something for him to play with. Now.'

She handed the package to him. 'You give it to him.' She put a brownie on her plate. Her hair was tied back in a French plait. She wore a blue cardigan and well-worn jeans. She'd been pregnant when he'd last seen her so he couldn't tell whether she'd gained weight or not compared to her previous self. In the last year, they'd spoken on the phone but not met. Her face had always been plump, and he couldn't see any difference, other than that expression of unmistakable happiness.

He bent down to bring Kabir to him. He opened the colourful foil wrapping slowly, knowing that Kabir was watching in concentration. Slowly. Slowly. He tore it off in circular motion. Kabir's eyes on his hands. He held up the rattle. *Chun. Chun. Chun.* A tinkling sound of old silver bells inside the silver filigree ball.

Kabir stretched out his hand and Monish wrapped the

boy's cute little fingers around the handle. Naaz seemed delighted. 'Is it antique, Monish? It's beautiful. You shouldn't have.'

Chun. Chun. Chun. 'Oh, I should have. This is nothing. Nothing at all. You have done so much for me.'

'I'm not doing it for you.'

'I know.' Yep, straight-talking Naaz. He wouldn't expect any less from her.

'Where is Deepak this weekend?' he asked. He was under no illusions. Naaz would not have come to visit him, baby in tow, unless Deepak was out of town.

'He's in Japan. He used to have just one customer there, for whose firm he produced uniforms each year. But now that customer has recommended Deepak to many of his friends, and Deepak keeps being called back to do the rounds of—' She broke off. Kabir was sitting at Naaz's feet and he'd thrown the rattle towards the door. Monish stood to pick it up and replace it in Kabir's little hand.

'Well, you know the Japanese like to build up a relationship first, somewhat formally,' Naaz said. 'So Deepak hasn't got any actual orders from these recommendations yet, but he makes it a priority to go when they ask him to come to see their stores and the current uniforms, as in this particular visit. He'll send some quotations—'

Chun Chun thud. Kabir had thrown the rattle again. Monish jumped up to fetch it.

'How many times are you willing to do that?' she asked. 'Shall we take it away from him? It'll get dented.'

'No, let him enjoy it. I'll tell you when I'm exhausted. It's an old rattle—many babies have thrown it; so what if it's dented. Makes it more precious.' Although he was a tiny bit worried about his parquet floor, but never mind.

Naaz smiled at him, her jaw and face lifting. 'Did you hear that I'm planning to have a party in August?'

'No. What's the occasion?'

'Hira and I are both born in August. Next August I'll be thirty-five and she'll be eight. We've decided to have a joint party. Hira gets to choose the theme and some of the food and invite her Delhi friends...'

'Wow, that's some forward planning. Six months ahead!'

'Yes...and I need you to back me up on this.'

'To whom? Why?'

'Waheeda. She's demurring. Probably because Nafis has balked at it, saying it's a crazy plan. It may be—but Hira loves the idea. And I do, too. Hira says we'll be princesses and wear gowns and tiaras, and have a joint ice-blue birthday cake with silver balls on it...and she's the one who excitedly told Nafis everything she's planning. She *is* a little madam, you know. He thinks *I'm* mad to indulge her and myself, I guess...' she pouted, 'but so what?'

'Right...' Monish got up again to bring back the rattle.

'If Wija mentions it to you, tell her not to spoil Hira's fun.'

He returned to his seat. At least Naaz had managed to drink her tea and polish off the brownie. 'She would never want to do that,' he said. 'She always tells me how difficult she finds it to be strict with Hira. Her father spoils her when she visits him; *you* cosset her; even Aseem-ji is soft on her; and Waheeda says it's left to her to be rigorous...'

He had no doubt about Waheeda's absolute devotion to Hira. She'd told him how she squirmed inside at her disciplinarian role. 'Ammi is so good at looking after Hira's needs that I don't like to pressure her with additional rules for my daughter,' she'd said. So it was she who ensured that Hira brushed her teeth at night (because I don't want her to have fillings or blame me for bad teeth later); only she who insisted Hira get 10/10 on her spelling tests and practiced for them (because she's bright enough and shouldn't slack off); only she who checked what exercise she'd gotten that week (for her health and for strong bones); and only she who read to Hira whenever she could (because all parents should do that). She'd told him she was looking for a dance teacher for Hira, because Hira seemed to love dancing and have natural rhythm.

'Of course, Monish. Hira is Wija's life. Like Kabir is mine. But if she sounds uncertain about this joint birthday bash, just give her a nudge in the right direction.'

'Sure. I will.' He nodded to assure her. 'Am I invited? Should I put it in the diary?'

He was joking but Naaz glanced at him in embarrassment. 'No, I think it will be for girls only. I mean, an all-female do. Girls and ladies.'

'And Kabir?' He'd tease her a bit more.

'Well, yes, he'll be there…he'll be the exception to the rule.'

'And Deepak?'

'Well, yes…'

'It's all right, Naaz. I understand.' *Chun chun chun* thud. He wanted to ask if Nafis would be there; he suspected not. He would be invited, perhaps, but it sounded like the sort of thing he would detest. He was already protesting.

Naaz pulled out an insulated bottle carrier patterned with kangaroos. She placed Kabir on her lap and he began sucking greedily from the bottle. 'He'll be drowsy soon,' she said. 'It'll be easier to strap him in his seat and drive home as he's falling asleep.'

'I'll escort you to your car,' he said as they stood by the lift. 'Thank you for coming to see me.'

Kabir was on her shoulder, dribbling into the cloth that Naaz had placed under his face. His eyes fluttered. They entered the lift, which jolted down once and stopped again on the floor below. Kriti got in. 'Hello. Going out for the evening?' she asked.

'No, I'm staying in.'

He saw her eyes widen as she clocked that he was holding

a handbag and a baby-changing-bag. 'Oh, hello,' she said to Naaz, realising that Naaz was with him. She stared at Kabir, whose eyes had closed. His little mouth had fallen open.

In the foyer Monish introduced Kriti and Naaz to each other. He walked Naaz to her car in the guest parking bay and helped her settle her son into the car seat. 'So that was Kriti,' Naaz said.

'Yes. You know of her? Has someone mentioned her to you?'

'Um—yes. I know she's your close friend. You two go back a long way, so I hear.' She spun her car keys expertly round her finger. 'People talk about her…a lot! She's stunning. Does she look like that all the time?'

'Yes…I think so. What do you mean people talk about her?'

Naaz made a face. 'You know, Monish. It means nothing. Or it does rather.' She got into the driver's seat. 'It means she's not a hypocrite. She doesn't care what people say. It means people are jealous. She's gorgeous. And brave. That's what I would say.'

TWENTY-SEVEN

April 1999

'Happy birthday, babe. Apparently you're gorgeous and brave.' Monish raised his new champagne glass in a toast. Kriti clinked her glass with his.

'Who said that about me?' She was curious.

He shrugged, 'Can't remember.' He didn't like champagne and wanted to spit it out, but he'd bought the Moet for her, at her request, and he would down some tonight, in solidarity, but leave most of it for her. 'Heard it somewhere.'

She went out into the balcony for a moment with her glass, then came back in. 'Look at this, Monish.' She waved an angry arm at the sky outside. It had been an overwhelming smoky orange when he was driving home, as the sun was setting; now it was dark and dulled. 'What have we done to our city? Did you read that article: "Delhi Pollution at par with 1952 London Smog"? Did you *see* that? It wasn't like this when we were young!'

'Careful, you're sounding like an old woman.' The air did feel solid with particulates. This would be one of the last evenings he would open the balcony door until September. Any hotter, and it would ruin the carefully cooled climate inside his flat. He should buy a house plant to decontaminate the air. 'Shall I close the doors?' he asked.

'No,' she sighed. 'I need to smoke.' She sat down and pulled the side table in front of her. Her wrap dress fell open slightly above her knees. It was in a navy, turquoise and white wave print. It looked cool: cotton, low v-neck, bare arms and legs. If he worked out for hours and hours in a gym, he could lounge here in a singlet and shorts, showing off whopping biceps like the current crop of Bollywood heroes. But he felt his limbs were too thin to be on display, and he was more comfortable in his jeans and tee.

She lit a joint. The doorbell rang. Kriti rolled her eyes and stubbed it out. He opened the door. Choppy's son said, 'Uncle, here are the printouts of the data you wanted. Papa said let him know if you need anything else.'

'Thanks.' Monish took the sheaf of papers from him.

The boy darted a look inside the living room. 'Hello, Kriti Auntie.'

'Hi.'

Monish was about to close the door, when she beckoned, 'Come here, come here.'

Choppy's son entered and stood in front of her. She examined him closely. 'How old are you now?'

'Seven,' he said proudly and smiled, showing her all his teeth and the gap on one side. *Wow*, Monish thought, *I've never elicited that smile from him. Even when I gave him a giant tube of Smarties.*

'This last year,' Kriti said to the boy, 'you've been a veritable fashion show.'

'Huh?'

'Your *patka*,' she pointed to the grey and green polka-dot turban covering his topknot. 'It always complements your clothes when you're dressed up to go somewhere. Even when you're just out to play, it seems. You like all these different colours and designs you wear?'

He nodded quite solemnly.

'You choose them?' she asked.

He shook his head and unleashed that toothy smile again.

'So your mom selects for you and ties on your *patka*?'

'Yes, auntie.'

'Great styling,' Kriti said. 'Both your mom and you. Go and tell her: I complimented you. What are you going to say?'

'Great styling,' he repeated. He touched his *patka*. 'Bye, auntie. Bye, uncle.'

'Isn't he adorable?' Kriti said, inhaling on her herb. 'What are those papers?'

'Choppy tells me that there's a Sikh joke: the children of Sardars and donkeys are the cutest of all. Then they grow up and…But he tells me only Sirds should make this joke. These papers? I asked him for some data. To shore up my argument against Falguni Lava. I didn't want to put a scare on my own agency.'

'What's happening with Fal?'

Monish placed the papers on the sideboard. 'She's pitching for the advertising business for Vani Paints. I should say she's demanding it; that's Fal for you. I've arranged for her to do the sell to Dad, so when I say no; or no to most of her agency's ideas, it won't be a direct snub from me. But I'll attend the pitch, with my marketing team…'

'Tell her to eff-off, Monny, if that's what you really want to do.'

'I can't.' He raised his hand. 'Don't ask, babe. It'll ruin my mood.' He sat down beside her on the sofa. 'Made any birthday resolutions?'

'Yes. Just one.'

'Oh?'

'I want a baby.'

Some of the champagne he was sipping dripped onto his T-shirt. He dabbed at it with his fingers. It would dry in a minute. 'Aren't you a bit young for that?' he said finally, after a minute of silence had elapsed.

She blew smoke at him. 'Thirty today.' She passed him the joint.

He took a toke. 'I know. Same as me. That's young. There's

no rush for…well, it's not my business, actually. If that's what you want and you've lined up a husband—' He settled back into the sofa. This relaxant effect must be psychological, he thought.

She gazed out of the balcony doors. 'No husband,' she murmured. 'I don't need one to have a baby.'

'Oh, Kriti,' he said softly. He couldn't think what advice to give. Do what you like? Don't do it?

'Who was that woman with her kid who came to visit you a few months ago?'

'Naaz? I introduced you, remember? Her husband, Deepak, is my friend.'

'Not *your* baby, then?'

He gaped at her. 'Are you kidding? Naaz is not…never mind. No way there's any baby of mine out there,' he said. 'You know how careful I am to make it clear that I'm not in the running for marriage and children. And if I don't already know the person well, I am *doubly* cautious—'

'That doesn't mean you haven't spawned—you might not even know—'

'I hope to God not.'

She passed him the last of the joint. He pulled at it and put it out.

'You might not know—'

He shifted uncomfortably. His eyes narrowed. 'Are you trying to tell me something? Is there something I don't know?' He glanced quickly at her abdomen. Her waist was small and tightly belted. No more than a normal curve under the belt.

She shook her head. 'Just saying.'

'Let's not talk about me. It's *your* birthday. Let's talk about you.'

'So that was what I was going to ask you.' She pushed away the little table with the ashtray. Her nails were painted dark blue.

'Sorry, what?'

'You can be my sperm donor.'

'You're mad. Seriously. No way.'

She opened a little tin in her orange pouch and brought out another joint.

'That's enough for now,' he said. 'You've barely digested that first one. Give it a break.'

Her eyes glittered as she sparked her lighter.

He felt hunger pangs. He walked to the kitchen (rather slowly he thought), returning with a bag of Jesse's corn puffs. He tore it open, but suddenly it reminded him of Fal and he left it on the dining table. Every savoury snack in his kitchen was Jesse's this or Jesse's that—the products that had made Fal's dad's fortune. He could see myriad packs of corn puffs floating round in his kitchen. He shook his head to clear it (he was out of practice with weed) and found a Tupperware box of *jeera mathi* that his mother had brought over last Sunday. He chomped on a large piece of *mathi*. Without a plate. Flakes of it fell on the floor and his clothes, but he was so chilled he didn't bother. 'Shall I heat up dinner, Kriti, or would you like to go out? Dancing? And I do have a mini chocolate cake for you in the fridge as well. (He'd put three golden candles on it.) Whatever you want to do. You're the boss.'

She was giving him the silent treatment. Oh dear, he didn't want her to sulk on her birthday. At least she'd stopped smoking after two or three tokes. She downed her champagne and scrutinised the blank wall above his sound system.

'You're being silly,' he said.

'All I'm asking for is sperm. You're happy to chuck it about usually. I'm asking for a good reason. As my *friend*. I'm not asking you to play Dad or anything.'

'Kriti, if you have a child and it bears even the slightest resemblance to me, everyone will know straightaway. If you

329

have a *"friend's"* child, everyone's going to look at *me*. I'm *not* doing it. How many times should I tell you this evening that I don't want kids? All these years, I've meant what I said. I don't want to be a father. Never. Never. *Never.* Whether a child calls me 'Dad' or not is not the point. I don't want there to *be* a child of mine. Get it?'

Still silent. He tried to imagine her heavily pregnant, her stomach distended, her breasts larger. He couldn't visualise it. He would have to see it in real life to be able to have that picture in his head. 'I don't understand why you're in such a rush. You can wait five years without a problem. Wait till you meet the right guy.'

'Of course you don't understand.' She slammed down her empty glass so hard the base and the stem broke. He took the top bowl from her fingers. It was good he had quick reflexes, even when stoned. He took the pieces to the kitchen and left it in a corner of the worktop. The glass rim was smeared with her peachy lip gloss. He came back with a duster to feel for any small bits of glass on the table. He would have to brush the carpet and be careful in his bare feet.

'If you were a woman, you'd be saying something different.' Kriti sat straight up, almost snarling at him. 'My women friends have the opposite reaction to you. They say: "If you want to have a child, there's no time to waste." They say: "Go for it, Kriti."' She stood up and followed him to the kitchen, where he put the duster in the bin. He checked his palms in the sink. There were tiny fragments sticking to him. He sloshed cold water till his palms felt smooth. Kriti said, 'Please, Monish. It's the only thing I'm asking of you.'

'Don't cry. Please don't cry.' He put his arms around her. 'Not on your birthday.' He felt close to tears himself. 'Don't ask me for something I can't give you.'

He hadn't even mentioned her medication to her and her mental health. Would she be OK with pregnancy and being a mother? He didn't know. Presumably she would've found out. He hoped. Already he was beginning to feel sorry for the next man who was reeled in by her loveliness. Watch out, you won't know what she's stealing from you.

'C'mon, let's go out,' he said. 'Let's go for basic Chinese, no-swank, come home and have cake; let's watch some Laurel & Hardy for old times' sake…' Her father had owned stacks of Laurel & Hardy films and Kriti and he used to cuddle in his den, watching the old flicks, high, laughing like idiots. Monish had a couple of L&H videos on his study shelf.

'We'll talk about this…resolution of yours…another day.'

She shook her head but stayed in his embrace. 'I need you to say yes. Tonight.'

He let her go. She put her things back in her pouch, tied the leather strings and marched to the door. She turned to him there. 'I thought…' Her tearful eyes looked deeply into his.

He came to the door to shut it. 'I may love you, but I'm not your slave.'

TWENTY-EIGHT

April 1999

'THREE ELECTIONS IN three years. Are we crazy fucking luna-
tics or what?' Monish turned up the air conditioning to full
blast.

Waheeda chewed on her lower lip. On a personal level,
the dissolution of Parliament was good news for her. On a
broader level, she agreed with Monish that it was a cata-
strophic waste of national resources. The previous Saturday,
the coalition government had failed to win a no-confidence
motion by *one* vote. The opposition had run hither and thither
trying to muster support for an alternative government but
failed. India would have to go to the polls again. She had six
months to voting day and everything to play for.

'How was your Sunday morning squash?' she asked to
deflect him. It was Monday evening and he looked hot and
bothered. She was relatively cool; Naaz had dropped her off
and she had several hours she could spend in the flat before
she returned to Naaz's home. She'd come in with the key
from under Kriti's door mat and freshened up. The morning
had been frenzied, as had Saturday and Sunday in Nulkazim.
She'd almost thought she'd have to cancel coming to Delhi,
but she had two interviews with journalists scheduled for this
morning, one with a national news magazine; and she'd been
honoured with an award by an NGO, a branch of an interna-
tional foundation for women's rights, for her work. Naaz had
come with her to the luncheon and then dropped her off at
Monish's building.

'Choppy beat me,' he growled. 'But it was this close.' He held up his thumb and forefinger together. 'Two games to one. Eight points to eleven on the last one.' He grinned. 'I'll get there yet.' He sat down beside her. 'And you will, too. But tell me this, Wija. We are a completely bonkers country, aren't we? Those jokers in the Lok Sabha will do my head in! Not you, I don't mean you...'

'I'm not in Parliament.'

'Soon. I'm betting on it. Waheeda Rela, MP.' He removed her hair clip. 'Will I have to treat you differently?' He said it teasingly.

Waheeda found she couldn't answer. Would she be able to see him? How could she carry on like this if she became an MP? Could she? 'Nothing will change,' she said. Her words sounded hollow to herself.

'Hmm. I see that. We remain furtive conspirators...never seeing the light of day...We'll spend two weeks setting up a meeting that lasts two hours...and what kind of man needs to make love more than once every new moon? Huh?'

Speak, Waheeda, she said to herself. Here it is, the opening. Take note of his complaints. He's giving you the chance to call it off. He doesn't have the guts to do it himself. You have the delicate phrases, you've thought of them long enough. *Speak, Waheeda.* What if she lost the election, though? Then: no proper job; no Monish. Life would be...

She twisted her body to look into his face. 'If there's something you want to say to me, Monish, say it. It's not as if I'll cry or anything.' Her voice broke. Oh no, she *would* cry.

He wound his arm around her waist and pulled her closer. 'Nobody's going to cry.' He ran his left hand through his hair. 'If I get fed up of creeping around...'—he brought his hand to her hip—'I'll tell you. But right now, everything I need is here. In this apartment. There's nothing I need from outside.

At this moment.' He pressed his lips on hers. The air conditioner juddered and switched off. A power surge, she thought. Or power cut.

'A million A/Cs being switched on,' he murmured against her mouth, as the lights blinked on and off and the electricity stabilizers made clicking noises. The ceiling lamp had gone out and the low drone of the fridge ceased. They were in darkness except for the low light from the bulb in the kitchen which stayed on during power cuts. It was connected to the inverter. He got up. 'One day soon this building will have its own generator. The committee keep talking about it. This summer will be a killer without it. I think by the end of summer all the residents will come on board and contribute to the cost of installing one.'

He padded his way to the dining area and lit two candles on the sideboard. 'How "morantic." Now all we need is a light breeze. Failing that, at least a dollop of air. Can I open the balcony doors?'

'No.' She looked at the drapes. They'd been closed when she came in; he must've instructed Malti to not let the sun in; but Waheeda had carefully overlapped them so there wouldn't be even a chink of light or visibility.

'Sometimes I think you're paranoid. But all right, no breeze to add to our romance. In that case we need ice.'

He loped off into the kitchen, unbuttoning his shirt as he went. She followed him. He shucked out ice cubes from an ice tray into a tall glass. 'You want ice, too, Wija? Here, you have this one.' She sucked a cube up into her mouth and crunched the lovely cold with her teeth, chilling the side recesses of her mouth deliciously slowly.

He filled another tall glass with the contents of a second ice tray. He tipped whisky into the glass. She watched the amber liquid fill all the nooks and rise to the rim. Again she heard his mother's voice in her head, from almost a year ago.

'I thought that was needed to keep warm, not the other way round,' she said, making him frown. What was it in her character, she wondered, that made her feel duty bound to process other people's expectations and requests? 'Do you need to pour so much? In one go?'

Monish returned to the sofa. 'Don't you know that rule, Wija: girlfriends don't nag; only wives do.' He said it lightly but he was annoyed. He leaned forward slightly. 'And you're not my mother,' he muttered to his feet. She caught it and decided to ignore it. This was the third occasion on which she'd tried to gently chide him, but the first time he'd become so irritable. She would not raise it again.

'Did I tell you I had an interview with *India Now*?' she asked. 'My interviewer said a little bird had told her that I was the one to watch in Dhoonpur. And Shakeel rang this morning to say that there's a request for an interview with BBC World Service. They might come to Nulkazim, to record the sounds in the old quarter, in the area outside the HQ.'

He squeezed her hand and lifted it to his exposed chest, pushing it onto his nipple. His expression softened. He crunched into an ice cube.

'There's one more thing. I wanted you to know first, before you read it in the papers,' she said. 'I'm going to stand as an Independent candidate.'

•

THE NEXT MORNING at breakfast Naaz said, 'I can see you hardly slept last night. You need some concealer under your eyes. Don't be stubborn, Wija, use mine.' She laughed. 'I don't understand it—your skin is radiant, your body looks like you're walking on air, but your eyes are dark-ringed. Actually, I do understand…What are your plans today before you head back to Nulkazim?' She had Kabir on her lap and he was pulling at her *mangalsutra*. He'd already broken it once.

'I'm going to meet Faisal and then Chetna. Separately. Now that things are hotting up again with an election on the horizon, the spats between them are increasing exponentially.' She buttered her third toast. 'I'm going to spend the morning ego-massaging before I set off for home.' She touched her bare ears and lowered her voice. 'I realised this morning when I was getting dressed that I left my earrings behind. The power came and went the whole evening and when it was time to leave, it was all dark and I didn't notice...'

'You'll get them back next time.'

'Yes...but...these were Abba's mother's emeralds...you saw them yesterday...and I only took them off because they were long drops and...' she went quiet. She'd taken them off because the heavy oval emeralds pulled at her ears once she'd lain down, and the backs of the hooks dug into her skin. She'd worn these valuable old emeralds rather than her usual small studs because of the formal luncheon.

'I noticed them,' Naaz said. 'How could you not? But I didn't realise they once belonged to Aseem-ji's mother. He gave them to *you*?' She placed Kabir onto the floor, admonishing him about trying to seize the knives on the table. He toddled off to the kitchen. 'Meera, Meera,' Naaz called out. 'Watch Kabir.'

Waheeda felt the familiar sorrow at explaining. 'Now that Abba is not going to have the daughters-in-law that he was saving these precious gems for, he occasionally presents me with something from the Zafar family collection. Sometimes I wonder if he thinks it absolves the need for other things in my life...perhaps he sees it as a kind of recompense...but whenever I receive something I would not have otherwise, I feel intensely sorry for him; more for him than for myself, even though I loved my brothers so much.'

Naaz listened sympathetically. 'Text Manisha,' she said. 'Ask her to keep the earrings safe.'

Waheeda nodded. Hopefully, Monish had already noticed in the morning and locked them away.

•

AT CHETNA MURA's home, she accepted a mug of coffee and salt-twists that Chetna had made that morning. They sat in Chetna's cool but dark sitting room. There was only one window and all she could see out of it was a hedge, its green broken by a passionflower vine. She loved the purple filaments and vivid yellow stamens of the flowers.

'I know you like flowers,' Chetna said, noticing her gaze. 'You've inherited your mother's keen interest in gardening.'

'Not really. I like looking. Appreciation of others' efforts is the extent of my gardening.' She laughed.

'It's nice to see you happy. And I keep my fingers crossed for even more happiness by the end of this year.' Chetna's large black bindi on her forehead went up and down in tune with her brow movement.

'If we're successful, Chetna, a lot of it will be down to you. Your efforts are not going unnoticed. Even Faisal-ji.' Waheeda set her mug down and spread out her fingers. 'I know you find him difficult, but just this morning he had fulsome praise for you.'

Chetna shrank her eyes at the mention of Faisal. 'He can't not applaud me. Who has raised the most? Already I have collected this much. See?' She thrust a sheet torn from a long register at Waheeda. 'It's not just Delhi people waking up. Even the person from Dubai, who donated before, is back, and in a big way.'

Waheeda scanned the sheet. 'May I keep this copy?'

'Yes, of course. Give it to your father. And take…a package…with you, if you're returning now.' She meant cash.

'I can't. I'm travelling alone. With Habib, but still. I will send Shakeel and a couple of others…'

'What about Aseem-ji? He comes very rarely to Delhi?'

337

'Yes, his visits are rare. But in fact I think he's due to visit next week and it's best if he meets you then.' If Chetna wanted Aseem, Waheeda would present him. She sought to keep Chetna sweet. Abba could come and say the same things she had; and Chetna would glow in his admiration. It felt odd to be sending him to flirt with Chetna, but then, all things considered, she was living a very odd life indeed. She did trust Aseem, though; and she had never mentioned to her mother that their Delhi chief had a crush on her husband. Aseem could carry back the money.

She looked down the list again before folding it in half. There were a few anonymous donors. 'Who is the Dubai person?' she asked.

Chetna pointed at the page with a long maroon fingernail. 'The largest anonymous donor. She lives in Dubai. She was born in Dhoonpur, she says, and she is overjoyed that there is a female candidate there; especially one who works sincerely.'

'She told you all this?'

'No. She sends her representative. To me, here. A young woman. Who tries not to give me too many details. *I* think she's a Muslim businesswoman in Dubai who is keen to see you win. Because she has some history there.'

'What does she want in return? Has she said?'

'No clue on that,' Chetna knocked her bent fingers on the table. 'The answer I get is: "nothing." If you win, you'll find out. Perhaps.'

TWENTY-NINE

May 1999

'How come you've quit your own party?' Falguni had barely said 'Hello' before she started her questioning. Her cheeks were pink as if she'd been in the sun all day.

'It's a strategic decision,' Waheeda explained. 'I have the absolute backing of NPF and Jehangir Wazan's party; which I would've received anyway, probably; but as an Independent, I might draw the support of one of the big parties. In fact, there's one party that is considering not fielding a candidate in Dhoonpur. As an NPF candidate I would not obtain the same backing as I can ask for now...I am free to make mutually beneficial pacts with the right kind of interested party...' She looked around at the opulent drawing room. The current maharaja of Tebilly lived in one wing of the old palace, a sprawling white building with a pillared portico and a balustrade roof. The other wing was a boutique hotel for birdwatchers, who were led on expeditions by a local expert.

'I note you're not naming any names.'

Waheeda shrugged. Fal leant forward but before she could say 'tell me,' Waheeda said, 'I can't just yet. I'm still making alliances. As you know, that's why I wanted to speak to Randhir.' Her eye was on the two stuffed tigers in glass cases. They looked very old, bits of them were dropping off.

'Wija, call him Binty. *Friends* know him as Binty.'

I'm not a friend, Waheeda wanted to say. I've not met him, although I have tried to set up a formal meeting. She'd also

339

tried for a lunch through Fal. Then, out of the blue, Fal had rung to invite her to dinner at his home. 'I'm staying over in Tebilly for a couple of days,' Fal had said, 'come and have dinner with us…this is an informal occasion, Wija, *be yourself*,' she'd stressed.

Waheeda had asked Aseem for his advice, saying that the maharaja had invited her via Fal, for dinner. She'd tried not to communicate her misgivings about Fal, but just hint at her uncertainty about visiting him. Aseem had said, 'Falguni's an old friend. It's good she's being helpful. (Although what is she doing with him?) If he's being elusive otherwise, then we should pursue this opportunity. There should be no harm in accepting his dinner invitation on this occasion. Ensure Fal chaperones you at all times.'

Waheeda looked across at Fal, who was stretching her back like a cat in her armchair. 'I'm not going to talk about politics, unless he does, just so you know…Don't push it.' Fal opened her mouth to speak just as Mr Randhir Bahar, aka the maharaja, entered the room, looking freshly showered and shaved. He was in a spotless white shirt and pressed linen trousers. He was wearing comfortable slip on sandals, two tan straps across his feet. Fal uncoiled herself and introduced them: 'Binty, Maharaja of Tebilly; Waheeda Rela,' Fal draped an arm around Waheeda. 'My dear friend from St. Ann's.'

Waheeda was about to put her hands together in a namaskar, but he proffered his hand so she shook it. She knew he was about thirty-five, once-divorced. He'd married into a royal family from the east, the bride selected for him when they were both young, but his wife and he had not got on. Unlike in the old days, when she'd have been stuck inside his palace, she'd decided to return home and run a business at *her* family palace. He must want to marry again, Waheeda thought, to beget a son. Surely it was imperative that the dynasty continue. Although it would continue, even if not in direct line from him; as there might be nephews who could be made head of the clan. But she knew the importance of the direct line; he must be thinking of it, too. Especially since the sudden death of his father. She looked into his large dark-brown eyes as he stared equally curiously at her. He had a magnetism about him; suave but slightly dangerous; she could see how he would appeal to Fal. 'What would you care to drink?' he asked.

'Something soft. Whatever you have. Or just water.'

He picked up a shiny golden brass bell and tinkled it. A man in a waiter's buttoned-up white uniform appeared at the door. 'Yes, your royal highness?' The man put his hand on his heart and bowed to Binty and towards her and Fal.

Fal gave a cool nod, murmuring 'Good evening.'

'Bearer, whisky *leke ao*, for two, yes, Fal?' and at her nod, Binty continued, 'And *nimbu-pani* for madam.' He gestured towards her.

Waheeda's long skirt swished pleasingly against her legs as she sat down. She'd heeded Fal's appeal to just be herself, and had dressed accordingly. The turquoise and yellow print skirt in crushed cotton was from a designer who hailed from Tebilly and used antique patterns. She realised the frescoes on the wall of the drawing room were in similar colours, but faded. Her long-sleeved white tunic was in plain linen and she'd embellished it by wearing a silver beaded chain with a tribal pendant. 'What did you do today?' she asked Fal. 'Did you get a tour of Tebilly?'

Fal's hair was done up in a side ponytail. She wore a pale beige shift dress that accentuated her height and leanness. A large piece of amber strung on black thread hung at her throat. A flat amber ring on her forefinger. 'We went for a run in the hunting grounds of Binty's grandfather. Nothing to hunt there anymore—'

'There are deer,' he interrupted.

'They are *protected*, Binty.' She tossed her head before continuing. 'Then we had brunch at the old hunting lodge. Binty's chef provided the most amazing picnic hamper. We came back here…had a nap in the afternoon.' Fal and he had sex with their eyes. Waheeda looked away. 'I had the most wonderful day,' Fal concluded.

The waiter arrived with a large salver that he put on a rose-wood table by the tall windows. Whisky in a crystal decanter; jug of water, ice bucket, glasses. Binty poured drinks for himself and Fal. The waiter returned with *nimbu-pani* and set it on the table in the middle. Fal came over to sit by Waheeda on the sofa, which was covered in silk navy scattered with a paisley motif embroidered in silver thread. Waheeda had already run her fingers along the embroidery and felt the real silver of the thread. As Fal brought her glass to her lips, the smell and taste of whisky swam into Waheeda's senses. How well she knew it, considering she didn't drink it. It reminded her of the taste of Monish's mouth and tongue, usually after their love-making, and of ice, the way he liked it. Catching the aroma now made her unreasonably sad.

'Are you enjoying politics?' Binty addressed her. He was not a big man, medium height, medium build, but he carried himself with authority. His voice was deep.

'Yes.' She was unsure whether this was the moment to leap in to ask for a proper meeting. Probably not. 'It's not what I thought it was. I've had setbacks, as you might know. Yet I find that you can do some good; you can cut through the cynicism, even of one's own family and friends—'

'Ah, you mean your artist husband and Fal, here—'

'No…I was speaking more generally…what about you? You've been elected pretty much unopposed the last three times, right? Do you *enjoy* your role?'

His dark-brown eyes fixed on hers. Again, she felt a slight

disquiet at the way his gaze tried to penetrate her. Like he was divining, guessing, deciding…'*I* serve my people. I have a duty to. For hundreds of years, the kings of Tebilly have served their subjects.'

'Of course.' Best not to say what *she* thought of royals-turned-politicians.

'It's one way for *ex-kings* to understand their own value, their history, and the privilege of their birth,' Fal added. 'If you can't rule one way, you assume the duties of a ruler another way.' She gave a wicked little laugh. 'It's a very good thing that Indira Gandhi ceased to recognize the titles of the maharajas and cut their government subsidies, don't you think, Binty? Imagine all of us paying our taxes to keep your father in the style to which he was accustomed.'

'It was the right thing for a democratic nation,' he said. 'I can't, hand on heart, say it was the right thing for us. It's a struggle to keep the buildings and treasures intact. There's never enough funds. Everything needs maintenance and restoration. The coffers need to be full. Suffice to say they're not.'

'You need to marry several enormously wealthy heiresses. Reinstate the wives' living quarters, instead of having bird-watchers and tourists lay their heads in those rooms.'

'Find me *one* who's willing to lavish her money on my palace, that'll be enough.'

Their banter went on, and Waheeda relaxed a bit. Until the start of dinner when Fal said, 'I met your friend Monish, recently.'

'Oh?' She gripped her fork, feeling that it would slip out of her suddenly warm hand. Could Fal really have brought this up now? In front of someone else? She could barely believe it. She felt Binty's eyes on her face. 'He's not a friend exactly; I've met him a couple of times, that's all.' She mumbled on, more quietly, at Fal, 'I've told you before.'

'That's not what *he* said.'

Waheeda stared at Fal, and she wasn't sure later if she'd been both shocked and pleading. What had come across? She shook her head and spoke as calmly as she could. 'He doesn't strike me as a liar, but I can't be responsible for what he said. I can do nothing about what's said behind my back.' She thought she caught a glint of approval in Binty's eyes.

Fal seemed displeased. 'When a man is a puppet, there's usually an intelligent woman pulling the strings, wouldn't you say, Wija?' She pushed across a dish of aromatic chicken korma. Her toned shoulders were framed by the gilded dining chair. Her green eyes were luminous. She could have been a painting.

Waheeda passed on the dish to Binty. She didn't reply. If Fal was blaming her for not immediately receiving business from Monish, she was on the right track. Waheeda had blocked it. Perhaps she'd made a big mistake. But the thought of Fal circling Monish, hugging him indiscriminately, and extracting information from him had been too much to bear.

'What do you think, darling?' Fal enquired of Binty.

'How would I know? I'm just a stupid man. I wouldn't even begin to know if you were pulling *my* strings, Falguni dear.'

Waheeda tried to eat so as not to betray further nervousness. She chewed tiny bites of chicken, followed by a small bite torn from her chapati. Binty replenished his wine glass and then Fal's; and he turned to Waheeda, bottle of white wine in hand. He had assumed a kindly expression. 'Care for some wine, Waheeda? This is a very good vintage, and a friend of mine owns this vineyard in south Burgundy.'

'No, thank you, I don't drink. I'm sure it's delicious.' She sipped her water.

'Don't corrupt her,' Fal said, suddenly on her side.

Binty's laugh was the hissing sort—the sound of a bicycle tyre rapidly deflating. 'I think she would cheerfully corrupt anybody, if it served her purposes. Don't underestimate your friend.'

'Oh, I would never do that.' And they were back on with their bantering for a few minutes, while Waheeda listened in silence.

Dessert was home-made *kulfi* ice cream, neatly cut up for them in small silver bowls. 'Pistachio, cardamom and rose-water flavour,' Binty said to her, 'the old way. That's how I like it. Do you prefer mango *kulfi*?'

'No, I prefer this. I like to eat mangoes fresh, in season. Hira loves them, too, and sometimes in the afternoons we put them in the freezer for a while and then have a feast...'

'Who's Hira?'

'Her daughter, Binty. I told you,' Fal said.

His expression changed at the word *daughter*. A softening? His eyes on her face again. 'What was it you wanted to see me about? You were trying to arrange a meeting with me, weren't you?'

'Yes. I'm standing in Dhoonpur.' Waheeda waved a hand. 'Next door to you.' He must know. 'I wanted to ask for your support for my campaign there. Just in Dhoonpur. There are some villages on the border of the constituency where the majority of people belong to your clan—'

'Why would I do this? You're not in my party.'

'No...but there are some reasons why I thought...I'm running as an Independent. Perhaps you might tacitly give support by not speaking against me; perhaps you could say you respect—'

'But what's in it for me? Why would I—'

'Because she's my friend,' Fal cut in.

Binty sat back. 'All right, set up an official meeting. We'll talk again about this. I'll hear you out.'

'I did contact your personal assistant. We didn't hear back...'

'I know. Try again. I've met you now.' His gaze moved

down her face, past her chin and throat, down to her triangle pendant and back up. He leant forward to whisper. 'I know who you *are*, Golden Oriole.'

He said goodbye in the dining room itself, shaking hands with her again. 'No doubt Fal has plenty of girly whisperings for you before you head home.'

Fal squeezed her shoulders in the hallway, and when Habib drove up into the portico, she hung back in the doorway, retreating further into the hall. Waheeda was slightly surprised because Fal's normal mode was to hug an exuberant goodbye at the point of departure. Waheeda reckoned she'd had plenty to drink and was itching to get smooching with her maharaja. She waved a hand at Fal from the car.

·

THE PHOTOGRAPH WAS grainy, she wasn't absolutely recognisable, but it was her. Habib was holding the back door of the car open, Waheeda was almost at the car. They were lit by the lights in the palace's portico. The accompanying article said it was a scoop: Waheeda Rela had dined alone with the Maharaja of Tebilly two nights ago. In his private apartments. She was returning home late. Here was the proof of her affair with him. More than that, see what she was wearing. She had worn a skirt to meet her lover, not the modest Indian costumes she wore for campaigning. Mrs Rela, an Independent candidate from Dhoonpur in the upcoming elections, is a Muslim married woman. Mr Randhir Bahar is a divorced Hindu man. Current MP for Tebilly, he is a member of the BJP, the Hindu nationalist party. What are the two of them up to? Waheeda Rela is an untrustworthy woman of low morals. A good man like the maharaja has been corrupted by her.

Waheeda rubbed at her eyes and read it all over again. The scoop was printed in a small-circulation Hindi paper, but even as she sat there, absorbing her infamy, she knew it would be re-reported in all the local papers. It was a juicy morsel if put in the context of local politics. It would be blown up out of all proportion, to her detriment. Binty was already 'the good one.' She wanted to throw the paper on the floor and stamp on it like a child. 'I just don't understand,' she said. 'Did *he* arrange this? But *why?*' She looked into the beleaguered faces of Umair, Aseem and Shakeel.

'We could deny that it's you,' Shakeel said. 'Say you've been framed…'

I certainly have been framed. But by Binty or Falguni? Both acting together?

Aseem hands were balled into fists. 'It's my fault,' he said. 'I advised you to go. I never thought he had such a scheme in mind. Using your trusted friend Falguni to trick you—'

Umair coughed, an expressive cough that meant he had significant news. They looked at him. 'I've called up the editor,' he said, pointing at the paper on the coffee table. 'Who sent him the photograph? When? Why did they publish when it's not really a story of importance that you went to dine among friends?'

'What was the weasel's excuse?' asked Shakeel. His face was tense in rage and she wondered if he was angry with her, too, if he thought there was some truth in it.

'On the evening in question he received a call from a *woman*, saying she was speaking from the palace and that he might be interested to know that Waheeda Rela was dining alone with the maharaja. The editor sent a photographer and a reporter. I don't know how they got inside the palace complex, but they did. It's probably not difficult. They saw your car and Habib, knew you were there. They hid and waited for you to emerge.'

'Did he identify the woman?' Aseem's concentration was palpable, like he was figuring out a jigsaw. 'Hope you put the screws on him, Umair.'

'He said he didn't know who it was. I got out of him what

number the call came from. It was a Delhi cell phone.' Umair glanced at Waheeda. 'I called it. No answer. But it seems to me your friend may not be your friend after all.' He handed a piece of paper with the number on it. Waheeda checked the number she had for Fal. She shook her head. 'Not the same number I have. But I believe it must've been her.'

'Why would she do this?' Aseem's fingers played the harmonium on the newspaper paper in a jittery motion. 'Or Randhir? What's in it for *anybody*? Would you do this just from malice?'

'Destroying Waheeda,' Shakeel said. 'There are enough people who want that. But I couldn't imagine that they would recruit Falguni or the Tebilly maharaja.' He put his hand in his kurta pocket and brought out the little notebook and capped pencil he carried. 'Did you spend time alone with him?' he asked Waheeda. His distrust pierced her.

'No. Only a few moments at the start of dinner when Fal went to the bathroom.'

'Or went to make the call,' Umair interrupted.

'But I wasn't completely alone. The server was laying out the dishes.'

'What happened later? What note did you end on?'

'He said he would give me a hearing. About support from his clan in Dhoonpur. He said to set up a meeting. His manner was agreeable…polite…nothing to suggest…'

•

BY THE EVENING they'd decided on a plan of action. Waheeda would try to arrange an immediate official meeting with Randhir Bahar. If he agreed, Umair and Shakeel would accompany her. She would ask him to speak to the editors of the papers to make them retract, or at the very least, put a stop to the story being repeatedly referred to. They were sure that he couldn't want this puerile rumour eddying on; it did nothing for him.

'May I use your office to call his personal assistant?' Waheeda asked Umair. She felt odd making the call in front of the three of them. She went into his concealed room behind the bookcases. They would be able to hear her, but not be peering at her expressions. She told Randhir's assistant who she was and that she wanted to urgently meet Mr Bahar. The woman at the other end of the phone line repeated her name. Waheeda felt from the tone-change that she'd read the paper or heard the gossip. Then the woman said, 'Hold on, I will call him on his mobile and come back to you. Stay on the line.' She had certainly not been this helpful before. She was back in a couple of minutes. 'He's in Delhi this evening. He'll be back in Tebilly tomorrow. He can see you at his office at four p.m. Also, give me your number, so I can call if there's a problem.'

'Well, that's one thing settled,' Umair said.

It was growing dark outside. Aseem said to her, 'You go home. Hira will be waiting for you. But just one more thing.' He cleared his throat. He seemed a bit embarrassed. 'Don't wear a skirt again. Anywhere. Anytime.'

'I don't understand why you did.' Shakeel seemed thoroughly irked.

Waheeda put a hand to her forehead. When she spoke her voice was louder than she intended. 'I don't understand why I did either. I just did. I took Fal at her word that it was an informal occasion. If you, Shakeel, wear kurta-pyjama one day and shirt and trousers the next, no one remarks on it. Do you not think I was modestly dressed? Look at that photo. My legs and arms are covered up. And did you know that a long skirt is an Indian outfit? Heard of the ghaghara worn by women in the Vedic period?'

'I'm not reproaching you, Wija, the paper is! There's no need to lecture *me*.'

Umair interceded. 'Well, we have to learn lessons from

everything. You may be right about the history of garments, but don't give anyone a stick to beat you with. People will comment on a woman's attire and not a man's, so now you have to live with that.'

'I know, Umair-ji. This was the first time in a while…and I guess, the last time…'

She thought to herself that she'd been a fool. She'd worn a skirt to be herself but also to impress the man she was going to meet. She'd wanted him to think she was attractive, and to notice the Tebilly connection (if he did) so he would be disposed to hear her state her case. She'd tried feminine wiles, and it had backfired spectacularly. She headed downstairs to the car. Shakeel followed her down the broad stairs. 'Wait a moment,' he said at the landing, and she turned.

'Nafis should come out and join you for a couple of rallies.'

Waheeda was silent for so long that he said, 'It will quell further slander if he shows his support. Will you call him when you get home tonight?'

She was quiet.

'Waheeda?' he asked.

'I can't do it, Shakeel. It's unfair to drag Nafis into this mire. I feel like everything bad that has happened is my fault…I have to fix it myself…and can you imagine Nafis with me in the campaign bus? Can you actually imagine him on a podium looking sanguine? Tell me if *you* can envisage that.'

•

RANDHIR BAHAR'S OFFICE was not accessible from the main portico of the palace but via a side entrance. Waheeda could see that it was in the same wing that he occupied as his home. The reception area was clean and neat but not spruced up. Compared to the sumptuous rooms she had been in on the evening of the dinner, the reception room was austere. The thick walls were in need of paint and the encaustic tiles on

the floor were mostly cracked; some of them had pieces missing. A male secretary directed them to a row of metal folding
chairs to wait. Binty appeared after a few moments. She
greeted him with a Namaskar, and he returned it. She introduced Shakeel, 'my brother-in-law,' and Umair to him. She
saw the steno flip open a pad and note the names. Binty ushered them into an office, less shabby than the reception. He
gestured at upholstered chairs for the three of them, and he
himself sat in the only armchair, which had his coat of arms
on the back. 'Will you have some tea or coffee?' he asked.

'Nothing, thank you,' all three of them said, more or less
in unison.

'Bring water for our visitors,' he said to the secretary. His
gaze took in the three of them aligned in front of him. 'What
can I do for you?'

Waheeda chewed at her cheek. How humiliating to have
to beg him to put an end to slander. And how to ask him who
had started this?

Shakeel spoke first, in his mild, firm manner. 'Are you aware
of some strange stories in the paper? A photo of Waheeda
was published as she left after dinner three evenings ago—
have you seen it?'

Binty nodded. Embarrassment crossed his face, too.

Umair said, 'Randhir, son, you must understand how distressing this is for Waheeda and her family. This false smear.
In the first instance, we're not even thinking about the reper-
cussions to her campaign…'

The secretary returned with glasses of water. He stood to
attention by the door. Umair looked towards him and sighed.

Binty said, 'I understand this is a delicate matter. More
than that, *I* am distressed. I have some questions to ask
Waheeda. I think she and I should talk in private.'

Waheeda felt Shakeel tense up beside her. Binty raised
a palm to deter any intervention. 'Umair-ji, please escort

Waheeda-ji into my private office, just here, and leave the door ajar. I am not an animal.' He looked at Shakeel, whose frown had sunk deep into his face, 'I assure you she will be safe. She requested this meeting. She intends to ask for my help, I believe; and if we are to clear the air, we must talk frankly. We do know each other and I'm sure she can vouch that I'm a gentleman.'

'Let me talk to him,' she muttered as she stood. 'There's no need to escort me.' She followed Binty into another room off the passage. She left the door wide open but he retraced his steps to partially close it. The office was lined with new wallpaper and adorned with historic family photographs. It was very much like Aseem's study had been before the death of her brothers. Those walls were still bare. The desk here, covered in green leather, was similar to Aseem's, too.

Binty went around to a chair behind the desk. 'Sit down, Waheeda.'

'Thank you for agreeing to see me at short notice, Randhir-ji.'

He raised his brows at her. 'Call me Binty. We're talking as friends now, right?'

'If you say so. I'm not sure alerting the press was a friendly act—'

'I did not create this situation. Let's be clear about that. Did *you* call that paper? Thinking it might—'

'*I did not.*' She stared at him. Could she tell him it was Fal? Hadn't he guessed? Did he know, and was he just playing with her? If he was still entangled with Fal, he wouldn't want to hear her accusations. He wouldn't want a showdown with Fal. Who would? 'Binty...this affects me terribly. It marks me in a way that...in a way it would never affect you. Forget my personal misery and horror, forget the shame my parents are suffering, you know how detrimental to my campaign any scandal or disgrace—'

'You don't think it's a disgrace for me? To be linked to you? You think this is something I want?'

Waheeda looked at the floor. An almost-threadbare Persian rug stretched from under the desk to halfway across the room.

He made a clicking sound of impatience with his tongue. 'What do you want me to do?'

'If you could call the editors of the papers and ask them to retract the story—'

'I'll try. I don't think they do retractions. Your ideas are too English sometimes, I think. I went to school in England, unlike you, yet I understand Uttar Pradesh better than you do, it seems.'

She twisted her hands in her lap. 'Then ask them to stop running or re-running it. They *will* listen to you, I know, and the story will peter out. The damage has been done, but you can contain it. In addition, I'd like you to issue a vehement denial of an affair, or even a friendship.'

'Really?'

'Yes, please if you could say: we respect each other's work, we met through mutual friends that evening, I did not dine alone with you; and that we spoke of my schemes for the education of women in my constituency…and the possibility of rolling them out into your—'

'Are you dictating what my statement should be? Are you *commanding me?*'

'No.' She fidgeted, before looking up into his face. 'Binty, I beg you to do what you can.'

He pulled open a drawer and found a pad of paper. He picked a pen from the engraved pewter pen pot on his desk. He began scribbling on the pad. She noticed the signet ring he wore on his third finger, with a blue monogram.

He looked up from his writing. 'I don't like to see you beg, Golden Oriole.'

He went back to scribbling on the pad. Green ink.

When he finished writing, he leaned back in his chair. 'Why do I have the feeling there's more you want from me? After I call the editors and issue a statement, that's it? You don't need another meeting with me, right? You go away and hope for the best.'

'Yes…I was going to talk about other matters, as you know. To do with the election. Before this happened. Perhaps we can look at that at some later point.'

'You want my support in some other way? That's what I suspected. Ask me now.'

'Now?'

'Do it now. While I'm in a reasonably helpful mood and feeling sorry for you. You won't have another opportunity.' He bent forward and whispered, 'Or you'll be stoking rumours of an affair.'

He was playing with her. He was as bad as Fal. She took a breath and began: 'As I explained at dinner, on the Dhoonpur border, your clan—'

He clicked his tongue impatiently again. 'I *know* what you want. Tell me what's in it for me. *Why* would I lend you my support?'

Her words tumbled out to convince him before he lost patience. 'Just as a second preference candidate. Some of your community don't care that much for the BJP nominee. Especially the women. Because of some past issues…' She waved a hand in the air. 'If they knew that you respected my work, that you had spoken well of me, as a *second* preference to your party's candidate, perhaps when it came to deciding on voting day—'

'They would choose the Golden Oriole lady. If they hated the guts of the other guy.'

She nodded.

'You haven't explained what's in it for me.' Once again he was watching her, divining, guessing…

'Other than helping you in return some day, other than securing my goodwill, I can't think of what might be in it for you.'

He smiled at her then. 'Good answer.' He smiled more broadly but there was something dangerous about him when he spoke. 'I will help you, dear girl. But I have some tight conditions.'

There was a knock on the half-closed door. She heard Umair's voice. 'Waheeda?'

'Come in,' Binty called.

Umair pushed open the door but didn't enter. 'Are you still talking?' He addressed Waheeda, who had turned towards him. 'Do you need us?'

'Sorry, it's taking time,' she said. 'We began discussing another request I'd made…'

'We're almost finished,' Binty said. 'Take a seat in here if you like. I was about to outline some terms of agreement to Waheeda-ji. This would have been between us, but if you must stay…'

Umair gazed at her for a cue. She shook her head. 'I'll leave you,' he said. 'But just a few more minutes, Wija.'

Binty walked to the door when Umair had gone and half-shut it again.

He returned to his seat and laughed suddenly. *Tsssssss.* That hissing sound. 'Oh my! They're going to follow you to heaven. How are you ever going to sneak off for a fling, eh?'

Before she could ask what he meant, he continued smoothly, 'But back to business. My conditions: I don't want you to encroach on Tebilly. No women's programmes. No toilet schemes. No talks on women's rights. I don't want you stepping foot in Tebilly on any official work.'

'Binty!' She was astonished at his demand. 'Some of that work is not political. Even if I lose, I'll carry on. It's for the good of the girls. Even in Tebilly.'

'You are not to cross the border on to my land for any

reason other than tourism. You are not to enter my constituency with any kind of charity scheme. Give me your word.'

'Yes...' she faltered, an axe cleaving into her stomach, 'Yes, OK.'

'You look nice in a sari.' His change of tone took her by surprise. He stood and she did, too. 'Oh?'

He came over to her. 'Don't be tempted to break your part of the bargain, Golden Oriole. You will regret it forever.' He placed his manicured thumbnail on the seam at her shoulder. He trailed his thumb lazily down the sleeve of her blouse to her inner elbow. Waheeda was too stunned to move.

He murmured, 'I know about your penchant for young Hindu men.'

•

SHAKEEL HURRIED TO her as they came out of Binty's office. 'What happened? You look so unwell!'

'I'm fine.'

'We've sorted matters to Waheeda's satisfaction, I believe.' Binty folded his hands and made a slight bow. 'Namaskar, Waheeda-ji. I hope these troubles will pass.'

'Namaskar, Randhir-ji.'

She walked in a daze to the car. Shakeel glowered at the path. At the car he opened the front passenger seat, and said, 'Umair-ji,' ushering him in. Waheeda pressed the handle of the back door, but Shakeel said, 'One moment.'

He stepped to the hibiscus hedge by the side of the path. There was a bright pink bloom just above his head and as he spoke, pollen brushed onto his hair. 'What did he do, Wija? Did he touch you? Because if he did I will go in there and break his nose—'

'No, no, nothing like that.'

'Something's not right. You look faint. You can tell me if he tried to act funny. I don't care who he thinks he is, I can go back in and—'

She caught his wrist. Umair must be watching and wondering. 'I *am* a bit stunned because he was brusque with me towards the end…he laid down some terms that I wasn't expecting…but all is good. I will explain everything in the car. We made a deal.'

THIRTY

May 1999

SHE UNWOUND THE double-strapped watch from her wrist and held it to her heart. She pushed away the news magazine on the bedside table and set the watch on its wooden surface. Sitting on the bed, palms prickling, heat still pulsing out from the back of her hands, she couldn't look away from the watch. It didn't have a hand to mark the seconds on the dial. The minute hand didn't seem perceptibly to be moving, although she knew it would. Time would tick on and the watch would keep running, as long as there was a battery in it, long after she'd stopped. Because she was primed to weep, she began to laugh. So it would be Falguni who brought the curtain down on her love life. She'd been foolish long enough.

The next time she was due to meet Monish they'd planned to commemorate two years to the day she'd attended the Jagjit Singh concert. She could text him now. Tell him, obliquely, what had happened to her today. 'I know I promised to see you next week, but in fact…this is it.'

She could ask Naaz to tell him, although Naaz would protest and refuse. She could call him herself. She reached over to grasp the phone. Fal was still in her thoughts. If she was Fal, her line would be: 'It's been a blast, dear boy, but let's call time on it. See you around.' But she was not Fal, it had not been a 'blast,' it had been madness, and she was not ready to say goodbye.

She would tell him face-to-face. Finally she would make that speech that she'd rehearsed often but never been able to deliver. He would hear the words he desired and rarely received from her.

•

THE LAST TIME they'd met they were recalling the evening of the concert and she'd asked him something she'd wanted to know but never asked before. 'Why me?'

'What?'

'Why did you surreptitiously give me that ticket? Out of the blue? I'm not exactly in the same mould as your other… good friends.'

'Variety?' Impish grin. He pushed back against the pillows. They were both sitting up, mellow, feet touching. Her legs were still jelly.

That was a thought which had occurred to her. She nudged his foot.

'Something about you didn't ring true that night,' he said. 'There were those clothes, so conservative, so subtle, but carefully put together; there was that restraint…and I became curious when we spoke. When we connected. I wanted to strip off your garments at once, and peel off your mannerisms to see who was underneath. I was *so* curious.'

His curiosity must be well-faded by now.

'There was something else. You reminded me of someone I had a crush on in my last year of school. Shabnam. She had dimples exactly like you.'

'Or, rather,' he added hastily on seeing her face, 'you have dimples like her. I mean…don't *mind* it. Not after two years!'

'Lara always says that you shouldn't ask questions you don't want to hear the answer to. Perhaps I should stick to that motto.'

'It's my turn. What brought you back to my flat that second night after you ran away the first time?'

Waheeda bent her head, grinning stupidly as she drew up her knees and re-positioned the sheet over herself. Lust, she thought, and insanity, but she said, 'Instinct, I suppose. When we talked, I felt instantly that I could trust you. Despite what…

'…you'd heard from Naaz or others.'

'Yes. How do you know what she said?'

'I can guess. But you obviously have good instincts, Wija.'

'Actually, I'm not sure they're that good. I fell in love with Nafis literally fifteen minutes after our first hello, and see how that turned out.'

Monish grimaced. 'He's an idiot. He left you alone in Delhi with a small child—'

She didn't want to argue. She got up and took her clothes into the bathroom. He was still sitting naked on the bed, the sheet drawn up to his waist, when she came out. 'Pass me my *dupatta*,' she said. It was on the armchair by him.

He placed it over his head so his face was under a transparent mauve veil embroidered with tiny white flowers. Waheeda reached out to touch the little flower that covered the edge of his left eyebrow.

'The world feels different from under here,' Monish said. 'A whole new way…a whole new world…'

She laughed. Hira could sing that song from 'Aladdin.'

She smoothed her fingers over his thin straight brows, feeling the texture of the chiffon between them.

'I want the truth.' The mauve chiffon went into Monish's lips when he spoke. 'What are your instincts saying? Right now. About me?'

She pressed an embroidered flower into the end of his chin, at the place where it grew into an almost pointed shape. 'You have a heart-shaped face. I hadn't realised before. Like my Hira, and my Ammi.'

'Yes, but what are your instincts saying, Wija?'

'Instincts? Honestly? That if I had any sense I wouldn't be here. If I felt I could do without this crazy feeling, I would…'

'…drop me in a heartbeat.'

She put her hand on his navel which rose and fell for two short breaths before he unveiled his face. 'I quite like how you tell the truth,' he said. 'Especially interesting is the way you phrased…how you love me.' The last few words were spoken tenderly to himself.

·

WHEN SHE SAW him next week he wouldn't have to be affectionate to himself. She would tell him how he'd been her angel in ways she couldn't describe. He'd been the monsoon to her parched heart. He'd been the flame tree bringing colour to her barren scrubland. They might laugh, but he liked sentimental words; he would have them to keep, while she tossed them away.

·

SHE WENT DOWNSTAIRS to find Hira prattling on the phone. Was she chatting to a friend? She stood still a few feet behind her to listen. Hira said, 'Bye, Abba,' and clicked off.

'Mama.' Hira turned and hurtled over to Waheeda. 'Abba is coming tomorrow. To stay for two days. I have to tell Nani.' She skipped to the kitchen. 'Nani! Nani!'

Hira returned to Waheeda, her face shining with happiness. 'Do you think Abba will bring a present for me?'

·

'DID SHAKEEL CALL you?' she asked Nafis when he arrived the next afternoon.

He gave a curt nod.

'You didn't have to rush down—'

'We'll talk later.'

That evening she let Hira be with him and stay up late after dinner. She entered Hira's room to kiss her goodnight. Nafis was pointing out things to her in the sketchbook that Hira jealously guarded to show him.

Waheeda waited for him to come speak to her once Hira was asleep, but it was past eleven when he turned the handle on the door of her bedroom. She was sitting up in her white cotton nightie with a sheet covering her, a magazine on her lap. The fan whooshed above the bed, creating a cool wind. From the foot of her bed, his light-brown eyes blazed at her.

'I can scarcely believe it.' He spoke through gritted teeth, his nose pinched in anger. 'A playboy, a politician, a slime-bag, a Hindu. He might think himself a maharaja but—'

'It's not true.'

'I'm surprised your father hasn't slapped you to high heaven. He seems to think it's somehow his fault.'

'Whatever's in the paper is false, Nafis.'

He sat heavily on the bed at a distance from her.

'All those things you said about Binty,' she began, and he squinted at her at the use of the nickname, 'they may be right but since when are they a disqualification for a man?'

'What?'

'He's a Hindu like I'm Muslim. Like you're "a Muslim." And the rest of it—'

'I got the rest of it from Shakeel.' He waved his hand. 'You're right, his religion doesn't matter to *me*. But it matters to every-one else around you! *What* are you thinking? Fooling around with someone like him. It's beyond my comprehension.'

'It's *not* true. It was a set-up by Falguni. Hasn't Shakeel told you that important fact?'

Nafis exhaled loudly. 'He has.'

When Waheeda thought of her husband in his absence, she remembered his temperate side and his deep moodiness. She forgot that he had a slow-boil temper. When he became seriously upset, it took him days to calm down. If he con-centrated on the *facts* to do with Binty, he wouldn't be so affronted, but she could see that for the moment he'd lost it.

'You didn't have to come.' She flattened her palm. 'I didn't call you.'

He stood. 'I know.' And at the door, 'You're a faithless woman.'

He left her seething.

Guilt crawled out of her pores as she pummelled her pillow in anger.

Nafis's words always hurt her, no matter what he said.

•

SHE CHECKED HIRA had packed her homework in her schoolbag, and peeked into her pencil case. She must get to a stationery shop to buy a new eraser. The one in her case was disintegrating. Nafis appeared on the drive to wave Hira off, too, as Ammi got in the car to take her to school. 'You can go to drop her today,' he said to Waheeda.

'Oh?' She was meant to be visiting NPF offices in two of the eastern towns of the constituency.

'Shakeel is driving me to Dhoonpur. You stay home today. Go, drop off Hira. You don't see enough of her.'

And you do? Hira would be late if she argued. Waheeda got into the front seat by the driver.

When she returned home, Nafis had gone. She called Shakeel on his phone. 'Was there a change of plan?' she asked. *That you didn't mention to me yesterday?*

Shakeel said, 'Ah, Wija…didn't Nafis tell you? I thought *he* should accompany me to meet some of our local officials on the ground.'

'What's he going to say, exactly?'

'Say? Nothing much. He'll just be charming.' She heard the smile in his voice, knowing his brother was listening to his side of the conversation. 'You know how well he can do that. It will dispel any doubts about…' Shakeel let it slide.

'Right.' Waheeda had to admit that Shakeel's ploy was a good one. Instead of the discomfort and dissonance of Nafis and herself sharing a car for all those hours, it would be just the two brothers; and two rumours laid to rest with one stroke. Her husband had come out to support her after the recent nastiness. He was best friends with his brother. He was not estranged from either Waheeda or Shakeel.

•

IN THE EVENING, as they all sat at the dinner table, Aseem at the head, Hira at the other end, Shakeel opposite Nafis, and Ammi opposite Waheeda, she finally heard how the visit to the towns had progressed. Shakeel filled in Aseem, who listened with his head to one side and at the end, grudgingly grunted towards Nafis, 'Good you came to stay, son. Good you went out to Dhoonpur.'

Ammi beamed and Waheeda knew that if it wasn't unseemly to do so she would've run around to hug Nafis. She'd always had a soft spot for him, and after her own sons had died, she seemed to have transferred more love to Nafis. She harboured hopes that all would be hunky-dory with Waheeda and him one day. She was very affectionate with Shakeel, too, and now she asked him again if he wanted to stay in Irfan's room. 'If you're going out again with Nafis tomorrow, stay the night here. I will give you a good breakfast in the morning. *Bhurji* the way you like it, with onions but no tomatoes. I'll pack *parathas* for your lunch. You don't have to go tonight to the guest house.'

Shakeel shook his head. His phone buzzed at that moment. Probably Parveen. She called several times a day for short catch-ups, even when he was out on the road, and even when there was barely enough signal so that Shakeel had to shout into the phone that he would call when he got close to a town. In the evenings, Waheeda knew, he had long chats with her when he had to stay over in Nulkazim, at the guest house near the HQ.

'Excuse me.' Shakeel went out into the hallway to answer the call.

Waheeda looked into Nafis's tired face and downturned mouth. 'You're going again tomorrow? To Dhoonpur? Just you and Shakeel?'

He wiggled his brows and bit his lip before he answered.

'That's the plan. I'm just following orders. Shakeel is the mastermind. I don't know which villages, but you can ask him, Wija. The names mean nothing to me…'

Aseem cleared his throat. He addressed Nafis. 'What reaction did you get? Your gut feel?'

'They were pleased to meet me in the local offices. Shakeel was touting me around as the "major" artist making a supreme effort to come down from my pedestal and speak coherently to the masses on behalf of my wife, the candidate. I didn't have to say anything but thank people for their support and the work they were doing on behalf of NPF.' Nafis shrugged. 'Shakeel tried to make me go into a mosque with him.' His tone suggested he had drawn a line at that. 'I don't think anyone was expecting anything of me. My presence is what mattered, according to Shakeel.'

'What're you saying about me?' Shakeel returned to his chair.

Aseem let slip a small satisfied smile, head bent towards his bowl of mango and ice cream.

'I'm your performing dog,' Nafis said.

Aseem's spoon thwacked down. Waheeda pushed back her chair. 'Come, Hira, let's get you ready for bed.'

•

AT TEN O'CLOCK Nafis knocked on her door, his face drawn. She felt sorry for him because he had another long day tomorrow. He was getting a taste of her gruelling schedule. He sat at the end of the bed again, setting down Hira's sketchbook on the sheet. She wondered what he'd come to say because he didn't speak.

After a few moments she asked, 'Did you and Shakeel get along all right today?'

He nodded, 'Yes,' a slightly asthmatic wheeze escaping him.

She was immediately concerned. 'Are you having an allergic reaction? To the fields and pollen and dust?'

'Just a bit. I'll be fine. I'll take an antihistamine tablet.'

'I'm sorry. You don't have to go tomorrow. I'll tell Shakeel—'

'Leave me to decide my life, please. I am fully capable of speaking to my brother. Although I do understand from him that he sees my wife much more than I see my wife.'

'Is that what he said?' She was intrigued at what they'd discussed. Nafis and Shakeel were close, but they'd always conducted a very formal relationship with each other. She wondered if Shakeel had urged Nafis to visit more often.

He gave a wry smile. 'He also says he sees my *begum* more than he sees his *own begum*.'

'Oh.'

Nafis removed his feet from his *kohlapuris* and wiggled his toes on the old mosaic floor of her room. His white *khadi* pyjama flapped over his feet.

'I'm grateful to Shakeel,' she said.

'Perhaps you should be grateful to Parveen. And make it known loud and clear.'

She gaped at him. 'What? That I'm grateful to Parveen?'

'She needs to hear it. She doesn't like him being in your clutches.'

'In my—? Nafis. Have you spoken to Parveen today? When?'

'Not today. But she speaks at length on the phone sometimes.'

'She confides in *you*?'

He lifted his chin. 'Why not? You depend on Shakeel. She's probably doing a tit-for-tat thing.'

'You seem to understand her well.'

'I do.'

Waheeda spread her hands out on her sheet. 'I know she must be resentful. But Shakeel never mentions any petulance on her part. She's always cold to me, so I just...let it slide.'

She could have done more, she supposed, been more vocal

to Parveen in appreciating her sacrifices. She could invite Parveen to help in her campaign. Waheeda desperately needed more women in her team. Parveen would be welcomed. 'She could join my team but I can't see her taking orders…'

Nafis was already shaking his head. 'No. She's incensed that you've superseded Shakeel. Then there's the fact that he spends so much time in Nulkazim in that impersonal guest-house. He's hardly in Lucknow during the campaign.'

'You know that Ammi asked him to stay in Irfan's room instead of the guest house. Any time he likes.'

'Please. Shakeel can't be spending the night here. He needs to get away from his work. He wouldn't get a break from Aseem-ji if he was here the whole time. And he must want some privacy.'

For the long conversations with his wife. Waheeda had seen how devoted Shakeel was to Parveen. Didn't his wife know how much she was loved? She wondered how she could help make things better. 'We should rent him a flat in Nulkazim instead of a room in that awful guest house. Then Parveen could stay here with him, and she would be close to him whenever he returned from a campaigning day. NPF should pay the rent.'

Nafis drummed his fingers on the mattress. 'Parveen has her friends and family in Lucknow. She won't want to spend the days alone here. She has to look after their apartment anyway.' He paused and looked carefully at his fingernails. He said, 'There's something else. She's envious because you have everything she doesn't.'

'I do?' Waheeda was tempted to laugh and mutter: *I don't live in my own apartment. I don't have an uxorious husband. I don't even have time to prettify myself as much as I want.*

'You have a child.'

Waheeda looked into Nafis's eyes. His eyes reflected the sadness in hers. 'Oh, Nafis. Are they trying and not succeeding?

I did wonder but I thought it too intrusive to ask Shakeel…'

'Don't speak to her about it. You'll just get up her nose.'

He opened the sketchbook. 'Last time Hira was in Theog I took her on a few walks and asked her to draw.' He held the book up so she could see a pastel illustration of blue wildflowers.

'It looks like *your* drawing,' Waheeda said. 'Hira did those?' She leaned forward.

He shifted slightly closer on the bed. 'She copied what I was drawing. But she's good. She's got the talent for it. The only thing is, she doesn't listen.' He smiled at the memory. 'I asked her to draw what she saw, but she insisted on copying what I was doing. She's so stubborn. Where does she get it from?' He glanced at her.

'From you,' Waheeda said at the same time as he said, 'From you!'

They both laughed. His laugh was a warm sound.

She moved forward to the middle of the bed and lifted the sketchbook, unsure what she was hoping for, that he would grasp her arm, hold her hand. She'd forgotten his touch but she knew the solidity of his arms and the curly hair on them and how it felt to whizz her palms up and down them.

He stood. 'You can return the sketchbook to her room later. I think my duties in Dhoonpur will be finished tomorrow, so I'll leave the day after.'

She gazed up into his handsome face. 'Are there many single women at that club you go to in the evenings?'

'The club?' Something amused him, a smile quivered on his lips. 'Unfortunately, no. Not at the club. C'mon, I'm in a one horse town. Literally. There is just the one horse. The club is a bastion of maleness. Having said that, there are the local wives who come there to play bridge.'

'I see.'

'There isn't a shortage of single women in the environs of

Theog. If that's what you're asking. There are women aplenty. I could be well supplied.'

No doubt Nafis could be 'well supplied' as he put it, if he was so inclined, but she was uncertain what was actually going on in his life. If he had a romantic life since leaving Delhi, it was more secret than her own. More likely that he had decided to live uncomplicatedly in Theog. Ease was his first regard. On the other hand, if he wanted to ensure zero complications and zero rumours in Theog, maybe his romantic life centred elsewhere, maybe in Delhi…maybe he loved someone…

'Nafis,' she said suddenly, surprising herself by not thinking it through first, 'If there is someone you want to marry, I'll—' She swung her feet to the floor.

'You'll what? You'll *let* me divorce you?' His eyes blazed again.

He was right, she'd been about to say something to that effect. The soles of her feet flattened on the coolness of the tiles while her stomach tightened in consternation.

'But it's important for *you* to be married to me. Can you imagine the fallout if I speak out *talaq* to you now?' He was so loud she worried that Ammi and Abba could hear. They'd hear him divorce her; they'd be witnesses.

'Shush,' she pleaded.

'I can divorce you when I like.' He clicked his fingers. 'Anytime.'

'I know,' she said softly. *But please don't. Not now. I said an idiotic thing. I wasn't thinking!*

He looked down at her and she saw him take in her neckline, the white nightgown pulled low. He just shook his head and she felt what he didn't say: He wouldn't divorce her. When he'd made that fateful decision to live in Theog permanently and she'd shielded him from everyone, neither of them had known what his payback would be.

•

SHE COULDN'T SLEEP, as often happened when he was in the house; she had visions of faceless women wrapped tight in his arms, and after a half-hour of tossing about, she got out of bed. At the switch-panel she moved the fan dial a notch higher, then went to open the window. A flicker of light by the swing seat. The end of a cigarette, bright, then not. Moving up and down. Nafis. Smoking out in the garden. She couldn't make him out but he would see her silhouette, yellow light behind her. She pulled shut the window, closed the drapes, and receded into her room.

THIRTY-ONE

June 1999

HOT AIR SWIRLED around Waheeda's face, raising the dust from the pavement so that it looked like it was dusk, although the sun had not slipped under the horizon yet. It dipped behind streaming pink and orange clouds, giving a kaleidoscope-tinge to her vision.

Her eyes watered as she entered Monish's building at a brisk pace. On spotting the security guard at the entrance steps, she slowed and passed by him with a regal nod. She was surprised that Monish was in the foyer, standing by the lift, waiting, his back to her. He hadn't noticed her. The creaking grew louder as the lift descended. Three people exited, and Monish leapt in as if he would miss it if he didn't hurry. He turned to press the button for his floor and met her eye. He opened his mouth but then didn't speak. She didn't want to hang around the lobby for any longer than necessary. She entered the small lift. Just before the doors closed a movement made her look towards the wall of steel letter boxes where a man raised a camera. A flash went off. The lift lurched upwards.

•

IN THE FLAT Monish tried to unclamp her clammy hands. 'Sit down,' he pleaded, 'sit down and we can talk. You can tell me again what spooked you.'

'I can't sit. Don't you understand? I must leave. But I don't know what to do. How to…what if that man is still in the building with his camera?'

'Who bloody cares?'

'I do. I can't have a picture of me with you.'

'You're in a lift, Wija. What's the picture going to mean? Nothing at all! That's if there's a picture. It was probably just some chap trying out his new camera. Taking a picture of his new letterbox or something equally stupid. People in this building have been known to do sillier things than that.' He grinned. 'Maybe he was taking a picture of the broken-down lift for management.'

'It's not funny. You don't know what happened to me last week—' Her right shoulder stooped under the weight of her heavy bag. 'How will they use this…' she murmured.

He gave her an impatient glance but spoke in a reasonable tone. 'It might be me they're stalking, not you. Ever since Dad did that interview last week with *India Now*, I've been pestered to agree to an interview, too. Pratish and I spoke to the main journalist at the office for brief profiles on us but we've been getting calls with nosy questions by other journalists. I hear that people are talking more nonsense about me. I'm a homo. Again! I'm being passed over as the heir to the business. Again! I'm a playboy who buys a platinum watch every day. How silly can you get! I asked for a mansion to agree to get married but my dad refused. I have illegitimate children. I drink and hit my father when I'm drunk. As if!' He ran his hand through his hair in exasperation. 'Wija, if there *was* someone sneaking a picture downstairs, it may have been some scoop-journalist-chappie who wants a picture of me in my private life.'

'They may be after you. Or after me. I don't know. It doesn't change anything. I can't have a photo of me with you!'

'Of course not,' Monish deadpanned, before his features twisted into frustration. 'That's if there really is anyone out there. Your eyes are red and watering. Do you want to just wash out your eyes first? Then we can have a drink—'

'You didn't see him. I saw him at the last second. I saw the camera rather than who was holding it. It was aimed in my direction. I saw the flash as the doors closed. You felt it, didn't you? Don't tell me I'm being paranoid. I *know* that someone was after me. Or you. Or us.'

She could tell he wanted to sit down. 'Even if you're right, Wija, this is becoming *a little bit* crazy. What kind of camera was it? Was it a proper press camera?'

'No, it was a small one. But if it was a person who shouldn't be there, he wouldn't draw attention to himself with a big—'

'You're having an extreme reaction. Sit down first and then—'

'Did you read last week's Nulkazim papers?'

'Not yet. We've been busy with—'

'I was framed by Falguni.' She placed her weighty hand-bag on the dining table. It slouched into itself, ungainly next to the blue ceramic bowl filled with *chiku* that took pride of place at the centre. 'When you see the papers you'll under-stand. I can't stay.' She clasped her right fist in her left palm. 'We must think. What is the best way to get out of the build-ing without—'

He pushed up his glasses to rub at his eyes. 'Wija…I can't do this. I rushed home to be with you and now you want to leave—' He went to the kitchen and returned with two glasses of water. He dunked one down.

'Do you love it?' he asked. She thought she'd misheard. Was he asking if she loved him?

'It?' she echoed.

'Your job. Your political *career*, if you want to call it that. Are you so happy in it that you wouldn't change course for something else?'

She stared at him. He knew happy wasn't the word. She was obsessed. Satisfyingly obsessed. It was her life. Where did the pursuit of happiness come into it?

'What sort of something else do you mean?'

'You could leave all this behind.' He gestured at the world

outside the flat, as he took a few steps into the sitting area.
'Forget the *netagiri*. Its bounds. Do whatever else you wanted
to do. Live in Australia, for example. At my home. Hira would
love it, too. I'll come and go often, whenever I can.'

That easy? What of Hira's father? And it wasn't marriage
he was proposing. She held his gaze, aware that she'd begun
squinting in anger. 'Live in Australia as what? Doing what?
Live on what? And what if…'

'No what ifs. If it doesn't work out, I'll always take care of
you and Hira. That's a promise I won't renege on, whatever
happens. You know me well enough to trust me on that, at
least. I won't let you down.'

Waheeda held on to the velvety back of the big armchair.
'I should be insulted,' she said haltingly, 'but why am I not
surprised? You want me to go from possibly being an MP to
being your chattel?'

'Being a chattel is no bad thing.' Something flamed in his
eyes, burning them to black pinpoints. 'Isn't that what you
want me to be? I was suggesting that you could stop this
circus and have a normal life. Then it wouldn't matter who
you went out with. Or if, god forbid, there was a photo of you
in a lift with—wait for it—a man!'

'It's not funny. Monish. It's not funny to me.'

'You're offended because I want to look after you? That's
insulting to your great principles?' He still sounded like he
wanted to laugh.

It stung enough for her to retort, 'I don't want to live on
your dirty money.'

His head tilted up at her words and his lips became a thin
white line of fury. He stood, stepping up to her and roughly
pulling her hands off the back of the armchair, then letting
them drop so she was standing unsupported. 'What did you
say?'

'Nothing…nothing…'

He grabbed her wrist. 'Let me tell you something, you stupid bloody woman. Let me tell you about dirty money. *Listen*. You know a woman called Chetna Mura? Ask her about cardboard shirtboxes. *Filled* with filthy money. To keep a sidey little regional party in the running. So that *someone's* campaign can be funded.'

Waheeda felt that faintness would overcome her. 'No…' she whispered.

It would be a relief to black out rather than look at him and speak. 'Please, no…I never asked you to…not once…'

'No, you didn't ask. That's true. You never asked for anything. But when my business is funding every type of fucking joker, from the most fascist to the most dim-witted, I thought why not include NPF in the distribution? Why not let my *dirty* money pay for saris to be bought for the women of Dhoonpur and cash to be gifted to the men of Nulkazim; for handouts to the committees of the villages and firearms for the security—'

'Monish! How could you? How could you be such a moron? Does Chetna *know*—'

'I'm an anonymous donor, Waheeda-ji.' He spoke coldly.

'Don't do this to me.' Her hands trembled and she pressed on the chair for support. 'Who gives Chetna the shirtboxes?' She knew, in her head, which anonymous donor he would turn out to be.

'I send Chanda.' He sounded weary. Of her, of everything.

Waheeda blinked. 'What does she say to Chetna? *Who* is it from?'

'A businesswoman in Dubai.'

She nodded. 'You've left a trail. A connection between us. If someone should want to follow it. *How could you?*' Her voice broke. She covered her eyes with her hands. 'I need to think. I need to go…And *Chanda* knows?'

"No, no. She doesn't. I told her I have a project in that area of U.P. My own project that I'm setting up with different partners. Not part of the Selvani umbrella.'

'Do you think Chanda has hay between her ears? After you've been telling me all this time she's totally switched on?'

'It's a big stretch to conflate my private business interests with an affair. I don't think she'll make that connection. Even if she did, I would trust her with my life—'

'But *I* wouldn't!'

'Take a moment, Wija. Breathe. Nothing has happened. Chanda doesn't know, Chetna doesn't know and nor does that fool in the foyer. You are in Kriti's flat for all he knows.' He went to the door suddenly and peered out through the viewer. 'Nothing there.' He came to her and took her wrist. 'All money is soiled, Wija.' His tone was soft. 'Aseem Zafar's money is the same as Arun Selvani's. It's the same stuff.'

He dropped her wrist, and she heard him inhale deeply. 'I could ask for a word of thanks. After all, you are standing on an edifice built on *my* money.'

She closed her eyes. 'Is there anything else you want to say to me?'

'Yes. You're lucky I'm giving you a choice, you know. You can stay in the fucking swamp or you can be with me.'

She pressed her thumb into the softness of the grey stripe on the chair. The tears at the back of her eyes needed to be banished before she could speak. *Remember, be gracious.* But what he'd done was unforgivable. His lies. All this time.

'I think I'll stay in the fucking swamp.' She picked up her bag from the dining table and walked out of his front door, clicking it shut behind her.

•

SHE STOOD IN the corridor feeling entirely foolish and bereft. The single bulb above Sodhi's door spilled its dim light on the landing. She hovered by the stairs. How was she going to get back to Naaz's home? Was that man with a camera waiting downstairs? She could just walk quickly from the building to the nearest taxi stand. Or dawdle, as if it was her intention, to Bengali Market. But these weren't the best moves. Speed and secrecy would be better. She could trouble Naaz. 'Come and get me.' Naaz would grumble, 'I can only go to Monish's flat so often you know. I'm a respectable married woman, not one of his coterie of single girls.' Waheeda could insist. 'Last time, Naaz. You won't have to fetch me from here again.'

•

MONISH'S FRONT DOOR opened. 'Come in; don't be stupid.'

An annoyed grunt when she didn't move. 'Come *in*, Waheeda. We'll sort out how to get you home.'

They were back facing each other in his living room. His lips still white and his face strained but he tried to speak calmly. 'Assuming you want to leave immediately…'

She nodded her agreement.

'Well, we've got two options. I can ask Sodhi to drop you off to Naaz's place. Only thing is, although Choppy's a great guy, really helpful, if he recognises you, he may pass it on as juicy gossip. I don't want to tell him not to talk, because most probably it won't click at all as to who you are. He'll just think I've double-booked or something.'

Double-booked? Waheeda didn't pursue it. 'What's the other option?'

'Well, you won't like this, but Kriti,'—he ignored her involuntary flinch—'can be trusted. She's not speaking to me at the moment, but if I need her help she'll come through, no questions asked. She's a good girl, really. I can call to see if she's home.'

Waheeda thought about this. Kriti, milk-skinned and willowy, as Naaz had described her, youthful, in white jeans, freshly-tonged hair, clutching an ostrich-skin pink purse, coming up one floor to rescue tiresome Waheeda, red-eyed, crumpled in her leaf-green *churidar kurta*, hauling a humongous black shoulder bag. It was all she needed. 'Ask Sodhi next door.'

•

MONISH RETURNED FROM Choppy's flat looking relieved. 'A smidgeon of luck. Choppy's out, but Mrs Sodhi said she could spare their driver. I told her Kriti had a friend round who needed to go home urgently, but I wasn't free to help just now; could she help? She's called up the driver and told him to deliver Kriti's friend to wherever she wants to go.' He held out a piece of paper, torn from a Pokémon notepad, on which he'd scribbled the numberplate. 'Take the lift directly to the basement car park; their bay is next to mine.'

She took the note, her finger touching his as she did so. The door shut behind her and she took the stairs, not the lift, running blindly down the five flights to the car park.

August 1999

TRUCKS WERE HEADING towards her with horns blaring. She cowered, one arm across face, other arm out, palm vertical, to stop a lorry careening into her, but it ploughed on and crashed into her jeep, overturning it. Habib was thrown wide, as was Shakeel, from the front passenger seat, while she was catapulted from the back, smashing through the glass of the windscreen, and rolling in the air before she hit earth.

Waheeda rose and fell in the air and bounced at the hard knock of earth. She was seated, her eyes were open now; she'd been dreaming. She was not alone in the back of the jeep; there were two women with her; and Habib was in the driving seat, a fierce frown on his face. Shakeel had turned around to her, saying something she couldn't hear. The horns were still blaring. There were not truck horns. It was the horn of their jeep. Habib was pressing on it to move the other vehicles out of their way.

Shakeel spoke again. 'You said something?'

She shook her head.

'You screamed. Are you all right?'

'Yes.' She felt herself bounce, as if she'd hit the earth again. 'No. Actually, I'm…STOP the horn. Please…'

Shakeel gestured to Habib, who held up both hands from the steering wheel in surrender. Other hooters clamoured all around them, truck horns the loudest with shrill sing-song tones, beep-beeps from cars, little squawks from the three-wheelers, and *brrr-zztts* from the motorcycles. The wooden barriers at the railway crossing they were stuck at had been raised. A mass of traffic was trying to get across from both sides, jellying into four lanes in a two-lane road and yes, Habib's palm had been glued to the horn because then people would look at the cream jeep, decide it was an important vehicle and give them way. Habib never tooted unnecessarily when she was in the vehicle. He knew she disliked it.

She must've fallen asleep while they waited at the crossing. Although the blaring horn distressed her, she knew they wouldn't cut through unless he leaned on it while Shakeel simultaneously waved angry hands at anyone who tried to slip ahead of them. They were already late for her next appointment at the school in Makeri.

'Sorry,' she mumbled to Shakeel. 'Let Habib do what he needs to.'

Shakeel gestured again and the jeep's piercing toots added to the cacophony. They began to inch forward.

'Are you sure you're all right?' Shakeel mouthed.

'I just fell asleep for a minute. I had a bad dream. I'm fine.'

She spoke to Nita on her left. 'Will the children be waiting at the school even if we're late? Shouldn't they be going home by this time?'

Nita looked at her as if she had asked a Very Stupid

Question. 'They will wait until you arrive,' she said. She might as well have said, *'Everyone waits for the neta. They bloody well have to. What do you think my organising skills are about?'*

The woman on Waheeda's right, Madhuri, gave her a slow understanding smile. 'Waheeda *didi* dislikes being late,' she declared to the jeep. 'She wouldn't want to keep children waiting.'

Waheeda twisted round to see that the rest of their convoy, vans with fluttering flags and posters glued to the sides of windscreens and windows, were managing to keep up with them in a bendy tail, with the aid of jangling horns, shouting drivers, and a toughie brandishing a *lathi* hanging out of every front passenger seat.

She looked ahead out of the windscreen at nothing in particular. She preferred the quieter trips she made, with fewer people and less rah-rah. But it was coming to crunch time, less than two months to go to the election and she was dutifully fulfilling the requests for mega-visits from local area managers. This afternoon she was visiting one of her own success stories; that made her feel good. She'd succeeded in raising the funds to have separate toilets built for female students in the school. Now there was a chance that more of the girls would stay on in education. Although it was her fervent wish that all the girls in all the villages were educated to a high standard, it was not something she stressed in her speeches. Privately she talked about it incessantly with the school principals she met. Publicly, she talked about education generally, because, of course, boys needed schooling, too, and to many of her supporters, boys needed education more urgently as they were likely to be the future breadwinners. The teenage boys she'd spoken to herself had told her that they wanted to learn English and not be subsistence-farmers or labourers. She wasn't sure she could fulfil their hopes, but it was right for them to aspire to anything they wanted.

'I am really looking forward to seeing this toilet block in Makeri,' she commented to Madhuri, who burst into giggles. Nita awarded her a stiff smile, too. Waheeda was pleased at having changed the atmosphere. They were making progress through the jam and soon traffic would begin to flow more normally and a breeze would bring them relief from the cloying humidity. Even though they were being ecologically unsound with the air-conditioning fan switched on in a vehicle with front window flaps opened, they were all perspiring. She drew out the notes for her speech from her bag. Pages covered with Sulabh's neat handwriting and soaring Hindi prose. Sulabh, Umair's protégé, turned out fine speeches, attuned to Waheeda's style and natural delivery. Umair wrote speeches to be delivered by an orator; Sulabh managed to capture what she'd said in her briefing session to him and compose a page or two that reminded her of the right words, the words she wanted to use. She repeated some phrases, silently moving her lips against the orchestra of horns, committing sentences to memory.

THIRTY-TWO

'HERE IT IS, this week's edition.' Arun Selvani slid the news magazine to Monish across the boardroom table. 'I'm happy with it. You can read it later and see what you think of *your* profile.'

Arun's face (slightly airbrushed) gazed out at Monish from the cover. Yes, Dad must be gratified. But what had been written about his older son? He couldn't tell if his father was displeased. 'What about my profile?' he asked. 'Didn't they follow the script?'

Pratish was flicking through the pages of another copy with a dampened middle finger, looking for the main article and for the piece on him. They'd been told the sons would receive a column each.

Monish received a curious look from his father. 'The journalist has called you "enigmatic." I'm not sure what you said to her.'

'I tried not to say much.'

'Mm-hmm. She also says: part-playboy, part-recluse.'

Monish scratched his ear. 'I can't be both. It makes no sense.' He picked up the magazine. 'I'll read it in my office.' It would be too embarrassing to sit there letting his father watch his reactions to whatever had been printed. The information-gathering and snooping seemed to have skewed the piece away from the prescribed version.

Pratish looked up from his copy. 'Read page twelve.' There was mischief in his tone.

'Why?'

'You'll see.'

•

AT HIS DESK Monish turned directly to page twelve.

Waheeda. A column on her. A small photo. She was cutting a red ribbon with outsize scissors at the inauguration ceremony of a new dry-fruit store in the old quarter of Nulkazim. The accompanying article was about her odds in the upcoming election and how she was utilising the tricks of her opponents in the contest: *Low blows all round…In with a chance…Congress caught in internal infighting as ticket goes to Singh's assistant and not deputy office-holders…BJP candidate facing criminal charges but declares himself innocent…Waheeda Rela, campaigner for toilets for women, can't be written off.*

•

THAT EVENING HE called Naaz again. 'Have you tried to speak to her?'

'I have. She's extremely preoccupied.'

'Yes, I understand that. But…' He sighed, aloud, so Naaz could hear and feel pity for him. 'I don't think it should end so messily. I was angry. I don't want that to be the last—'

'I *have* passed on your messages. I don't know what you did. Whatever it was is "unforgivable." If she won't answer your texts, I can't force her to. I know you like order, but *you* can't have your way always…'

If Waheeda hadn't told Naaz what the issue was, he wouldn't either, although he could tell she was keen to know. 'Look, just once…it's not like I'm asking to meet her again and again. It's over, it has to be. She's got a different sort of life to lead whatever happens. But. There are things to say. Look, I mean, inform her I want to apologise. I want to say sorry to her, face-to-face, not via you. And she forgot to pick up her earrings. She must want those back. They're emeralds!'

'She's asked me to collect them from you when I can.'

'Naaz…' Thunder rumbled far off in the sky.

'Yes?'

'Fix it for me, please.' Raindrops began to beat on the balcony railing. The sparrows perched there scuttled away.

'I'll try. It's our joint birthday party next week. For Hira and me. Wija hasn't even brought Hira to Delhi to try on her dress. I'll have to keep my tailor on standby to make last minute alterations! Anyway, they'll be here for a couple of days; and I'll speak to her before the party to see if we can arrange a short visit.'

'I won't be at my flat. I'll be at the farmhouse. I really should've gone to Queensland to escape this darn humidity. Or to London like all normal people do.'

'Of your set.' Naaz's tone was dry.

Affectionate upbraiding, he decided. 'Yes, I meant my friends, not the whole country. But the thing is…I don't feel like travelling until October. Until after the…I feel like I need to see this out.'

'I understand.'

'I'm at the farmhouse for the week. Just me, and my trusty man Friday. And his disabled wife, who lives with him in the quarter. Wija knows. I'll keep her earrings with me. In case she has the chance to drop by. Tell her: we need to speak. In a more cordial manner than we did last time. Tell her I want to explain why I…'

'Did whatever it is you did. All right. I'll try my best.'

•

WHEN THE RAIN ceased, he opened the balcony doors and stepped out into the dark evening. Cleansed damp air. Wonderful. He could hear chattering below. A gaggle of girls in the cul-de-sac. Wasn't it just past eight o'clock? Had they delayed coming out until the rain stopped? He caught the flash of sequinned blouses when they turned towards the lamppost. They must be heading to a birthday party or some big celebration. They would stay out until morning, because they wouldn't be allowed back into the hostel now until seven a.m. He stared down at the group, wanting to see who would arrive to pick them up. Motorcycles, scooters, cars? How many? Young men? How young?

One of the girls waved to him. He wasn't sure if it was the impetuous one whom Kriti had described. He looked keenly at the figure. Tall, yes. Short hair? He thought so, but couldn't be sure. He raised his hand in a slow acknowledgement. He was smiling, despite not wanting to. Who could see in the dark anyhow?

The one who had waved moved to stand a little apart from the group. She must have said something to the others because they turned *en masse* to look up at his balcony. Hastily he withdrew into his sitting room, drink in hand. He backed all the way to the dining table, setting his glass down there. Idiot. Now they'd gossip about him.

His phone was on the table. He wondered about texting Waheeda again. 'Did you see this week's *India Now*? We're both in it.'

Strange, wasn't it? That this coincidence would happen this week. When their relationship was irreparably broken. She would read the mag at some point. If not today, in a couple of days. She skimmed through it before bed, she'd told him. She wasn't going to respond to his messages, it was no use. She was wrong to behave like this. OK, so she felt she was the injured party and he'd betrayed her trust. He got that. But the rest of it? If he'd been livid, so had she. She could apologise, too, for the things she'd said.

He spoke aloud to her as if she was there in the flat with him. 'You're being childish. You're likely to spend a lot of time in Delhi. One day our paths will cross. And when that happens, everything that needed to have been said should have been aired. The past safely buried. Otherwise, I don't know what we do. Do we pretend we don't know one another? Do we shake hands? Are you going to look daggers at me as if you're nursing some deep hurt? You can't. So what are you going to do, huh, Wija?'

•

'CALL ME AGAIN in five minutes, but on my cell phone,' Waheeda muttered into the house telephone. She replaced it on its cradle and sprinted up to her room.

'Lara,' she began, when her mobile bleeped. 'I haven't had the chance to tell you about Falguni.' She filled her in.

'I can't understand why she would do such a thing,' Lara said. 'But I fear what I have always suspected is true. Hyper is a viper.'

They both laughed and Waheeda felt better instantly.

'Have you had it out with her?' Lara asked.

'No…reason being, we decided, Abba and Umair-ji and I, that playing it cool would be best. If I upset her further, she could do worse. We don't have evidence so accusing her will become a battle of her word against mine. I have other battles to fight. I'm ignoring her.'

'I'm happy to yell at her. I can be your attack hound. If you want.'

'No. I have to concentrate on other—'

'How *is* your campaign going?'

'Very well. It's hard to believe, but seriously, many people seem to think there's a good chance…' she trailed off, slightly embarrassed.

'Wija, that's great. I'm so pleased to hear that. I won't call you again until after the election, I know you must be busy.'

'Yes, thanks.'

'And by the way, how is the Luxurious Hermit?'

'Oh.' Waheeda's chin trembled. She should have antici-pated the question. She couldn't control her tearful reaction. She couldn't speak.

'Hello? Hello?' Lara echoed. 'Are you there?'

'Yes.'

'I'm sorry.' Lara sensed something amiss. 'Have I upset you?'

'I'm fine. The hermit is fine. I haven't seen her lately. And I won't be...'

'Oh.' They were both silent. Waheeda wondered if Monish had been in touch with Lara already and told her. Or whether she would call him now. They did occasionally ring each other.

'Right.' Lara's tone was absurdly cheery. 'I must go and tuck my girls into bed now. You carry on with your evening. Give Hira a big kiss from me. And...don't forget, you want to keep those industrialist types in your pocket.'

'I do?' Waheeda was incredulous.

'Yes, don't let it end badly. That's the counsel I would give. But don't mind me. I give advice unasked. You take care.'

August 1999

SHE STOOD IN a daze of indecision in Naaz's polished hallway, gazing at Naaz's fingernails, painted in the same light blue as Hira's nails, tapping the console by her white telephone.

'Will you call him?' Naaz asked.

'Tell me again, what did he say exactly.'

'Wija. I've told you. Twice. He wants you to call him at the farmhouse. If you can possibly see him...He wants to apologise, explain...and return your earrings.'

Waheeda stared at the telephone. She shook herself, violently. She should not be crying on the day of Hira's birthday party. 'I'll think about it.' She put a palm on her forehead. 'I have a bit of a headache. I'll just do some yoga in my room before I dress for the evening.' She could hear Hira upstairs, playing a basic form of hide-and-seek with Kabir. Hira running into a room and calling: 'Where am I?' Kabir toddling behind to 'find' her.

She said to Naaz, 'I'm sorry to leave you with all the preparation...'

'It's all under control. There's nothing for you to do. Be ready by six-thirty. We'll eat early for the kiddies. I've told all the guests. To bed by nine!'

•

SHE SAT ON the bed, stretched out her legs, rotated her ankles. She lifted her arms up to the ceiling, reaching further. She brought her arms down and her fingers massaged the back of her neck. Breathe. Breathe. Don't think about Monish. She twisted in a half-hearted spinal rotation, first left, then right. *Every moment was tainted.* That's what he'd done with his lies. How much time did she have before guests arrived? She should first dress Hira in her pale blue strapless gown and do her hair. She'd spiral some strands from the front and pin them up. Somewhere in her cosmetics case there were some bobby pins. Ice blue; why hadn't she bought blue or silvery pins? *He had made a fool of her.* He'd been buying her and she hadn't known it.

He was a moron who had no clue how much danger he'd put her in. She missed him. Terribly. He hadn't told her about funnelling money because she wouldn't have seen him any-more. That's what he was going to say. *I did it for you, Wija.* She could bet on it. She could see his tapering eyes as he said those words.

Stop. Lay out your clothes. Rosewater to freshen up your face. Twist and pin up your own hair. *Australia.* What did he think she was? Didn't he know her master-plan?

Guilt scorched her intestines. His funds were being used efficaciously. There was no way to send them back without being the architect of her own ruin.

'Hira, let me check you one last time. Do a twirl, yes, super, you really are a princess.' Hira's straight hair fell to her shoulders in a shiny curtain at the back. The pulled-back fronds at her temple brought out her large eyes and high cheekbones. The blue silk set off the bronze of her thin shoulders and arms. Waheeda kissed her hair, her forehead, her soft cheeks.

'Lipstick, mama?' her daughter asked. 'Naaz *masi* said—'

'No darling. Eight-year-olds don't wear lipstick.' Hira pouted just like Naaz did. 'All right, try this…' Waheeda rubbed a gloss on Hira's lips and then thumbed on a light lipstick. Hira skipped off in her silver sandals to check herself in the bathroom mirror and came out satisfied.

•

NAAZ HAD FASTENED bunches of red and blue balloons to the door handles of the sitting room and dining room. It was difficult to squeeze past them to enter the rooms but the children didn't seem to mind. Hira's friends from her old kindergarten dashed between the rooms while the balloons popped and their mothers sipped calmly at their cold drinks, dotting themselves about on the chairs and sofas. Naaz had invited eight guests for Hira (not counting their accompanying parent) and eight for herself. As Waheeda began to greet her acquaintances, she heard bawling from behind the sofa. Kabir was stuck there. The noise of the balloons bursting must've scared him. She scooped him up. Amongst all the little-girl-princesses and decked-up ladies he looked out of place in his tatty cowboy outfit. He was the only male in the room, a twenty-one-month-old representative of his gender. He'd refused Hira's coaxing to dress as a prince; wrinkling his nose and shutting his eyes in distaste at the brocade jacket she was trying to fit him in. He'd dug in his play basket for his cowboy costume and Naaz had relented.

Deepak was meant to be here, maintaining gender solidarity with his son, but had flown to Japan the previous day, telling Naaz that a huge order was in sight. Before he departed he hung a garland of ashoka leaves on the front door for good luck and to leave his blessings for the party.

'Daddy…daddy…' Kabir whimpered in her arms.

'*Shhh. Shhh*. I'm taking you to your mummy,' she said. Where was Naaz? She wasn't in the dining room where two little girls were exchanging princess ornaments: a tiara in return for an imitation gold forehead *tikka*; a mish-mash of Indian and western models. Hira had not asked for a crown but was thrilled that she'd been allowed to wear tiny diamond-like studs in her ears. 'Mummy…mummy…' Kabir hit at her face with his little fists.

Waheeda followed the delicious frying smell wafting out of the kitchen. Naaz was supervising operations in there, and spotting Kabir's bewildered expression, she lifted him from Waheeda's arms into her own, her dress straining as she did. Her gown, like Hira's, was in pale blue satin but Naaz had sensibly added shoulder straps and eschewed the large bow at the back. Despite her dress being narrow and tight she was managing to look cool and unruffled, if a little incongruous standing next to her cook, dressed all in dark brown, his brow sweating furiously.

'What're you fattening us up with next?' Waheeda asked her and then answered the question herself. '*Kachori!*' She watched them being spooned out from the *kadai* and placed on paper towels. 'One of the things I like best.'

'I know, dear. This is one of Hira's choices for the evening's menu. But Wija, I'll bring some to you. Get back to the sitting room. Please. You're the guest of honour!'

'Hira's the guest of honour, not me. It's her birthday party. And *yours*.'

'Yes, but everyone wants to talk to you. The influential MP-to-be.'

'All right. I'll follow instructions, madam.' She gave a little salute.

•

STRIPS OF BLUE and red rubber from the balloons stuck to the floor and the rugs.

Hira ran up to nuzzle against her, like a cat. 'When will I see the cake, mama?'

Before Waheeda could answer, a lady whom Waheeda didn't know, wearing a white sequinned corset with her hair heavily 'set' spoke to her. 'Your daughter is so lovely. What's her name?'

'Thank you. This is Zahira.'

'A beautiful name. Did you choose it?'

She hesitated. 'Her father...my husband chose it and I agreed with him.'

'Have *you* already seen the cake, mama?'

But the white-sequinned woman was still talking. 'Zahira doesn't look like you. I heard she resembles your mother.'

'Yes, people say that.' How does one say: *And you are?*

'Tie up my bow, mama.' Hira turned her back. Waheeda fussed with the lengths of satin.

'Where is your papa now? At home in Nulkazim?' Hair-sprayed woman cunningly addressed this question to Hira.

Fortunately, Hira had been coached over the last two years in the art of giving out minimal information while being truthful. 'My Abba is in Theog.'

'Theog...where...in Himachal?'

'Yes.'

'Is he there for business?'

'He likes the mountains.'

Naaz's maid entered the room holding a tray of mini-samosas and tiny sandwiches. Hira danced away to help herself. Waheeda was rescued by her ex-colleague Mandira.

'Grey suits you,' Mandira said, eyeing up Waheeda's outfit.

'And you,' Waheeda smiled back. 'Although I see you're not into the "frock" dictum.'

'When you're my weight, a sari is a more forgiving garment.' Mandira's sari was in silver grey with a gold and cream border. 'You've deviated from the dress code, too.'

Waheeda had chosen a shot-silk grey buttoned kurta that

came to her knees and a narrow pink *salwar*. Her silk *dupatta* was in *bandhini* grey and pink. 'How are things at work?' she asked.

'Same old, same old. We miss you in the department.'

'Hmm…'

'But we understand, serving the people of our nation is *far* more important—'

'Will you believe me,' broke in Waheeda, 'if I tell you it really is? I know I used to say I could never be more satisfied than when I was teaching. But I *am* more useful now. People approach me believing that somehow I might be able to help them, and when I find out that I *can*, even if it's just because I know the system, or the right people, when I find that I can *do* something, it makes me light up inside. It—'

'Do you actually get anything done?' Mandira's tone was drier than a prune. 'In Nulkazim and Dhoonpur?'

'Everything takes more time than you expect, and finds a winding path, but if you struggle on, yes, it gets done.'

'Meet our future leader, historian turned sage and politician,' Mandira addressed the air innocently.

•

SHE HOPED HER weariness didn't show, but it must have, because as she entered the kitchen again, Naaz said, 'Look at that frown! Are they petitioning you with their personal agendas already?'

'I'm escaping Mrs Sinha,' whispered Waheeda, referring to white-corset.

'Ah, I see. When Deepak's sister asked if she could bring *her* sister-in-law, I couldn't refuse.'

'Oh, that's how you know her. I wondered. She's name-dropped every half-famous person in the Rajya Sabha twice over and now she's insisting she will hold a celebratory reception for me. I can guess she's well-connected, she doesn't *need* to impress me. I did stress that the election is still four weeks away. Who knows what will happen? She bludgeoned on. I told her I wouldn't attend any events that she organised. I mean, I tried to tell her, without actually saying those words. It's tricky to be polite when people are so pushy. Now I know why we lie all the time and promise we'll be there for this or that function.'

She stopped. 'Oh Naaz…Rant over. Sorry. I have a head-ache.' She put a palm to her forehead.

Naaz picked up a pile of bright blue paper plates. "I'm just setting up the cake in the dining room.' She towed Waheeda into the hallway. 'A sweaty kitchen is no place for you, my lady. Do you want to sit in your room for a while? I'll tell Mrs Sinha you're unwell. I must clear all the kids out of the dining room before I place the cake there.'

Waheeda's eye was caught by Naaz's white phone. She stumbled. She sat on the chair by the phone. 'Give me a few moments,' she said. 'Then I'll go back and mingle.'

How much longer did she have to paste on her smile? She smoothed out her face with her fingers, letting them run over her forehead, her eyes, her cheeks, her chin. She smiled once, a quick practice. Now her face was awake, alert. What was the time? She checked her watch. Instead of the watch her eyes fastened on the pale band of skin above it, a less-tanned stripe of skin that had been under the double strap that she used to wear. She was wearing her old watch. Monish's gift had been placed at the very top of the cupboard under old winter clothes that were barely used. She'd needed a step-ladder to put it there.

Eight-forty-five. Heat arcing from her belly to her throat. Her hand reaching out to pick up the white telephone. Push-ing at numbers lodged in her head.

He picked up. 'Naaz?' he asked, sounding surprised.

'No…it's me,' she was breathless.

'Oh. Hi.'

'Hi.'

There was an awkward silence. She filled it. 'I was thinking of stopping by. Just for five minutes.' *What was she saying?*

'I'm not at my flat. I'm at the farmhouse.'

'I know, Naaz told me. Do you have company?'

She'd made him laugh. She could hear it in his tone. 'No. I'm quite alone, if you don't count Jagjit Singh on the player and the stars in the sky, which I can actually see tonight. The caretaker can be sent to his quarter. But…Stopping by, did you say?'

'Well, yes…because if I came out there it would be for a few minutes. To pick up my earrings. You have them with you?' *We didn't do our goodbyes properly, like they do in the movies. I should have a last hug. After two secret years, I should have a big secret hug, I should be able to kiss you below your lip, if that's what I want. I want. I want.*

'I see. Now I get five minutes. I have your earrings. Moon-raker, it's good you called because we need to talk. Is the birthday party over? Already?'

'Not yet. But after we've cut the cake, I can slip away…I've just thought of a plan. This moment.'

'I want to say…stupidly I'm finding it difficult to say… sorry about that last time. I don't know what I might have said—'

'I can't talk right now.'

'All right. Come over as soon as you can. Make peace, not war.'

'Yes.'

'I know where I stand.' He adopted his sardonic voice. 'Allotted time: five minutes.' And just as she was putting the receiver back in its cradle, her hands electric with shock, she heard him say, 'Be careful.'

•

NAAZ HAD CLOSED the door to the dining room. Hira was

waiting outside and as Waheeda approached she put her arms around her, nuzzling her waist and yawning. Waheeda bent down to her. 'Are you tired?' The over-excitement of two days had led to fatigue.

Hira nodded.

'I was thinking...we should return to Sangeet Vihar tonight.' Waheeda spoke in a low voice to her daughter. 'I have a small work errand first, shall we go for a long drive? On the way home?'

Hira nodded enthusiastically. 'But mama, what about my cake?' She pointed at the shut door.

'Of course! We won't leave until you and Naaz *masi* have cut your cake.'

Hira's eyes gleamed. 'Are we cutting it now?' She rapped on the door. 'Naaz *masi*, Naaz *masi*.' The door opened.

'A castle!' Hira squealed in delight and Naaz's face was a picture of satisfaction. The cake was a splendid tiered confection, a rising white fairy castle topped with eight blue towers. 'Happy Birthday, Hira' was iced onto the lowest tier. Eight blue candles flickered.

'Call everyone,' Naaz instructed Waheeda, as Hira jumped up and down. 'Quickly.'

In the sitting room some of the girls were drooping, sitting in their mothers' laps, because Kabir had taken up the sofa, sweetly asleep, his head resting on his folded hands. Waheeda couldn't decide whether to pick up her camera or pick up Kabir. What should she do? She rounded up everyone and took a quick shot of Kabir before joining the others in the dining room, her camera raised and ready-to-go. The walls resounded with off-key renditions of 'Happy Birthday' twice over, once for Hira, once for Naaz. After Hira had blown out the eight candles Naaz and she cut the cake together. Waheeda clicked away.

As the slices of cake were being distributed, Naaz came up

to her. 'My baby is asleep. I've just realised. And Hira looks exhausted, too.'

Waheeda whispered to her. 'I'm going to take Hira for a drive now. We'll return to Sangeet Vihar after.'

'I thought you were staying here tonight.'

'Change of plan. Sudden.'

Naaz raised a perfectly-threaded eyebrow. 'Oh. I get it.'

'I'm leaving my bags here. I'll pick them up tomorrow. There'll be a time lag before I get home this evening…would be best if you told our guests that Hira and I are feeling unwell and resting in our room. So they don't insist on saying goodbye personally.'

'Will do.'

'Mama.' Hira had come up to them. She held out her plate to Waheeda. 'I'm too full to eat my cake.'

'Don't worry,' Naaz said, taking the plate. 'I'm going to wrap a few slices and put them in a bag for you. You can have it tomorrow.' When Hira had turned away, she looked meaningfully at Waheeda. 'Take a slice for Miss Doctorwala, too. From me.'

'If you insist.'

Waheeda went into the guest room to retrieve her small evening bag. It had a long thin strap and she wore it cross body over her *kameez*. She picked up her mobile from the bed and dialled Habib. 'We're coming out. I have to pick up some important papers. Then we'll go home to Sangeet Vihar.'

Naaz and Hira came into the room, Hira clutching two paper bags.

'The lighter one is to give away,' Naaz instructed her.

Waheeda checked once more that she had the keys for her flat in her little bag. She took Hira's hand and they sidled out of the guest room into the tiny front garden. Waheeda walked out of Naaz's gate quickly and pulled Hira into the car.

She waited until Habib had turned onto the main road, then said, 'We're going to Mehrauli.'

He seemed to stiffen. 'Mehrauli, *Didi*?' he asked, his tone surly.

'Yes. After that, home. I have to pick up some papers. I'll show you the way to the house once we get to Mehrauli.'

Hira cuddled into her and yawned again. 'If you're drowsy,' she said to Hira, 'put your head on my lap and go to sleep.'

The roads were still clogged with traffic, although it would ease up towards the outskirts of the city. Aseem's words came to her for some reason, how he scoffed at the 'so-called farm-houses.' He would say, 'These are just mansions of the rich; neutered architecture set on big tracts of party lawns.' He liked the Mughal heritage buildings, which still survived in the old village, but objected to estates masquerading as residences of the agriculturally-minded.

The car turned into a bumpy path lined with trimmed hedges.

'This is the way, *Didi*? Are you sure?' Habib was hesitant.

'Yes, this way. Keep going. Straight on and then turn in at the big gate. It will be on the left.'

The gate had been left open, so they wouldn't have to halt outside. Waheeda leaned forward. 'Actually, drive on. Past the gate. Pull up here.'

Habib was puzzled but he stopped the car to the side of the path, in blackness.

She listened out for other motors. There were no cars on this stretch of road. No other lights that she could see. 'Now reverse and drive up through the gate. Park to one side of the house; I'll show you where.'

The porch light was on but the house itself was in darkness. She eased Hira's head off her lap and slowly got out of the car. She left the door almost closed, but didn't shut it, not wanting any sound to wake Hira.

She spoke into Habib's window, both paper bags in her hands. 'I won't be long. Just ten minutes or so. Keep an eye on Hira. Come and ring the bell *at once* if she awakes.'

She handed him the heavier bag. 'Have some cake while you wait.'

Her heels clattered on the steps to the front door. The hall light inside came on. The door opened soundlessly, like a ghost was operating it. No one in sight. She entered the house, her pulse quickening. Monish was behind the door. He guided her into the living room, where the drapes were closed and the lights dimmed.

THIRTY-THREE

'Naaz sent you a slice of birthday cake.' Waheeda set the paper bag on the oval coffee table.

'That's nice of her. How was the party?'

'Great. Hira loved it. Poor Naaz was intensely busy, but I think she did enjoy herself.'

'And you?'

'My pleasure came from seeing Hira and Naaz have their dream evening.'

Looking into Monish's face was too painful. She moved her eyes down to the rug. Cream wool crisscrossed with black in a diamond pattern. He hadn't asked her to sit. They stood there like strangers, two feet between them, in self-conscious silence.

'Your earrings,' he said, going over to a shelf where a hi-fi system was set up. He picked up a brown envelope and handed it to her. 'This is what you came for, right?'

'Monish.' It hurt to say his name. 'I came to say a proper goodbye.' She placed the envelope in her bag and moved it to the side of her hip again, so it was not impeding her.

'A proper goodbye. How do we do that?' He slanted a roguish smile at her, his eyes scrunched.

Tears pushed up from her lower lids. She was going to be silly! He was going to be jokey and cold. But she heard him take a slow breath and he came one step closer. 'I still don't quite know how to say…but you know I am…sorry. About anything I said. I didn't mean to be nasty. Not like that, not to you.'

'I don't care about what you said. It's what you did. What you hid from me. You don't know how you've made me feel. *Everything is ruined.*'

'Don't say that, Wija. It's just money.'

'But it's not. I wanted "us" to be separate from everything else in my life; I wanted what we had to be different. I *couldn't* have been with you if I'd known—'

He held her wrist. 'That's why I couldn't tell you. Listen to me, just for a moment. Listen to what *I* wanted. I wanted one of us to get to where we want to be.'

'I thought you'd say that.'

'And I knew you'd say what you have.'

They were both silent again, but smiling. Or he was smiling, she thought, and her mouth was tremulous. She put her hands on his arms, waiting. It seemed like he wouldn't respond, but then he did, encircling her with his arms and drawing her closer.

His voice was gentle. 'You're sure of your choices?' he asked. 'A lifetime of gagging on warm milk in dingy huts.'

She let her body loosen, fall slightly into his. She spoke into the soft cotton of his shirt. It was the same shirt he'd worn on the night of the concert, that first time she'd gone with him to his flat. 'That's an occupational hazard. A niggle.'

He stood back. 'My cow dung girl. It's all ahead of you.'

'Monish—' His name came out sad.

'Don't worry about me. I'm a free and happy man.'

She nodded. *Kiss me. Let me kiss you.* 'I should go. Hira might have woken up.'

'Is she at Naaz's home?'

'No, she's outside in the car.'

'Here? You brought her here?'

'Habib drove us both here. She's asleep in the back seat. We'll return to Sangeet Vihar now. It was the only way I could think of to—'

'But what did you *say*? To your bodyguard?'

'That I needed to pick up some important papers.'

'Where are those documents?'

'Oh.' She looked around. What had happened to her brain? This whole evening she'd not been herself. One minute she was sluggish, the next she was reckless. She spread out her empty fingers. Her small bag was slung on her, but other than the cake she hadn't brought in anything. Even her phone was in the car; she'd placed it on the ledge at the back when Hira lay down. She'd not made a show of taking folders inside, as for a meeting; but she needed to emerge with something, to keep her story straight.

Monish looked at his watch. 'Well, I've taken up more than my allotted time. It's been ten minutes at least. But wait here, Wija. Let me find a sheaf of papers for you. And one last question. For the future. Just so I don't get it wrong. We know each other, yes? We're acquainted?'

'Yes, Monish, we are.'

She heard his footsteps in the rooms upstairs. He returned with a blue plastic folder, the type that closed with a band. She opened it to look inside. He'd stuffed in two newspapers. With the band closed it looked right: a folder filled with documents. 'Thank you.'

His hands squeezed her shoulders and he bent to kiss her forehead.

'Go home,' he said. 'Win. Show them.'

He hid behind the front door again as he opened it for her. She went down the steps in the dim light. She looked towards the car. All four doors were wide open. Where was Habib? She strained to see in the dark. There was no one standing by the car. 'Habib?' she called. Was Hira awake? Her gaze still on the car, she stumbled on the last step and fell, the folder dropping from her hands. 'Hira!' A strange panic overcame her as she scrabbled on her hands and knees trying to stand. 'Hira!'

She heard Monish come down the steps behind her but she was up by herself and running on a twisted heel to the car. Hira was still asleep on the back seat. She'd turned on her front. But that wasn't right. She didn't sleep like that. Waheeda bent over her. Hira's dress was wet. She'd wet her satin dress? Wet and sticky. Stickiness pouring. From Hira. Blood.

A madwoman was screaming hoarsely. Waheeda's own voice was stuck in her throat, stuck on the word *Help. Somebody. Help.* Waheeda tried to turn Hira over, to check her pulse, her airway, to see her face, but the madwoman screamed 'Hira! Hira!' until she was pushed aside. She was punched and thrown on the ground.

•

WAHEEDA COULD HEAR them talking. In other rooms. Or were they right by her? Where was she? She struggled to open her eyes but couldn't. There was a hand on her face; she smelt her mother's talcum powder. There was another smell, a sour smell, something crusted on her clothes. Her hand moved on her *kameez*. Gone solid.

Frenzied screams from a madwoman. Waheeda tried to block her out. To think. A new voice in the room. A pinprick. No, no. She couldn't wrench her arm away. I am trying to remember. Hira. Hira.

•

IT MUST HAVE been hours later when she sat up. Large black ants had been marching over her eyes, digging into the flesh of her lids, but she'd managed to pick them away. She was in her bed in Sangeet Vihar. Bring me my daughter. Someone was screeching. It was her. 'Hira,' she called. A terrible rasping sound. It was from her. Go away, crazy person. Bring me my daughter.

A new voice in the room. Nafis. The shape of him by the bed. Physically holding back someone. 'No, don't inject her. Not yet. I want to speak to her.'

Another person in the room. Aseem. 'Son, don't question

her. When we've got back to Nulkazim, all of us, there you can…'

Nafis. Speaking above the commotion of hoarse calling, and the voices of Rehana and Aseem and someone else. 'Can you all leave the room. *Now*.'

A slap across her face. Not hard, but shocking. Her hand went to her cheek and her mouth fell open. It stopped making sounds. The room was silent. Nafis pulled a chair up to the bed. 'What is it that I don't know?' he asked. 'What is your Abba keeping from me?' His car keys were in his hand. Had he just driven down from Theog? Or was he going somewhere? What was the time?

'Where is Hira?' she mumbled.

'You don't know?'

She held out a pleading hand. 'Bring my daughter to me.'

Outside the room, voices were raised and a phone kept ringing. The doorbell rang, too.

Nafis leaned forward. 'Hira is in the police morgue. I'm going there now.'

The madwoman began screaming uncontrollably. Waheeda tried to speak through her, 'I'm coming with you. I need to be with her.' She tried to put her feet on the floor.

Who had pulled her off when she refused to leave Hira? Who had hit her so she blacked out? She'd been manhandled into the floor of the car. Doors had slammed. She'd lain moaning, frozen, in and out of consciousness, in a moving car.

Hospital, he'd shouted.

A man, unfamiliar to her, came into the room. His demeanour calm, his hands smelling of chemicals and medical solutions. Nafis held her down. A needle in her arm.

'Dr Tarun,' she heard Ammi speak to the man, 'leave the tablets with me. Come back tomorrow early morning.'

•

WAHEEDA TIPTOED TO the bathroom. Ammi, asleep on an

armchair, dark agate prayer beads fallen on her lap, didn't stir. Dawn light outside the high window rectangle. She smelled, everything smelled strongly. The room, the bathroom, her. It was the spoor of the ants. Tiny stinging red ants had joined the large black ants to feast on the whites of eyes. She'd fought them off and awakened. She didn't flush. Too noisy. She reached up to open the window a crack. Birds were carolling. She caught sight of herself in the mirror. She was in the clothes from the birthday party. Her *kameez* was stiff with—

She knew that, she knew that. There was no need to scream. No need. Ammi closing the window. Nafis returning her to the bed.

Ammi again. Tea and a tablet. Take it, take it. You must have some tea. I'll bring some toast. No. No. I need to be with my daughter. Take it, take it or we'll have to force you. Here, the tablet is halved. Two halves with some sips of tea. Shall we change your clothes? Let's get you into fresh—

She spat out the tablet and clutched at her kurta. No! No! I won't change. In the background a woman rambled on a loop: Go to the farmhouse. Find Habib. Where is he? A whispering mad woman who came at Waheeda so that she fell back on the pillows. 'Hospital. He said, hospital.' She spilled out a phone number. 'Call. Find out. Where is everyone? Where have they gone?'

Ammi on the phone to Dr Tarun. 'We can't get anything down her.' Saying to the room, 'He's on his way.'

Aseem's voice. 'This is what needs to stop. We can't have it. I'm doing everything I can. But she has to be *quiet*.'

•

A FEW HOURS later she woke to find she was in the room alone. Hira, my darling, she whispered. Come to your mama.

An argument in the sitting room. She strained to hear. If she turned on the lamp or made a sound someone would come in. Daylight bathed the world outside and enough light seeped in under the two closed doors so that she could make out everything in the bedroom. She remembered an hour of clarity at dawn. Then the impassive Dr Tarun had arrived to befuddle her. She knew what they were doing. They didn't want to have to wrestle with her as she tried to leave the flat.

When she listened intently, she could make out what Aseem was saying in the sitting room. 'I'm getting the body released today. We will go home to Nulkazim tomorrow. We've arranged the burial for the day after.'

Nafis shouting. 'You've *arranged* it? Who do you think you are?'

'What do you want to do, son? *Not* bury your daughter? In the right manner?'

Tears wet Waheeda's cheeks. Perhaps it was good to be kept brain-dead. No one was asking *her*. She wanted to lie in the morgue with Hira. Why wouldn't they let her out? If they buried Hira, then she wanted to lie in the ground with her. When they came in, she would tell them in no uncertain terms.

'She will be buried in Lucknow. With the Rela family.' Nafis was firm. He wasn't asking her either. 'Or she can be with me in Theog. On *my* property.'

Waheeda heard her mother's voice. Beseeching.

'If you really want that,' Nafis responded heavily, 'then you have to have me, too. I want to be placed to rest with my daughter when I go. You have to save a place for me in the Zafar plot.'

She tried to stand. What had happened to her? She had a sore bump on her head. She rubbed at it. Her ankle was swollen and painful. She hopped out of the bedroom to tell them she had to be with Hira. No one listened to her. Her entrance created a commotion in the sitting room. Even her maid, Bhavna, paid her no heed as Waheeda commanded them all to get their hands off her.

•

IT WAS EVENING. She could tell from how dim it was in the room. It stank. The bed, the room.

Dr Tarun stood over her, being firm. He was unperturbed at the expletives she'd begun flinging at him. 'Now Waheeda, if you don't have tea and toast I will admit you to the hospital and put you on an IV drip. You don't want that; I don't want that. Your family want to take you home tomorrow. Eat something tonight and I can give you permission to travel tomorrow. Have an egg—'

Her stomach churned and her torso rose in a spasm of nausea.

'Just toast,' he said hurriedly. 'Toast and butter will be fine. Drink sweet tea with your tablets. Plenty of water, too. Now, Waheeda.' He looked into her face solemnly, his grey beard and longish white hair giving him the look of an artist. 'Let your mother sponge you. Brush your teeth after tea. I will see you early tomorrow morning.'

•

'LET ME COMB your hair, Wija. When we leave the flat tomorrow you need to look decent. Have a shower tonight. Bhavna and I will help. Or I can call Naaz. She can assist you if you prefer.'

'Naaz?' Waheeda looked dully at her mother. 'Naaz?'

She remembered being pushed into Naaz's arms and blacking out again. She remembered being left on the hallway floor. Someone shouting. Naaz stepping over her, running here and there. Naaz was in a cotton dressing gown. Naaz talking rapidly into the phone. Waheeda had managed to get herself to standing, she remembered that, first on hands and knees, then supporting herself against the wall. Her left ankle had twisted painfully to the floor on the broken heel of her sandal. She'd taken off her sandals and made it outside the house, hadn't she? Before she could cross the road, Naaz's maid had dragged her back.

'I will only go where Hira is.' She lifted her arm. It felt weak. She noticed the needle and cap on her hand, plasters holding it in place. 'Why can't I move? What have you done to me?'

'Hira will be with us tomorrow. We are taking her home in the morning. All of us together. *You* need to look right.'

'Ammi, what have you heard from the police? Where is Habib? What did he do? Somebody tell me.'

A whisper started, a hissing: Bring me Habib. What happened? Call the police. The whisper became a hoarse cry: 'Hospital. He said, hospital.'

'*Shh.*' Ammi pushed out two tablets from a blister pack.

The front door slammed making them both look up in fear.

Nafis entered the room. He loomed over her. 'Is she lucid? I need to talk to her.'

'Nafis.' Waheeda held out her limp arm. 'Have you been with Hira?' His car keys were in his hand.

'I've been to see Naaz. Is it true? What she told me.'

Waheeda attempted to raise her head off the pillows, but she couldn't hold it upright. 'It must be,' she whispered. 'Naaz wouldn't lie to you.'

'Oh no?'

'Not now, no…'

'*Beta*, this is not the time—' Ammi began.

'You.' He turned on her. 'I can understand Aseem-ji keeping things from me but *you*—'

'I was never going to conceal anything from you.' Ammi spoke with some dignity. 'We're just trying to get home to Nulkazim, where everything can be handled better.'

Nafis shook Waheeda's shoulders, the car keys dropping onto the sheets. 'Is it true?'

'Wija must have these tablets now,' Ammi intervened.

'*Leave*,' he said.

'We have to give them to her before it gets unmanageable.'

'I will give them to her.' He broke one tablet into two halves and filled a glass with water. 'Leave.'

Wearily she pulled the door closed behind her.

He hauled Waheeda up by her shoulders. 'You killed Hira. Do you hear me, Waheeda? You did this. You went to see your sleazy lover and got Hira murdered.' He let her drop back down. 'Well done.'

She closed her eyes. Four lines of red and black ants ran down her face and neck, stung her nipples, then crammed into her eyes. Their nest, their mound. They were building a network of tunnels. She wanted them there in the flesh and lobes behind her eyes. The ants would take her to Hira.

Nafis's voice shook with fury. 'Don't ignore me, Wija, or I swear I will—'

She opened her eyes against the weight of the ants. It took an effort but she found some control over her thickened tongue. She put her hand on his and brought it to her throat. 'Kill me, Nafis. That's what you want to do. I deserve it.'

He looked into her eyes and recoiled. His thumb was still on her throat. He pressed lightly. 'That would be too easy. Do you know how Hira suffered? While you're just lying here?'

He pushed half a tablet into her mouth and put her fingers around the glass of water. It was heavy. She let it drop to her lap and water spilt onto the sheets. He brought her arm up to her mouth and held the glass there. She swallowed.

'Nafis,' she tried to speak again, coherently. 'What happened to Hira?'

He set the glass on the table. He sat down on the chair by the bed, scrutinising his palms. His eyes sank inwards. His cheeks were puffy, as if he'd been weeping for hours. 'She was stabbed. Her heart was punctured. You must know that.' He inspected the backs of his hands. 'How could you do it? You took *my* daughter to your rendezvous with—'

'Knife?' she interrupted. She could hear the high pitch of

her own voice. 'Habib killed her with a knife? *Why?*' Her legs were shaking uncontrollably.

'You better have this.' He pushed another half tablet onto her tongue and brought the water to her lips. Her body heaved as she swallowed. He threw a small towel on her lap. But it was a dry spasm and then she collapsed back on her pillows. 'You *will* need to eat,' he muttered, 'like the doctor says. Or we can't make the journey.'

Her tongue began to swell but she was still able to speak. Lucid, he'd said she was lucid. Was she making sense? Could he understand what she was saying?

'Nafis, I asked—'

'I know what you asked. We don't know if Habib did it. Or someone else. Habib is still missing.'

'Are the police hunting him?'

'The police.' He gave a grim laugh. 'Aseem-ji is in charge of the police.'

'Is he pulling all the strings he can? Making sure the investigation is—'

'Oh yes he's strong-arming everyone. So that there's no investigation. Once we've taken the body tomorrow, the records might show an accidental death from some other reason, not murder.'

'No! No. Follow the leads, send the police to interrogate...'

'At the farmhouse?'

'Yes, please, Nafis. I must find who did this to—'

'So that you can—'

'I will—'

'Kill him? Whoever it is?'

'Yes.'

She lay back. She would kill with her bare hands when she got hold of the murderer. When she could move. She would battle the army of ants to escape their knoll and she would, with her bare hands, throttle...Her hands began trembling.

KAVITA A. JINDAL

Nafis's eyes were drawn to them, to the cannula. He broke another tablet into halves. 'We are looking for Habib. Privately. The family in his village is surrounded, but they say they have no news of him.'

'Did he hate me? How could he hurt Hira? I told him to look after her. I gave him her birthday cake.' The ants were washed away by the rivulets running down her face.

Nafis's voice became a touch softer. 'Habib was in debt. He must've been working for someone…We'll probe more once we're back in Nulkazim. Right now, Aseem-ji is concentrating on…making everything watertight here. He's been telling people about Hira dying suddenly after her party and about the planned funeral, but I don't know what story he's spinning. Whatever it is, it's not an assassination. Now I know why. I didn't understand before why he wanted to hide that it was murder…when clearly Habib was…Aseem-ji told me to trust that he was doing the right thing, which I didn't believe. But he wasn't able to tell me about…*you.* Now I know why we're warping the truth. He said he'll spread two different causes of death and people will repeat them and squabble among themselves as to who has the correct information.'

'You can't let him do that. You don't believe in cover-ups.'

'I don't believe in anything anymore. Or anyone.'

He was so broken. She had done that to him.

There was a knock on the door.

'Yes?' he growled.

Her mother's timid tired face around the door. 'Has she had her medication?'

'I don't want it, Ammi,' Waheeda burst out. She tried to swing her feet to the ground. 'I'm going now to Mehrauli to question—' She put her weight on her palms to push herself off the bed.

Her mother looked pleadingly at Nafis.

'There's nothing in Mehrauli,' he said. 'According to your

410

statement, and Naaz's, you were at her home when…it happened.'

'It can't be,' she whispered.

He went to the door. 'Leave it with me,' she heard him reassure her mother, who said something back in a low voice. 'Yes, I *know*,' he snapped at her. 'I understand very well.'

'Don't listen to her, Nafis. Let's go now. To the police.'

He lifted her legs back onto the bed and dragged her body back towards the headboard. 'Let me speak to your father,' he said. 'He'll be back any minute. Here, have this; last half.'

•

SHE HEARD THE walls echoing with their quarrelling voices. Nafis yelling. Her mother's soothing tones. Nafis quietening. Aseem's gruff tone when he lobbed questions at Nafis. Aseem sounded hysterical, too; she had done that to him. She knew he couldn't bear to look at her. He was throwing himself into keeping the machine running. She had brought them all down. She'd slipped down on the pillows into a half-lying position, one ear muffled, but she heard some of the words Aseem spoke; they soaked into her torpor. 'Interrogate Naaz and Waheeda? And the Selvani boy. You really want that? After Naaz's staff have been paid off? You want them to change their story now.'

'Give the police leads? The actual location. Let them sell the whole sordid tale to the press? About our family? Your wife? You do that, son, you do that.'

Nafis, she wanted to call, don't be swayed by him, but she couldn't speak.

He came in. He must've heard her silent calls. 'Have some tea,' he said. 'Then brush your teeth. Ammi will sponge you. Change your clothes, comb your hair. Dr Tarun will come in the morning before we set off to give you an injection for the journey.'

He seemed to be speaking to himself, although he used her name. 'Do as you're told, Wija. Stay quiet.'

THIRTY-FOUR

15 August 1999

MONISH JUMPED WHEN his home phone rang. He answered cautiously.

'Aren't you coming over for lunch today?' his mother asked.

He'd forgotten to cancel. 'No, Ma, something's come up. I have to help Gaurav and Diljit with their move.'

He did have to do that, but he was letting them down, too, because he was waiting for Naaz. She'd rung him to say she needed to see him. She would find an excuse and leave Deepak minding his son at home for a couple of hours. She couldn't give him a fixed time. He'd promised to wait in for her.

There was a short silence at the other end of the line. His mother lowered her voice. 'Have you heard the sad news?'

'What sad news?'

'Your friend…Waheeda…her daughter…'

He gripped the phone. 'No, I haven't. What's happened?'

His mother's voice hushed. 'The poor little girl has passed away. You don't know?'

'What? No, I don't know. How? Where did you hear—'

'From a good friend of the Zafar family. The little girl died of rabies.'

'*What?*'

'She must have been bitten by a stray dog. They probably didn't even know she'd been infected. It's terrible news. You must call Waheeda, give your condolences.'

'We're not in touch; I've told you.'

'But…in this situation…I've heard she's in complete shock. Not speaking at all.'

'I…yes, I'll send a message…' He shivered. 'This is terrible news.' He loosened his grip on the receiver and took a breath, trying to speak normally. 'I must go. I'll call you later. Oh, something I forgot to tell you. I took your cream shawl from your cupboard in the farmhouse. Don't be blaming Ashwin for stealing it.'

'Oh. You were cold? It's been so hot and humid!'

'I was lazy about turning down the air conditioning and I'd forgotten to keep a sweatshirt handy. I liked using your *pashmina*. I'm keeping it, Ma. It reminds me of you.' *It comforts me.*

'Keep it.' She sounded pleased.

He wandered unshaven to his sitting room, trailing the shawl behind him like Linus's blanket.

Rabies?

Aseem Zafar was a master.

He sat on the couch and drew the shawl around himself, putting his head in his hands.

Was it only three days ago? That black night, that white car in the dim light, all the doors open.

•

WAHEEDA STUMBLING AT the bottom of the steps. He saw her struggle to get up and ran down to help her. She managed to stand just as he got to her and she began calling out as she half-hobbled half-ran to her car.

He followed her but even before he reached the car, a wailing had gone up. For a second or two he didn't understand. She was bent into the back seat of the car. He couldn't see. He tried to pull her out. She'd ceased screaming for a brief minute. She turned her head and didn't focus, but she knew someone was there. 'Ambulance, call an ambulance.' Then she was bent inside, calling her child's name.

He'd run to the other side. He put his hands out to straighten the child who was slipping out of Waheeda's grasp. That's when he knew. Her thin arm fell lifelessly to the floor. Waheeda clambered in and blew breaths into Hira's nose and mouth. He put his hands on the girl's shoulders to steady her. He wondered about CPR, gently moving a hand down to touch her breastbone, while Waheeda blew breaths. Blood spurted over his hands. He couldn't pump on that. He backed out, nauseous, bumping into Ashwin, who appeared behind him.

Hoarse animal keening filled the air. He went around to the front of the car. The keys were in the ignition. He turned them with his sticky hands and switched on the inside light. He tugged at Waheeda. Her head hit the roof as he dragged her out of the back. He held her jaw with his hands so she couldn't scream. 'I don't know of any hospital nearby that can send an ambulance.' He spoke in a rush, but loud so she could hear and understand. 'I can call an ambulance from South Delhi. But they won't know how to find us here. It will take too long.' Her dazed eyes on his face. Him holding her jaw closed. 'I'm going to drive you to a hospital that has an emergency department.'

He felt rather than saw Ashwin sprint towards the house.

'Get in the front seat,' he said to her. 'I'll drive you there NOW.'

'No! No! I'm not leaving Hira.'

He held her in a grip that he knew must hurt. Her *dupatta* trailed on the ground. He pulled it off her, a sudden moment of clarity. He bent into the backseat to tie it tightly around the child's torso. Her slippery unwieldy body, even though she was only a small thing…If he could stem the bleeding…perhaps…although he knew what he'd touched. Even as he thought it, he wondered how it could be, just a few minutes…

Waheeda pulled at him. She seemed not to know that she was screaming in his face. 'Hira. Hira.'

'Please, Wija, if you just sit—' She wasn't listening. Bent into the back seat. 'Hospital!' he yelled in her ear. Pushed her roughly so she would sit down on the floor. She wouldn't budge. He pushed. Down she went and silent, confused. Concussed? She whimpered, clutching at Hira's hand that dangled down.

'The quickest way to get help is to drive you to Emergency,' he said.

Ashwin standing by the car with towels. Clear-thinking Ashwin. Monish grabbed a towel and wiped his hands and brushed the towel quickly over his face and chest. He threw it on the ground. 'Where is Habib? Have you seen their driver? Anywhere here?'

Ashwin shook his bald head, wrinkling his brow.

Monish got in the car. 'Ashwin, run and tell your wife you have to drive me into town. Grab my car keys and follow me. We're going to The Medical Institute.'

As he got to the main road he spotted another pair of headlights behind him, keeping close. His own car. Ashwin had made good time and caught up with him. Monish was driving fast but not too fast, wary of jolts, aware of Waheeda on the floor and the bleeding body on the back seat.

•

Monish put his fingers in his ears. 'Quiet,' he said. 'Shush. Quiet.'

Music. Perhaps music. But no, that was no help. Nothing stilled the turmoil in his head.

He jumped again. It was only the doorbell. He peered suspiciously into the viewer. Naaz. Just Naaz.

'I don't want anything,' she said, when he offered her a drink. But he made a pot of tea and set it down on the dining table. They each took a chair.

She was seething. 'I want to know what happened.' She spoke flatly.

'I get nightmares,' Monish said. 'Since that night, I haven't been able to sleep. I have these nightmares where—'

'Do you think *anyone* is sleeping?' She glared at him like he was a monster. He looked down at the glass top, letting the walls of his stomach, his lungs, his intestines, his liver, take the heat, the roiling, the bad blood that flowed in him. He looked at his feet. Socks. Why was he wearing socks? Socks and shoes were for the office. He shivered.

'I don't have much time.' Her tone was harsh. 'I need to know what happened. What *did* you do to my Hira?'

He shuddered. 'Excuse me,' he retrieved his mother's shawl from the sofa, wrapping it around his T-shirt. Let her think what she liked, that he was an odd one. He came back to his seat. He swallowed. Naaz wasn't interested in his nightmares. No one was. A child had died. His face reflected in Naaz's eyes was a murderer's face.

'I can only tell you what I know. You might know more than me about who…'

'You were there, Monish.'

'How is she?'

'Wija? She's heavily sedated. They've all returned to Nulka-zim today for the funeral.'

'I take it Dr Tarun proved himself useful,' he said, looking longingly at the teapot. But if Naaz didn't pour a cup for herself he didn't feel he could drink.

Naaz's eyes glittered at him with both hatred and a smidgeon of gratitude. 'How did you know that I should call him?'

'I'd heard his name around the table at home. Whenever there was something a family wanted hushed up. A reputable trusted doctor who never broke his code of silence.' His voice wavered. One of his school friends had committed suicide when she was sixteen. So long ago, but even then, Dr Tarun is whom they'd called. Monish and his friends, they'd all known it was suicide, but that wasn't in the news, or spoken at the funeral, and whenever the family talked about her death it was vague; an accident that happened in some other city. They never gave anyone hard facts.

'From a while back,' he said, 'Dr Tarun is the go-to guy.'

He shivered again, his shoulders hunching and his feet trembling in their socks. He gave in and poured out a cup of tea for himself and for Naaz.

She eyed the cup suspiciously. 'This is not a social call. I don't care about you—'

'I know—'

'*What* happened out at your farmhouse? And how could you think of dropping everything on me? *Everything.* On *me.* Nightmares, let me tell you about nightmares, you bastard—'

'Naaz, please. I did it for her. It was a last-minute decision...but when I thought it, in that moment it seemed absolutely the only thing to do...' He gulped down the warm tea. 'I *knew* that it was too late for...the child...I don't know how I knew so surely, but—'

He told her all he remembered, everything that made any sense in the haze that clouded his mind; he spoke with his eyes shut, trying to recall his actions.

•

HE WAS NEARING South Delhi, and he spoke to Waheeda, who was crumpled on the back floor. 'Almost at the hospital. Almost there.'

He heard nothing. He slowed slightly to risk a glance. She seemed to be drifting in and out of consciousness. He looked at the seat quickly. No change there.

What would he say at the hospital? Waheeda and he had come out of the house and found the little girl unconscious and bleeding severely. Had someone attacked her? He would say, yes, he thought so. But he didn't *know* anything. He couldn't even give them details about the bodyguard, other than the name.

What was he thinking? Monish Selvani arrives at Accident & Emergency with a semi-conscious Waheeda Rela and a dead child. Waheeda Rela, the current front-runner for Dhoonpur, is brought to Accident & Emergency in the late evening by Monish Selvani, son of the industrialist Arun. Waheeda Rela and her dead daughter are deposited at a Delhi hospital by a man who then runs away. In a BMW. He is traced and turns out to be Monish Selvani. Mrs Rela was inside the farmhouse with him when someone attacked her child.

At the next roundabout Monish found that the steering wheel took a turn to the left, one exit before the road to the hospital. Left, he went left, towards Naaz's house. He parked across the road. He was in a fevered state, propelled by adrenalin, he felt his own blood vessels inflate as his brain laboured and the actions he should take became clear, absolutely clear in his head.

Ashwin parked behind him. Monish darted to his car. 'Do you have your phone?' Please God, he breathed. Ashwin nodded and fished it out from his pocket.

Monish dialled Naaz's number. 'It's me. This is urgent. Open your front door and—'

'What's wrong? What's happened?'

'Just listen, Naaz, just listen! I want *you* to open your front door. I want you to call an ambulance from Greybridge hospital. It's an emergency. Ask them to send Dr Tarun to you. Whenever they can. Remember the name: Tarun. But first, get an ambulance sent immediately. Then call Waheeda's father. Then call the police. I don't have the number for Greybridge on me but get it from directory enquiry; it won't take long. Do this first; yes, do this first. NOW.'

He ran back to Waheeda's car. He opened the back door and lifted her up from the floor. 'Come, let's get you inside.' She let out a whimper as she sagged against him. He dragged her across the road and stood impatiently at Naaz's front door. Waheeda stared at it uncomprehendingly. She reached out at the garland of ashoka leaves strung on the door. 'Hospital?' she murmured, dazed again. She slumped and pulled at the garland. It broke. She turned. 'Hira. I'm not leaving her.' Her voice rose. 'Hira.' He gripped her.

The door opened and he pushed Waheeda on to Naaz who stepped backwards, the weight of Waheeda engulfing her. Naaz was trying to hold her up, and her own face was held high trying to hear him. He issued more frenzied instructions. 'It happened here. Remember that, Naaz. It happened here.'

'What—'

'She was about to go home, but she came in to—I don't know what—use the bathroom? You think of something. That's when—'

Waheeda screamed, 'Let me go to Hira.' She tried to stand, pushing herself off Naaz's body, but it seemed one foot couldn't take her weight. She held a hand to the wall, her clothes stained, her hair in disarray, her hands blood-ied, staining Naaz's wall. She hopped towards the door, her keening more hoarse—

He shut the front door. He slid into the passenger seat of his own car. 'Take me home, Ashwin. As fast as you can, but without attracting attention with excessive speed.'

•

He didn't tell Naaz about the clean-up. The bonfire of the towels, (Christ, *white* towels that Ashwin had run inside for) and the clothes he and Ashwin had been wearing. The cash he'd put in Ashwin's and his wife's palms the next afternoon, after making them swear on each other's lives and on their idols of Radha-Krishna, whom they worshipped, that they would not speak of the incident to anyone.

On that night he'd wandered through the grounds with a torch searching but not finding anything. Ashwin had fol-lowed him around, but not come across anyone or anything out-of-place either. Monish had wandered the rooms in the house, patrolling, seeking, until the weak light of dawn tinged the windows. He realised his hands were frozen, and he had held his arms across his chest for two hours, his shoulders hunched inwards. He opened his mother's wardrobe and found a solitary shawl on a shelf. He wound it around himself.

He'd walked on the road leading to the farmhouse in the morning. Looking under hedges and bushes; looking for what, he didn't know; a weapon; a knife, but finding nothing.

Smoke drifted in the air, goat bells chimed in the distance and birds chirruped crazily.

•

HE POURED ANOTHER cup of tea. It was lukewarm and tasted of nothing, but he sipped and swallowed. Naaz was lost in thought, eyes screwed up, tapping the table with her nails. Chipped light blue varnish. Her face hard and her mouth set tight, like she couldn't bear to speak to him.

'Naaz, I heard…rabies. How can that be?'

Her round eyes opened fully. 'Already? Even before the funeral? Who did you hear from?'

'My mother.'

'God, she's plugged in. I thought it was your Dad who knew everything.' She shook her head angrily. He didn't know if it was disgust at his parents, or disgust at the world.

'I know Aseem Zafar can do almost anything, certainly in Nulkazim, but how can the Delhi police go along with that story?' he asked.

'They're not. They have an investigation into murder. Committed on *my* road. But Aseem-ji has sorted something: confidentiality; as much as is possible; and a low-profile case; and no public statements. Which means that even if some people hear the rumour of murder from a police source, and some hear rabies, and others something else; there's enough confusion sowed. No one's going to question the immediate family for *facts*; everyone can see what a *shock* it is.' Naaz's lip quivered. She turned away from him to wipe at her eyes.

He didn't know what to say to comfort her. Instead, he asked the question uppermost in his mind. He knew he'd asked before but the answer was unsatisfactory. 'How is she?'

Naaz's face filled with anger. 'How do you *think*?' She seemed to be condemning him for something he'd done. 'She won't speak to me. She blames *me* for betraying her.'

'What? Why?'

'I did what everyone asked. First I did what *you* asked. I called Dr Tarun. And I put Aseem-ji in touch with him on the phone, even before he began driving down to Delhi. I told the ambulance and the police when they arrived that it had happened outside my home, while I was inside clearing up after the party. I told my maid and cook to stick with my story, not that they knew anyway where Wija was; *they* didn't know she'd left the house. Then Aseem-ji took over when he arrived and no one asked me anything anymore. Dr Tarun told the police and even Deepak, when he returned, that I was too distressed and couldn't express myself clearly.' She slumped in her chair. 'But Wija wanted to speak out. She kept insisting on being with Hira, wherever she was; and on finding Habib; and although she never said your name, she demanded: "check the farmhouse; have you checked at the farmhouse?" And she screamed when she wasn't let out of the flat. I mean, *screamed*. They silenced her with strong sedatives.'

Naaz raised her head and looked out towards the balcony and the heavy monsoon sky. 'I did what Aseem-ji asked. I lied to everyone, even my own Deepak. Lies, Lies, Lies. The only person I didn't lie to was Nafis. But I should have done what my friend asked. *She* wanted me to speak the truth. She expected that from me.' Tears dripped from her eyes.

Again, Monish was at a loss. If he moved to put his arm around her, she would strike him, he could see that. 'You did the right thing,' he murmured.

'You didn't.' She stood up. 'If you'd taken Hira directly to the hospital she might've been saved.'

'No.' He leapt up. 'No…'

But Naaz had gone.

•

HE CLAWED AT himself. Was he a monster? He wasn't. He'd done what he'd thought was best. For Waheeda. Had his hasty decision been wrong? Was he saving his own skin? Hadn't he saved Wija? She would be finished and have nothing left. Nothing.

He switched on the television in his bedroom. The Prime Minister's speech was being replayed cut with old scenes of January's Republic Day Parade. The armed might of the nation. Rapprochement with Pakistan. It would be a wonderful thing, Monish thought, if it happened in his lifetime. But he doubted it. Rhetoric was one thing. Infiltration another. Violence against civilians yet another. Inciting division between religions, hatred for religions—those things were not going to die when he died. The agenda of those who didn't want peace always won out. Always. He had held a dead child in his arms as he wrapped a *dupatta* around her chest and stomach. He didn't *know* anything, but could it be her killing was a punishment aimed at Aseem? Or was it aimed at Hira's mother? For not being in thrall to made-up rules of her religion. Waheeda had argued against certain imams on the subject of educating girls. 'The Prophet Mohammad, peace be upon him, believed in education for women,' she had said. 'The Prophet's first wife was a businesswoman. Remember that. The Prophet did not issue a call for head-to-toe coverings. The Prophet's later utterings are being misused and misinterpreted. Learn from the life of The Prophet,' she had said.

Monish leaned towards the television, shutting off the PM mid-clip.

Who? At his farmhouse, who had killed? Habib, who'd

disappeared? Suspicions plagued Monish. He wondered who was crazy, who was malevolent. Every single person he'd seen since he'd come back to his apartment made him distrustful. The doorman in the foyer. Malti. If he thought of people, he thought of them with mistrust. Who could've organised such a thing? Chanda? His father? His brother? Chetna Mura? No, no. They were all normal people; they wouldn't organise a murder; there was no reason. *Who* could have a motive for killing a *child*? On his family property.

THIRTY-FIVE

WAHEEDA'S MOTHER HELPED her into the room just inside the gate of the cemetery. Hira lay on a raised stone slab on the centre. Waheeda hobbled to her and half fell on the small body. This is why the dead are swaddled in white sheets, she thought. To make the bodies feel like they are in their mother's arms, loved and safe. But just to make sure, to be sure that Hira knew, Waheeda put her arms around the white shroud and embraced her daughter. 'Hira,' she whispered in her ear. She laid her head on her daughter's body, too afraid to lift the sheet, to uncover Hira's mutilated torso. She would gather strength to do that, she would have the courage in a moment. A warm hand stroked her stomach. She gasped out, 'Hira, you're awake.' But it was Nafis's warm hand under her. He lifted her up, off her sleeping child, and to one side of the raised slab.

Waheeda tried to shake him off, but his grip was tight. The room was shadowed and chilly, with high rectangular windows, which let in some light. A strange woman hovered by Hira, tinkering with little boxes on a tall narrow table.

'Who's she?' Waheeda tried to speak clearly, although her tongue was thickened, and she could barely make sense of the words that came out of her.

Her mother's cold hand on her arm. 'She's the lady who... prepares for burial...she's just confirming that—'

The woman wore white like the rest of them. She smelled. The room smelled. Waheeda checked her own clothes. She didn't remember who had dressed her and when; she, too, was in a white *salwar-kameez,* and the *dupatta* covering her head was white muslin.

'Go away,' she pushed at the woman. 'Go away. Leave my daughter alone.'

'Let her finish,' Rehana said, inclining her head once in the direction of the woman, who moved to bend over Hira's face.

'*Send* her away.' Waheeda couldn't hear herself. Had she articulated anything?

What other rituals could there be? They were at the *cemetery*. She understood that. In a few minutes Hira would be buried. These were her last minutes in the open air. Or not even that. This little room, where she was being administered to until she was brought out for burial, was stuffy and dank.

'What more?' Waheeda knew she was slurring. What did they keep injecting her with that stopped her speaking intelligibly? What was Aseem afraid of? That she was going to shout: *'It was me. It was me. I did this.'*

The strange woman with her frizzy hair and pursed lips lifted Hira's eyelids and, using a thin silver wand, lined her eyes.

'Stop that.' Waheeda found a surge of energy to shake off Nafis and chop her hands on the woman's shoulders. 'Stop that. What are you doing?'

'*Shh.*' Ammi held her back again. 'She's just putting *surma* in her eyes.'

'I never allowed Hira to have a black dot on her face. Never.' Waheeda crumbled backwards into Nafis. 'No *kajal*, no *surma,* no black dot.' *It was me.* Was she screaming? She couldn't be sure. Her voice sounded muffled and distant. She herself was wrapped in five white old cotton sheets. It felt good. She could stay like this, in the clothes of the dead, but someone woke her, someone was lifting her up. Nafis. She must've slipped towards the floor. He spoke slowly, with his arm around her waist, 'Wa-hee-da. Hold on to me. Keep holding on to me, this afternoon.'

'It was me. I never let her have a black spot on her face. She wasn't protected from evil. It was *me.*'

'*Shh.*' He veiled her head again, clumsily patting her *dupatta* into place. 'Please. Don't say anything. Stay silent now.'

Mute, that's what they want. I should stay mute. Rage clamoured at her tongue, yet she was helpless to express it. The woman placed a yellow marigold between Hira's pink lips. Nafis reached out immediately to remove it. He threw the flower on the blackened floor. 'Enough,' he growled to the room. To all the women in it.

He rested his palm on the white-sheeted form. Waheeda, grasped in his other arm, could feel his need to linger, to be alone with his daughter, to talk to her; but it wasn't going to happen, he wasn't going to speak, not with his mother-in-law in attendance, and his drugged wife and the alien woman who tended to the corpses, preparing them to look like corpses in ways that the corpse and its parents wouldn't want, would never want!

Nafis turned Waheeda towards the door and took her outside into the blazing sunshine. They stood together as Hira was brought out. He kept Waheeda propped up by holding her arm, and she, in turn, heeded his instruction to be silent. They followed their daughter as she was carried on her pallet to her grave. Waheeda's ankle hurt, even in her medicated state, but she dragged it along to keep up with Nafis.

They stood by the pit looking down. People were grouping behind them; Waheeda could feel their breath and sighs and sobs but she didn't turn to look. She heard recitations but they came from afar. Her mother propped her up. Why had Nafis left her?

He was helping to lower Hira into the grave.

Before they'd left home, Waheeda had been given a pair of sunglasses. Someone, she didn't know who, had tried to place them on her face, but she'd knocked the glasses away. She should have worn them, because now she was forced to squeeze her eyes open just the tiniest bit, to be there for Hira;

to witness her funeral; but not open enough that she would meet someone's eyes.

She clung at Nafis as he stepped out of the grave and he put his arm around her waist to steady her. Through her daze she realised that he was remaining by her side, although he was perhaps meant to be standing on the other verge. Her mother and Parveen, beside them, wiped at their faces, both of them wearing oversized dark glasses. On the opposite verge there were lines of men, six deep. Aseem and Shakeel at the head. Segregated from the men, standing a short distance behind, two rows of women mourners.

This is the small private funeral that Nafis requested? Waheeda squeezed her eyes and bent her head. She would not look up. No one should look into her face. No one but Hira, who was in the earth, except the sheet had been pulled over to cover her face. A wooden board was laid across her. Waheeda put out a hand, and slumped into Nafis, crying. She felt her legs buckling.

She heard Shakeel urgently whispering to Nafis. He must've crossed over to them. Nafis said, 'Wa-hee-da. I'm sending you home. Parveen and Shakeel will take you home.'

'Who will talk to all these people?' she asked thickly. 'Who are these people...Who told them they could come?'

'*Shh*...it will be taken care of. Your Ammi is here, your Abba is here, I'm here...'

He thrust a handful of soil in her hand. 'Do this with me,' he said, and he moved her arm so that they threw the soil on the grave. Three times they threw soil over Hira.

An embroidered *chaddar* was opened and spread over the grave.

Where did that come from? Did Nafis know about it? Or like everything else, had it been arranged for them? Had Rehana and Aseem decided that Hira's mother and father were not *au-fait* with the correct rituals of their own religion? True, in the past, Nafis and she had been unwilling to conform to traditions just for the sake of it. But this was different.

This is really what religion was for: funerals. Hira would return to God in a proper way, and be brought into the fold. There could not be a more beautiful tribute than the silk and wool blanket that had just been unfolded. Verses from the Qu'ran. Poetry in green embroidered on a plain cream background. Dainty stalks and flowers in violet. In death, Hira was being looked after properly by her grandmother. Unlike her lousy mother, who couldn't get it right while her daughter had lived.

She trembled.

'Parveen, Waheeda really *must* go home now.' Nafis spoke fairly loudly as he handed her over like she was a sack of grain. 'Go now,' he said to her.

Parveen held her roughly and pulled her along. Waheeda couldn't find the will to resist. Shakeel had walked ahead at a faster pace and when they reached the cemetery gate he was waiting at the wheel of an unfamiliar car.

Was this Parveen's car? Waheeda didn't know.

'What *are* they giving her?' Parveen burst out as soon as they were in the back. She spoke as if Waheeda, sitting next to her, couldn't hear, when in fact she was still conscious. 'I can hear you,' she wanted to say, but was too fatigued to make the effort. Shakeel began to drive without answering his wife, but after a while, he half-turned towards the back and said, 'She will need to lie down. When we get there, take her straight to her bedroom. Settle her on her bed. Put a pillow under her head. She might need a light blanket.'

Parveen let out a heavy annoyed sigh.

THIRTY-SIX

September 1999

THE SECOND MONDAY in September, the atmosphere in the house changed. From early in the morning, there was a flurry of activity around her. Either that, thought Waheeda, or she was noticing things more.

She found that she was responding to all the impatient posturing around her, although she didn't want to. A few days earlier, Nafis had taken to checking the dosage on the new tablets her mother regularly fed her. Waheeda had not been able to sneak a look at the packaging, but ever since Hira's funeral she'd obligingly downed the pills anytime they were offered. If she tried to speak, the family shushed her. If she screamed, they drugged her. Fine. Anything not to be aware of who and what she was. Nafis, mouth twisted in a grimace, informed her she was 'on' Valium. 'Get out of this cycle,' he said. 'I'm cutting your dose.' Typically, he told her at two a.m., and she'd been too tired to argue.

That Monday afternoon, Lara telephoned from Singapore. Waheeda had not accepted a single call since the evening of Hira's party, refusing to talk to Lara and even Naaz. But here Ammi stood, in her room, holding out the phone, mouthing 'Lara, calling again, from Singapore,' as if this repetition would make her change her mind. Waheeda shook her head firmly at the receiver. Her mother's face and body stiffened, but she showed no inclination to leave. Waheeda heard Lara's 'hello… hello?' at the other end. Wearily, she stretched out an arm. 'Hello' she whispered into the phone, as Ammi glided away.

After replying to 'How are you?' with 'I'm well, as well as can be,' she was ready to hang up. Lara sounded pained at her indifference, but she completely surprised Waheeda by not offering any of her regular homilies. She didn't even say the 'sorry' word: 'So sorry to hear the news...so sorry about your loss.' Those words were guaranteed to make Waheeda cringe. Secretly, she commended her friend. Condolence was superfluous.

Waheeda astounded herself with these thoughts, with the clarity of her own emotions and analysis. She willed the drift to take over, forcibly returning herself to the red ants that burned their path behind her eyes. There lay a safer land than the one in which friends, those who didn't have the delicacy of Lara, or her own relatives with kindest intentions, tried to tell her what to do, tried to empathise with something they would never understand, never. Had any of them killed a daughter?

•

ON WEDNESDAY, NAAZ arrived with the afternoon haze. 'Just a quick trip from Delhi,' she breathed over Waheeda's bed, as Waheeda squirmed under her sheet and scrunched her eyes shut. 'I had to come to see you. I had to see how you were doing. And it's so close now to the...' She let it hang. The *e* word. Elections. Wasn't that another life?

'Fine, I'm doing fine...you see?' Waheeda waved a feeble hand.

She gave Naaz permission to bring a tray into her room and let her sip at her tea and munch on a *parantha*, although she herself declined food or coffee in sheer defiance. Coffee. How she liked to have coffee and biscuits with Naaz. But no. No. That was the old normality. She didn't deserve it. Not with Hira in the ground and her above it, tasting the world's goodies.

Naaz was returning to Delhi the same day, and the least she could do was let her be looked after by Ammi. All those hours that Naaz was spending travelling in a car on a futile mission. Naaz offered her news of Deepak's travels. She was careful not to mention Kabir. Waheeda felt for her and eventually asked gently, 'How is Kabir?'

That broke Naaz's dam. She left the room weeping. Waheeda lay back on her pillows. If everybody was weeping for Hira, what was she? Just her mother. Just the person who'd set her in harm's way.

Naaz returned to the bedroom. But as she drew close to the bed, Waheeda said, 'Don't touch me, Naaz. I can't bear anybody.'

Naaz brought up another tray. Eventually, she set down her fourth cup of tea—she'd been draining them in the extended silences—and said, 'You're still on the ballot paper, you know.'

Waheeda subjected her to the cold fish gaze she used when this topic was mentioned. She noted the exasperation on Naaz's face—the thin eyebrows pulled together, the lips bitten in. 'You *have* to leave this room, Wija. You have to start living life.'

'What life?'

'Whatever life. Whatever you can bear to do. If it's too much for you to be here or in Delhi, you can go abroad. If that's what you want.'

'I don't want anything.' *Please go away*, thought Waheeda. *Go abroad*. The default running away option. Go where? And she didn't want to run away, couldn't they see? She didn't care about anything. She was either where Hira was, or she was in hell, or she was nowhere. That would suffice. *Go abroad*. What did that remind her of?

She must've been screaming. Naaz was saying, 'I don't know what I said.' Nafis was holding down her shoulders. '*Stop.*' She quietened. 'I'm not having this,' he said. 'You hear me, Wija?' She nodded.

'I think she's tired,' he said to Naaz. 'She has not let anyone visit her before.' He looked at her keenly.

'I'll leave soon,' Naaz said. 'Give me a couple of minutes alone with her.'

She took Waheeda's hand. 'Don't waste it all, Wija, please.'

Waheeda hauled herself up from the bed and opened the door for her.

'Don't waste it all,' Naaz repeated. Then, softly 'Khuda Hafiz.'

Waheeda murmured 'mmm hmmm' because it would be rude to not say something that sounded like a farewell. She shut the door and thought, *What's happening to me? Why do I care to greet her hello or goodbye? I care about nothing. I care about nothing.'*

•

HALF AN HOUR later, she heard the creak of the swing-seat in the garden. She walked slowly to the window to look out. Nafis was sitting on the swing in a fresh sky-blue shirt. Naaz was perched beside him. Waheeda moved away from the glass window panel to hover at the side of the frame. She stretched her neck out for another quick glance. Their heads dipped towards each other; they seemed rapt in an intense conversation. She felt a twinge of jealousy. What exactly did Nafis and Naaz have in common besides her? When had they discovered they had so much to talk about? Nafis surely knew by now that Naaz had been Waheeda's alibi for her clandestine assignations, yet he seemed to be getting on with her. Looking at them with increasing resentment she realised suddenly that she was awake. Fully awake, observing, noting and *feeling*.

Sunlight splashed onto the wall. Everything in her room was so bright. The bed didn't seem overly creased, the sheet she'd been hiding under didn't seem overly soiled. She peeped out of the window again. It looked like the kind of day where there was a soft breeze, carrying the fragrance of flowers, and the temperature was perfectly suited to human-kind. What could Naaz and Nafis be discussing? Who was sharing confidences, in that head-bent serious manner? And about whom?

•

ANOTHER DAY PASSED.

Waheeda nibbled at her toast and tea but thought about other foods all day. In the early evening she had a shower, without anyone begging her. She was drying her hair, flip-ping it with a towel, when the smell of onions frying reached her. She felt ravenous. For chilli sauce. For some odd reason she craved a Chinese meal. She wanted to sit in Akasaka with a friend and slurp forkfuls of greasy noodles. That was something she could never do now. Something she would never do. How could she? Greasy noodles made her sick, yes, just the thought of them. What she wanted was for the armies of red and black ants marching behind her eyes to continue their wars. Build their anthill fortresses in her burning brain. What she wanted was to stay in her room and not be asked to appear before the world, not be asked to account for herself in all the eyes that looked into hers, all the heads that swivelled her way, and not to partake ever in any sympathy directed her way. She was not deserving of that and she couldn't be hypocritical about it. It was OK to be hypocritical about everything else in the world, if your vocation so demanded it. But this was one step too far. Noo-dles. She craved a plateful.

That night, very late, Nafis opened the door of her bed-room. She was not asleep. She'd become nocturnal so that she could lapse into exhausted, fretful sleep during the day. It was always during the day that people tried to bother her, to talk to her, to bring messages, to feed her, to medicate her, to ask what she wanted to eat, to encourage her to comb her hair, to check if she was ready to go back to a life outside her room. At night they left her alone.

She was propped up on her pillows musing at the night colours of the wall, powerfully aware that she was not in a stupor, that there was plenty she could see in the dark. How by force of will she could cross from the realm of the ants to focusing only on the shadows and shapes in the room, and how by force of will she could block the events and thought patterns that led her to scream.

She heard the door open and recognised Nafis from his tread. He switched on the overhead light, but as she frowned into it and reached for her bedside lamp he turned it off. He sat heavily by her feet, his face out of the low lamplight. His bare feet on the rug were illuminated, his toes turned towards her. The white wide hem of his pyjama made his feet look more brown than she remembered them.

'I'm leaving tomorrow.'

He shifted his weight on her bed. Their bed: as it had been for a few years on their visits home. How many years ago was that? And how many years since she had killed her child? His child. One part of her mind knew that it wasn't years, it was still days, just days, not even thirty days, since Hira's death. Another part of her mind insisted that she, Waheeda, had been a murderer for years.

'Did you hear me?'

She was bereft. There was no reason to be, and no reason to show it. 'Does Ammi know?' she asked tiredly. Ammi would be more bereft than she was.

'Yes. She knows I have to go back to Theog sometime. And she agrees that it's the right time now.'

'She agrees?'

'Reluctantly.' There was a trace of a smile. 'She might seem the most fragile but she's the strongest of us all. A core of steel. She's a bit like our nation—resilient, no matter what horror and insanity you throw at her.' His tone became serious. 'She understands…'

'What?'

'That I have to go home. We all have to get on with our lives.'

'We do? I see.'

'I've told her to completely stop the damn sedatives.' He smacked the sheet near her feet. 'Even in minuscule doses. There's no need to check with a doctor. We just stop. You don't need medication, Wija. Clear?'

Her hand came up to her neck. How was he so sure he would be obeyed?

'I won't be here and you won't do the screaming thing anymore. Clear?'

'I won't?'

'No.'

'Because you've decided? What, you and Naaz have decided?' She couldn't help herself.

'Naaz?' Nafis repeated. 'Naaz? What I heard from Naaz is—' He broke off.

Waheeda straightened up on her pillows.

'There are many people who are suffering along with you. This pathetic style doesn't suit you. What I wanted to say to you was…it could have happened anywhere. It could have happened when she was with me. I've left her with the *ayah* for an hour or two sometimes. If there was somebody out there whose mind was set on…on…killing, it could have happened in Theog, too. I don't blame you.'

'You did blame me.'

'I did. But that's what I came to say. I don't blame you. Hira was our beautiful guest. She's gone.' He swallowed. 'We're here. Look at us.' He spread out his big hands, his palms thick and callused. 'We're here. And we have to love Hira, the memory of her, and love ourselves, and…well, you've got to get out of this room, go downstairs and receive all the condolences for a start. And after that—'

'Who's been getting to you?' she burst out. 'Why do you sound like Abba?'

His toes curled at the intended insult. 'I sound like myself,' he said quietly. 'It's you who doesn't sound like you. I want you to come off this…you are too intelligent for hysterical drama, Waheeda. When I'm gone tomorrow morning, you'll go downstairs and start living. I've told Ammi.'

'Just like that? What about the person who did this? Are we looking for him? Punishing him? Or am I to be gagged till I die? Why do I scream?' Her voice rose high. 'Because there is someone we have to find.'

A deep exhalation from him. Like his breath was pulsing out in sorrow. She felt badly about the furrows she had added to his handsome face. Deep grooves down his cheeks. Her actions had done this to him. Her foolhardiness had made him complicit in the cover-up, not Aseem's entreaties.

'Do we know who it was?' he asked her, not for the first time.

'If we find Habib, we'll know if it was him or not. Who else could it be? And why? We *have* to find—'

'Apparently, we are trying, still, to find out who committed the…we *are* trying, privately, in our own way. Your father assures me on that. But Wija, whoever it is, his punishment will track him. Justice finds its way.'

'You believe that?'

'I have to. And we have to go back to living proper lives, with meaning.'

'Just like that?'

'It's what you can do for me.'

That certainly wasn't true, she thought. He hated what he was asking her to do, hated what she would spend her life doing if she did step out of her room. And yet, it could be true that he hated her lying in bed, a hopeless case, even more.

'You don't understand anything,' she said. 'I killed her. I alone am responsible. I can't begin to look in the mirror, let alone look at people look at me…'

'Lameness doesn't suit you, Wija.'

'Do I look like I care?'

'You're wasting everything. Why do you think that Selvani guy did what he did?'

She felt herself flinch. She shuffled back on her pillows, shut her eyes. '*Why* are you bringing him up? If it wasn't for him…she…she…' She found herself stammering. 'Hospital…he said…'

'There was a reason he left you at Naaz's.'

'I hate him for that. I never want to hear him mentioned *ever*.'

'I don't give a damn about him either. But what I heard from Naaz is that he knew there was nothing he could do for Hira.' He swallowed again. 'He tried to salvage something for you.'

'Don't mention…don't mention…'

'All right. If you want to pour cold water on everyone's efforts, I can't stop you. I'm just telling you what I think you should do. Starting tomorrow.'

'You're telling me. With what right?'

'Remaining son of this family?'

She felt the trace of another smile emanate from him and the tears begin in her eyes. He wouldn't hug her of course, although that was all she wanted. But he didn't get up to leave straightaway. He sat there, giving her the solidity of his presence, while she heaved through her sobs. After a while, he said, 'It's very late. Try to sleep a bit.' From the door he said, 'I'm taking the photographs from Hira's room.'

•

SHE PUT HER head down on her bent knees. His last words rang in her ears. 'I'm taking the photos.' He had those same

437

photos in Theog. But she knew why he was packing the ones from Hira's room. He wanted the frames from Hira's bedside; her kisses imprinted in some intangible way on the picture of him. He was taking away her laughing photo, too. He was taking away Hira's spirit, his and hers, and leaving nothing for Waheeda.

She slept fitfully. In her dream the yellow sun rose high while red ants circled it endlessly. They crawled over her, demanding her guilt, her blood, her unborn screams. She was soaked in sweat. The dream faded into another. The pale orange orb of the sun slid into an indigo ocean. Hira peeked out from behind the setting sun, her eyes glinting with mischief. 'Magic carpet, Mama,' she said. Waheeda awoke. The bedside clock showed it was seven in the morning. She pushed off the damp sheet, pulled on her bottle-green dressing gown and ran downstairs. 'Nafis,' she called. 'Nafis! Wait for me.'

Ammi was weeping at the front door.

'Has he gone?'

Ammi nodded, a small white hanky to her cheek, like in a film.

She could hardly believe it. He never travelled this early. He liked to rise a bit later and eat a good breakfast. But he'd departed. How had he known that something would change in the night and she would come running out of her room to stop him?

Her mother tried to give her a consoling hug, but Waheeda couldn't bear to comfort her in return. She had stubbornly resisted everyone's touch and methods of comfort. If she gave in now to receiving solace and giving comfort in return, she would sob for a lifetime. The lifetime she didn't want anymore. She would not spend it sobbing.

There was no sign of Aseem. 'Where is Abba?' she asked through her unbrushed marshy mouth.

'He's gone to Dhoonpur. You were due to make your final campaign speech there today. He didn't cancel because until yesterday…he thought…he believed you'd be there. He's gone in lieu of you.'

'Abba is going to address a rally?'

'Yes. And so will some others.'

Waheeda heard a delicate cough behind them. Umair had stepped out of Aseem's study. 'I thought I heard your voice,' he said. 'How are you feeling, *beti*?"

'I look a fright. You shouldn't see me like this! I feel worse than I look.' She was talking. Conversing. Like a normal person. She could hear her own voice. She was coherent. Her ears were clear. She could hear properly. 'What are you doing here, Umair-ji, so early in the morning?'

'I was just working on your speech.'

'Mine? At this time?'

'Nafis called me late last night. He said that perhaps you would be able to campaign today.'

'Nafis said? *Nafis* said…?'

He nodded. 'Shakeel is standing by to take you to Dhoonpur if you're ready to go. Your speech is ready—you can read and tweak it on the way there. All the newspapers are saying that the electorate is with you. You have a very good chance of getting the majority of the votes…if you show up…if you show yourself willing and able…'

Ammi was propping up Waheeda as if she was afraid she would keel over. Waheeda released her mother's fingers from her elbow.

'Look at me,' she said, standing up squarely to Umair. 'The people want to see this?'

'Yes. If you wash and get dressed…Rehana-ji will help you to—'

'I don't need help,' Waheeda snapped. 'I don't need help. I don't need…anybody.'

She walked to the stairs, keeping her back straight and forcing her shaky legs to remain upright. 'Leave me alone,' she mumbled, 'Everybody, leave me alone.'

She held on to the banister at the first step. 'Help me, Hira,' she whispered. 'Smile for your mama.'

She turned around. 'Call Shakeel. I'll be ready to go in half an hour.'

THIRTY-SEVEN

October 1999

MONISH KEPT THE television on through the evening as the results rolled in. When he heard the announcer say, 'And more results have come in from Uttar Pradesh,' he stood right in front of the screen staring at it. The results for Tebilly were announced. Binty had won by a landslide. Predictable. Bastard. In another neighbouring constituency of Dhoonpur, the Samajwadi lady was on top. *Wow.* Then, Dhoonpur, and he tensed, every inch of him flexed, and he couldn't breathe. An independent candidate, Waheeda Rela, had won the seat. By a small margin of three hundred votes.

He was numb. The only thought that flickered instantly was, there's no comment about her being backed by the Nulkazim Peace Forum. Interesting. All that sort of information would be reported in analysis. Or perhaps another channel was providing more background details on the candidates. He unclenched his hands, took off his glasses, put them back on.

Was there whooping where she was? Or were they being subdued, suppressing their delight, in keeping with the mourning they were in.

The TV announcer had moved on to other constituencies and other numbers. Monish was no longer listening. He picked up his drink, swished the whisky around the ice in his glass for a few moments, staring into it before he took a gulp and switched off the TV.

He went out on to his balcony. The moon was high in the sky and partly obscured by ragged grey clouds. From the balcony below, he heard voices, Kriti's high excited pitch, a man's expectant sensual timbre. Snatches of an old song floated out of Kriti's living room. Monish couldn't help a wry smile. Her music collection was such an imitation of his. Kishore Kumar singing '*Har koi chahta hai ek muthi aasman.*' 'Everyone desires a fistful of sky.'

ACKNOWLEDGMENTS

THANKS TO—

Michele Roberts for her belief in me and for nudging this book along to the finish line.

The early readers at Brighthorse Books who understood this book and chose my manuscript as one of the finalists and to Jonis Agee and Brent Spencer for selecting it as the winner.

This novel has been many years in the making, and members of various writing groups have seen brief excerpts from previous versions.

Birkbeck College friends: John, Maggie, Cordelia, Robert, Dorothy, Linda, and Jamie. Collier Street Fiction Group: Gul, Deirdre, Sue, Rob, Katy, Nada, and Sherry.

The Whole Kahani: Reshma, Mona, Alex, Radhika, Catherine, Shibani, Rohan, Deblina, Nadia, and especially Farrah.

Alison and Karen, who read a later version, for immersing themselves so completely in this story.

My longstanding walking group, for the chance to clear my head in the park before the return to my desk: Kasumi, Elaine, Yvonne, and Jenny.

Old friends whose conviction in me and my work is uplifting, even when I'm wavering. And to all those people, not mentioned here by name, who stepped forward to support this book in big and small ways. You are hugely appreciated.

ABOUT THE AUTHOR

Kavita A. Jindal is a prize-winning writer whose work has appeared in literary journals, newspapers and anthologies around the world and been broadcast on BBC Radio, Zee TV and European radio stations. She is an acclaimed poet, with selected poems having been translated into Arabic, German, Punjabi, Spanish and Romanian. Her poem 'Kabariwala' is included in *100 Great Indian Poems* published by Bloomsbury in 2018. Kavita is the author of two poetry books, *Patina* and *Raincheck Renewed*. She is the co-founder of *The Whole Kahani* writers' collective. In addition, she collaborates with musicians, artists and filmmakers across a range of projects. *Manual for a Decent Life* was the 2018 winner of the Brighthorse Prize in the Novel.

www.kavitajindal.com
@writerkavita